D0057578

Work, Culture, and Society
in Industrializing America

Work, Culture, and Society in Industrializing America

ESSAYS IN AMERICAN WORKING-CLASS AND SOCIAL HISTORY

Herbert G. Gutman

VINTAGE BOOKS
A Division of Random House / New York

FIRST VINTAGE BOOKS EDITION, March 1977
Copyright © 1966, 1968, 1973, 1976 by Herbert Gutman

"Work, Culture, and Society in Industrializing America, 1815–1919" originally appeared in *The American Historical Review*, June 1973. "Protestantism and the American Labor Movement: The Christian Spirit in the Gilded Age" originally appeared in *The American Historical Review*, October 1966.

See following page for continuation of Acknowledgments

Library of Congress Cataloging in Publication Data

Gutman, Herbert George, 1928-
Work, culture, and society in industrializing America.

Includes bibliographical references and index.
1. Labor and laboring classes—United States—History—Addresses, essays, lectures. 2. Industrial relations—United States—History—Addresses, essays, lectures. 3. United States—Social conditions—1865-1918—Addresses, essays, lectures. 4. United States—Social conditions—To 1865—Addresses, essays, lectures. I. Title.
[HD8072.G98 1977]   301.44′42′0973   76-40901
ISBN 0-394-72251-5

Manufactured in the United States of America
B9876543210

Acknowledgments continued

"The Negro and the United Mine Workers of America: The Career and Letters of Richard L. Davis and Something of Their Meaning, 1890–1900" originally appeared in *The Negro and the American Labor Movement*, 1968.

"The Reality of the Rags-to-Riches 'Myth': The Case of the Paterson, New Jersey Locomotive, Iron, and Machinery Manufacturers, 1830–1880" originally appeared in *Nineteenth Century Cities, Essays in the New Urban History*, edited by Stephen Thernstrom and Richard Sennett, Yale University Press, 1969. Reprinted by permission.

"Class, Status, and Community Power in Nineteenth Century American Industrial Cities—Paterson, New Jersey: A Case Study" originally appeared in *The Age of Industrialism in America: Essays in Social Structure and Cultural Values*, Free Press, 1968. Copyright © 1968 by The Free Press, a div. of Macmillan Publishing Co., Inc. Used by permission of the publisher.

"Trouble on the Railroads in 1873–1874: Prelude to the 1877 Crisis?" originally appeared in *Labor History*, Spring 1961. Copyright © 1961 by *Labor History*. Used by permission of the publisher.

"Two Lockouts in Pennsylvania, 1873–1874" originally appeared in *Pennsylvania Magazine of History and Biography*, July 1959.

*For my mother
and
in memory of my father*

Contents

Introduction

"The United States," the sociologist Norman Birnbaum has written, "insofar as major aspects of its past are concerned, remains an unknown country. . . . We are at the beginning of a voyage of self-discovery that may yet revise some of our notions of our social provenance." The essays collected in this volume are a part of that voyage. Published over the past fifteen years, they all share a common theme—a concern to explain the beliefs and behavior of American working people in the several decades that saw this nation transformed into a powerful industrial capitalist society. They differ in emphasis from the work of able but more conventional labor historians. That work is not less important but different in focus, giving primary attention to the worker as trade unionist. My own work goes beyond the boundaries fixed by that conventional approach. The differences between the "old" and the "new" labor history are indicated in the first essay reprinted in this collection and need not be repeated here.

The subjects in these essays range widely in order to explore the beliefs and behavior of ordinary working Americans. One essay compares the behavior of Pennsylvania coal miners living in different company towns. Another examines the patterns of violence in scattered railroad strikes prior to the great 1877 upheaval. One focuses on black workers; it deals with the neglected role black coal miners played in the formative years of the United Mine Workers of America. Other essays have different themes: the social origins of manufacturers in a New Jersey industrial town, the powerful strains of premillennial Protestant belief among Gilded Age trade unionists and labor radicals, and the difficulties encountered by capitalists in imposing decisions upon their workers because they lacked popular sanction. Overall, the essays divide evenly in their emphasis. Those published prior to 1966 focus on the "community." They mainly explore the relationships between nineteenth-century workers, their employers, and the surrounding community. Since that time, my interests have shifted in emphasis. Much greater attention has been given to working-class belief and behavior, to its diverse sources, and to the meaning of particular working-class experiences in industrializing America. The most recently published essay reprinted in this collection, "Work, Culture, and Society in Industrializing America, 1815–1919" (1973), is a preliminary synthesis of many of these earlier essays. It also indicates the direction of my current and future work. Far too much attention in a little-studied field ("labor history") has emphasized only the ways in which the coming of American capitalism transformed generations of working people. That remains an essential subject for continuing study. But altogether too little attention has been given to the ways in which the behavior of working people affected the development of the larger culture and society in which they lived. That, too, needs to be studied. But such relationships can come only after there is rich and detailed study of the many varieties of past American working-class experiences.

The essays reprinted in this volume are sometimes described as part of the "new social history." That description pleases but also disturbs me. Much in the new social history soundly examines greatly neglected but important aspects of past working-class experience. But too much of it is too narrowly classificatory, too narrowly statistical and behavioral. Such studies often describe with some precision regularities in behavior. But they fail to explain them. Moreover, the new social history suffers from a very limiting overspecialization. Let me illustrate briefly these dangers by taking the case of an "Irish born Catholic female Fall River Massachusetts textile worker and union organizer involved in the disorderly 1875 strike." Contemporaries called that event "the long vacation." The balkanizing thrust in the new social history might carve up this individual in nine different specialized substudies:

1. The person moved to Fall River: Mobility History.
2. The person was Irish: Immigration History.
3. The person was female: Women's History.
4. The person was married: Family History.

5. The person lived in Fall River: Urban History.
6. The person worked in a textile mill: Business History.
7. The person was a Catholic: Religious History.
8. The person was a union officer: Labor History.
9. The person engaged in a disorder: Collective Behavior History.

If enough women of her kind labored in New England textile mills, yet a tenth specialized study might be written. Their number could be counted and cross-tabulated with diverse "variables." She would then become a part of "quantitative" history. Something is learned from such specialized studies, but in themselves such works often substitute classification for meaning and wash out the wholeness that is essential to understanding human behavior. Such work, moreover, ignores the wise stricture placed upon the social historian decades ago by G. M. Trevelyan. That historian, Trevelyan insisted, needs "to know more in some respects than the dweller in the past knew about the conditions that enveloped and controlled his own life."

Much remains to be learned about the past history of the American working class, much of which will enlarge our understanding of the larger social and economic processes that have shaped the development of late twentieth-century American society. And there is much to be learned about the individual men and women who made up that changing class. A final illustration belongs in this brief introduction. In the early twentieth century, Mary White Ovington, not yet the co-founder of the National Association for the Advancement of Colored People, was already deeply involved in efforts to improve the condition of New York City's rapidly increasing black working-class population. The poet Claude McKay remembered her as a person who "radiated a quiet silver shaft of white charm which is lovely when it's real." Ovington reported a "story" ("whose every word I can vouch for"):

　　An Irish friend was talking on trade union matters, and she said: "Do you know, yisterday I dined wid a naygur.

Little did I ivir think I wud do sich a thing, but it was this way. You know my man is sicretary of his union, and the min are on strike, and who should come to the door at twelve o'clock but a big black naygur. 'Is Brother O'Neill at home?' says he. 'Brother O'Neill,' thinks I; 'well, if I'm brother to you I'd better have stayed in Ireland.' But I axed him in, and in a minute my man comes and he shakes the naygur by the hand, and says he, 'You must stay and ate wid us.' So I puts the dinner on the table and I sat down and ate wid a naygur." "Well," I said, "how did he seem?" "To tell you the truth," she said, "he seemed just like anybody else."

So much needs yet to be known about the worlds that shaped the lives of Brother O'Neill, his wife, and their black friend. They remain part of our unknown country and to learn more about them is a part of the process of self-discovery.

My debts as a labor historian are numerous but belong mostly to the larger study of American industrial and social development of which these essays have been a byproduct. I want to thank Angus Cameron for encouraging their publication in this form. A few of these essays, however, were published long enough ago for me to express my appreciation for a fine teacher and a good friend who encouraged me when labor history was not too popular a field of study. Henry David sparked my initial interest in such study, and once it began the late Ray Ginger prodded me in critical ways (sometimes quite harsh but always concerned and helpful) that proved invaluable. I like to think he knew that before his death. I shall never forget it. I also owe a great deal to Marta and Nell Gutman and especially to Judith Mara Gutman. They know why, and that is what matters.

Nyack, New York
June 1975

PART I

An Overview

Work, Culture, and Society in Industrializing America, 1815–1919

I

THE WORK ETHIC remains a central theme in the American experience, and to study this subject afresh means to re-examine much that has been assumed as given in the writing of American working-class and social history. Such study, moreover, casts new light on yet other aspects of the larger American experience that are usually not associated with the study of ordinary working men and women. Until quite recently, few historians questioned as fact the ease with which most past Americans affirmed the "Protestant" work ethic.[1] Persons much more

1. See especially the splendid essays by Edmund S. Morgan, "The Labor Problem at Jamestown, 1607–18," *American Historical Review*, 76 (1971), 595–611, and C. Vann Woodward, "The Southern Ethic in a Puritan World," in

Earlier versions of this paper were delivered at the Anglo-American Colloquium in Labour History sponsored by the Society for the Study of Labour History in London, June 1968; and at the meeting of the Organization of American Historians in Philadelphia, April 1969. Several friends and colleagues made incisive and constructive criticisms of these drafts, and I am in their debt: Eric Foner, Gregory S. Kealey, Christopher Lasch, Nancy Lane, Val Lorwin, Stephan Thernstrom, Robert Webb, Alfred F. Young, and especially Neil Harris and Joan Wallach Scott. So, too, it has profited much from comments by graduate seminar students at the University of Rochester. My great debt to E. P. Thompson should be clear to those who even merely skim these pages.

prestigious and influential than mere historians have regularly praised the powerful historical presence of such an ethic in the national culture. A single recent example suffices. In celebrating Labor Day in 1971, the nation's president saluted "the dignity of work, the value of achievement, [and] the morality of self-reliance. None of these," he affirmed, "is going out of style." And yet he worried somewhat. "Let us also recognize," he admitted, "that the work ethic in America is undergoing some changes." [2] The tone of his concern strongly suggested that it had never changed before and even that men like Henry Ford and F. W. Taylor had been among the signers of the Mayflower Compact or, better still, the Declaration of Independence.

It was never that simple. At all times in American history—when the country was still a preindustrial society, while it industrialized, and after it had become the world's leading industrial nation—quite diverse Americans, some of them more prominent and powerful than others, made it clear in their thought and behavior that the Protestant work ethic was not deeply ingrained in the nation's social fabric. Some merely noticed its absence, others advocated its imposition, and still others represented an entirely different work ethic. During the War of Independence a British manufacturer admitted that the disloyal colonists had among them many "good workmen from the several countries of Europe" but insisted that the colonists needed much more to develop successful manufactures. "It is not enough that a few, or even a great number of people, understand manufactures," he said; "the spirit of manufacturing must become the general spirit of the nation, and be incorporated, as it were, into their very essence. . . . It requires a long time before the personal, and a still longer time, before the national, habits are formed." This Englishman had a point. Even in the land of Benjamin Franklin, Andrew Carnegie, and Henry Ford, nonindustrial cultures and work habits regularly thrived

---

his *American Counterpoint, Slavery and Racism in the North-South Dialogue* (Boston, 1971), 13–46.

2. Quoted in *The New York Times*, April 2, 1972.

and were nourished by new workers alien to the "Protestant" work ethic. It was John Adams, not Max Weber, who claimed that "manufactures cannot live, much less thrive, without honor, fidelity, punctuality, and private faith, a sacred respect for property, and the moral obligations of promises and contracts." Only a "decisive, as well as an intelligent and honest, government," Adams believed, could develop such "virtues" and "habits." Others among the Founding Fathers worried about the absence of such virtues within the laboring classes. When Alexander Hamilton proposed his grand scheme to industrialize the young republic, an intimate commented, "Unless God should send us saints for workmen and angels to conduct them, there is the greatest reason to fear for the success of the plan." Benjamin Franklin shared such fears. He condemned poor relief in 1768 and lamented the absence among English workers of regular work habits. "Saint *Monday,*" he said, "is as duly kept by our working people as *Sunday;* the only difference is that instead of employing their time cheaply at church they are wasting it expensively at the ale house." Franklin believed that if poorhouses shut down "Saint Monday and Saint Tuesday" would "soon cease to be holidays." [3]

Franklin's worries should not surprise us. The Founding Fathers, after all, lived in a preindustrial, not simply an "agrarian" society, and the prevalence of premodern work habits among their contemporaries was natural. What matters here, however, is that Benjamin Franklin's ghost haunted later generations of Americans. Just before the First World War the International Harvester Corporation, converted to "scientific management" and "welfare capitalism," prepared a brochure to

3. "A Manufacturer," London *Chronicle*, March 17, 1778, quoted in *Pennsylvania Magazine of History and Biography*, 7 (1883), 198–99. John Adams to Tench Coxe, May 1792, quoted in *National Magazine*, 2 (1800), 253–54, in Joseph Davis, *Essays in the Earlier History of the American Corporation* (New York, 1917), 1: 500; Thomas Marshall? to Alexander Hamilton, September/October 1971, in Harold C. Syrett, ed., *The Papers of Alexander Hamilton* (New York, 1965), 9: 250–52; Benjamin Franklin, *Writings, 1767–1772*, ed. A. H. Smith (New York, 1907), 5: 122–27, 534–39.

teach its Polish common laborers the English language. "Lesson One," entitled "General," read:

> I hear the whistle. I must hurry.
> I hear the five minute whistle.
> It is time to go into the shop.
> I take my check from the gate board and hang it
>   on the department board.
> I change my clothes and get ready to work.
> The starting whistle blows.
> I eat my lunch.
> It is forbidden to eat until then.
> The whistle blows at five minutes of starting time.
> I get ready to go to work.
> I work until the whistle blows to quit.
> I leave my place nice and clean.
> I put all my clothes in the locker.
> I must go home.

This document illustrates a great deal. That it shows the debasement of the English language, a process closely related to the changing ethnic composition of the American working population and the social need for simplified English commands, is a subject for another study. Our immediate interest is in the relationship it implies between Americanization, factory work habits, and improved labor efficiency.[4]

4. Gerd Korman, "Americanization at the Factory Gate," *Industrial and Labor Relations Review*, 18 (1965), 402. See also his *Industrialization, Immigrants, and Americanization: The View from Milwaukee* (Madison, 1967). These instructions should be compared to those issued in February 1971 by LaGrange, Illinois, General Motors officials to engine division supervisory personnel: "BELL TO BELL POLICY: It is the policy of the [electromotive] division that all employe[e]s be given work assignments such that all will be working effectively and efficiently during their scheduled working hours except for the time required for allowable personal considerations. EACH EMPLOYEE WILL BE INSTRUCTED ON THE FOLLOWING POINTS: 1. Be at their work assignment at the start of the shift. 2. Be at their work assignment at the conclusion of their lunch period. 3. All employe[e]s will be working effectively

Nearly a century and a half separated the International Harvester Corporation from Benjamin Franklin, but both wanted to reshape the work habits of others about them. Machines required that men and women adapt older work routines to new necessities and strained those wedded to premodern patterns of labor. Half a century separated similar popular laments about the impact of the machine on traditional patterns of labor. In 1873 the Chicago *Workingman's Advocate* published "The Sewing Machine," a poem in which the author scorned Elias Howe's invention by comparing it to his wife:

> *Mine is not one of those stupid affairs*
> *That stands in the corner with what-nots and chairs . . .*
> *Mine is one of the kind to love,*
> *And wears a shawl and a soft kid glove . . .*
> *None of your patent machines for me,*
> *Unless Dame Nature's the patentee!*
> *I like the sort that can laugh and talk,*
> *And take my arm for an evening walk;*
> *And will do whatever the owner may choose,*
> *With the slightest perceptible turn of the screws.*
> *One that can dance—and possibly flirt—*
> *And make a pudding as well as a shirt;*
> *One that can sing without dropping a stitch,*
> *And play the housewife, lady, and witch . . .*

and efficiently until the bell of their scheduled lunch period and at the end of their scheduled shift. 4. Employe[e]s are to work uninterrupted to the end of the scheduled shift. In most instances, machines and area clean-up can be accomplished during periods of interrupted production prior to the last full hour of the shift." These instructions came to my attention after I read an earlier version of this paper to students and faculty at Northern Illinois University. Edward Jennings, a student and a member of Local 719, United Automobile Workers, delivered the document to me the following day. See also the copy of the work rules posted in 1888 in the Abbot-Downing Factory in Concord, New Hampshire, and deposited in the New Hampshire Historical Society. Headed "NOTICE! TIME IS MONEY!" the rules included the following factory edict: "There are conveniences for washing, but it must be done outside of working hours, and not at our expense." I am indebted to Harry Scheiber for bringing this document to my attention.

What do you think of my machine,
Ain't it the best that ever was seen?
'Tisn't a clumsy, mechanical toy,
But flesh and blood! Hear that my boy.

Fifty years later, when significant numbers of Mexicans lived in Chicago and its industrial suburbs and labored in its railroad yards, packing houses, and steel mills (in 1926, 35 percent of Chicago Inland Steel's labor force had come from Mexico), "El Enganchado" ("The Hooked One"), a popular Spanish tune, celebrated the disappointments of immigrant factory workers:

I came under contract from Lorelia.
To earn dollars was my dream,
I bought shoes and I bought a hat
And even put on trousers.
For they told me that here the dollars
Were scattered about in heaps
That there were girls and theatres
And that here everything was fun.
And now I'm overwhelmed—
I am a shoemaker by trade
But here they say I'm a camel
And good only for pick and shovel.
What good is it to know my trade
If there are manufacturers by the score
And while I make two little shoes
They turn out more than a million?
Many Mexicans don't care to speak
The language their mothers taught them
And go about saying they are Spanish
And denying their country's flag . . .
My kids speak perfect English
And have no use for Spanish,
They call me "fadder" and don't work
And are crazy about the Charleston.

> *I am tired of all this nonsense*
> *I'm going back to Michogan.*

American society differed greatly in each of the periods when these documents were written. Franklin personified the successful preindustrial American artisan. The "sewing girl" lived through the decades that witnessed the transformation of preindustrial into industrial America. Harvester proved the nation's world-wide industrial supremacy before the First World War. The Mexican song served as an ethnic Jazz Age pop tune. A significant strand, however, tied these four documents together. And in unraveling that strand at particular moments in the nation's history between 1815 and 1920, a good deal is learned about recurrent tensions over work habits that shaped the national experience.[5]

The traditional imperial boundaries (a function, perhaps, of the professional subdivision of labor) that have fixed the territory open to American labor historians for exploration have closed off to them the study of such important subjects as changing work habits and the culture of work. Neither the questions American labor historians usually ask nor the methods they use encourage such inquiry. With a few significant exceptions, for more than half a century American labor history has continued to reflect both the strengths and the weaknesses of the conceptual scheme sketched by its founding fathers, John R. Commons and others of the so-called Wisconsin school of labor history.[6] Even their most severe critics, including the orthodox

5. "The Sewing Machine," *Workingman's Advocate* (Chicago), August 23, 1873; "El Enganchado," printed in Paul Taylor, *Mexican Labor in the United States: Chicago and the Calumet Region* (Berkeley, 1932), vi–vii.

6. Helpful summaries of recent scholarship in American labor history are Thomas A. Kruger, "American Labor Historiography, Old and New," *Journal of Social History*, 4 (1971), 277–85; Robert H. Zieger, "Workers and Scholars: Recent Trends in American Labor Historiography," *Labor History*, 13 (1972), 245–66; and Paul Faler, "Working Class Historiography," *Radical America*, 3 (1969), 56–68. Innovative works in the field that have broken away from the traditional conceptual framework include especially Richard B. Morris, *Government and Labor in Early America* (New York, 1946); David Brody, *Steelworkers*

"Marxist" labor historians of the 1930s, 1940s, and 1950s and the few New Left historians who have devoted attention to American labor history, rarely questioned that conceptual framework.[7] Commons and his colleagues asked large questions, gathered important source materials, and put forth impressive ideas. Together with able disciples, they studied the development of the trade union as an institution and explained its place in a changing labor market. But they gave attention primarily to those few workers who belonged to trade unions and neglected much else of importance about the American working population. Two flaws especially marred this older labor history. Because so few workers belonged to permanent trade unions before 1940, its overall conceptualization excluded most working people from detailed and serious study. More than this, its methods encouraged labor historians to spin a cocoon around American workers, isolating them from their own particular subcultures and from the larger national culture. An increasingly narrow "economic" analysis caused the study of American working-class history to grow more constricted and become more detached from larger developments in American social

---

in America: The Non-Union Era (Cambridge, 1960); Stephan Thernstrom, *Poverty and Progress: Social Mobility in a Nineteenth Century City* (Cambridge, 1964); David Montgomery, *Beyond Equality: Labor and the Radical Republicans, 1862–1872* (New York, 1967); Montgomery, "The Working Class of the Preindustrial American City, 1780–1830," *Labor History*, 9 (1968), 1–22; Montgomery, "The Shuttle and the Cross: Weavers and Artisans in the Kensington Riots of 1844," *Journal of Social History*, 5 (1972), 411–46; Alfred F. Young, "The Mechanics and the Jeffersonians: New York, 1789–1801," *Labor History*, 5 (1964), 247–76; and Alexander Saxton, *The Indispensable Enemy: Labor and the Anti-Chinese Movement in California* (Berkeley, 1971).

7. The best example of orthodox "Marxist" labor history is Philip S. Foner, *History of the Labor Movement in the United States* (New York, 1947–1965). Emphasis in so-called New Left history on the relationship between "corporate liberalism" and American labor is found in James Weinstein, *Corporate Ideal in the Liberal State, 1900–1918* (Boston, 1968), and in Ronald Radosh, *American Labor and United States Foreign Policy* (New York, 1969). A different approach is found in Jesse Lemisch, "Jack Tar in the Streets: Merchant Seamen in the Politics of the American Revolution," *William and Mary Quarterly*, 25 (1968), 371–407.

and cultural history and from the writing of American social and cultural history itself. After 1945 American working-class history remained imprisoned by self-imposed limitations and therefore fell far behind the more imaginative and innovative British and Continental European work in the field. In Great Britain, for example, the guideposts fixed by Sidney and Beatrice Webb have been shattered by labor and social historians such as Asa Briggs, Eric Hobsbawm, Henry Pelling, Sidney Pollard, George Rudé, E. P. Thompson, and Brian, J. F. C., and Royden Harrison, among other scholars who have posed new questions, used new methods, and dug deeply into largely neglected primary materials.[8] As a consequence, a rich and subtle new history of the British common people is now being written. Much of value remains to be learned from the older American labor historians, but the time has long been overdue for a critical re-examination of their framework and their methodology and for applying in special ways to the particularities of the American working-class experience the conceptual and methodological breakthroughs of our colleagues across the ocean.

The pages that follow give little attention to the subject matter usually considered the proper sphere of labor history (trade-

8. This essay draws especially on the methods of analysis in the following works: E. P. Thompson, *Making of the English Working Class* (London, 1963); Thompson, "Time, Work-Discipline, and Industrial Capitalism," *Past and Present*, 38 (1967), 56–97; Thompson, "The Moral Economy of the English Crowd in the Eighteenth Century," *Past and Present*, 50 (1971), 76–136; Sidney Pollard, *Genesis of Modern Management* (Cambridge, 1965); Pollard, "Factory Discipline in the Industrial Revolution," *Economic History Review*, 16 (1963), 254–71; Eric Hobsbawm, *Primitive Rebels and Social Bandits* (Manchester, 1959); Hobsbawm, *Labouring Men* (London, 1964) and especially the essay on "Custom Wages and Workload," 344–70; George Rudé, *Crowd in History* (New York, 1964); George Rudé and Eric Hobsbawm, *Captain Swing* (New York, 1968); Brian Harrison, "Religion and Recreation in Nineteenth Century England," *Past and Present*, 38 (1967), 98–125; Brian Harrison, *Drink and the Victorians* (Pittsburgh, 1971); Asa Briggs, ed., *Chartist Studies* (New York, 1954); Royden Harrison, *Before the Socialists* (London, 1965); J. F. C. Harrison, *The Quest for the New Moral World: Robert Owen and the Owenites in Britain and America* (New York, 1969).

union development and behavior, strikes and lockouts, and radical movements) and instead emphasize the frequent tension between different groups of men and women new to the machine and a changing American society. Not all periods of time are covered: nothing is said of the half-century since the First World War when large numbers of Spanish-speaking and rural Southern white and black workers first encountered the factory and the machine.[9] Much recent evidence describing contemporary dissatisfactions with factory work is not examined.[10] Neither are

9. The best recent work is Robert Coles, *South Goes North* (Boston, 1972).

10. The publication in late 1972 of "Work in America" by the Upjohn Institute for Employment Research, a study financed by the U.S. Department of Health, Education, and Welfare, revealed widespread dissatisfactions with work among contemporary blue- and white-collar workers and even their supervisors. The dispute over this finding in government circles is described in *Newsweek*, January 1, 1973, pp. 47–48, and Howard Muson, "The Ranks of the Discontent," *The New York Times*, December 31, 1972. Other evidence of dissatisfaction among factory workers with work routines is reported in *The New York Times*, January 23, April 2, and September 3, 1972. The April dispatch reported that a University of Michigan survey team described twenty-five aspects of their jobs to factory workers and then asked the workers to rank them in order of importance. Interesting work ranked first; pay was listed second. Absenteeism, the three large Detroit automobile manufacturers reported, had doubled between 1965 and 1972, "increasing from 2 to 3 percent . . . to 5 to 6 percent." In some plants, up to 15 percent of the workers were absent "on Fridays and Mondays." Quite interesting discussions of contemporary work dissatisfactions are found in Bennett Kremen, "No Pride in This Dust. Young Workers in the Steel Mills," *Dissent* (Winter 1972), 21–28, and Steve Kline, "Henry and His Magic Kabonk Machine," *Boston Globe Magazine*, July 16, 1972, pp. 8–10, 20–24. See also Rochester (N.Y.) *Times-Union*, November 29, 1971, for a discussion of obstinate work and leisure habits among Southern white workers fresh to Northern-owned factories. And a brief feature story in the Rochester (N.Y.) *Democrat and Chronicle*, April 30, 1972, told about an artisan Santo Badagliacca who seemed to belong to another era. He had moved to Rochester from Sicily in 1956 with his wife and five-year-old daughter. He was then forty and worked for nearly twelve years as a "tailor" for the National Clothing Company, Timely Clothes, and Bond Clothes, Inc. He quit the clothing factories in 1968 and opened a small custom tailoring shop in his home. In four years, not a single order came for a custom-made suit. Three or four persons visited his place weekly but only to have alterations made. Badagliacca explained his decision to quit the factory: "Each day, it's just collars, collars, collars. I didn't work forty years as a tailor just to do that." See also Richard Sennett and

bound workers (factory slaves in the Old South) or nonwhite free laborers, mostly blacks and Asian immigrants and their descendants, given notice. These groups, too, were affected by the tensions that will be described here, a fact that emphasizes the central place they deserve in any comprehensive study of American work habits and changing American working-class behavior.

Nevertheless the focus in these pages is on free white labor in quite different time periods: 1815–1843, 1843–1893, 1893–1919. The precise years serve only as guideposts to mark the fact that American society differed greatly in each period. Between 1815 and 1843, the United States remained a predominantly preindustrial society and most workers drawn to its few factories were the products of rural and village preindustrial culture. Preindustrial American society was not premodern in the same way that European peasant societies were, but it was, nevertheless, premodern. In the half-century after 1843 industrial development radically transformed the earlier American social structure, and during this Middle Period (an era not framed around the coming and the aftermath of the Civil War) a profound tension existed between the older American preindustrial social structure and the modernizing institutions that accompanied the development of industrial capitalism. After 1893 the United States ranked as a mature industrial society. In each of these distinctive stages of change in American society, a recurrent tension also existed between native and immigrant men and women fresh to the factory and the demands imposed upon them by the regularities and disciplines of factory labor. That state of tension was regularly revitalized by the migration of diverse premodern native and foreign peoples into an industrializing or a fully industrialized society. The British economic historian Sidney Pollard has described well this process whereby "a society of peasants, craftsmen, and versatile labourers

Jonathan Cobb, *The Hidden Injuries of Class* (New York, 1972), and William Serrin, *The Company and the Union: The "Civilized Relationship" of the General Motors Corporation and the United Auto Workers* (New York, 1973).

became a society of modern industrial workers." "There was more to overcome," Pollard writes of industrializing England,

> than the change of employment or the new rhythm of work: there was a whole new culture to be absorbed and an old one to be traduced and spurned, there were new surroundings, often in a different part of the country, new relations with employers, and new uncertainties of livelihood, new friends and neighbors, new marriage patterns and behavior patterns of children within the family and without.[11]

That same process occurred in the United States. Just as in all modernizing countries, the United States faced the difficult task of industrializing whole cultures, but in this country the process was regularly repeated, each stage of American economic growth and development involving different first-generation factory workers. The social transformation Pollard described occurred in England between 1770 and 1850, and in those decades premodern British cultures and the modernizing institutions associated primarily with factory and machine labor collided and interacted. A painful transition occurred, dominated the ethos of an entire era, and then faded in relative importance. After 1850 and until quite recently, the British working class reproduced itself and retained a relative national homogeneity. New tensions emerged but not those of a society continually busy (and worried about) industrializing persons born out of that society and often alien in birth and color and in work habits, customary values, and behavior. "Traditional social habits and customs," J. F. C. Harrison reminds us, "seldom

---

11. Pollard, "The Adaptation of the Labour Force," in *Genesis of Modern Management* (Cambridge, 1965), 160–208. Striking evidence of the preindustrial character of most American manufacturing enterprises before 1840 is found in Allen Pred, "Manufacturing in the American Mercantile City, 1800–1840," *Annals of the American Association of Geographers*, 56 (1966), 307–25. See also Richard D. Brown, "Modernization and Modern Personality in Early America, 1600–1865: A Sketch of a Synthesis," *Journal of Interdisciplinary History*, 2 (1972), 201–28.

fitted into the patterns of industrial life, and they had . . . to be discredited as hindrances to progress." That happened regularly in the United States after 1815 as the nation absorbed and worked to transform new groups of preindustrial peoples, native whites among them. The result, however, was neither a static tension nor the mere recurrence of similar cycles, because American society itself changed as did the composition of its laboring population. But the source of the tension remained the same, and conflict often resulted. It was neither the conflict emphasized by the older Progressive historians (agrarianism versus capitalism, or sectional disagreement) nor that emphasized by recent critics of that early twentieth-century synthesis (conflict between competing elites). It resulted instead from the fact that the American working class was continually altered in its composition by infusions, from within and without the nation, of peasants, farmers, skilled artisans, and casual day laborers who brought into industrial society ways of work and other habits and values not associated with industrial necessities and the industrial ethos. Some shed these older ways to conform to new imperatives. Others fell victim or fled, moving from place to place. Some sought to extend and adapt older patterns of work and life to a new society. Others challenged the social system through varieties of collective associations. But for all—at different historical moments—the transition to industrial society, as E. P. Thompson has written, "entailed a severe restructuring of working habits—new disciplines, new incentives, and a new human nature upon which these incentives could bite effectively." [12]

Much in the following pages depends upon a particular definition of culture and an analytic distinction between culture and society. Both deserve brief comment. "Culture" as used here has little to do with Oscar Lewis's inadequate "culture of poverty" construct and has even less to do with the currently fashionable but nevertheless quite crude behavioral social his-

---

12. J. F. C. Harrison, *Learning and Living* (London, 1961), 268; Thompson, "Time, Work-Discipline, and Industrial Capitalism," *op. cit.*, 57.

tory that defines class by mere occupation and culture as some kind of a magical mix between ethnic and religious affiliations.[13] Instead this paper has profited from the analytic distinctions between culture and society made by the anthropologists Eric Wolf and Sidney W. Mintz and the exiled Polish sociologist Zygmunt Bauman. Mintz finds in culture "a kind of resource" and in society "a kind of arena," the distinction being "between sets of historically available alternatives or forms on the one hand, and the societal circumstances or settings within which these forms may be employed on the other." "Culture," he writes, "is *used;* and any analysis of its use immediately brings into view the arrangements of persons in societal groups for whom cultural forms confirm, reinforce, maintain, change, or deny particular arrangements of status, power, and identity." Bauman insists that for analytic purposes the two (culture and society) need always be examined discretely to explain behavior:

> Human behavior, whether individual or collective, is invariably the resultant of two factors: the cognitive system as well as the goals and patterns of behavior as defined by culture systems, on the one hand, and the system of real contingencies as defined by the social structure on the other. A complete interpretation and apprehension of social processes can be achieved only when both systems, as well as their interaction, are taken into consideration.

Such an analytic framework allows social historians to avoid the many pitfalls that follow implicit or explicit acceptance of what

13. Valuable and convincing theoretical criticisms of the culture of poverty construct appear in detail in Eleanor Burke Leacock, ed., *The Culture of Poverty: A Critique* (New York, 1971). See also William Preston's withering comments on the faulty application of the culture of poverty to a recent study of the Industrial Workers of the World: William Preston, "Shall This Be All? U.S. Historians versus William D. Haywood *et al.,*" *Labor History*, 12 (1971), 435–71. The use of crude definitions of class and culture in otherwise sophisticated behavioral social history is as severely criticized in James Green, "Behavioralism and Class Analysis," *Labor History*, 13 (1972), 89–106.

the anthropologist Clifford Geertz calls "the theoretical dichotomies of classical sociology—*Gemeinschaft* and *Gesellschaft*, mechanic and organic solidarity, [and] folk and urban cultures." Too often, the subtle historical processes that explain particular patterns of working-class and other behavior have been viewed as no more than "the expansion of one at the expense of the other." [14] An analytic model that distinguishes between culture

14. Eric Wolf, "Specific Aspects of Plantation Systems in the New World: Community Sub-Cultures and Social Class," in *Plantation Systems of the New World* (Washington, 1949), 142; Sidney W. Mintz, "Foreword," in Norman Whitten and John F. Szwed, eds., *Afro-American Anthropology: Contemporary Perspectives* (New York, 1970), 1–16, but especially 9–10; Zygmunt Bauman, "Marxism and the Contemporary Theory of Culture," *Co-Existence*, 5 (1968), 171–98; Clifford Geertz, *Old Societies and New States* (Glencoe, Ill., 1963), 32–54, 109–10, 154–55. See also Emilio Willems, "Peasantry and City: Cultural Persistence and Change in Historical Perspective, A European Case," *American Anthropologist*, 72 (1970), 528–43, in which Willems disputes the proposition that "peasant culture is incompatible with industrialization" and shows that in the German Rhineland town of Neyl there existed significant "cultural continuity of urban lower class and peasantry rather than cultural polarity between the two segments." A brilliant article which focuses on West Indian slaves but is nevertheless methodologically useful to students of all lower-class cultures is S. W. Mintz, "Toward an Afro-American History," *Journal of World History*, 13 (1971), 317–33. The confusion between race and culture greatly marred early twentieth-century American labor history, and no one revealed that more clearly than John R. Commons in *Races and Immigrants in America* (New York, 1907), 7, 11–12, 153–54, 173–75, *passim*. "Race differences," Commons believed, "are established in the very blood and physical condition" and "most difficult to eradicate." Changes might take place in language and other behavioral patterns, "but underneath all these changes there may continue the physical, mental and moral incapacities which determine the real character of their religion, government, industry, and literature." The behavior of the recent immigrants confused historians like Commons. His racial beliefs and the crude environmentalism he shared with other Progressive reformers encouraged that confusion. "Ireland and Italy," he could write, "have nothing to compare to the trade-union movement of England, but the Irish are the most effective organizers of the American unions, and the Italians are becoming the most ardent unionists. Most remarkable of all, the individualistic Jew from Russia, contrary to his race instinct, is joining the unions." "The American unions, in fact," Commons concluded, "grow out of American conditions, and are an American product." But he could not explain how these "races" so easily adapted to American conditions. How could he when he believed that "even the long series of crimes against the Indians, to which the term 'Century of Dishonor' seems to have

and society reveals that even in periods of radical economic and social change powerful cultural continuities and adaptations continued to shape the historical behavior of diverse working-class populations. That perspective is especially important in examining the premodern work habits of diverse American men and women and the cultural sanctions sustaining them in an alien society in which the factory and the machine grew more and more important.

Men and women who sell their labor to an employer bring more to a new or changing work situation than their physical presence. What they bring to a factory depends, in good part, on their culture of origin, and how they behave is shaped by the interaction between that culture and the particular society into which they enter. Because so little is yet known about preindustrial American culture and subcultures, some caution is necessary in moving from the level of generalization to historical actuality. What follows compares and contrasts working people new to industrial society but living in quite different time periods. First, the expectations and work habits of first-generation predominantly native American factory workers before 1843 are compared with first-generation immigrant factory workers between 1893 and 1920. Similarities in the work habits and expectations of men and women who experienced quite different premodern cultures are indicated. Second, the work habits and culture of artisans in the industrializing decades (1843–1893) are examined to indicate the persistence of powerful cultural continuities in that era of radical economic change. Third, evidence of premodern working-class behavior that parallels European patterns of premodern working-class behavior in the early phases of industrialization is briefly described to suggest that throughout the entire period (1815–1920) the changing composition of the American working class caused the recurrence of "premodern" patterns of collective behavior usually only associated with the early phases of industrialization.

---

attached itself with no protest, must be looked upon as a mob spirit of a superior race bent on despoiling a despised and inferior race"?

And, finally, attention is given to some of the larger implications resulting from this recurrent tension between work, culture, and society.

II

THE WORK HABITS and the aspirations and expectations of men and women new to factory life and labor are examined first. Common work habits rooted in diverse premodern cultures (different in many ways but nevertheless all ill fitted to the regular routines demanded by machine-centered factory processes) existed among distinctive first-generation factory workers all through American history. We focus on two quite different time periods: the years before 1843 when the factory and machine were still new to America and the years between 1893 and 1917 when the country had become the world's industrial colossus. In both periods workers new to factory production brought strange and seemingly useless work habits to the factory gate. The irregular and undisciplined work patterns of factory hands before 1843 frustrated cost-conscious manufacturers and caused frequent complaint among them. Textile factory work rules often were designed to tame such rude customs. A New Hampshire cotton factory that hired mostly women and children forbade "spirituous liquor, smoking, nor any kind of amusement . . . in the workshops, yards, or factories" and promised the "immediate and disgraceful dismissal" of employees found gambling, drinking, or committing "any other debaucheries." A Massachusetts firm nearby insisted that young workers unwilling to attend church stay "within doors and improve their time in reading, writing, and in other valuable and harmless employment." Tardy and absent Philadelphia workers paid fines and could not "carry into the factory nuts, fruits, etc.; books or paper." A Connecticut textile mill owner justified the twelve-hour day and the six-day week because it kept "workmen and children" from "vicious amusements." He forbade "gaming . . . in any private house." Manufacturers elsewhere worried about the example "idle" men set for women and children. Massachusetts family heads who rented "a piece of land on shares" to grow corn and potatoes while their wives and children labored in factories worried one manufacturer. "I would prefer giving constant employment at some sacrifice," he said, "to having a man of the village seen in the streets on a rainy day at leisure." Men who worked in Massachusetts woolen mills upset expected work routines in other ways. "The wool business requires more man labour," said a manufacturer, "and this we study to avoid. Women are much more ready to follow good regulations, are not captious, and do not clan as the men do against the overseers." Male factory workers posed other difficulties, too. In 1817 a shipbuilder in Medford, Massachusetts, refused his men grog privileges. They quit work, but he managed to finish a ship without using further spirits, "a remarkable achievement." An English visitor in 1832 heard an American complain that British workers in the Paterson cotton and machine shops drank excessively and figured as "the most beastly people I have ever seen." Four years later a New Jersey manufacturer of hats and caps boasted in a public card that he finally had "4 and 20 good, permanent workmen," not one infected with "the brutal leprosy of blue Monday habits and the moral gangrene of 'trades union' principles." Other manufacturers had less good fortune. Absenteeism occurred frequently among the Pennsylvania ironworkers at the rural Hopewell Village forge: hunting, harvesting, wedding parties, frequent "frolicking" that sometimes lasted for days, and uproarious Election and Independence Day celebrations plagued the mill operators. In the early nineteenth century, a New Jersey iron manufacturer filled his diary with notations about irregular work habits: "all hands drunk"; "Jacob Ventling hunting"; "molders all agree to quit work and went to the beach"; "Peter Cox very drunk and gone to bed. Mr. Evans made a solemn resolution any person or persons bringing liquor to the work enough to make drunk shall be liable to a fine"; "Edward Rutter off a-drinking. It was reported he got drunk on cheese." [15]

15. *Mechanic's Free Press* (Philadelphia), January 17, 1829; Edith Abbott, *Women in Industry* (New York, 1910), 374–75; Silesia Factory Rules, German-

Employers responded differently to such behavior by first-generation factory hands. "Moral reform" as well as what Sidney Pollard calls carrot-and-stick policies meant to tame or to transform such work habits. Fining was common. Hopewell Furnace managers deducted one dollar from Samuel York's wages "for getting intoxesitated *[sic]* with liquor *[sic]* and neglecting hauling 4 loads wash Dird at Joneses." Special material rewards encouraged steady work. A Hopewell Village blacksmith contracted for nineteen dollars a month, and "if he does his work well we are to give him a pair of coarse boots." In these and later years manufacturers in Fall River and Paterson institutionalized traditional customs and arranged for festivals and parades to celebrate with their workers a new mill, a retiring superintendent, or a finished locomotive. Some rewarded disciplined workers in special ways. When Paterson locomotive workers pressed for higher wages, their employer instructed an underling: "Book keeper, make up a roll of the men . . . making *fulltime;* if they can't support their families on the wages they are now getting, they must have more. But the other men, who are drunk every Monday morning, I don't want them around the shop under any circumstances." Where factory work could be learned easily, new hands replaced irregular old ones. A factory worker in New England remembered that years before the Civil War her employer had hired "all American girls" but later shifted to immigrant laborers because "not coming from country homes, but living as the Irish do, in the town, they take no vacations, and can be relied on at the mill all year round." Not

town *Telegraph*, November 6, 1833, reprinted in William Sullivan, *Industrial Worker in Pennsylvania* (Harrisburg, 1955), 34; letters of Smith Wilkinson and Jedidiah Tracy to George White, n.d., printed in George White, *Memoir of Samuel Slater* (Philadelphia, 1836), 125–32; Carroll D. Wright, *Industrial Evolution of the United States* (New York, 1901), 296; Rowland T. Berthoff, *British Immigrants in Industrial America* (Cambridge, 1953), 146; Card of H. B. Day, 1836, printed in Paterson (N.J.) *Guardian*, August 6, 1886; J. E. Walker, *Hopewell Village* (Philadelphia, 1966), 115–16, 256, 265–68, 282–83, 331, 380–84; "The Martha Furnace Diary," in A. D. Pierce, *Iron in the Pines* (New Brunswick, 1957), 96–105; Sidney Pollard, "Factory Discipline in the Industrial Revolution," *Economic History Review*, 16 (1963), 254–71.

all such devices worked to the satisfaction of workers or their employers. Sometime in the late 1830s merchant capitalists sent a skilled British silk weaver to manage a new mill in Nantucket that would employ the wives and children of local whalers and fishermen. Machinery was installed, and in the first days women and children besieged the mill for work. After a month had passed, they started dropping off in small groups. Soon nearly all had returned "to their shore gazing and to their seats by the sea." The Nantucket mill shut down, its hollow frame an empty monument to the unwillingness of resident women and children to conform to the regularities demanded by rising manufacturers.[16]

First-generation factory workers were not unique to premodern America. And the work habits common to such workers plagued American manufacturers in later generations when manufacturers and most native urban whites scarcely remembered that native Americans had once been hesitant first-generation factory workers.[17] To shift forward in time to East and South European immigrants new to steam, machinery, and electricity and new to the United States itself is to find much that seems the same. American society, of course, had changed greatly, but in some ways it is as if a film—run at a much faster speed—is being viewed for the second time: primitive work rules for unskilled labor, fines, gang labor, and subcontracting were commonplace. In 1910 two-thirds of the workers in twenty-one major manufacturing and mining industries came from Eastern and Southern Europe or were native American blacks, and studies of these "new immigrants" record much evidence of

16. Walker, *Hopewell Village, passim;* Walker, "Labor-Management Relations at Hopewell Village," *Labor History,* 14 (1973), 3–18; *Voice of Industry* (Lowell), January 8, 1847; New York *Tribune,* June 29, July 4, August 20, 1853; Paterson *Guardian,* September 13, 1886; Massachusetts Bureau of Labor Statistics, *First Annual Report, 1869–1870* (Boston, 1870), 119; Paterson *Evening News,* November 21, 1900.

17. Fining as means of labor discipline, of course, remained common between 1843 and 1893. See, for examples, *Illinois Bureau of Labor Statistics, Fourth Annual Report, 1886* (Springfield, 1887), 501–26; Pennsylvania Bureau of Labor Statistics, *Fourteenth Annual Report, 1886* (Harrisburg, 1887), 13–14.

preindustrial work habits among the men and women new to American industry. According to Moses Rischin, skilled immigrant Jews carried to New York City town and village employment patterns, such as the *landsmannschaft* economy and a preference for small shops as opposed to larger factories, that sparked frequent disorders but hindered stable trade unions until 1910. Specialization spurred anxiety: in Chicago Jewish glovemakers resisted the subdivision of labor even though it promised better wages. "You shrink from doing either kind of work itself, nine hours a day," said two observers of these immigrant women. "You cling to the variety . . . , the mental luxury of first, finger-sides, and then, five separate leather pieces, for relaxation, to play with! *Here* is a luxury worth fighting for!" American work rules also conflicted with religious imperatives. On the eighth day after the birth of a son, Orthodox Jews in Eastern Europe held a festival, "an occasion of much rejoicing." But the American work week had a different logic, and if the day fell during the week the celebration occurred the following Sunday. "The host . . . and his guests," David Blaustein remarked, "know it is not the right day," and "they fall to mourning over the conditions that will not permit them to observe the old custom." The occasion became "one for secret sadness rather than rejoicing." Radical Yiddish poets, like Morris Rosenfeld, the presser of men's clothing, measured in verse the psychic and social costs exacted by American industrial work rules:

> *The Clock in the workshop,—it rests not a moment;*
> *It points on, and ticks on: eternity—time;*
> *Once someone told me the clock had a meaning,—*
> *In pointing and ticking had reason and rhyme. . . .*
> *At times, when I listen, I hear the clock plainly;—*
> *The reason of old—the old meaning—is gone!*
> *The maddening pendulum urges me forward*
> *To labor and still labor on.*
> *The tick of the clock is the boss in his anger.*
> *The face of the clock has the eyes of the foe.*

The clock—I shudder—Dost hear how it draws me?
It calls me "Machine" and it cries [to] me "Sew"! [18]

Slavic and Italian immigrants carried with them to industrial
America subcultures quite different from that of village Jews,
but their work habits were just as alien to the modern factory.
Rudolph Vecoli has reconstructed Chicago's South Italian
community to show that adult male seasonal construction gangs
as contrasted to factory labor were one of many traditional
customs adapted to the new environment, and in her study of
South Italian peasant immigrants Phyllis H. Williams found
among them men who never adjusted to factory labor. After
"years" of "excellent" factory work, some "began . . . to have
minor accidents" and others "suddenly give up and are found in
their homes complaining of a vague indisposition with no
apparent physical basis." Such labor worried early twentieth-
century efficiency experts, and so did Slavic festivals, church
holidays, and "prolonged merriment." "Man," Adam Smith
wisely observed, "is, of all sorts of luggage, the most difficult to
be transported." That was just as true for these Slavic immigrants as for the early nineteenth-century native American
factory workers. A Polish wedding in a Pennsylvania mining or
mill town lasted between three and five days. Greek and Roman
Catholics shared the same jobs but had different holy days, "an
annoyance to many employers." The Greek Church had "more
than eighty festivals in the year," and "the Slav religiously
observes the days on which the saints are commemorated and
invariably takes a holiday." A celebration of the American Day
of Independence in Mahanoy City, Pennsylvania, caught the eye
of a hostile observer. Men parading the streets drew a handcart
with a barrel of lager in it. Over the barrel "stood a comrade,

---

18. Moses Rischin, *Promised City: New York's Jews, 1870–1914* (Cambridge,
1962), 19–33, 144–99 but especially 181–82; New York *Tribune*, August 16, 1903;
William Herd and Rheta C. Dorr, "The Women's Invasion," *Everybody's
Magazine*, March, 1909, pp. 375–76; Melech Epstein, *Jewish Labor in the United
States* (New York, 1950), 280–85, 290–91.

goblet in hand and crowned with a garland of laurel, singing some jargon." Another sat and played an accordion. At intervals, the men stopped to "drink the good beverage they celebrated in song." The witness called the entertainment "an imitation of the honor paid Bacchus which was one of the most joyous festivals of ancient Rome" and felt it proof of "a lower type of civilization." Great Lakes dock workers "believed that a vessel could not be unloaded unless they had from four to five kegs of beer." (And in the early irregular strikes among male Jewish garment workers, employers negotiated with them out of doors and after each settlement "would roll out a keg of beer for their entertainment of the workers.") Contemporary betters could not comprehend such behavior. Worried over a three-day Slavic wedding frolic, a woman concluded: "You don't think they have souls, do you? No, they are beasts, and in their lust they'll perish." Another disturbed observer called drink "un-American, . . . a curse worse than the white plague." About that time, a young Italian boy lay ill in a hospital. The only English words he knew were "boots" and "hurry up." [19]

More than irregular work habits bound together the behavior of first-generation factory workers separated from one another by time and by the larger structure of the society they first encountered. Few distinctive American working-class populations differed in so many essentials (their sex, their religions, their nativity, and their prior rural and village cultures) as the Lowell mill girls and women of the Era of Good Feelings and the South and East European steelworkers of the Progressive Era. To describe similarities in their expectations of factory labor is not to blur these important differences but to suggest

19. William M. Leiserson, *Adjusting Immigrant and Industry* (New York, 1924), ch. 1; R. J. Vecoli, "Contadini in Chicago: A Critique of 'The Uprooted,'" *Journal of American History*, 51 (1964), 404–27; Phyllis H. Williams, *South Italian Folkways in Europe and America* (New Haven, 1938), 30–32; A. Rosenberg, *Memoirs of a Cloak Maker* (New York, 1920), 42, quoted in Louis Levine, *Women's Garment Workers* (New York, 1924), 42; Peter Roberts, *New Immigration* (New York, 1912), 79–97, 118–19; Roberts, *Anthracite Communities* (New York, 1904), 49–56, 219, 236, 291, 294–95.

that otherwise quite distinctive men and women interpreted such work in similar ways. The Boston Associates, pioneer American industrialists, had built up Lowell and other towns like it to overcome early nineteenth-century rural and village prejudices and fears about factory work and life and in their regulation of lower-class social habits hoped to assure a steady flow of young rural women ("girls") to and from the looms. "The sagacity of self-interest as well as more disinterested considerations," explained a Lowell clergyman in 1845, "has led to the adoption of a strict system of moral police." Without "sober, orderly, and moral" workers, profits would be "absorbed by cases of irregularity, carelessness, and neglect." The Lowell capitalists thrived by hiring rural women who supplemented a distant family's income, keeping them a few years, and then renewing the process. Such steady labor turnover kept the country from developing a permanent proletariat and so was thought to assure stability. Lowell's busy cotton mills, well-ordered boarding-houses, temples of religion and culture, factory girls, and moral police so impressed Anthony Trollope that he called the entire enterprise a "philanthropic manufacturing college." John Quincy Adams thought the New England cotton mills "palaces of the Poor," and Henry Clay marveled over places like the Lowell mills. "Who has not been delighted with the clock-work movements of a large cotton factory?" asked the father of the American System. The French traveler Michel Chevalier had a less sanguine reaction. He found Lowell "neat and decent, peaceable and sage," but worried, "Will this become like Lancashire? Does this brilliant glare hide the misery and suffering of the working girls?" [20]

Historians of the Lowell mill girls find little evidence before 1840 of organized protest among them and attribute their

20. Anthony Trollope, quoted in Howard Gitelman, "The Waltham System and the Coming of the Irish," *Labor History*, 8 (1967), 227–54; John Quincy Adams and Henry Clay quoted in Seth Luther, *An Address to the Workingmen of New England* (Boston, 1832), title page; Michel Chevalier, *Society, Manners, and Politics in the United States* (Boston, 1939; reprinted New York, 1969), 133–44; Henry Miles, *Lowell As It Is and Was* (Lowell, 1845), 128–46.

collective passivity to corporation policing policies, the frequent turnover in the labor force, the irregular pace of work (after it was rationalized in the 1840s, it provoked collective protest), the freedom the mill girls enjoyed away from rural family dominance, and their relatively decent earnings. The women managed the transition to mill life because they did not expect to remain factory workers too long. Nevertheless frequent inner tension revealed itself among the mobile mill women. In an early year, a single mill discharged twenty-eight women for such reasons as "misconduct," "captiousness," "disobedience," "impudence," "levity," and even "mutiny." The difficult transition from rural life to factory work also caused tensions outside the mills. Rural girls and women, Harriet Robinson later recalled, came to Lowell in "outlandish fashions" and with "queer names," "Samantha, Triphena, Plumy, Kezia, Aseneth, Elgardy, Leafy, Ruhamah, Almaretta, Sarpeta, and Florilla . . . among them." They spoke a "very peculiar" dialect ("a language almost unintelligible"). "On the broken English and Scotch of their ancestors," said Robinson, "was engrafted the nasal Yankee twang." Some soon learned the "city way of speaking"; others changed their names to "Susan" or "Jane"; and for still others new clothing, especially straw hats, became important. But the machines they worked still left them depressed and with feelings of anxiety. "I never cared much for machinery," Lucy Larcom said of her early Lowell years. "I could not see into their complications or feel interested in them. . . . In sweet June weather I would lean far out of the window, and try not to hear the unceasing clash of sound inside." She kept a plant beside her and recollected an overseer who confiscated newspaper clippings and even the pages of a "torn Testament" some women had slipped into the factory. Years after she had left the textile mills, Lucy Larcom ridiculed her mill-girl poems: "I continued to dismalize myself at times quite unnecessarily." Their titles included "The Early Doomed" and "The Complaint of a Nobody" (in which she compared herself to "a weed growing up in a garden"). When she finally quit the mill, the paymaster asked, "Going where you can earn more money?" "No," she remembered answering, "I am going where I can have more time." "Ah, yes!" he responded, "time is money." [21]

Even the *Lowell Offering* testified to the tensions between mill routines and rural rhythms and feelings. Historians have dismissed it too handily because the company sponsored it and refused to publish prose openly critical of mill policies. But the fiction and poetry of its contributors, derivative in style and frequently escapist, also often revealed dissatisfactions with the pace of work. Susan, explaining her first day in the mill to Ann, said the girls awoke early and one sang, "Morning bells, I hate to hear./Ringing dolefully, loud and clear." Susan went on:

> You cannot think how odd everything seemed to me. I wanted to laugh at everything, but did not know what to make sport of first. They set me to threading shuttles, and tying weaver's knots and such things, and now I have improved so that I can take care of one loom. I could take care of two if I only had eyes in the back of my head. . . . When I went out at night, the sound of the mill was in my ears, as of crickets, frogs, and Jew-harps, all mingled together in strange discord. After, it seemed as though cotton-wool was in my ears. But now I do not mind it at all. You know that people learn to sleep with the thunder of Niagara in their ears, and the cotton mill is no worse.

Ellen Collins quit the mill, complaining about her "obedience to the ding-dong of the bell—just as though we were so many living machines." In "A Weaver's Reverie," Ella explained why the mill women wrote "so much about the beauties of nature":

> Why is it that the delirious dreams of the famine-stricken are of tables loaded with the richest viands? . . . Oh, tell me

21. Roll Book of the Hamilton Company, 1826–1827, printed in Caroline Ware, *Early New England Cotton Manufacture* (Boston, 1924), 266–67; Harriet Robinson, *Loom and Spindle* (New York, 1898), 62–69; Lucy Larcom, *A New England Girlhood* (Boston, 1889), 138–43, 152–55, 174–76, 180–85, 209–19, 226–31.

why this is, and I will tell you why the factory girl sits in the hours of meditation and thinks, not of the crowded, clattering mill, nor of the noisy tenement which is her home.

Contemporary labor critics who scorned the *Lowell Offering* as little more than the work of "poor, caged birds," who "while singing of the roses . . . forget the bars of their prison," had not read it carefully. Their attachment to nature was the concern of persons working machines in a society still predominantly "a garden," and it was not unique to these Lowell women. In New Hampshire five hundred men and women petitioned the Amoskeag Manufacturing Company's proprietors in 1853 not to cut down an elm tree to allow room for an additional mill: "It was a beautiful and goodly tree" and belonged to a time "when the yell of the red man and the scream of the eagle were alone heard on the banks of the Merrimack, instead of two giant edifices filled with the buzz of busy and well-remunerated industry." Each day, the workers said, they viewed that tree as "a connecting link between the past and the present," and "each autumn [it] remind[s] us of our own mortality." [22]

Aspirations and expectations interpret experience and thereby help shape behavior. Some Lowell mill girls revealed dissatisfactions, and others made a difficult transition from rural New England to that model factory town, but that so few planned to remain mill workers eased that transition and hampered collective protest. Men as well as women who expect to spend only a

22. William Scoresby, *American Factories and Their Mill Operatives* (Boston, 1845), 21–23, 58–66, *passim;* Norman Ware, *Industrial Worker*, 1840–1860 (New York, 1924), 85; "New York Industrial Exhibition," *Sessional Papers* (Commons) 1854, vol. 26, p. 10; Ray Ginger, "Labor in a Massachusetts Cotton Mill," *Business History Review*, 28 (1954), 67–91 (a brilliant study of mobility among New England factory women). Useful works on the early New England cotton mills and their female workers include Caroline Ware, *op. cit.;* Hannah Josephson, *Golden Threads, Mill Girls and Magnates* (New York, 1949); Vera Shlakman, "Economic History of a Factory Town: A Study of Chicopee, Massachusetts," *Smith College Studies in History*, 20, nos. 1–4 (1934–1935); Edith Abbott, *op. cit.*

few years as factory workers have little incentive to join unions. That was just as true of the immigrant male common laborers in the steel mills of the late nineteenth and early twentieth centuries (when multiplant oligopoly characterized the nation's most important manufacturing industry) as in the Lowell cotton mills nearly a century earlier. David Brody has explained much about the common laborers. In those years, the steel companies successfully divorced wages from productivity to allow the market to shape them. Between 1890 and 1910, efficiencies in plant organization cut labor costs by about a third. The great Carnegie Pittsburgh plants employed 14,359 common laborers, 11,694 of them South and East Europeans. Most, peasant in origin, earned less than $12.50 a week (a family needed fifteen dollars for subsistence). A staggering accident rate damaged these and other men: nearly 25 percent of the recent immigrants employed at the Carnegie South Works were injured or killed each year between 1907 and 1910, 3,723 in all. But like the Lowell mill women, these men rarely protested in collective ways, and for good reason. They did not plan to stay in the steel mills long. Most had come to the United States as single men (or married men who had left their families behind) to work briefly in the mills, save some money, return home, and purchase farmland. Their private letters to European relatives indicated a realistic awareness of their working life that paralleled some of the Lowell fiction: "if I don't earn $1.50 a day, it would not be worth thinking about America"; "a golden land so long as there is work"; "here in America one must work for three horses"; "let him not risk coming, for he is too young"; "too weak for America." Men who wrote such letters and avoided injury often saved small amounts of money, and a significant number fulfilled their expectations and quit the factory and even the country. Forty-four South and East Europeans left the United States for every one hundred that arrived between 1908 and 1910. Not a steelworker, a young Italian boy living in Rochester, New York, summed up the expectations of many such immigrant men in a poem he wrote after studying English just three months:

> *Nothing job, nothing job,*
> *I come back to Italy;*
> *Nothing job, nothing job,*
> *Adieu, land northerly. . . .*

> *Nothing job, nothing job,*
> *O! sweet sky of my Italy;*
> *Nothing job, nothing job,*
> *How cold in this country. . . .*

> *Nothing job, nothing job,*
> *I return to Italy;*
> *Comrades, laborers, good-bye;*
> *Adieu, land of "Fourth of July."* [23]

Immigrant expectations coincided for a time with the fiscal needs of industrial manufacturers. The Pittsburgh steel magnates had as much good fortune as the Boston Associates. But the stability and passivity they counted on among their unskilled workers depended upon steady work and the opportunity to escape the mills. When frequent recessions caused recurrent unemployment, immigrant expectations and behavior changed. What Brody calls peasant "group consciousness" and "communal loyalty" sustained bitter wildcat strikes after employment picked up. The tenacity of these immigrant strikers for higher wages amazed contemporaries, and brutal suppression often accompanied them (Cleveland, 1899; East Chicago, 1905; McKees Rock, 1909; Bethlehem, 1910; and Youngstown in 1915 where, after a policeman shot into a peaceful parade, a riot caused an estimated one million dollars in damages). The First World War and its aftermath blocked the traditional route of overseas outward mobility, and the consciousness of immigrant steelworkers changed. They sparked the 1919 steel strike. The steel mill had become a way of life for them and was no longer

23. David Brody, *Steelworkers in America: The Non-Union Era* (Cambridge, 1960), 26–28, 36, 96–111, 119–20, 125–46, 180–86, *passim;* Brody, *Labor in Crisis* (Philadelphia, 1965), 15–45; "Song of an Italian Workman," Rochester (N.Y.) *Post-Express*, n.d., reprinted in *Survey,* 21 (1908), 492–93.

the means by which to reaffirm and even strengthen older peasant and village life-styles.[24]

III

LET US SHARPLY SHIFT the time perspective from the years before 1843 and those between 1893 and 1919 to the decades between 1843 and 1893 and also shift our attention to the artisans and skilled workers who differed so greatly in the culture and work-styles they brought to the factory from men and women bred in rural and village cultures. The focus, however, remains the same—the relationship between settled work habits and culture. This half-century saw the United States (not small pockets within it) industrialize as steam and machinery radically transformed the premodern American economic structure. That so much attention has been given to the Civil War as a crucial divide in the nation's history (and it was, of course, for certain purposes) too frequently has meant neglect by historians of common patterns of behavior that give coherence to this period. Few contemporaries described these large structural changes more effectively if indirectly than the Boston labor reformer Jennie Collins in 1871:

If you should enter a factory and find the water-wheels in the garret, the heaviest machinery in the seventh story, and the dressing and weaving in the basement, you would find the machinery and system less out of joint than at present it seems to be in this strange country of ours. The structure of our society is like a building for which the stones were carefully designed and carved, but in the construction of which the masons seized upon whatever block came handiest, without regard to design or fitness, using window-sills for partition walls, capstones for the foundation, and chink-pieces for the corner-stone.

24. Brody, *Steelworkers in America, op. cit., passim;* Brody, *Labor in Crisis, op. cit.,* 15–45.

The magnitude of the changes noticed by Collins cannot be understated. In 1869 half of the country's manufacturing enterprises still managed on water power. The nation in 1860 counted more slaves than factory workers. In his unpublished study of six upstate New York counties Richard L. Ehrlich has found that in five counties during that same year employment in manufacturing plants having at least fifty workers accounted for 37 percent or less of their respective labor forces. In the six counties (Albany, Erie, Monroe, Oneida, Onondaga, and Rensselaer) the average number of persons employed by firms engaging fewer than fifty employees was less than nine. In the year of Abraham Lincoln's election as president, the United States ranked behind England, France, and Germany in the value of its manufactured product. In 1894 the United States led the field: its manufactured product nearly equalled in value that of Great Britain, France, and Germany together. But such profound economic changes did not entirely shatter the older American social structure and the settled cultures of premodern native and immigrant American artisans. "There is no such thing as economic growth which is not, at the same time, growth or change of a culture," E. P. Thompson has written. Yet he also warns that "we should not assume any automatic, or over-direct, correspondence between the dynamic of economic growth and the dynamic of social or cultural life." That significant stricture applies as much to the United States as to England during its industrial revolution and especially to its native and immigrant artisans between 1843 and 1893.[25]

It is not surprising to find tenacious artisan work habits before the Civil War, what Thompson calls "alternate bouts of intense labour and of idleness wherever men were in control of their

---

25. Jennie Collins, *Nature's Aristocracy* (Boston, 1871), 4; Richard L. Ehrlich, "The Development of Manufacturing in Selected Counties in the Erie Canal Corridor, 1815-1860," (Ph.D. dissertation, State University of New York, Buffalo, 1972); Stuart Bruchey, *Roots of American Economic Growth* (New York, 1965), 139; George Rogers Taylor, *Transportation Revolution, 1815-1860* (New York, 1951), 249; Thompson, *Making of the English Working Class, op. cit.,* 97, 192.

working lives." An English cabinetmaker shared a New York City workplace with seven others (two native Americans, two Germans, and one man each from Ireland, England, and France), and the readers of *Knight's Penny Magazine* learned from him that "frequently . . . after several weeks of real hard work . . . a simultaneous cessation from work took place." "As if . . . by tacit agreement, every hand" contributed "loose change," and an apprentice left the place and "speedily returned laden with wine, brandy, biscuits, and cheese." Songs came forth "from those who felt musical," and the same near-ritual repeated itself two more times that day. Similar relaxations, apparently self-imposed, also broke up the artisans' work day in the New York City shipyards, and a ship carpenter described them as "an indulgence that custom had made as much of a necessity in a New York shipyard as a grind-stone":

In our yard, at half-past eight a.m., Aunt Arlie McVane, a clever kind-hearted but awfully uncouth, rough sample of the "Ould Sod," would make her welcome appearance in the yard with her two great baskets, stowed and checked off with crullers, doughnuts, ginger-bread, turnovers, pieces, and a variety of sweet cookies and cakes; and from the time Aunt Arlie's baskets came in sight until every man and boy, bosses and all, in the yard, had been supplied, always at one cent a piece for any article on the cargo, the pie, cake and cookie trade was a brisk one. Aunt Arlie would usually make the rounds of the yard and supply all hands in about an hour, bringing the forenoon up to half-past nine, and giving us from ten to fifteen minutes "breathing spell" during lunch; no one ever hurried during "cake-time."

Nor was this all:

After this was over we would fall to again, until interrupted by Johnnie Gogean, the English candyman, who came in always at half-past ten, with his great board, the size of a medium extension dining table, slung before him, covered with all sorts of "stick," and several of sticky candy, in one-cent lots. Bosses, boys and men—all hands, everybody —invested one to three cents in Johnnie's sweet wares, and another ten to fifteen minutes is spent in consuming it. Johnnie usually sailed out with a bare board until 11 o'clock at which time there was a general sailing out of the yard and into convenient grog-shops after whiskey; only we had four or five men among us, and one apprentice—not quite a year my senior—who used to sail out pretty regularly ten times a day on the average; two that went for whiskey only when some one invited them to drink, being too mean to treat themselves; and two more who never went at all.

In the afternoon, about half-past three, we had a cake-lunch, supplied by Uncle Jack Gridder, an old, crippled, superannuated ship carpenter. No one else was ever allowed to come in competition with our caterers. Let a foreign candyboard or cake basket make their appearance inside the gates of the yard, and they would get shipped out of that directly.

At about five o'clock p.m., always, Johnnie used to put in his second appearance; and then, having expended money in another stick or two of candy, and ten minutes in its consumption, we were ready to drive away again until sundown; then home to supper.

Less well-ordered in their daily pleasures, the shoemakers in Lynn, Massachusetts, nevertheless surrounded their way of work with a way of life. The former cobbler David Johnson recorded in minute detail in *Sketches of Old Lynn* how fishermen and farmers retained settled ways first as part-time shoemakers in small shops behind their homes. The language of the sea was adapted to the new craft:

There were a good many sea phrases, or "salt notes" as they were called, used in the shops. In the morning one would hear, "Come Jake, hoist the sails," which simply was a call to roll up the curtains. . . . If debate ran high upon some exciting topic, some veteran would quietly remark, "Squally, squally, today. Come better *luff* and bear away."

At times a shoemaker read from a newspaper to other men at work. Festivals, fairs, games ("trolling the tog"), and excursions were common rituals among the Lynn cobblers. So was heavy drinking with the bill often incurred by "the one who made the most or the fewest shoes, the best or the poorest." The man "paid 'the scot.' " "These were the days," Johnson reminded later and more repressed New England readers, "when temperance organizations were hardly known." [26]

Despite the profound economic changes that followed the American Civil War, Gilded Age artisans did not easily shed stubborn and time-honored work habits. Such work habits and the life-styles and subcultures related to them retained a vitality long into these industrializing decades. Not all artisans worked in factories, but some that did retained traditional craft skills. Mechanization came in different ways and at different times to diverse industries. Samuel Gompers recollected that New York City cigarmakers paid a fellow craftsman to read a newspaper to them while they worked, and Milwaukee cigarmakers struck in 1882 to retain such privileges as keeping (and then selling) damaged cigars and leaving the shop without a foreman's permission. "The difficulty with many cigarmakers," complained a New York City manufacturer in 1877, "is this. They come down to the shop in the morning; roll a few cigars and then go

26. Thompson, "Time, Work-Discipline, and Industrial Capitalism," *op. cit.,* 73; "A Workingman's Recollections of America," *Knight's Penny Magazine,* 1 (1846), 97–112; Richard D. Trevellick, in *Fincher's Trades Review,* n.d., reprinted in George E. McNeill, ed., *The Labor Movement: the Problem of To-day* (New York, 1887), 341–42; David Johnson, *Sketches of Old Lynn* (Lynn, 1880), 30–31, 36–49. The relationship between drink, work, and other artisanal communal activities was described inadvertently in unusual detail for dozens of British crafts and trades on nearly every page of John Dunlop's *The Philosophy of Artificial and Compulsory Drinking Usage in Great Britain and Ireland* (6th ed.; London, 1839), a 331-page temperance tract. There is good reason to believe that the craft customs described in this volume were known to American artisans and workers, too.

to a beer saloon and play pinnocio or some other game, . . . working probably only two or three hours a day." Coopers felt new machinery "hard and insensate," not a blessing but an evil that "took a great deal of joy out of life" because machine-made barrels undercut a subculture of work and leisure. Skilled coopers "lounged about" on Saturday (the regular payday), a "lost day" to their employers. A historian of American cooper-age explained:

> Early on Saturday morning, the big brewery wagon would drive up to the shop. Several of the coopers would club together, each paying his proper share, and one of them would call out the window to the driver, "Bring me a Goose Egg," meaning a half-barrel of beer. Then others would buy "Goose Eggs," and there would be a merry time all around. . . . Little groups of jolly fellows would often sit around upturned barrels playing poker, using rivets for chips, un-til they had received their pay and the "Goose Egg" was dry.
>
> Saturday night was a big night for the old-time cooper. It meant going out, strolling around the town, meeting friends, usually at a favorite saloon, and having a good time generally, after a week of hard work. Usually the good time continued over into Sunday, so that on the following day he usually was not in the best of condition to settle down to the regular day's work.
>
> Many coopers used to spend this day [Monday] sharpen-ing up their tools, carrying in stock, discussing current events, and in getting things in shape for the big day of work on the morrow. Thus, "Blue Monday" was something of a tradition with the coopers, and the day was also more or less lost as far as production was concerned.
>
> "Can't do much today, but I'll give her hell tomorrow," seemed to be the Monday slogan. But bright and early Tuesday morning, "Give her hell" they would, banging away lustily for the rest of the week until Saturday which was pay day again, and its thoughts of the "Goose Eggs."

Such traditions of work and leisure—in this case, a four-day work week and a three-day weekend—angered manufacturers anxious to ship goods as much as it worried Sabbatarians and temperance reformers. Conflicts over life- and work-styles occurred frequently and often involved control over the work process and over time. The immigrant Staffordshire potters in Trenton, New Jersey, worked in "bursts of great activity" and then quit for "several days at a time." "Monday," said a manufacturer, "was given up to debauchery." After the potters lost a bitter lockout in 1877 that included torchlight parades and effigy burnings, the *Crockery and Glass Journal* mockingly advised:

> Run your factories to please the crowd. . . . Don't expect work to begin before 9 a.m. or to continue after 3 p.m. Every employee should be served hot coffee and a bouquet at 7 a.m. and allowed the two hours to take a free perfumed bath. . . . During the summer, ice cream and fruit should be served at 12 p.m. to the accompaniment of witching music.

Hand coopers (and potters and cigarmakers, among others) worked hard but in distinctly preindustrial styles. Machine-made barrels pitted modernizing technology and modern habits against traditional ways. To the owners of competitive firms struggling to improve efficiency and cut labor costs, the Goose Egg and Blue Monday proved the laziness and obstinacy of craftsmen as well as the tyranny of craft unions that upheld venerable traditions. To the skilled cooper, the long weekend symbolized a way of work and life filled with almost ritualistic meanings. Between 1843 and 1893, compromise between such conflicting interests was hardly possible.[27]

27. Samuel Gompers, *Seventy Years of Life and Labor* (New York, 1925), 1: 42–53, 63–82; Thomas Gavett, *Development of the Labor Movement in Milwaukee* (Madison, 1965), 43 ff.: New York *Herald*, November 17, 1877; Franklin E. Coyne, *The Development of the Cooperage Industry in the United States* (Chicago, 1940), 7–26 but especially 21–22; *Crockery and Glass Journal*, n.d., reprinted in *Labor Standard* (N.Y.), September 9, 1877; Frank Thistlethwaite, "Atlantic

Settled premodern work habits existed among others than those employed in nonfactory crafts. Owners of already partially mechanized industries complained of them, too. "Saturday night debauches and Sunday carousels though they be few and far between," lamented the *Age of Steel* in 1882, "are destructive of modest hoardings, and he who indulges in them will in time become a striker for higher wages." In 1880 a British steelworker boasted that native Americans never would match immigrants in their skills: " 'adn't the 'ops, you know." Manufacturers, when able, did not hesitate to act decisively to end such troubles. In Fall River new technology allowed a print cloth manufacturer to settle a long-standing grievance against his stubborn mule spinners. "On Saturday afternoon after they had gone home," a boastful mill superintendent later recollected, "we started right in and smashed a room full of mules with sledge hammers. . . . On Monday morning, they were astonished to find that there was not work for them. That room is now full of ring frames run by girls." Woolen manufacturers also displaced handjack spinners with improved machinery and did so because of "the disorderly habits of English workmen. Often on a Monday morning, half of them would be absent from the mill in consequence of the Sunday's dissipation." Blue Monday, however, did not entirely disappear. Paterson artisans and factory hands held a May festival on a Monday each year ("Labor Monday") and that popular holiday soon became state law, the American Labor Day. It had its roots in earlier premodern work habits.[28]

The persistence of such traditional artisan work habits well into the nineteenth century deserves notice from others besides labor historians, because those work habits did not exist in a cultural or social vacuum. If modernizing technology threatened and even displaced such work patterns, diverse nineteenth-

Migration of the Pottery Industry," *Economic History Review*, 10 (1957–1958), 264–73.

28. *Age of Steel*, August 5, 1882 (courtesy of Lynn Mapes); Berthoff, *op. cit.*, 54–55, 146; announcement of "Great Festival" on "Labor Monday," Paterson *Labor Standard*, May 29, 1880.

century subcultures sustained and nourished them. "The old nations of the earth creep on at a snail's pace," boasted Andrew Carnegie in *Triumphant Democracy* (1886), "the Republic thunders past with the rush of an express." The articulate steelmaster, however, had missed the point. The very rapidity of the economic changes occurring in Carnegie's lifetime meant that many, unlike him, lacked the time, historically, culturally, and psychologically, to be separated or alienated from settled ways of work and life and from relatively fixed beliefs. Continuity not consensus counted for much in explaining working-class and especially artisan behavior in those decades that witnessed the coming of the factory and the radical transformation of American society. Persistent work habits were one example of that significant continuity. But these elements of continuity were often revealed among nineteenth-century American workers cut off by birth from direct contact with the preindustrial American past, a fact that has been ignored or blurred by the artificial separation between labor history and immigration history. In Gilded Age America (and afterward in the Progressive Era despite the radical change in patterns of immigration), working-class and immigration history regularly intersected, and that intermingling made for powerful continuities. In 1880, for example, 63 of every 100 Londoners were native to that city, 94 coming from England and Wales, and 98 from Great Britain and Ireland. Foreign countries together contributed only 1.6 percent to London's massive population. At that same moment, more than 70 of every 100 persons in San Francisco (78), St. Louis (78), Cleveland (80), New York (80), Detroit (84), Milwaukee (84), and Chicago (87) were immigrants or the children of immigrants, and the percentage was just as high in many smaller American industrial towns and cities. "Not every foreigner is a workingman," noticed the clergyman Samuel Lane Loomis in 1887, "but in the cities, at least, it may almost be said that every workingman is a foreigner." And until the 1890s most immigrants came from Northern and Western Europe, French- and English-speaking Canada, and China. In 1890, only 3 percent of the nation's foreign-born residents—

290,000 of 9,200,000 immigrants—had been born in Eastern or Southern Europe. (It is a little recognized fact that most North and West European immigrants migrated to the United States after, not before, the American Civil War.) When so much else changed in the industrializing decades, tenacious traditions flourished among immigrants in ethnic subcultures that varied greatly among particular groups and according to the size, age, and location of different cities and industries. ("The Irish," Henry George insisted, "burn like chips, the English like logs.") Class and occupational distinctions within a particular ethnic group also made for different patterns of cultural adaptation, but powerful subcultures thrived among them all.[29]

Suffering and plain poverty cut deeply into these ethnic working-class worlds. In reconstructing their everyday texture there is no reason to neglect or idealize such suffering, but it is time to discard the notion that the large-scale uprooting and exploitative processes that accompanied industrialization caused little more than cultural breakdown and social anomie. Family, class, and ethnic ties did not dissolve easily. "Almost as a matter of definition," the sociologist Neil Smelzer has written, "we associate the factory system with the decline of the family and the onset of anonymity." Smelzer criticized such a view of early industrializing England, and it has just as little validity for nineteenth-century industrializing America. Family roles changed in important ways, and strain was widespread, but the immigrant working-class family held together. Examination of household composition in sixteen census enumeration districts in Paterson in 1880 makes that clear for this predominantly working-class immigrant city, and while research on other ethnic working-class communities will reveal significant variations, the overall patterns should not differ greatly. The Paterson immi-

29. Andrew Carnegie quoted in Henry Pelling, *America and the British Left* (New York, 1957), 52; Samuel Lane Loomis, *Modern Cities and Their Religious Problems* (New York, 1887), 68–73; Henry George quoted in Carl Wittke, *Irish in America* (Baton Rouge, 1956), 193.

TABLE 1. MALE OCCUPATIONAL STRUCTURE AND HOUSEHOLD COMPOSITION BY ETHNIC GROUP, PATERSON, NEW JERSEY, 1880, ENUMERATION DISTRICTS 150–53, 161–72[a]

	British	German	Irish	Native White
Total Males 20 and Older	2090	927	2841	1461
Total Females 20 and Older	1941	804	3466	1689
Male Occupational Structure				
Unskilled Laborer	8.2%	9.8%	43.6%	20.8%
Skilled Worker	75.5%	64.3%	44.8%	62.5%
Nonlaborer	16.3%	25.9%	11.6%	16.7%
Household Composition				
Number of Kin-related Households	1402	686	2142	905
Number of Subfamilies[b]	117	41	158	125
Nuclear Households	73.9%	78.1%	73.1%	65.7%
Extended Households	13.5%	10.3%	13.6%	18.7%
Augmented Households[c]	14.6%	13.1%	15.3%	19.0%
Percent of Households and Subfamilies with a Husband and/or Father Present	87.2%	91.6%	81.1%	78.9%

[a] I am indebted to Carol Waserloos for gathering the raw Paterson data from the 1880 federal manuscript census schedules.

[b] A subfamily is defined as a complete or incomplete nuclear family residing with another nuclear family.

[c] Augmented households include lodgers. The sum of nuclear, augmented, and extended households is greater than 100 percent because some households included both relatives and lodgers and have been counted twice.

grant (and native white) communities were predominantly working class, and most families among them were intact in their composition. For this population, at least (and without accounting for age and sex ratio differences between the ethnic groups), a greater percentage of immigrant than native white households included two parents. Ethnic and predominantly working-class communities in industrial towns like Paterson and in larger cities, too, built on these strained but hardly broken familial and kin ties. Migration to another country, life in the city, and labor in cost-conscious and ill-equipped factories and workshops tested but did not shatter what the anthropologist Clifford Geertz has described as primordial (as contrasted to civic) attachments, "the 'assumed' givens . . . of social existence: immediate contiguity and kin connections mainly, but beyond them, the givenness that stems from being born into a particular religious community, speaking a particular language, and following particular social patterns." Tough familial and kin ties made possible the transmission and adaptation of European working-class cultural patterns and beliefs to industrializing America. As late as 1888, residents in some Rhode Island mill villages figured their wages in British currency. Common rituals and festivals bound together such communities. Paterson silk weavers had their Macclesfield wakes, and Fall River cotton mill workers their Ashton wakes. British immigrants "banded together to uphold the popular culture of the homeland" and celebrated saints' days: St. George's Day, St. Andrew's Day, and St. David's Day. Even funerals retained an archaic flavor. Samuel Sigley, a Chartist house painter, had fled Ashton-under-Lyne in 1848, and built American trade unions. When his wife died in the late 1890s a significant ritual occurred during the funeral: some friends placed a chaff of wheat on her grave. Mythic beliefs also cemented ethnic and class solidarities. The Irish-American press, for example, gave Martin O'Brennan much space to argue that Celtic had been spoken in the Garden of Eden, and in Paterson Irish-born silk, cotton, and iron workers believed in the magical powers of that town's "Dublin Spring." An old resident remembered:

There is a legend that an Irish fairy brought over the water
in her apron from the Lakes of Killarney and planted it in
the humble part of that town. . . . There were dozens of
legends connected with the Dublin Spring and if a man
drank from its precious depository . . . he could never leave
Paterson [but] only under the fairy influence, and the wand
of the nymph would be sure to bring him back again some
time or other.

When a "fairy" appeared in Paterson in human form, some
believed she walked the streets "as a tottering old woman
begging with a cane." Here was a way to assure concern for the
elderly and the disabled.[30]

Much remains to be studied about these cross-class but
predominantly working-class ethnic subcultures common to
industrializing America. Relations within them between skilled
and unskilled workers, for example, remain unclear. But the
larger shape of these diverse immigrant communities can be
sketched. More than mythic beliefs and common work habits
sustained them. Such worlds had in them what Thompson has
called "working-class intellectual traditions, working-class community patterns, and a working-class structure of feeling," and
men with artisan skills powerfully affected the everyday texture
of such communities. A model subculture included friendly and
benevolent societies as well as friendly local politicians, commu-
nity-wide holiday celebrations, an occasional library (the Balti-

30. Neil Smelzer, *Social Change in the Industrial Revolution* (Chicago, 1959),
193; Clifford Geertz, *Old Societies and New States* (Glencoe, 1963), 109–10; Lillie
B. Chace Wyman, "Studies in Factory Life," *Atlantic Monthly*, 62 (1888), 17–29,
215–21, 605–21, and 63 (1889), 68–79; Berthoff, *op. cit.*, 147–81, *passim;* Paterson
Labor Standard, October 2, 1897; Thomas N. Brown, *Irish-American Nationalism*
(Philadelphia, 1966), 32; Paterson *Evening News*, October 27, 1900. Except for
the fact that nuclear households declined greatly at the expense of households
containing lodgers (augmented households), examination of the household
composition among immigrant Jews and Italians in Lower Manhattan in 1905
shows that powerful familial and kin ties bound together later immigrant
communities, too. The data are summarized briefly in Table 3 (see appendix to
this essay, page 77).

more Journeymen Bricklayer's Union taxed members one dollar a year in the 1880s to sustain a library that included the collected works of William Shakespeare and Sir Walter Scott's *Waverley* novels), participant sports, churches sometimes headed by a sympathetic clergy, saloons, beer gardens, and concert halls or music halls and, depending upon circumstances, trade unionists, labor reformers, and radicals. The Massachusetts cleric Jonathan Baxter Harrison published in 1880 an unusually detailed description of one such ethnic, working-class institution, a Fall River music hall and saloon. About fifty persons were there when he visited it, nearly one-fourth of them young women. "Most of those present," he noticed, were "persons whom I had met before, in the mills and on the streets. They were nearly all operatives, or had at some time belonged to that class." An Englishman sang first, and then a black whose songs "were of many kinds, comic, sentimental, pathetic, and silly. . . . When he sang 'I got a mammy in the promised land,' with a strange, wailing refrain, the English waiter-girl, who was sitting at my table, wiped her eyes with her apron, and everybody was very quiet." Harrison said of such places in Fall River:

> All the attendants . . . had worked in the mills. The young man who plays the piano is usually paid four or five dollars per week, besides his board. The young men who sing receive one dollar per night, but most of them board themselves. . . . The most usual course for a man who for any reason falls out of the ranks of mill workers (if he loses his place by sickness or is discharged) is the opening of a liquor saloon or drinking place.

Ethnic ties with particular class dimensions sometimes stretched far beyond local boundaries and even revealed themselves in the behavior of the most successful practitioners of Gilded Age popular culture. In 1884, for example, the pugilist John L. Sullivan and the music-hall entertainers Harrigan and Hart promised support to striking Irish coal miners in the Ohio

Hocking Valley. Local ties, however, counted for much more and had their roots inside and outside of the factory and workshop. Soon after Cyrus H. McCormick, then twenty-one, took over the management of his father's great Chicago iron machinery factory (which in the early 1880s employed twelve hundred men and boys), a petition signed by "Many Employees" reached his hands:

> It only pains us to relate to you . . . that a good many of our old hands is not here this season and if Mr. Evarts is kept another season a good many more will leave. . . . We pray for you . . . to remove this man. . . . We are treated as though we were dogs. . . . He has cut wages down so low they are living on nothing but bread. . . . We can't talk to him about wages if we do he will tell us to go out side the gate. . . . He discharged old John the other day he has been here seventeen years. . . . There is Mr. Church who left us last Saturday he went about and shook hands with every old hand in the shop . . . this brought tears to many mens eyes. He has been here nineteen years and has got along well with them all until he came to Mr. Evarts the present superintendent.

Artisans, themselves among those later displaced by new technology, signed this petition, and self-educated artisans (or professionals and petty enterprisers who had themselves usually risen from the artisan class) often emerged as civic and community leaders. "Intellectually," Jennie Collins noticed in Boston in the early 1870s, "the journeymen tailors . . . are ever discussing among themselves questions of local and national politics, points of law, philosophy, physics, and religion." [31]

---

31. Thompson, *Making of the English Working Class, op. cit.,* 194; Richard T. Ely, *Labor Movement in America* (New York, 1886), 125; Jonathan Baxter Harrison, *Certain Dangerous Tendencies in American Life and Other Essays* (Boston, 1880), 178–88; *National Labor Tribune* (Pittsburgh), December 13, 1884; Robert Ozanne, *Century of Labor-Management Relations at McCormick and International Harvester* (Madison, 1967), 10–28; Collins, *op. cit.,* 94.

Such life-styles and subcultures adapted and changed over time. In the Gilded Age piece-rates in nearly all manufacturing industries helped reshape traditional work habits. "Two generations ago," said the Connecticut Bureau of Labor Statistics in 1885, "time-work was the universal rule." "Piece-work" had all but replaced it, and the Connecticut Bureau called it "a moral force which corresponds to machinery as a physical force." Additional pressures came in traditional industries such as shoe, cigar, furniture, barrel, and clothing manufacture, which significantly mechanized in these years. Strain also resulted where factories employed large numbers of children and young women (in the 1880 manuscript census 49.3 percent of all Paterson boys and 52.1 percent of all girls aged eleven to fourteen had occupations listed by their names) and was especially common among the as yet little-studied pools of casual male laborers found everywhere. More than this, mobility patterns significantly affected the structure and the behavior of these predominantly working-class communities. A good deal of geographic mobility, property mobility (home ownership), and occupational mobility (skilled status in new industries or in the expanding building trades, petty retail enterprise, the professions, and public employment counted as the most important ways to advance occupationally) reshaped these ethnic communities as Stephan Thernstrom and others have shown. But so little is yet known about the society in which such men and women lived and about the cultures which had produced them that it is entirely premature to infer "consciousness" (beliefs and values) only from mobility rates. Such patterns and rates of mobility, for example, did not entirely shatter working-class capacities for self-protection. The fifty-year period between 1843 and 1893 was not conducive to permanent, stable trade unions, but these decades were a time of frequent strikes and lockouts and other forms of sustained conflict.[32]

32. *Connecticut Bureau of Labor Statistics, First Annual Report, 1885* (Hartford, 1885), 70–73; Stephan Thernstrom, *Poverty and Progress, Social Mobility in a Nineteenth Century City* (Cambridge, 1964), *passim;* and Thernstrom and Richard Sennett, eds., *Nineteenth Century Cities* (New Haven, 1969), *passim.*

Not all strikes and lockouts resulted in the defeat of poorly organized workers. For the years 1881 to 1887, for example, the New Jersey Bureau of Labor Statistics collected information on 890 New Jersey industrial disputes involving mostly workers in the textile, glass, metal, transportation, and building trades: 6 percent ended in compromise settlements; employers gained the advantage in 40 percent; strikers won the rest (54 percent). In four of five disputes concerning higher wages and shorter hours, New Jersey workers, not their employers, were victorious. Large numbers of such workers there and elsewhere were foreign-born or the children of immigrants. More than this, immigrant workers in the mid-1880s joined trade unions in numbers far out of proportion to their place in the labor force. Statistical inquiries by the Bureau of Labor Statistics in Illinois in 1886 and in New Jersey in 1887 make this clear. Even these data may not have fully reflected the proclivity of immigrants to seek self-protection. (Such a distortion would occur if, for example, the children of immigrants apparently counted by the bureaus as native-born had remained a part of the ethnic subcultures into which they had been born and joined trade unions as regularly as the foreign-born.) Such information from Illinois and New Jersey suggests the need to treat the meaning of social mobility

Table 2. Organized Workers, Male Whites
in Nonagricultural Pursuits,
Illinois (1886) and New Jersey (1887)

| | Illinois 1886 | | New Jersey 1887 | |
Nativity	Bread-winners	Organ-ized	Bread-winners	Organ-ized
Number				
Native-born	423,290	25,985	243,093	24,463
Foreign-born	308,595	57,163	137,385	26,704
Percent				
Native-born	57.8%	31.3%	63.9%	47.8%
Foreign-born	42.2%	68.7%	36.1%	52.2%

with some care. So does the sketchy outline of Hugh O'Donnell's career. By 1892, when he was twenty-nine years old, he had already improved his social status a great deal. Before the dispute with Andrew Carnegie and Henry Clay Frick culminated in the bitter Homestead lockout that year, O'Donnell had voted Republican, owned a home, and had in it a Brussels carpet and even a piano. Nevertheless this Irish-American skilled worker led the Homestead workers and was even indicted under a Civil War treason statute never before used. The material improvements O'Donnell had experienced mattered greatly to him and suggested significant mobility, but culture and tradition together with the way in which men like O'Donnell interpreted the transformation of Old America defined the value of those material improvements and their meaning to him.[33]

Other continuities between 1843 and 1893 besides those rooted in artisan work habits and diverse ethnic working-class subcultures deserve brief attention as important considerations in understanding the behavior of artisans and other workers in these decades. I have suggested in other writings that significant patterns of opposition to the ways in which industrial capitalism developed will remain baffling until historians re-examine the relationship between the premodern American political system and the coming of the factory along with the strains in premodern popular American ideology shared by workers and large numbers of successful self-made Americans (policemen, clergymen, politicians, small businessmen, and even some "traditional" manufacturers) that rejected the legitimacy of the modern factory system and its owners.[34] One strain of thought

33. Table on New Jersey and Illinois trade-union membership in Isaac Hourwich, *Immigration and Labor: The Economic Aspects of European Immigration to the United States* (New York, 1912), 524; Leon Woolf, *Lockout: The Story of the Homestead Strike of 1892* (New York, 1965), 187–88.

34. See, for examples, H. G. Gutman, "The Worker's Search for Power: Labor in the Gilded Age," in H. Wayne Morgan, ed., *The Gilded Age: A Reappraisal* (Syracuse, 1963), 38–68; Gutman, "Protestantism and the American Labor Movement: The Christian Spirit in the Gilded Age," *American Historical Review*, 72 (1966–1967), 74–101; Gutman, "Class, Status, and Community Power in Nineteenth Century American Industrial Cities: Paterson, New Jersey, a Case

common to the rhetoric of nineteenth-century immigrant and native-born artisans is considered here. It helps explain their recurrent enthusiasm for land and currency reform, cooperatives, and trade unions. It was the fear of dependence, "proletarianization," and centralization, and the worry that industrial capitalism threatened to transform "the Great Republic of the West" into a "European" country. In 1869, the same year that saw the completion of the transcontinental railroad, the chartering of the Standard Oil Company, the founding of the Knights of Labor, and the dedication of a New York City statue to Cornelius Vanderbilt, some London workers from Westbourne Park and Notting Hill petitioned the American ambassador for help to emigrate. "Dependence," they said of Great Britain, "not independence, is inculcated. Hon. Sir, this state of things we wish to fly from . . . to become citizens of that great Republican country, which has no parallels in the world's history." Such men had a vision of Old America, but it was not a new vision. Industrial transformation between 1840 and 1890 tested and redefined that vision. Seven years after their visit, the New York *Labor Standard*, then edited by an Irish socialist, bemoaned what had come over the country: "There was a time when the United States was the workingman's country, . . . the land of promise for the workingman. . . . We are now in an *old country*." This theme recurred frequently as disaffected workers, usually self-educated artisans, described the transformation of premodern America. "America," said the Detroit *Labor Leaf*, "used to be the land of promise to the poor. . . . The Golden Age is indeed over—the Age of Iron has taken its place. The iron law of necessity has taken the place of the golden rule." We need not join in mythicizing preindustrial American society in order to suggest that this tension between the old and the new helps give a coherence to the decades between 1843 and 1893 that even the trauma of the Civil War does not disturb.[35]

Study," in Frederic C. Jaher, ed., *The Age of Industrialism: Essays in Social Structure and Cultural Values* (New York, 1968), 263–87.

35. *Reynold's Newspaper* (London), March 28, 1869; *Labor Standard* (N.Y.), May 6, 1876; Detroit *Labor Leaf*, September 30, 1885.

As early as the 1830s, the theme that industrialism promised to make over the United States into a "European" country had its artisan and working-class advocates. Seth Luther then made this clear in his complaint about "gentlemen" who "exultingly call LOWELL the Manchester of America" and in his plea that the Bunker Hill monument "stand *unfinished,* until the time passes away when aristocrats talk about mercy to mechanics and laborers, . . . until our rights are acknowledged." The tensions revealed in labor rhetoric between the promises of the Republic and the practices of those who combined capital and technology to build factories continued into the 1890s. In 1844 New England shoemakers rewrote the Declaration of Independence to protest that the employers "have robbed us of certain rights," and two years later New England textile workers planned without success a general strike to start on July 4, 1846, calling it "a second Independence Day." The great 1860 shoemakers' strike in Lynn started on George Washington's birthday, a celebration strikers called "sacred to the memory of one of the greatest men the world has ever produced." Fear for the Republic did not end with the Civil War. The use of state militia to help put down a strike of Northeastern Pennsylvania workers in 1874 caused *Equity,* a Boston labor weekly, to condemn the Erie Railroad as "the George III of the working-man's movement" and "the Government of Pennsylvania" as "but its parliament." ("Regiments," it added, "to protect dead things.")[36]

Such beliefs, not the status anxieties of Progressive muckrakers and New Deal historians, gave rise to the pejorative phrase "robber baron." Discontented Gilded Age workers found in that phrase a way to summarize their worries about dependence and centralization. "In America," exploded the *National Labor Tribune* in 1874, "we have realized the ideal of republican government at least in form." "America," it went on, "was the

36. Luther, *Address to the Workingmen of New England, passim;* Ware, *op. cit.,* 38–48; Philip S. Foner, *History of the Labor Movement in the United States* (New York, 1947), 1: 202–09, 241–45, 292; *Equity* (Boston), 1 (1874), quoted in James Dombrowski, *Early Days of Christian Socialism* (New York, 1936), 81.

star of the political Bethlehem which shone radiantly out in the
dark night of political misrule in Europe. The masses of the old
world gazed upon her as their escape." Men in America could be
"their own rulers"; "no one could or should become their
masters." But industrialization had created instead a nightmare:
"These dreams have not been realized. . . . The working people
of this country . . . suddenly find capital as rigid as an absolute
monarchy." Two years later, the same Pittsburgh labor weekly
asked, "Shall we let the gold barons of the nineteenth century
put iron collars of ownership around our necks as did the feudal
barons with their serfs in the fourteenth century?" The rhetoric
surrounding the little-understood 1877 railroad strikes and riots
summed up these fears. Critics of the strikers urged repressive
measures such as the building of armories in large cities and the
restriction of the ballot, and a few, including Elihu Burritt, even
favored importing "British" institutions to the New World. But
the disorders also had their defenders, and a strain in their
rhetoric deserves notice. A radical Massachusetts clergyman
called the strikers "the lineal descendants of Samuel Adams,
John Hancock, and the Massachusetts yeomen who began so
great a disturbance a hundred years ago . . . only now the kings
are money kings and then they were political kings." George
McNeill, a major figure in the nineteenth-century labor movement and later a founder of the American Federation of Labor,
denied that the Paris Commune had come to America: "The
system which the pilgrims planted here has yet a residue of
followers. No cry of 'commune' can frighten the descendants of
the New England commune. This is the COMMONWEALTH, not
the *Class* wealth, of Massachusetts." A discharged Pittsburgh
brakeman put it differently in blaming the violence on a general
manager who treated the railroad workers "no better than the
serfs of Great Britain, sir, . . . introduced into this country a lot
of English ideas and customs, [and] made our men wear
uniforms and traveling bags." "A uniform," he worried, "con-
stantly reminds them of their serfdom, and I for one would
rather remain out of work than wear one." An amazed reporter
wondered how this man could "assert his rights as a free born

American, even if in so doing himself and family starved." [37]

This Pittsburgh brakeman revealed values that persisted throughout the decades of industrialization, that expressed themselves most commonly in the rhetoric and behavior of artisans and skilled workers, and that worried other influential Americans besides railroad magnates and industrial manufacturers. In 1896 an army officer won a prize for writing the best essay submitted to the *Journal of the Military Service Institutions of the United States.* Theodore Roosevelt helped to judge the contest. The officer insisted that "discipline" needed to be more rigorous in an American as opposed to a European army. Even though he knew little about European societies, his insistence that "means of discipline are entirely artificial productions of law" in the United States counted as a profound insight into a social condition that plagued industrialists and sparked frequent discontent among skilled and other workers in industrializing America:

Discipline should be as a rod of iron. It may seem hopelessly illogical to claim that the army of a free people needs to be kept in stricter discipline than any other army, with wider space between the officers and the enlisted men, yet there are natural reasons why it should be so. The armies of Europe are drawn from people who for countless generations have lived under monarchical institutions and class government, where every man is born and bred to pay homage to some other man, and the habit of subordination to the will of another is a matter of heredity. It is natural that when such a man finds himself in the army he is not only amenable to discipline, but any relaxation on the part of the officer would be accepted as a matter of grace.

With us these conditions are reversed. Every man is born and bred in the idea of equality, and means of discipline are

37. *National Labor Tribune* (Pittsburgh), December 12, 1874, and October 14, 1876; Jesse Jones, "Railroad Strike of 1877," and George McNeill, "An Address," *Labor Standard* (N.Y.), August 26, and September 30, 1877; Robert, Pittsburgh dispatch, Chicago *Inter-Ocean*, September 11, 1877.

entirely artificial productions of law, not only without support from traditional habit, but they have that habit to overcome, and familiarity on the part of the officer would breed contempt of authority.

Two decades earlier, the London editor of the *Industrial Review* and increasingly conservative British trade-union leader, George Potter, posed the same problem somewhat differently. The disorders incident to the 1877 railroad strikes convinced him that Americans then lived through an earlier stage of English history, before "habit" had "begotten" men to "use their combinations peaceably and wisely." "The state of things that existed then in England," Potter insisted, "exists now in the United States. It was at one time believed that this was impossible within the borders of the great Republic, but it has proved itself wrong." Potter believed that the widespread violence in 1877 had been caused by men "suddenly or newly brought together to defend an interest" and therefore lacking "that wisdom of method that time and experience develop." But Potter was wrong. The men who quit work in 1877 (and before and after that) included many deeply rooted in traditional crafts and worried that the transformation of the American social and economic structure threatened settled ways of work and life and particular visions of a just society. Their behavior—in particular the little-understood violence that accompanied the strikes (including the burning and destruction of the Pennsylvania Railroad's Pittsburgh yards and equipment)—makes this clear. It had specific purposes and was the product of long-standing grievances that accompanied the transformation of Old America into New America.[38]

38. Major George Wilson, "The Army: Its Employment During Times of Peace and the Necessity for Its Increase," *Journal of the Military Service Institutions of the United States*, 18 (1896), 8–9; George Potter, "The American Labour Riots," *Industrial Review* (London), August 4, 1877, p. 9.

I V

QUITE DIVERSE PATTERNS of collective lower-class behavior (some of them disorderly and even violent) accompanied the industrialization of the United States, and certain of them (especially those related to artisan culture and to peasant and village cultures still fresh to factory labor and to the machine) deserve brief attention. Characteristic European forms of "premodern" artisan and lower-class protest in the United States occurred before (prior to 1843), during (1843–1893), and after (1893–1919) the years when the country "modernized." The continuing existence of such behavior followed from the changing composition of the working-class population. Asa Briggs's insistence that "to understand how people respond to industrial change it is important to examine what kind of people they were at the beginning of the process" and "to take account of continuities as well as new ways of thinking," poses in different words the subtle interplay between culture and society that is an essential factor in explaining lower-class behavior. Although their frequency remains the subject for much further detailed study, examples of premodern lower-class behavior abound for the entire period from 1815 to 1919, and their presence suggests how much damage has been done to the past American working-class experiences by historians busy, as R. H. Tawney complained more than half a century ago, "dragging into prominence forces which have triumphed and thrusting into the background those which have been swallowed up." Attention is briefly given to three types of American artisan and lower-class behavior explored in depth and with much illumination by European social historians ("church-and-king" crowds, machine-breaking, and food riots) and to the presence in quite different working-class protests of powerful secular and religious rituals. These occurred over the entire period under examination, not just in the early phases of industrial development.[39]

39. Asa Briggs, review of Thompson, *Making of the English Working Class*, in *Labor History*, 6 (1965), 84–91; R. H. Tawney, *Agrarian Problem in the Sixteenth Century* (London, 1912), 177.

Not much is yet known about premodern American artisan and urban lower-class cultures, but scattered evidence suggests a possible American variant of the European church-and-king phenomenon. Although artisan and lower-class urban cultures before 1843 await their historians, popular street disorders (sometimes sanctioned by the established authorities) happened frequently and increasingly caused concern to the premodern elite classes. Street gangs, about which little is yet known except the suggestion that some had as members artisans (not just casual or day laborers) and were often organized along ethnic lines, grew more important in the coastal and river towns after 1830. New York City, among other towns, had its Fly Boys, Chichesters, Plug Uglies, Buckaroos, and Slaughterhouse Gangs, and their violence against recent immigrants provoked disorderly counterthrusts. Political disorders on election days, moreover, were apparently well-organized and may have involved such gangs. The recurrence of such disorders through the pre-Civil War decades (including the nativist outbursts in nearly all major Northern and Southern cities in the 1850s) may have meant that local political parties, in their infancy, served as the American substitute for the king and the church, a third party "protecting" artisans and even day laborers from real and imagined adversaries and winning clanlike loyalty. Although the testimony of Mike Walsh, a Tammany leader and later the publisher of the *Police Gazette*, must be read with care, he suggested an interesting relationship between the decline of premodern lower-class entertainments and the rise of modern political "machines." Election politics, Walsh noted in the *Subterranean*, saw "the Goth-and-Vandal-like eruption of the shirtless and unwashed democracy" which Walsh connected to the disappearance of popular lower-class entertainments. A "gloomy, churlish, money-worshipping . . . spirit" had "swept nearly all the poetry out of the poor man's sphere," said the editor-politician. "Ballad-singing, street dancing, tumbling, public games, all are either prohibited or discountenanced, so that Fourth of July and election sports alone remain." Workers flocked to political clubs and labored hard for a party to "get a taste of the equality which they hear so much preached, but never, save there, see even partially practiced." If Walsh's insight has merit, political parties quite possibly competed with early craft unions in adapting older forms of popular entertainment and ritual to changing needs. That process, once started, had a life beyond the early years of the premodern political party and continued as the composition of the working class changed. The ethnic political "boss" created a new dependence that exploited well-understood class feelings and resentments but blunted class consciousness. The relationship, however, was not simple, and in the 1880s the socialist Joseph P. McDonnell exploited that same relationship to convince local New Jersey politicians to respond to pressures from predominantly immigrant workers and thereby to pioneer in the passage of humane social legislation, a process that began well before the stirring of the middle- and upper-class conscience in Progressive America.[40]

Available evidence does not yet indicate that machine-breaking of the "Luddite" variety was widespread in the United States. There are suggestive hints in reports that Ohio farm laborers burnt and destroyed farm machinery in 1878 and that twenty years later in Buffalo a crowd of Polish common day laborers and their wives rioted to break a street-paving machine, but the only clear evidence found of classic machine-breaking occurred early in the Civil War among rural blacks in the South Carolina Sea Islands, who resisted Yankee missionary and military efforts to make them plant cotton instead of corn and therefore broke up cotton gins and hid the iron work. "They do not see the use of cotton," said a Northern woman school-

40. Mike Walsh, *Subterranean* (New York, n.d.), quoted in M. R. Werner, *Tammany Hall* (New York, 1932), 49–51 (courtesy of Paul Weinbaum). On gangs, nativism, politics, and antebellum street violence, see A. F. Harlow, *Old Bowery Days* (New York, 1931), *passim;* Ray Billington, *Protestant Crusade, 1800–1860* (New York, 1938), *passim;* and McNeill, *Labor Movement*, 344. The ways in which McDonnell used machine politics and politicians to push social reform in the 1880s are described in Gutman, "Class, Status, and the Gilded Age Radical: The Case of a New Jersey Socialist," Gutman and Gregory S. Kealey, eds., *Many Pasts: Readings in American Social History* (Englewood Cliffs, 1973), 2: 125–51.

teacher, and a Yankee entrepreneur among them added that "nothing was more remote from their shallow pates than the idea of planting cotton for 'white-folks' again." (Some time later, this same man ordered a steam-run cotton gin. "This engine," he confided, "serves as a moral stimulus to keep the people at work at their hand-gins, for they want to gin all the cotton by hand, and I tell them if they don't by the middle of January I shall get it by steam.") If white workers rarely broke machines to protest their introduction, they sometimes destroyed the product of new technology. In the early 1830s Brooklyn ropemakers paraded a "hated machine" through town and then "committed to the flames" its product. Theirs was not an irrational act. They paid for the destroyed hemp, spun "a like quantity" to allow the machine's owner to "fulfill his engagement for its delivery," and advertised their product in a newspaper, boasting that its quality far surpassed machine-made rope "as is well known to any practical ropemaker and seaman." Silk weavers in the Hudson River towns of New Jersey broke looms in 1877 but only to prevent production during a strike. A more common practice saw the destruction of the product of labor or damage to factory and mining properties to punish employers and owners. Paterson silk weavers regularly left unfinished warps to spoil in looms. Crowds often stoned factories, burned mine tipples, and did other damage to industrial properties (as in the bitter Western Pennsylvania coke strikes between 1884 and 1894) but mostly to protest the hiring of new hands or violence against themselves by "police." Construction gangs especially in railroad work also frequently destroyed property. In 1831, between two and three hundred construction workers, mostly Irish, punished an absconding contractor by "wantonly" tearing up track they built. Similar penalties were meted out by Italian construction gangs between 1880 and 1910 and by unorganized railroad workers, mostly native-born repairmen and trainmen, between 1850 and 1880, who tore up track, spiked switches, stole coupling links and pins, and did other damage to protest changing work rules or to collect back wages.[41]

41. *Labor Standard* (N.Y.), September 28, 1878; Edward S. Abdy, *Journal of a Residence and Tour in the United States from April 1833 to October 1834* (London,

"Luddism" may have been rare, but classic "European" food riots occurred in the United States, and two in New York City—the first in 1837 and the second in 1902—that involved quite different groups of workers are briefly examined to

1838), 1: 77–79; Gutman, "Class, Status, and Community Power"; Pennsylvania Bureau of Labor Statistics, *Fifteenth Annual Report, 1887* (Harrisburg, 1888), F1–F18, and *Nineteenth Annual Report, 1891* (Harrisburg, 1892), D1–D18; *Niles' Weekly Register*, 40 (1831), 338–39; New York *Tribune*, May 2, 1857; *John Swinton's Paper* (N.Y.), February 24, 1884; New York *Tribune*, October 21, 1893; *New York State Board of Mediation and Arbitration, Eleventh Annual Report, 1898* (New York, 1899), 139–42; Gutman, "Trouble on the Railroads in 1873–1874," *Labor History*, 2 (1961), 215–35. The materials on the Sea Island blacks are found in Laura Towne, *Letters and Diaries of Laura S. Towne 1862–1884, Written from the Sea Islands of South Carolina*, ed. Rupert S. Holland (Cambridge, Mass., 1910), 16–17, 20–21; Elizabeth Ware Pearson, ed., *Letters from Port Royal, 1862–1868* (Boston, 1906), 221–22, 236–37, 250; Willie Lee Rose, *Port Royal Experiment: Rehearsal for Reconstruction* (Indianapolis, 1964), 141; Jane and William Pease, *Black Utopias* (Madison, 1963), 134, 143, 149–50. Although American blacks are not included in these pages, the behavior and thought of rural and urban blacks fits the larger patterns suggested here in a special way. Their experiences first as slaves and then as dependent laborers in the rural South as well as in the industrial North (where most manufacturing industries remained closed to them until the First World War) distinguished most lower-class blacks from all immigrant and native white workers. In still little-understood but profoundly important ways enslavement followed by racial exclusion sustained among blacks a culture that despite change remained preindustrial for more than merely two or three generations. Despite this significant difference, similarities in behavior between blacks and native and immigrant white workers can be noticed. Visitors to the Richmond tobacco factories in the 1850s found industrial slaves there who practiced "Blue Monday." Joseph C. Roberts, *The Story of Tobacco in America* (New York, 1949), 86–91. Blacks themselves made comparisons to whites who shared difficult premodern rural experiences: "I have never heard any songs like those [slave songs] anywhere since I left slavery, except when in Ireland. . . . It was during the famine of 1845–1846." Frederick Douglass said that. Quoted in Harriet Beecher Stowe, *Men of Our Times* (Hartford, 1868), 395. Contemporary observers who noticed black work habits after emancipation rarely told of "laziness" but nearly always noticed irregularity, and in 1909 W. E. B. Du Bois quoted approvingly a writer who suggested that "what is termed Negro 'laziness' may be a means of making modern workingmen demand more rational rest and enjoyment rather than permitting themselves to be made machines." W. E. B. Du Bois, *Negro-American Family* (Atlanta, 1909), 42. See also Du Bois's discussion of the same matter in *World's Week*, 103 (1926), quoted in Asa H. Gordon, *Sketches of Negro Life and History in South Carolina* (Industrial College, Ga., 1929), 10–11.

illustrate the ways in which traditional cultural forms and expectations helped shape lower-class behavior. (Other evidence of similar disorders, including the Confederate food riots led by white women in Mobile, Savannah, and Richmond, await careful study.) In February 1837, thousands gathered in City Hall Park to protest against "monopolies" and rising food prices. Some months before, that park had witnessed yet another demonstration against the conspiracy trial of twenty-five striking journeymen tailors. In their rhetoric the protesters identified the trial with the betrayal of the premodern "Republic." "Aristocrats" had robbed the people of "that liberty bequeathed to them, as a sacred inheritance by their revolutionary sires" and "so mystified" the laws that "men of common understanding cannot unravel them." "What the people thought was liberty, bore not a semblance to its name." Resolutions compared the tailors to that "holy combination of that immortal band of Mechanics who . . . did throw into Boston Harbor the Tea." In 1837 a crowd dumped flour, not tea, and in its behavior revealed a commonplace form of premodern protest, a complaint against what Thompson calls "the extortionate mechanisms of an unregulated market economy." The crowd in City Hall Park heard protests about the high price of rent, food, and especially flour and denunciations of "engrossers," and the New York *Herald* called the gathering "a flour meeting—a fuel meeting—a rent meeting—a food meeting—a bread meeting—every kind of a meeting except a political meeting." But a New York newspaper had printed advice from Portland, Maine, that "speculating" flour dealers be punished with "some mark of public infamy," and after the meeting adjourned a crowd (estimates range from two hundred to several thousand) paraded to Eli Hart's wholesale flour depot. A speaker advised it to "go to the flour stores and offer a fair price, and if refused take the flour." Crowd members dumped two hundred barrels of flour and one thousand bushels of wheat in the streets, broke windows, did other minor damage, and chased the city's mayor with stones and "balls of flour." At first, little looting occurred, and when wagons finally appeared to carry home sacks of flour "a tall athletic fellow in a carman's frock" shouted: "No plunder, no plunder; destroy as much as you please. Teach these monopolists that we know our rights and will have them, but d--n it don't rob them." The crowd moved on to other flour wholesalers and continued its work. It smashed the windows of B. S. Herrick and Son, dumped more flour, and finally stopped when "a person of respectable appearance" came from inside the building to promise that what remained untouched would be distributed gratis the next day to the "poor." The crowd cheered and melted away. More than twenty-eight persons were arrested (among them "mere boys," a few "black and ignorant laborers," a woman, and as yet unidentified white men), but the *Herald* found "mere humbug . . . the unholy cry of 'It's the foreigners who have done all this mischief.' " The daily press, including the *Herald*, denounced the crowd as "the very canaille of the city," but the *Herald* also pleaded for the reimposition of the assize of bread. "Let the Mayor have the regulation of it," said the *Herald.* "Let the public authorities regulate the price of such an essential of life." (In 1857, incidentally, New Yorkers again filled the City Hall Park to again demand the restoration of the assize of bread and to ask for public works.)[42]

More than half a century later different New York City workers re-enacted the 1837 food "riot." Unlike the rioters of 1837 in origins and rhetoric, the later rioters nevertheless displayed strikingly similar behavior. In 1902, and a few years

42. John R. Commons and others, eds., *Documentary History of American Industrial Society* (Cleveland, 1910), 5: 314–22; New York *Herald*, February 13–16, 1837; New York *Evening Post*, February 14, 16, 1837; New York *Sun*, n.d., quoted in Thomas Brothers, *United States of America as They Are* (London, 1840), 374–76; E. P. Thompson, "The Moral Economy of the English Crowd in the Eighteenth Century," *Past and Present*, 50 (1971), 76–136 but especially 134. On the Confederate bread riots, see Paul Angle and Earl S. Miers, eds., *Tragic Years, 1860–1865* (New York, 1960), 1: 526–28; William J. Kimball, "The Bread Riot in Richmond," *Civil War History*, 7 (1961), 149–54. Early American patterns of price regulation involving foodstuffs and the disputes over them are detailed splendidly in Richard B. Morris, *Government and Labor in Early America* (New York, 1946), *passim,* and Sam Bass Warner, *The Private City* (Philadelphia, 1968), ch. 1.

before Upton Sinclair published *The Jungle*, orthodox New York City Jews, mostly women and led by a woman butcher, protested the rising price of kosher meat and the betrayal of a promised boycott of the Meat Trust by retail butchers. The complaint started on the Lower East Side and then spontaneously spread among Jews further uptown and even among Jews in Brooklyn, Newark, and Boston. The Lower East Side Jews demanded lower prices. Some called for a rabbi to fix for the entire New York Jewish community the price of meat, as in the East European *shtetl*. Others formed a cooperative retail outlet. But it is their behavior that reveals the most. The nation's financial metropolis saw angry immigrant women engage in seemingly archaic traditional protest. Outsiders could not understand its internal logic and order. These women did not loot. Like the 1837 demonstrators, they punished. Custom and tradition that reached far back in historical time gave a coherence to their rage. The disorders started on a Wednesday, stopped on Friday at sundown, and resumed the following evening. The women battered butcher shops but did not steal meat. Some carried pieces of meat "aloft on pointed sticks . . . like flags." Most poured kerosene on it in the streets or in other ways spoiled it. "Eat no meat while the Trust is taking meat from the bones of your women and children," said a Yiddish circular apparently decorated with a skull and crossbones. The New York police and *The New York Times* came down quite hard on these Jewish women. A "dangerous class . . . very ignorant," said *The Times*, explaining:

> They mostly speak a foreign language. They do not understand the duties or the rights of Americans. They have no inbred or acquired respect for law and order as the basis of the life of the society into which they have come. . . . The instant they take the law into their own hands . . . they should be handled in a way that they can understand and cannot forget. . . . Let the blows fall instantly and effectively.

. . .

Two days later, *The Times* reflected on a British Royal Commission then examining the effects of Jewish immigration on British society. "Stepney," *The Times* of New York noted, also was "becoming a foreign town. . . . Perhaps when the Royal Commission reports on what England should do about its un-English Londoners we shall learn what to do about these not yet Americanized New Yorkers whose meat riots were stranger than any nightmare." *The Times* found comfort in what it felt to be a "fact." Immigrant Jews had sparked the 1902 troubles. "The attempted incendiarism," it believed, "could not happen in an American crowd at all." *The New York Times* had done more than idealize a world that had never been lost in suggesting that premodern Americans had been little more than ordered and expectant entrepreneurs. In comparing its response in 1902 to that of the New York *Herald* in 1837, we measure some of the distance that proper Americans had traveled from their own, premodern American roots.[43]

Even though American society itself underwent radical structural changes between 1815 and the First World War, the shifting composition of its wage-earning population meant that traditional customs, rituals, and beliefs repeatedly helped shape the behavior of its diverse working-class groups. The street battle in 1843 that followed Irish efforts to prevent New York City authorities from stopping pigs from running loose in the streets is but one example of the force of old styles of behavior. Both the form and the content of much expressive working-class behavior, including labor disputes, often revealed the powerful role of secular and religious rituals. In 1857 the New York City unemployed kidnapped a musical band to give legitimacy to its parade for public works. After the Civil War, a Fall River cotton manufacturer boasted that the arrival of fresh Lancashire

---

43. New York *Herald*, April 21, 23, May 15–30, 1902; New York *Tribune*, April 19, 21, May 11, 16–27, June 15, 1902; New York *World*, May 16–19, 1902; New York *Commerical Advertiser*, May 15, 17, 24, 26, 1902; *New York Times*, May 23–26, June 7, 1902; New York *Journal*, May 15, 1902; *People* (N.Y.), May 14, 15, 20, 23, 26, 1902. Food riots occurred again among immigrant New York City Jews in the spring of 1917.

operatives meant the coming of "a lot of greenhorns here," but an overseer advised him, "Yes, but you'll find they have brought their horns with them." A few years later, the Pittsburgh courts prevented three women married to coal miners from "tin-horning" nonstrikers. The women, however, purchased mouth organs. ("Tinhorning," of course, was not merely an imported institution. In Franklin, Virginia, in 1867, for example, a Northern white clergyman who started a school for former slave children had two nighttime "tin horn serenade[s]" from hostile whites.) Recurrent street demonstrations in Paterson accompanying frequent strikes and lockouts nearly always involved horns, whistles, and even Irish "banshee" calls. These had a deep symbolic meaning, and, rooted in a shared culture, they sustained disputes. A Paterson manufacturer said of nonstrikers: "They cannot go anywhere without being molested or insulted, and no matter what they do they are met and blackguarded and taunted in a way that no one can stand . . . which is a great deal worse than actual assaults." Another manufacturer agreed:

> All the police in the world could not reach the annoyances that the weavers have at home and on the street that are not offenses—taunts and flings, insults and remarks. A weaver would rather have his head punched in than be called a "knobstick," and this is the class of injury they hate worst, and that keeps them out more than direct assault.

But the manufacturers could not convince the town's mayor (himself a British immigrant and an artisan who had become a small manufacturer) to ban street demonstrations. The manufacturers even financed their own private militia to manage further disorders, but the street demonstrations continued with varying effectiveness until 1901 when a court injunction essentially defined the streets as private space by banning talking and singing banshee (or death) wails in them during industrial disputes. In part, the frequent recourse to the courts and to the state militia after the Civil War during industrial disputes was the consequence of working-class rituals that helped sustain long and protracted conflicts.[44]

Symbolic secular and, especially, religious rituals and beliefs differed among Catholic and Jewish workers fresh to industrial America between 1894 and the First World War, but their function remained the same. Striking Jewish vestmakers finished a formal complaint by quoting the Law of Moses to prove that "our bosses who rob us and don't pay us regularly commit a sin and that the cause of our union is a just one." ("What do we come to America for?" these same men asked. "To bathe in tears and to see our wives and children rot in poverty?") An old Jewish ritual oath helped spark the shirtwaist strike of women workers in 1909 that laid the basis for the International Ladies Garment Workers Union. A strike vote resulted in the plea, "Do you mean faith? Will you take the old Jewish oath?" The audience responded in Yiddish: "If I turn traitor to the cause, I now pledge, may this hand wither and drop off at the wrist from the arm I now raise." (Incidentally, during this same strike a magistrate who advised troublesome Jewish women that "you are on strike against God" provoked Bernard Shaw's classic quip, "Delightful, medieval America always in the most intimate personal confidence of the Almighty.") Immigrant Catholic workers shared similar experiences with these immigrant Jews. A reporter noticed in 1910 at a meeting of striking Slavic steelworkers in Hammond, Indiana: "The lights of the hall were extinguished. A candle stuck into a bottle was placed on a platform. One by one the men came and kissed the ivory image on the cross, kneeling before it. They swore not to scab." Not all rituals were that pacific. That same year, Slavic miners in Avelia, Pennsylvania, a tiny patch on the West Virginia border,

44. Billington, *op. cit.,* 196; New York *Herald,* November 12, 1857; Fall River *Weekly News,* January 21, 1875; L. H., Pittsburgh, to the editor, *John Swinton's Paper* (N.Y.), September 28, 1884; A. B. Corliss, Franklin, Va., to the editor, *American Missionary,* 11 (1867), 27–28; Paterson *Press,* August 2, 1877; Paterson *Guardian,* August 2, 1877; Gutman, "Class, Status, and Community Power," *op. cit.,* 283–87; Gutman, "Social Structure and Working-Class Life and Behavior in an Industrial City, Paterson, New Jersey, 1830–1905," unpublished manuscript.

crucified George Rabish, a mine boss and an alleged labor spy. An amazed journalist felt their behavior "in the twentieth century . . . almost beyond belief":

> Rabish was dragged from his bed and driven out into the street amid the jeers of the merciless throng. . . . Several men set about fashioning a huge cross out of mine timbers. They even pressed a crown of thorns upon his temples. After they had nailed him to the cross, the final blasphemy was to dance and sing about the still living man.

That event was certainly unusual, but it was commonplace for time-honored religious symbols as well as American flags to be carried in the frequent parades of American workers. Western Pennsylvania Slavic and Italian coal miners in a bitter strike just east of Pittsburgh (eighteen of twenty thousand miners quit work for seventeen months when denied the right to join the United Mine Workers of America) in 1910 and 1911 carried such symbols. "These rural marches," said Paul Kellogg, "were in a way reminiscent of the old time agrarian uprisings which have marked English history." But theirs was the behavior of peasant and village Slavs and Italians fresh to modern industrial America, and it was just such tenacious peasant-worker protests that caused the head of the Pennsylvania State Police to say that he modeled his force on the Royal Irish Constabulary, not, he insisted, "as an anti-labor measure" but because "conditions in Pennsylvania resembled those in strife-torn Ireland." Peasant parades and rituals, religious oaths and food riots, and much else in the culture and behavior of early twentieth-century immigrant American factory workers were cultural anachronisms to this man and to others, including Theodore Roosevelt, William Jennings Bryan, Elbert Gary, and even Samuel Gompers, but participants found them natural and effective forms of self-assertion and self-protection.[45]

45. Rischin, *op. cit.*, 144–94; Levine, *op cit.*, 154; Graham Adams, *Age of Industrial Violence, 1910–1915* (New York, 1966), 105–16, 188–94; Chicago

V

THE PERSPECTIVE EMPHASIZED in these pages tells about more than the behavior of diverse groups of American working men and women. It also suggests how larger, well-studied aspects of American society have been affected by a historical process that has "industrialized" different peoples over protracted periods of time. Fernand Braudel reminds us that "victorious events come about as the result of many possibilities," and that "for one possibility which actually is realized, innumerable others have drowned." Usually these others leave "little trace for the historian." "And yet," Braudel adds, "it is necessary to give them their place because the losing movements are forces which have at every moment affected the final outcome." Contact and conflict between diverse preindustrial cultures and a changing and increasingly bureaucratized industrial society also affected the larger society in ways that await systematic examination. Contemporaries realized this fact. Concerned in 1886 about the South's "dead"—that is, unproductive—population, the Richmond *Whig* felt the "true remedy" to be "educating the industrial morale of the people." The *Whig* emphasized socializing institutions primarily outside of the working class itself. "In the work of inculcating industrial ideas and impulses," said the *Whig*, "all proper agencies should be enlisted—family discipline, public school education, pulpit instruction, business standards and requirements, and the power and influence of the workingmen's associations." What the *Whig* worried over in 1886 concerned other Americans before and after that time. And the resultant tension shaped society in important ways. Some are

Socialist, January 31, 1910, quoted in Brody, *Steelworkers in America, op. cit.*, 125–46; Cleveland *Plain Dealer*, April 24, 1910 (courtesy of Robert D. Greenberg); Paul Kellogg and Shelby M. Harrison, "The Westmoreland Strike," *Survey*, 25 (1910), 345–66; *Report on the Miners' Strike in the Bituminous Coal Fields in Westmoreland County, Pennsylvania, in 1910–1911* (Washington, 1912), *passim*. A recent work which convincingly disputes earlier views that Slavic coal miners were difficult to organize into trade unions is Victor H. Greene, *Slavic Community on Strike* (Notre Dame, 1968).

briefly suggested here. In a *New York Times* symposium ("Is America by Nature a Violent Society?") soon after the murder of Martin Luther King, the anthropologist Clifford Geertz warned: "Vague references to the frontier tradition, to the unsettledness of American life, to our exploitative attitude toward nature or to our 'youthfulness' as a nation, provide us with prefabricated 'explanations' for events we, in fact, not only do not understand, but do not want to understand." More needs to be said than that Americans are "the spiritual descendants of Billy the Kid, John Brown, and Bonnie and Clyde." It has been suggested here that certain recurrent disorders and conflicts relate directly to the process that has continually "adjusted" men and women to regular work habits and to the discipline of factory labor. Sidney Pollard reminds us that this "task, different in kind" is "at once more subtle and more violent from that of maintaining discipline among a proletarian population of long standing." [46]

The same process has even greater implications for the larger national American culture. Hannah Arendt has brilliantly suggested that the continual absorption of distinctive native and foreign "alien" peoples has meant that "each time the law had to be confirmed anew against the lawlessness inherent in all uprooted people," and that the severity of that process helps explain to her why the United States has "never been a nation-state." [47] The same process also affected the shaping and reshaping of American police and domestic military institutions. We need only realize that the burning of a Boston convent in 1834 by a crowd of Charlestown truckmen and New Hampshire Scotch-Irish brickmakers caused the first revision of the Massachusetts Riot Act since Shays' Rebellion, and that three years later interference by native firemen in a Sunday Irish funeral

46. Richmond *Whig*, June 15, 1886 (courtesy of Leon Fink); Clifford Geertz, "We Can Claim No Special Gift for Violence," *New York Times Magazine*, April 28, 1968, pp. 24–25; Pollard, "Factory Discipline in the Industrial Revolution," *op. cit.*, 254–71.

47. Hannah Arendt, "Lawlessness Is Inherent in the Uprooted," *New York Times Magazine*, April 28, 1968, pp. 24–25.

procession led to a two-hour riot involving upward of fifteen thousand persons (more than a sixth of Boston's population), brought militia to that city for the first time, and caused the first of many reorganizations of the Boston police force.[48] The regular contact between alien work cultures and a larger industrializing or industrial society had other consequences. It often worried industrialists, causing C. E. Perkins, the president of the Chicago, Burlington, and Quincy Railroad to confide in a friend in the late nineteenth century, "If I were able, I would found a school for the study of political economy in order to harden men's hearts." It affected the popular culture. A guidebook for immigrant Jews in the 1890s advised how to make it in the New World: "Hold fast, this is most necessary in America. Forget your past, your customs, and your ideals. . . . A bit of advice to you: do not take a moment's rest. Run, do, work, and keep your own good in mind." [49] Cultures and customs, however, are not that easily discarded. So it may be that America's extraordinary technological supremacy—its talent before the Second World War for developing labor-saving machinery and simplifying complex mechanical processes—depended less on "Yankee know-how" than on the continued infusion of prefactory peoples into an increasingly industrialized society.[50] The same process, moreover, may also explain why movements to legislate morality and to alter habits have lasted much longer in the United States than in most other industrial countries, extending from the temperance crusades of the 1820s and the 1830s to the violent opposition among Germans to such rules in the 1850s and the 1860s and finally to formal prohibition earlier in this century.[51] Important relationships also exist

48. Oscar Handlin, *Boston's Immigrants* (New York, 1968), 186–91; Roger Lane, *Policing the City: Boston* (Cambridge, Mass., 1967), chs. 1–2.

49. Sidney Fine, *Laissez Faire and the General Welfare State* (Ann Arbor, 1956), 54, 56, 103; Rischin, *op. cit.,* 75.

50. John Higham, in C. Vann Woodward, ed., *Comparative Approaches to American History* (New York, 1968), 101; H. J. Habakkuk, *American and British Technology in the Nineteenth Century* (Cambridge, 1967), *passim.*

51. Although the literature on American temperance and prohibition movements is vast, nothing yet written about them approaches in clarity of analysis

between this process and the elite and popular nativist and racist
social movements that have ebbed and flowed regularly from the
1840s until our own time, as well as between this process and
elite political "reform" movements between 1850 and the First
World War.[52]

---

and use of evidence Brian Harrison, *Drink and the Victorians: The Temperance
Question in England, 1815-1872* (Pittsburgh, 1971). Much information on the
relationship between temperance and late nineteenth-century American factory
labor is found in the little-used *U.S. Commissioner of Labor, Twelfth Annual
Report, 1897* (Washington, 1897), a detailed analysis of the replies about
working-class drinking habits from the owners of more than seven thousand
establishments which together employed about 1,750,000 workers. For the later
period see (but with great care) Herman Feldman, *Prohibition: Its Economic and
Industrial Aspects* (New York, 1927), especially pages 200-12. Feldman, who
surveyed representative manufacturing firms about the impact of Prohibition on
work patterns, learned that "many plants in pre-Prohibition days had the
five-day week long before Henry Ford ever thought of it, because so many
workers were absent after pay-day." Employers used "considerable ingenuity" to
cut down Monday absenteeism. Some had shifted pay-day from Saturday to a
midweek work day, and others paid wages less frequently. Feldman received
replies from 287 firms. Two-thirds said improved attendance at work followed
Prohibition. A New Hampshire shoe manufacturer no longer had to "reckon
with the after-effects of celebrations, holidays, and weekends" as he did "years
ago." And a St. Louis metal manufacturer told that the Saturday paycheck no
longer meant "the usual 'Blue Monday.'" "Now," he explained, "we have
changed to Friday, and as we are paying by the check system this enables the
men to deposit their checks in one of the local banks that stay open on Friday
evenings. We have no Saturday absences." Not all sounded so optimistic. "The
stuff available to labor," said an employer of Delaware River tugboat and barge
workers, "and there is plenty of it, is so rotten that it takes the drinking man two
to three days to get over his spree." And a Connecticut manufacturer feared that
new technology threatened regular attendance at work more than traditional or
spurious spirits. "Cheap automobiles," he said, "make more employees tardy
than does liquor."

52. Detailed local studies are badly needed here, and these should focus on
the clear continuities between antebellum municipal "reform" movements and
the issues that dominated much of local politics in the Gilded Age. Such studies
will reveal neglected elements of continuity in political issues, patterns of elite
reform, and patterns of political centralization that started before the Civil War
and continued into the Progressive Era. Few saw this more clearly than
President Andrew D. White of Cornell University who reminded delegates to the
First Lake Mohonk Conference on the Negro Question in 1890 that "in 1847"
New York had "sank back toward mobocracy." "We elected judges on small

The sweeping social process had yet another important consequence: it reinforced the biases that otherwise distort the ways in which elite observers perceive the world below them. When in 1902 *The New York Times* cast scorn upon and urged that force be used against the Jewish women food rioters, it conformed to a fairly settled elite tradition. Immigrant groups and the working population had changed in composition over time, but the rhetoric of influential nineteenth- and early twentieth-century elite observers remained constant. Disorders among the Jersey City Irish seeking wages due them from the Erie Railroad in 1859 led the Jersey City *American Standard* to call them "imported *beggars*" and *"animals,"* "a mongrel mass of ignorance and crime and superstition, as utterly unfit for its duties, as they are for the common courtesies and decencies of civilized life." (According to their historian Earl Niehaus, the antebellum New Orleans Irish fared so badly in the "public" view that many non-Irish criminals, Germans and even blacks among them, assumed Irish names.) Although the Civil War ended slavery, it did not abolish these distorted perceptions and fears of new American workers. In 1869 *Scientific American* welcomed the "ruder" laborers of Europe but urged them to

salaries for short terms," said White; "we did the same thing with the governors. We have swung backward or forward . . . out of that. We now elect men for longer terms. In many ways, we have returned to more conservative principles." Isabel Barrows, ed., *First Lake Mohonk Conference on the Negro Question* (Boston, 1890), 120. See also Samuel P. Hays, "The Politics of Reform in Municipal Government in the Progressive Era," *Pacific Northwest Quarterly,* 55 (1964), 157–69. The pattern Hays uncovered for Progressive Pittsburgh was not new because its roots rested in elite fears of immigrant and working-class domination of municipal governments (and especially the influence of those groups on local fiscal and educational policies), fears that revealed themselves powerfully before the Civil War and retained much importance during the Gilded Age. The focus on municipal corruption has hidden such important social and political processes from historians. See the original and convincing study by Douglas V. Shaw, "The Making of an Immigrant City: Ethnic and Cultural Conflict in Jersey City, New Jersey, 1850–1877" (Ph.D. dissertation, University of Rochester, 1972), that demonstrates conclusively (for that city at least) that antebellum elite nativism did not end with the Civil War but continued into the postwar decades.

"assimilate" quickly or face "a quiet but sure extermination." Those who retained their alien ways, it insisted, "will share the fate of the native Indian." Elite nativism neither died out during the Civil War nor awaited a rebirth under the auspices of the American Protective Association and the Immigration Restriction League. In the mid-1870s, for example, the Chicago *Tribune* called striking immigrant brickmakers men but "not reasoning creatures," and the Chicago *Post-Mail* described that city's Bohemian residents as "depraved beasts, harpies, decayed physically and spiritually, mentally and morally, thievish and licentious." The Democratic Chicago *Times* cast an even wider net in complaining that the country had become "the cess-pool of Europe under the pretense that it is the asylum of the poor." Most Chicago inhabitants in the Gilded Age were foreign-born or the children of the foreign-born, and most English-language Chicago newspapers scorned them. The Chicago *Times* told readers that Slavic Chicagoans were descended from "the Scythians," "eaters of raw animal food, fond of drinking the blood of their enemies whom they slew in battle, and [men] who preserved as trophies the scalps and skins of enemies whom they overthrew." "The old taste for the blood of an enemy has never been obliterated," said this proper Chicago newspaper. And the Slavs had now "invaded the peaceful republic." In words echoed differently in *The New York Times* fifteen years later, the Chicago *Times* advised: "Let us whip these slavic wolves back to the European dens from which they issue, or in some way exterminate them." Here, as in the Jersey City *American Standard* (1859) and *The New York Times* (1902), much more was involved than mere ethnic distaste or "nativism." In quite a different connection and in a relatively homogeneous country, the Italian Antonio Gramsci concluded of such evidence that "for a social elite the features of subordinate groups always display something barbaric and pathological." The changing composition of the American working class may make so severe a dictum more pertinent to the United States than to Italy. Class and ethnic fears and biases combined together to worry elite observers about the diverse worlds below them and to distort gravely their perceptions of these worlds. Few revealed these perceptual difficulties and genuine fears more clearly than John L. Hart in 1879:

> About one half of our poor can neither read nor write, have never been in any school, and know little, positively nothing, of the doctrines of the Christian religion, or of moral duties, or of any higher pleasures than beer-drinking and spirit-drinking, and the grossest sensual indulgence. . . . They have unclear, indefinable ideas of all around them; they eat, drink, breed, work, and die; and while they pass through their brute-like existence here, the rich and more intelligent classes are obliged to guard them with police and standing armies, and to cover the land with prisons, cages, and all kinds of receptacles for the perpetrators of crime.

Hart was not an uneducated "nativist." He had been professor of rhetoric, the English language, and literature at the College of New Jersey and also the principal of the New Jersey State Normal School. These words appeared in his book entitled *In The School-Room* (1879) where he argued that "schoolhouses are cheaper than jails" and that "teachers and books are better security than handcuffs and policemen." We have returned to Lesson One.[53]

53. Jersey City *American Standard*, September 20, 1859 (courtesy of Douglas V. Shaw); Earl Niehaus, *Irish in New Orleans* (Baton Rouge, 1965), 186; *Scientific American*, June 19, 1869, pp. 393–94; Chicago *Tribune*, May 11, 1876; Chicago *Post and Mail*, n.d., reprinted in Chicago *Tribune*, July 25, 1876; Chicago *Times*, April 25, 1874; Chicago *Times*, May 6, 1886 (courtesy of Steven Hahn); Antonio Gramsci, quoted in Charles Tilly, "Collective Violence in European Perspective," in Hugh D. Graham and Ted R. Gurr, eds., *Violence in America* (New York, 1969), 12; John L. Hart, *In The School-Room* (Philadelphia, 1879), 252–57 (courtesy of Barbara Berman). See also John Kober, *Capone, The Life and World of Al Capone* (New York, 1972), 344, for an extraordinary description of Alcatraz prison routine in the 1930s: "Midmorning. Bell. Recess. Bell. Work. 11:30. Bell. Prisoners Counted. Bell. Noon. Bell. Lunch. 1 P.M. Bell. Work. Midafternoon. Bell. Recess. Work. 4:30. Bell. Prisoners Counted. Bell. 6:30. Bell. Lockup. 9:30. Bell. Lights Out."

V I

THESE PAGES HAVE FRACTURED HISTORICAL time, ranging forward and backward, to make comparisons for several reasons. One has been to suggest how much remains to be learned about the transition of native and foreign-born American men and women to industrial society, and how that transition affected such persons and the society into which they entered. "Much of what gets into American literature," Ralph Ellison has shrewdly observed, "gets there because so much is left out." That has also been the case in the writing of American working-class history, and the framework and methods suggested here merely hint at what will be known about American workers and American society when the many transitions are studied in detail. Such studies, however, need to focus on the particularities of both the groups involved and the society into which they enter. Transitions differ and depend upon the interaction between the two at specific historical moments. But at all times there is a resultant tension. Thompson writes:

> There has never been any single type of "the transition." The stress of the transition falls upon the whole culture: resistance to change and assent to change arise from the whole culture. And this culture includes the systems of power, property-relations, religious institutions, etc., inattention to which merely flattens phenomena and trivializes analysis.

Enough has been savored in these pages to suggest the particular importance of these transitions in American social history. And their recurrence in different periods of time indicates why there has been so much discontinuity in American labor and social history. The changing composition of the working population, the continued entry into the United States of nonindustrial people with distinctive cultures, and the changing structure of American society have combined together to produce common modes of thought and patterns of behavior. But these have been experiences disconnected in time and shared by quite distinctive first-generation native and immigrant industrial Americans. It was not possible for the grandchildren of the Lowell mill girls to understand that their Massachusetts literary ancestors shared a great deal with their contemporaries, the peasant Slavs in the Pennsylvania steel mills and coal fields. And the grandchildren of New York City Jewish garment workers see little connection between black ghetto unrest in the 1960s and the kosher meat riots seventy years ago. A half-century has passed since Robert Park and Herbert Miller published W. I. Thomas's *Old World Traits Transplanted*, a study which worried that the function of Americanization was the "destruction of memories." [54]

Not all fled such a past. Born of Croatian parents in McKeesport, Pennsylvania, in 1912 (his father and brother later killed in industrial accidents), Gabro Karabin published a prize-winning short story in *Scribner's Magazine* (1947) that reflected on the experiences replayed in different ways by diverse Americans and near-Americans:

> Around Pittsburgh, a Croat is commonplace and at no time distinctive. As people think of us, we are cultureless, creedless, and colorless in life, though in reality we possess a positive and almost excessive amount of those qualities. Among ourselves, it is known that we keep our culture to ourselves because of the heterogeneous and unwholesome grain of that about us. . . . We are, in the light of general impression, just another type of laboring foreigner . . . fit only as industrial fuel.

The native-born American poet William Carlos Williams made a similar point. He lived near the city of Paterson and grasped

54. Ralph Ellison and James Alan McPherson, "Indivisible Man," *Atlantic*, 226 (1970), 57; Thompson, "Time, Work-Discipline, and Industrial Capitalism," *op. cit.*, 80; Park and Miller, *op. cit.*, 281. I am indebted to Leon Stein, the editor of *Justice*, for calling to my attention the fact that W. I. Thomas, whose great study of the Polish immigrant leaves us all in his debt, was the author of *Old World Traits Transplanted.*

its tragic but rich and deeply human interior textures far more incisively than temporary visitors such as Alexander Hamilton and William D. Haywood and illustrious native sons such as William Graham Sumner and Nicholas Murray Butler. The poet celebrated what gave life to a city in which men, women, and children made iron bars and locomotives and cotton and silk cloth:

> *It's the anarchy of poverty*
> *delights me, the old*
> *yellow wooden house indented*
> *among the new brick tenements*
>
> *Or a cast iron balcony*
> *with panels showing oak branches*
> *in full leaf. It fits*
> *the dress of the children*
>
> *reflecting every stage and*
> *custom of necessity—*
> *chimneys, roofs, fences of*
> *wood and metal in an unfenced*
> *age and enclosing next to*
> *nothing at all: the old man*
> *in a sweater and soft black*
> *hat who sweeps the sidewalk—*
>
> *his own ten feet of it—*
> *in a wind that fitfully*
> *turning his corner had*
> *overwhelmed the entire city.*

Karabin and Carlos Williams interpreted life and labor differently from the Chicago *Times* editor who in the centennial year (1876) boasted that Americans did not enquire "when looking at a piece of lace whether the woman who wove it is a saint or a courtesan." [55]

55. Gabro Karabin, quoted in George J. Prpic, *Croatian Immigrants in America* (New York, 1971), 331–32; William Carlos Williams, "The Poor," in

APPENDIX

TABLE 3. MALE OCCUPATIONAL STRUCTURE AND
HOUSEHOLD COMPOSITION, SELECTED JEWS AND ITALIANS,
NEW YORK CITY, 1905

	Jews	Italians
Total Males 20 and Older	6250	4518
Total Females 20 and Older	4875	3433
Male Occupational Structure		
Unskilled Laborer	7.7%	39.1%
Clothing Worker	44.7%	18.0%
Skilled Worker (Nonclothing)	21.5%	29.2%
Nonlaborer	26.1%	13.7%
Household Composition		
Percentage of All Households with a Nuclear Kin-related Core	96.6%	94.5%
Number of Kin-related Households	3584	2945
Number of Subfamilies	159	262
Nuclear Households	48.6%	59.9%
Extended Households	11.8%	23.2%
Augmented Households	43.1%	21.1%
Percentage of Households and Subfamilies with a Husband and/or Father Present	93.2%	92.9%

Note: As in 1880 the percentages again total more than 100 percent because a small number of households that included both lodgers and relatives are counted twice.

The data are drawn from the New York State 1905 manuscript census schedules, and I am indebted to Mark Sosower, Leslie Neustadt, and Richard Mendales for gathering this material. As with the 1880 Paterson data, they cast grave doubts on the widely held belief that working-class family disruption commonly occurred as the byproduct of immigration, urbanization, and factory work. The 1905 Jews studied lived on the Lower East Side (Rutgers, Cherry, Pelham, Monroe, Water, Pike, Jefferson, Clinton, Madison, Livingston, Henry, Division, Montgomery, Delancey, Rivington, Norfolk, Suffolk, and East Third Streets, East Broadway, and Avenue B). The Italians resided on Hancock, Thompson, Mulberry, Bayard, Mott, Canal, Baxter, Elizabeth, Spring, Prince, Grand, Hester, MacDougal, Sullivan, West Houston, Bleecker, Bedford, Downing, and Carmine Streets, and the Bowery. The table above deserves another brief comment. Clothing workers are listed as a separate occupational category because census job descriptions make it impossible to determine their skill levels. A large percentage of those listed as nonlaborers engaged in petty enterprise (including peddling): 10.9 percent of all the Jewish males and 8.3 percent of all the Italian males. On early twentieth-century immigrant households and family behavior, see Virginia Yans McLaughlin, "Patterns of Work and Family Organization Among Buffalo's Italians," *Journal of Interdisciplinary History*, 2 (1971), 299–314, and McLaughlin, "Like the Fingers of the Hand: The Family and Community Life of First-Generation Italian-Americans in Buffalo, New York" (Ph.D. dissertation, State University of New York, Buffalo, 1970).

2

Protestantism and the American Labor Movement

THE CHRISTIAN SPIRIT IN THE GILDED AGE

LABOR HISTORIANS and others have puzzled over precisely how and why American workers, especially those critical of the new industrial order, reacted to the profound changes in the nation's social and economic structure and in their own particular status between 1850 and 1900, but in seeking explanations they have studied almost exclusively working-class behavior and trade-union organization and have neatly catalogued the interminable wranglings between "business" unionists, "utopian" dreamers, and "socialist" radicals. Although their works have uncovered much of value, the "mind" of the worker—the modes of thought and perception through which he confronted the industrialization process and which helped shape his behavior—has received scant and inadequate attention. American workers, immigrant and native-born alike, brought more than their "labor" to the factory and did not view their changing circumstances in simple "economic" terms. So narrow an emphasis ignores the complexity of their lives and experiences and, in general, distorts human behavior. "Events, facts, data, happenings," J. L. Talmon reminds us, "assume their significance from the way in which they are experienced." [1] These

1. J. K. Talmon, "The Age of Revolution," *Encounter*, 21 (September 1963), 14. See also Richard Hofstadter, *The Paranoid Style in American Politics and*

pages examine one of several important but overlooked influences on the disaffected worker's thought: the way certain
strands of pre-Gilded Age Protestantism affected him in a time
of rapid industrialization and radical social change.

Before 1850 relatively few Americans had direct contact with
an industrial *society,* but after that date rapid industrialization
altered the social structure, and the process left few untouched.
Depending upon circumstance, these social changes meant more
or less opportunity for workers, but nearly all felt greater
dependence and profoundly different patterns of work discipline. In addition, urbanization and immigration changed the
structure and composition of the working class and affected its
style of life. In ways that have not yet been adequately explored,
class and status relationships took on new meaning, too.[2] And a
new ideology that sanctioned industrial laissez faire emerged
because, as Ralph Gabriel has perceptively written, "the mores
of a simpler agricultural and commercial era did not fit the
conditions of an age characterized by the swift accumulation of
industrial power."[3] The era found much "truth" in the frequent
judgments of the Chicago *Times* that "the inexorable law of
God" meant that "the man who lays up not for the morrow
perishes on the morrow," that "political economy" was "in
reality the autocrat of the age" and occupied "the position once
held by the Caesars and the Popes."[4]

Legal and political theory, academic economics, amoral

Other Essays (New York, 1965), ix–x. Urging the study of popular ideology in
order to understand more fully political thought and behavior, Hofstadter
writes: "The political contest itself is deeply affected by the way in which it is
perceived." "This does not mean," he hastens to warn, "that the material
interests of politics can be psychologized away or reduced to episodes in
intellectual history." A similar admonition is essential in studying labor thought.

2. Evidence on differing contemporary estimates of the status of industrialists
and workers in large cities and small industrial towns is found in H. G. Gutman,
"The Worker's Search for Power: Labor in the Gilded Age," in *The Gilded Age:
A Reappraisal*, ed. H. Wayne Morgan (New York, 1963), 38–68.

3. Ralph Gabriel, *The Course of American Democratic Thought* (New York,
1956), 154.

4. Chicago *Times*, August 24, 1874, August 26, 1876.

"social science," and institutional Protestantism emphasized that in industrial America interference with the entrepreneur's freedom violated "divine" or "scientific" laws, and historians have given much attention to the many ways Gilded Age social thought bolstered the virtues of "Acquisitive Man." [5] Two seemingly contradictory ideas especially sanctioned industrial laissez faire. Related to the decline of traditional religious sanctions and the growing importance of secular institutions and values, the first insisted that no connection existed between economic behavior and moral conduct. Gilded Age business practices, Edward C. Kirkland has argued, cannot be understood without realizing that for most entrepreneurs "economic activity stood apart from the sphere of moral and personal considerations." [6] Much contemporary evidence supports this view.[7] The second concept, identified with traditional Calvinist doctrine, reinforced the business ethic by equating poverty and failure with sin.[8] Evidence gathered primarily from national

5. An able summary of the defense of laissez faire in the Gilded Age is found in Sidney Fine, *Laissez Faire and the General-Welfare State: A Study of Conflict in American Thought, 1865–1901* (Ann Arbor, Mich., 1956), 3–166. On the process of legitimizing newly achieved power, see Max Weber, *Essays in Sociology*, tr. and ed. H. W. Gerth and C. W. Mills (New York, 1946), 271.

6. Edward C. Kirkland, "Divide and Rule," *Mississippi Valley Historical Review*, 43 (June 1956), 3–17.

7. Economist Arthur Perry explicitly said that "the grounds of economy and morals are independent and incommensurable," while the president of the American Exchange Bank found the "laws" of economics separate from but "as sacred and obligatory as . . . those of the Decalogue." Chicago, Burlington, and Quincy Railroad President C. E. Perkins explained: "The question of political economy is not, What is noble? What is good? What is generous? What are the teachings of the Gospel?—But what, if anything, is it expedient to do about [the] production, distribution and consumption of property or wealth?" Like many other men of new wealth and power, this railroad leader worried about those who denounced "the economic law of Adam Smith . . . as too cruel and heartless for a Christian People." (Quoted in Fine, *op. cit.*, 54, 56, 103; Kirkland, *op. cit.*; and Thomas Cochran, *Railroad Leaders, 1845–1890: The Business Mind in Action* [Cambridge, Mass., 1953], 436–37.)

8. This view is identified most frequently with Henry Ward Beecher and Russell Conwell. "The general truth will stand," Beecher argued, "that no man in this land suffers from poverty unless it be more than his fault—unless it be his

denominational weekly and monthly periodicals, together with a
Gilded Age premillennial evangelism (typified by the popular
Dwight Moody) that insisted that "until Christ returned none of
the basic problems of the world could be solved," convinces its
historians that the Protestant denominations and their leaders
mostly "lost their sense of estrangement from society" and
"began . . . to bless and defend it in a jargon strangely
compounded out of the language of traditional Christian
theology, common-sense philosophy, and *laissez-faire* economics." [9] Henry May, Aaron Abell, and Charles Hopkins have
shown that a small but quite influential group of Protestant
clergymen and lay thinkers broke free from institutional Protestantism's social conservatism and traveled a difficult route in
pioneering the social gospel,[10] but in the main Gilded Age
Protestantism is viewed as a conformist, "culture-bound" Christianity that warmly embraced the rising industrialist, drained the

---

sin." (Quoted in Henry F. May, *Protestant Churches and Industrial America* [New
York, 1949], 69.) Conwell made the same point another way: "The number of
poor to be sympathized with is very small. . . . To sympathize with a man whom
God has punished for his sins, thus to help him when God will still continue a
just punishment, is to do wrong, no doubt about it." (Quoted in Marquis Childs
and Douglas Cater, *Ethics in a Business Society* [New York, 1954], 137.) A
variant of this theme urged passivity upon complaining workers as when the
Methodist *Christian Advocate* lectured readers: "John the Baptist set a good
example . . . when he advised the Roman soldiers, 'Be content with your
wages.' . . ." (Quoted in William G. McLoughlin, Jr., *Modern Revivalism:
Charles Grandison Finney to Billy Graham* [New York, 1959], 267–68.)

9. Sidney E. Mead, "American Protestantism Since the Civil War," *Journal of
Religion*, 36 (January 1956), 1–15. See also Winthrop Hudson, *American
Protestantism* (Chicago, 1961), 136–40. Hudson also relates these developments
to the new theology, "the doctrine of Incarnation, interpreted as divine
immanence, which sanctified the 'natural' man and invested the culture itself
with intrinsic redemptive tendencies." The new theology therefore surrendered
"any independent basis of judgment." Excellent analysis of the post-Civil War
evangelism typified by Dwight Moody is found in McLoughlin, *op. cit.,* 166–281,
and Bernard A. Weisberger, *They Gathered at the River: The Story of the Great
Revivalists and Their Impact upon Religion in America* (Boston, 1958), 160–219.

10. May, *op. cit., passim,* but esp. 91–111, 163–203; A. I. Abell, *The Urban
Impact on American Protestantism, 1865–1900* (Cambridge, Mass., 1943), *passim;*
and C. H. Hopkins, *The Rise of the Social Gospel in American Protestantism,
1865–1915* (New Haven, Conn., 1940), *passim.*

aspiring rich of conscience, and confused or pacified the poor. The writings of an articulate minority suggest to historians that the wealthy busied themselves memorizing Herbert Spencer's aphorisms and purchasing expensive church pews, that the middle classes chased wealth and cheered Horatio Alger, and that the wage-earners, busy laboring, found little time to ponder existential questions and felt separated from institutional Protestantism. Workers wandered from the fold, and the churches lost touch with the laboring classes.

Accurate in describing certain themes characteristic of Gilded Age social and religious thought, this view nevertheless tells little about the relationship between Protestantism and the working class because the many functions of religion, particularly its effects on the lower classes, cannot be learned by analyzing what leading clergymen said and what social philosophy religious journals professed. Unless one first studies the varieties of working-class community life, the social and economic structure that gave them shape, their voluntary associations (including churches, benevolent and fraternal societies, and trade unions), their connections to the larger community, and their particular and shared values, one is likely to be confused about the relationship between the worker, institutional religion, and religious beliefs and sentiments.[11] It is suggested, for example, that a close tie between laissez faire and Gilded Age Protestantism developed partly because the post-Civil War "burst of technological and industrial expansion . . . created unbridled cheerfulness, confidence, and complacency among the American people" and because "the observational order coincided in a high degree with the conceptual order and . . . such coincidence defines social stability."[12] Such was probably the case for successful entrepreneurs and many lesser folk who benefited

11. See the penetrating and original study of the role of voluntary associations and community institutions among Irish immigrant workers and their children in Newburyport, Massachusetts, between 1850 and 1880 in Stephan Thernstrom, *Poverty and Progress: Social Mobility in a Nineteenth Century City* (Cambridge, Mass., 1964), 166–91.

12. Hudson, *op. cit.*; Mead, *op. cit.*

from rapid industrialization and the era's massive material
gains, but the same cannot be inferred for those whose
traditional skills became obsolete, who felt economic dependence for the first time, who knew recurrent seasonal and cyclical
unemployment, and who suffered severe family and social
disorganization in moving from farm and town to city and in
adapting to industrial and urban priorities and work discipline
patterns different from traditional norms. Day-to-day experiences for many such persons ("the observational order") did not
entirely coincide with the religious and secular ideas and values
("the conceptual order") they carried with them from the
immediate past. Some withdrew from the tensions stirred by
such conflict, and others changed their beliefs. Many found in
Gilded Age Protestantism reason to cheer material progress or
comfort in premillennial evangelism. But some, especially trade
unionists and labor reformers and radicals, discovered that
preindustrial ideology heightened rather than obliterated the
moral dilemmas of a new social order and that the Protestantism
of an earlier America offered a religious sanction for *their*
discontent with industrial laissez faire and "Acquisitive Man." A
preindustrial social order had nurtured particular religious
beliefs that did not disappear with the coming of industrialism
and did not easily or quickly conform to the Protestantism of a
Henry Ward Beecher or a Dwight Moody and the secular
optimism of an Andrew Carnegie or a Horatio Alger. The
material conditions of life changed radically for these workers
after 1850, but not the world of their mind and spirit. They saw
the nation transformed, but were not themselves abruptly
alienated from the past. Older traditions and modes of thought
(religious and secular in origin) did not succumb easily to the
imperatives of a disorganized industrial society, but, depending
upon particular circumstances, often clung tenaciously and even
deepened tensions generally characteristic of an early industrializing society.

The recent perspective emphasized by British historians of
early industrial England helps clarify the particular relationship
between Protestantism and Gilded Age labor reform. "In order

to understand how people respond to industrial change," Asa Briggs has written, "it is necessary to examine fully what kind of people they were at the beginning of the process, to take account of continuities and traditions as well as new ways of thinking and feeling." [13] Edward P. Thompson has gathered and organized a mass of data in *The Making of the English Working Class* to argue persuasively that the English working class was not "the spontaneous generation of the factory-system" and that the early social history of industrial England was more than "an external force—the 'industrial revolution'—working upon some nondescript undifferentiated raw material of humanity." [14] Applied to the United States, this general point is quite simple although its particular American characteristics demand a level of conceptualization and a method of research not yet typical of "labor history." Protestantism in its many and even contradictory forms, but particularly the Christian perfectionism of pre-Civil War evangelical and reform movements, lingered on among many discontented postbellum workers. [15] It was no different in the United States than in Great Britain where labor and religious historians have documented the close relationship

13. Asa Briggs, review of Edward P. Thompson, *The Making of the English Working Class, Labor History*, 6 (Winter 1965), 84.

14. Edward P. Thompson, *The Making of the English Working Class* (London, 1963), 194 *et passim.*

15. See esp. Timothy L. Smith, *Revivalism and Social Reform in Mid-Nineteenth Century America* (New York, 1957), *passim.* Smith does not carry his important findings on the relationship between pre-Civil War evangelism, Christian perfectionism, and social reform beyond the Civil War. Clifton E. Olmstead argued that perfectionism "increased steadily in American evangelical Protestantism throughout and beyond the Civil War." It "flourished primarily in urban areas," Olmstead maintained, "where the social problems and the individual frustrations presented a peculiar challenge to those who believed that Christianity could 'work' to the betterment of mankind." (C. E. Olmstead, *History of Religion in the United States* [Englewood Cliffs, N.J., 1960], 352.) But Olmstead offered no concrete evidence to support this valuable insight. Although he makes little of the strain of labor Protestantism emphasized in these pages, W. G. McLoughlin offers a suggestive framework for understanding the effects of pietistic perfectionism on American social movements in his essay "Pietism and the American Character," *American Quarterly*, 17 (Summer 1965), 163–86.

between Protestant Nonconformity, especially Methodism, and labor reform.[16] None of this should surprise students of social movements. "The bulk of industrial workers in all countries," Eric Hobsbawm notes, "began . . . as first-generation immigrants from preindustrial society . . . and like all first-generation immigrants, they looked backwards as much as forwards." The new industrial world "had no pattern of life suited to the new age," and so men and women often "drew on the only spiritual resources at their disposal, preindustrial custom and religion." [17]

An additional point stressed in Thompson's recent work offers insight into the Gilded Age labor reformer. "Behind every form of popular direct action," Thompson notes, "some legitimising notion of right is to be found." [18] Thus Boston labor leader and editor Frank K. Foster insisted in 1888: "The dry names and dates furnish but a small part of the history of the labor movement. To understand its real meaning one must comprehend the spirit animating it." [19] Leaders and followers of social movements that challenge an established order or question the direction of a rapidly changing society (such as the United States after the Civil War) are usually "animated" by a "spirit" that sanctions and legitimizes the particular alternative they espouse. It is not enough for them merely to criticize and to offer alternatives. This is the case whether they advocate trade unions in a society hostile to collective activity or urge even more thorough and fundamental social reorganization. They must *feel* that what they propose is justified by values that transcend the particular social order they criticize. For this reason, they often crudely reinterpret the historical past. They either project "new"

16. Thompson, *op. cit.*, 350–400; Eric Hobsbawm, *Labouring Men: Studies in the History of Labour* (London, 1964), 23–33; Robert F. Wearmouth, *Methodism and the Working-Class Movements of England, 1800–1850* (London, 1937), *passim.*

17. E. J. Hobsbawm, *Social Bandits and Primitive Rebels: Studies in Archaic Forms of Social Movement in the 19th and 20th Centuries* (Glencoe, Ill., 1959), 108, 130.

18. Thompson, *op. cit.*, 68.

19. *Labor Leader* (Boston), September 15, 1888.

values or, as is more frequently the case, reinterpret vague and broadly shared national values to sanction their behavior. Then, they can argue that their critique of the dominant order and its ideology is "consistent with very basic values." [20] Such was the case with the generation of trade unionists, labor reformers, and labor radicals who felt the transition from a preindustrial to an industrial society and who bore the social, economic, and psychological brunt of the American industrializing process after 1860.

Two broadly shared preindustrial national traditions especially offered the discontented nineteenth-century American worker a transcendent and sanctioning "notion of right." The first—the republican political tradition—is beyond the scope of these pages. The second was traditional American Protestantism. Frank Foster could explain in 1887: "John on Patmos, Jack Cade at the head of the populace, . . . Krapotine indicting Russian imperialism, the rising wrath of American Democracy —these are all of kinship." Commenting on the American labor movement, Foster went on:

> The "cross of the new crusade" is the cross of an old crusade, old as the passions of the human heart. An idea may take different forms of expression and its ethical purport may be the same, and in whatever direction men may strive for this ambiguous thing we call social reform, if they mean anything at all, they but echo—be they Jew or Gentile, Greek or Christian, Deist or Atheist, Knight of Labor or Socialist—that carol of welcome which was sung to greet the coming of the Carpenter's Son in the centuries long gone by, "peace on earth, good will to men."

"Looking afar off, over the broad ocean of time and space," the Boston editor concluded, "we have faith, like St. Simon at death's door, [we] may exclaim, 'The future is ours.' " [21]

---

20. Alvin and Helen Gouldner, *Modern Sociology* (New York, 1963), 634–36.
21. *Labor Leader*, August 27, 1887.

Similarly, the *Union Pacific Employees Magazine* comforted fearful trade unionists by reminding them that after the Crucifixion "the rabble rejoiced." "Time," this journal insisted in explaining the difficulties encountered by trade-union advocates, "corrects errors. . . . The minority continue to urge their views until they become the majority or the fallacy of them be proven. Advance is made only thus. Time must be had to prepare the way for every step." [22] In another connection, the American Railway Union's *Railway Times* called "sublime idiocy . . . the idea that workingmen of the present, or of any other century, were the first to call attention to the rapacity of the rich." Instead, "The arraignment of the rich by God Himself and His Son, the Redeemer, set the pace for all coming generations of men who would be free from the crushing domination of wealth." Labor's complaints had "the unequivocal endorsement of the Holy Writ." [23] Here, then, was a religious faith that justified labor organization and agitation, encouraged workers to challenge industrial power, and compelled criticism of "natural" economic laws, the crude optimism of social Darwinism, and even the conformist Christianity of most respectable clergymen.

Protestantism affected the American working class in many ways, and a brief essay cannot encompass its varied manifestations. But it is possible to indicate some of them.

A subordinate but distinct theme drew from pessimistic premillennialism the apocalyptic tradition that prophesied doom and imminent catastrophe before "redemption." In a period of rapid, unpredictable social and economic change, change itself meant decay and destruction to some. For them, the Christian prophetic tradition did not buoy up the spirit and command reform, but stimulated withdrawal. A Massachusetts ship joiner predicted destructive world-wide war as the result of "the sin of the people, 'covetousness.' " [24] A regular *Coast Seaman's Journal*

22. *Union Pacific Employees Magazine*, n.d., reprinted in the *Journal of the Nights of Labor* (Philadelphia), July 16, 1891. The Crucifixion was but one example this journal cited. It also pointed to the mobbing of William Lloyd Garrison, the hanging of John Brown, and the jailing of Voltaire.

23. *Railway Times* (Chicago), June 15, 1896.

24. *Labor Standard* (Boston), February 22, 1879.

columnist more than once made the same point.[25] Readers of the Denver *Labor Enquirer* learned from several sermons by Mrs. P. C. Munger of "the World's Final Crisis." She urged violence to speed the end of an evil social order and praised dynamite as a "blessing" from God:

> Socially, the ruling world is a dead leper. In the name of God and man bury it deep in the earth it has corrupted. . . . Dynamite in its line is the last scientific fruit of the Holy Ghost. . . . It is in every way worthy of the giver—God. . . . I thank, I praise, I bless God for dynamite. It is the blast of Gabriel's trumpet. . . . It does the deeds of God. . . . Its fruits are peace, love, joy, goodness, gentleness, meekness, and truth displayed in decent life and government. Is not this boon of heaven worth a blow; worth a blast on the trumpet of doom? . . . Dynamite is a weapon to win; a weapon to conquer, a weapon to kill. It is your only one. God Himself allows you no other; use it or tamely submit and sign your death warrant.[26]

Such violent and apparent psychotic anguish, however, was not typical of even the most extreme premillenarian visionaries. More characteristic was the complaint of an Indiana coal miner's wife who believed that "according to history" a "visitation" took place every two thousand years and quietly complained, "I have heard my mother talk about her girlhood days and how good and religious people were." The world had changed for the worse. "It is no wonder," she feared, "that God sends His voice in thunder through the air as wicked as this world stands to-day. . . . We are living in a land where shadows are continually falling in our pathway." [27] The extraordinary psychological strains of early industrialism thus found expression in the rejection of the secular order and the acceptance of a Protestantism of doom, despair, and destruction.[28]

25. *Coast Seaman's Journal* (San Francisco), November 28, 1888, January 30, 1889.

26. *Labor Enquirer* (Denver), April-May 1883.

27. *United Mine Workers' Journal* (Columbus, Ohio), March 8, 1900.

28. Hobsbawm, *Labouring Men, op. cit.,* 376.

More widespread than these premillennial prophecies was a postmillennial Christian justification of trade unionism and even more radical social reform. Conservative trade unionists and radical anarchists and socialists (except for the zealous followers of Daniel De Leon) often appealed to Christianity for its sanction. A pre-Civil War utopian and afterward a Knight of Labor and builder of cooperatives, John Orvis claimed "the labor question" was "here in the Providence of Almighty God" and meant "the deliverance, exaltation, and ennobling of labor and the laboring classes to the first rank." [29] Conservative craft unionist and president of the Amalgamated Association of Iron, Steel, and Tin Workers, John Jarrett told a gathering of clergymen that "the climax of the mission of the Savior, beyond a question, . . . is that He came here so that the gospel would be preached to the poor." [30] After being sentenced to death in the aftermath of the Haymarket affair, German immigrant anarchist August Spies linked his beliefs to Thomas Münzer. "He," Spies said of Münzer, "interpreted the Gospel, saying that it did not merely promise blessings in heaven, but that it also commanded equality and brotherhood among men on earth." Spies insisted that "the spirit of the Reformation was the 'eternal spirit of the chainless mind,' and nothing could stay its progress." [31] This sentiment—radical criticism and labor discontent sanctioned by an appeal to Christian tradition—did not diminish by the end of the nineteenth century and remained as common in the 1890s as in the 1860s. No apparent connection existed between a particular brand of labor reform and Christianity; all shared in it.

Prophetic Protestantism offered labor leaders and their followers a transhistoric framework to challenge the new industrialism and a common set of moral imperatives to measure their rage against and to order their dissatisfactions. The intensity of religious commitment varied among individuals: it depended

29. *American Workman* (Boston), June-July 1869.

30. *Labor: Its Rights and Wrongs* (Washington, D.C., 1886), 252–61.

31. *The Accused, the Accusers. The Famous Speeches of the Eight Chicago Anarchists in Court . . . On October 7th, 8th and 9th, 1886* (Chicago, 1886), 5–6.

upon particular life experiences, and its sources drew from the many strands that made up the web of Protestant tradition. But the influence of the Christian perfectionism and postmillennialism identified with Charles G. Finney and other pre-Civil War and preindustrial evangelical revivalists seems predominant.[32] Even this tradition, which emphasized God's redemptive love and benevolence and insisted that "progress, in all its forms, was divinely directed toward the perfection of the world," took many forms.[33] A few examples suffice. In the 1860s, William Sylvis, that decade's most prominent trade unionist, pitted the God of Christian perfectionism against Malthusian doctrine and asked: "Is it not reasonable, is it not Christian, to suppose that the all-wise Being who placed us here, and whose attributes are benevolence and love, could find other means of controlling population than by war, famine, pestilence, and crime in all its forms?" [34] More than thirty years later, George E. Ward hailed the coming of the American Railway Union by arguing that "God is infinite and eternal justice" so that "he who strives to promote and establish justice upon earth is a co-worker with God." It followed that union men were "the rapidly-evolving

32. McLoughlin, *op. cit.*, 65–165; Smith, *op. cit., passim;* Olmstead, *op. cit.*, 347–62. See also the subtle but significant distinctions between the prophetic and the apocalyptic impulses stressed by Martin Buber in his essay "Prophecy, Apocalyptic, and Historical Hour" (1954), reprinted in *id., Pointing the Way: Collected Essays* (New York, 1957), 192–207. Although authoritative conclusions cannot yet be drawn, it appears that the prophetic rather than the apocalyptic tradition characterized the dominant religious sentiment of dissident Gilded Age workers.

33. McLoughlin, *op. cit.*, 167. There is little direct reference to Finney in post-Civil War labor thought. An exception is found in the *Iron Molder's Journal* (Cincinnati), October 1876, which reported the following story about Finney: "He was passing an iron foundry when the works were in full blast and heard a workman swearing terribly. 'Young man,' said the revivalist, addressing the swearer, 'how hot do you suppose hell is?' The workman recognized the questioner, and placed his arms akimbo, and looking him squarely in the face, said, 'Well, Mr. Finney, I suppose it's so hot there that if somebody brought you a spoonful of melted iron, you'd swear 't was ice cream.' Mr. Finney had nothing more to say."

34. James Sylvis, *Life, Speeches, Labors and Essays of William H. Sylvis* (Philadelphia, 1872), 152–65.

God-men—the *genus homo* vivified by the eternal truths and energizing principles of the gospel of Christ." [35] Another perfectionist strain, more "emotional," told of man's "sin," but was nevertheless distinctly postmillennial. Celebrating Thanksgiving, a Midwestern worker assured the Chicago *Knights of Labor:*

> God has given the earth to the children of men; that a few have stolen it all and disinherited the masses, is no fault of God's, but the wickedness of man. . . . We could not know the wickedness of man, could we not see the goodness of God. . . . It is perfectly safe to pray for His kingdom to come, and in that prayer you anathematize the present system as bitterly as words could do it. . . . [36]

"Pumpkin Smasher," a Newcomb, Tennessee, coal miner, typified extreme labor evangelism:

> Labor has made this country into a bed of roses so that a few may lie therein, and bask in the beautiful God-given sunshine, while the laborer or the creator of all this splendor is roaming in rags all tattered and torn. . . . Cheer up, my brothers, the longest night comes to an end. It may end by an honest use of the ballot box, but as that can never be until the great and glorious millennium with all its attendant beauties set in, brothers we need not look for deliverance through the medium of the ballot box. But it will come just the same. It may come like it did to the Israelitish serfs from down yonder in Egypt, or it may come like it did in France in those long days of rebellion. Or, my brothers, it may come as it did to the colored slaves of the South by sword and fire. Let us be ready to eat the Paschal lamb at any moment the trumpet sounds. [37]

35. *Railway Times*, January 15, 1894.
36. *Knights of Labor* (Chicago), November 20, 1886.
37. *United Mine Workers' Journal*, March 29, 1894.

Even the more "conservative" *American Federationist* found room for labor evangelism. A contributor to the American Federation of Labor's official journal asked for nothing less than "A living Christ moving, living, breathing and dominant in the hearts of a people, not a dead Christianity, dreaming of a dead Christ, but live Christians as live Christs, scattering the table of the money changers in the temples, . . . going down in the poverty-stricken alleys of the robbed industrial slaves, and raising up its victims." This Christianity he called *"the real article!"* [38]

Not surprisingly, the labor evangels found the most essential characteristics of the rapidly developing new industrial social order un-Christian and violative of God's will. As early as the 1860s "Uncle Sam" told readers of *Fincher's Trades Review* that "the present system of labor . . . is a system begotten by the *evil one, hell-born*" and that it "warred against the heaven-born creation, the system instituted by *God* for the good of man." [39] And the Boston *Daily Evening Voice* justified a living wage and condemned the maldistribution of wealth by appealing to God: "It is because He has made of one blood all men—because all are brethren—that the differences instituted by men—the chief of which is the money difference—are so morally disastrous as they are. . . . The elevation of a false god dethrones the real one." [40]

Self-protection and trade unionism especially enjoyed the blessings of God. A Louisville cigarmaker argued: "The toilers are coming out of darkness into light and . . . have dared to organize, to come in closer touch with our Lord's will and the teachings of Jesus Christ." He prophesied: "The time is not far distant when the wage earners shall stand on the rock of independence and sing, 'Nearer, My God, to Thee.' We need not fire and sword, but [to] organize, unionize. . . ." [41] During the

38. Louis Nash, "Is This A Christian Civilization?" *American Federationist*, 1 (January 1895), 252.

39. *Fincher's Trades Review* (Philadelphia), February 2, 1864.

40. Boston *Daily Evening Voice*, September 2, 1865.

41. *Cigar-Makers' Official Journal*, 19 (January 1894), 3.

bitter bituminous coal strike of 1897 the *United Mine Workers'
Journal* editorialized: "Blessed are the union men. They are the
salt of the earth which keeps uncontaminated the pure principles
of brotherhood in the breast of their fellow toilers, and which, if
allowed to die, would make us doubt the fatherhood of God." [42]
Biblical "history" served well J. A. Crawford, Illinois district
president of the United Mine Workers, as he preached the
divinity of unions:

> The first labor organization mentioned in history, either
> profane or divine, was the one founded just outside of the
> historic Garden of Eden, by God Himself; the charter
> members being Adam and Eve. . . . Noah's campaign
> among the Antediluvians favorably reminds us of the
> organizing campaigns of the United Mine Workers. . . .
> The third attempt at organizing labor was made by the
> authority of Jehovah, instituted and carried to a successful
> termination by "The Walking Delegates," Moses and
> Aaron, for the purpose of redeeming Israel from Egyptian
> task-masters. . . . The next labor movement of importance
> recorded in sacred history, begins with the beginning of the
> ministry of the "Nazarene," opposed to all forms of
> oppression of the poor and antagonistic to the operation
> of "Wall street" in the house of His Father, the sanctuary of
> worship. . . . Choose you this day whom you shall serve. If
> plutocracy be God, serve it; if God be God, serve Him. [43]

A *Railway Times* writer summed it up by insisting that "so-
called 'labor agitators,' who are such, *not* for the love of money,
but for the love of humanity, are true followers of Christ and are
striving to establish upon earth the kingdom of God, for which
disciples are taught to pray." [44] Labor organizers had only to
push ahead. "Brother Knights," a fellow unionist advised,

---

42. *United Mine Workers' Journal*, September 30, 1897.
43. *Ibid.*, June 15, 1893.
44. *Railway Times*, January 15, 1894.

"allow me to say that Moses, while fleeing from bondage and endeavoring to deliver his people from the hands of the Egyptian destroyer, received the imperative command from God, to 'go forward.' The same injunction still comes to us, 'go forward.' " [45]

The historic and divine person of Jesus Christ loomed large in the rhetoric and imagery of labor leaders. He served as a model to emulate, a symbol to inspire. An Illinois coal miner later elected to the state assembly admiringly described trade unionist Richard Trevellick: "While not a preacher of Jesus and Him crucified, yet he was one of His most exemplary followers. . . . My wife thought Dick Trevellick the second Jesus Christ." [46] Much was made of the argument that "the Saviour Himself" had associated "with common fishermen and carpenters." [47] A West Coast seaman reminded his brothers that "Peter and James and John, . . . three sailors, were the chosen of our Saviour." [48] *Railway Times* called Jesus "an agitator such as the world has never seen before nor since, . . . despised and finally murdered to appease the wrath of the ruling class of His time." [49] William Mahon, the international president of the motorman's union, lectured the Businessman's Bible Class of the Detroit First Congregational Church that Christ was "crucified for disturbing the national order of things . . . [by] the conservative goody good people, whose plans Jesus spoilt." The businessmen learned that the speaker belonged to "the organiza-

---

45. *Journal of United Labor* (Philadelphia), September 1882.
46. O. T. Hicks, *Life of Richard Trevellick* (Joliet, Ill., 1898), 198–200.
47. *Craftsman* (Washington, D.C.), May 30, 1885.
48. *Coast Seaman's Journal*, February 25, 1891. See also the editorials in the *National Labor Tribune* (Pittsburgh), February 3, March 7, 1877, in which trade-union organizers and labor reformers are called the "Apostles of Labor" and urged to go among the workers and talk with them as did the early Christians. The Apostles, the *Tribune* reminded readers, "were teachers who traveled without pay, and for no other reason than to spread the new gospel." "Looking back," it noted, "we may wonder how a few simple-minded men, without education, with nothing but plain, simple honesty, could make such mighty changes."
49. *Railway Times*, February 1, 1897.

tions . . . fighting for the very principles laid down by Jesus
Christ." [50] The *Coast Seaman's Journal* explained Christ's death:

> Christ taught that all men had souls and were therefore
> equal in the finality of things. For that He was put to death.
> But it was not for preaching the doctrine of a common
> equality before God that the Saviour suffered. The Powers
> have never objected to changing the conditions and rela-
> tions of the future: it is the conditions and relations of today
> they object to altering. Christ was crucified because the
> doctrine of common equality hereafter, which He preached,
> led inevitably to the doctrine of common equality now. This
> is the essence of Christ's teaching. [51]

Christ in an industrializing America would suffer as a labor
leader or even as a "tramp" suffered. "Had Christ lived in
Connecticut, he would have been imprisoned for asking for a
cup of water," believed the Washington *Craftsman*. [52]

If Gilded Age businessmen make sense only when it is

50. *The Motorman and Conductor*, 5 (January 1899), 1–3. See also *Labor
Standard* (New York), January 6, 1877. The socialist *Standard* condemned the
New York *Herald* for praising Christ's life among the poor and for finding in it
"a theory of the conduct of life and of society." The *Standard* believed that "if
any man were to follow Christ's example by going amongst the brokers and
doing as he did, he would soon find himself an inmate of a Lunatic asylum or a
Jail." "Who in these days," asked the *Standard*, "does unto others as he wishes to
be done by?"

51. *Coast Seaman's Journal*, February 22, 1897.

52. *Craftsman*, December 19, 1885; see also W. J. M., "Christmas Greeting,"
Coast Seaman's Journal, December 21, 1887. The identification of Christ with
"tramps" occurred earlier, too, especially during the antitramp hysteria of the
middle and late 1870s. Defending "tramps," the *Weekly Worker* reminded
readers: "About the only consolation left the truly unfortunate tramp is the
thought that Christ was a tramping vagabond. . . ." (*Weekly Worker* [Syracuse,
N.Y.], August 15, 1875.) The *National Labor Tribune* and other labor journals
echoed this point in the 1870s. "Christianity," the *Tribune* insisted, "was ushered
into existence by tramps. . . . Great movements come from the bottom layer of
society, who [sic] possess the truest instincts and noblest instincts. Our tramps
are but the beginning of a worn-out system." (*National Labor Tribune*, December
23, 1876.)

realized that for them "economic activity stood apart from moral considerations," the opposite is true for most Gilded Age labor leaders. Protestantism helped many of them restore what Oscar Handlin calls "the sense of human solidarity infused with religious values." [53] Prominent Gilded Age trade unionists, labor reformers, and even radicals—with the notable exception of Samuel Gompers and De Leon—shared a common faith in a just God, effused perfectionist doctrine, and warned of divine retribution against continuing injustice.[54] They often condemned the insensitivity of institutional Protestantism to the suffering brought about by rapid industrialization, but their speeches and writings also made frequent allusion to essential religious "truths" that gave meaning to their lives and that sanctioned organized opposition to the new industrialism.[55] Trade unionists and reformers from Catholic backgrounds such as Joseph P. McDonnell, who had studied for the priesthood, and Terence V. Powderly frequently quoted the Sermon on the Mount.[56] Important trade unionists and labor radicals reared as Protestants did the same. Sylvis found no contradiction between

53. Oscar Handlin, *The Americans* (Boston, 1963), 308.

54. An unusual example of Gompers making a direct appeal to religion occurred in an April 1891 Pittsburgh speech after the Morewood, Pennsylvania, murder of several East European coke workers. Gompers said: "I say to the capitalists, don't turn your backs on organized labor; don't widen the chasm. . . . Even the Bible lesson of our early childhood will change and we may be compelled to say, 'Whither thou goest I cannot go. . . . Thy people were not my people; thy God is not my God.'" (*United Mine Workers' Journal*, April 23, 1891.) But see more typically Gompers's 1898 attack on "the church and the ministry as the apologists and defenders of the wrong committed against the interests of the people, simply because the perpetrators are possessors of wealth . . . whose real God is the almighty dollar. . . ." (quoted in Hopkins, *op. cit.*, 85), and other examples of his critical attitude toward organized religion in Bernard Mandel, *Samuel Gompers: A Biography* (Yellow Springs, Ohio, 1963), 9–12.

55. A good summary of the criticism by labor reformers and radicals of institutional Protestantism and "clerical *laissez-faire*" is found in May, *op. cit.*, 216–23.

56. See, e.g., Powderly's speeches in the *Journal of United Labor*, July 17, 1890, December 28, 1892, and McDonnell's editorials in the Paterson *Labor Standard*, December 24, 1881, May 15, 1886, and in *Bakers' Journal*, December 1, 1888.

his sympathies for the First International and his belief that the worker's "task" was "to found the universal family—to build up the City of God" through trade unions which Sylvis called an "association of souls" formed by "the sons of God." America's distinctiveness rested for Sylvis on "God's ordained equality of man . . . recognized in the laws and institutions of *our* country." [57] Early trained for the Baptist ministry, Knights of Labor founder Uriah Stephens called excessive hours of work "an artificial and man-made condition, not God's arrangement and order" and insisted the Knights build upon "the immutable basis of the Fatherhood of God and the logical principle of the Brotherhood of Man." Labor organizations had come "as messiahs have ever come, when the world was ready for them." The Knights brought workers together in local assemblies:

> The tabernacle—the dwelling-place of God—is among men. No longer shall men pine for justice, or perish for lack of judgment. "And He will dwell with them, and they shall be His people." "God and Humanity." How inseparably connected! God, the Universal Father; Man, the Universal Brother! [58]

Trevellick found in God reason to ennoble human labor and asked: "Is He less because His mechanical hand formed the mountains? . . . No fellow toilers; He is not less because He worked; neither are you." [59] Eugene V. Debs bristled with Christian indignation at human suffering and cannot be understood outside that framework. From his prison cell after the Pullman debacle, Debs publicly celebrated Labor Day by declaring that it "would stand first in Labor's Millennium, that prophesied era when Christ shall begin in reign on the earth to continue a thousand years." [60] He compared his jailing with

57. Sylvis, *op. cit.,* 96–117, 443–46.

58. Terence V. Powderly, *Thirty Years of Labor* (Columbus, Ohio, 1886), 160–72, 176–77.

59. *National Labor Tribune*, March 18, 1882.

60. *Writings and Speeches of Eugene V. Debs*, ed. Arthur M. Schlesinger, Jr. (New York, 1948), 4–6.

Daniel's treatment by the Persians.[61] Released from Woodstock jail, Debs told an admiring Chicago throng in an oration punctuated with religious images and analogies:

> Liberty is not a word of modern coinage. Liberty and slavery are primal words, like good and evil, right and wrong; they are opposites and coexistent. There has been no liberty in the world since the gift, like sunshine and rain, came down from heaven, for the maintenance of which man has not been required to fight. . . . Is it worth[while?] to reiterate that all men are created free and that slavery and bondage are in contravention of the Creator's decree and have their origin in man's depravity?

Courts, like the Supreme Court, had been "antagonizing the decrees cf heaven since the day when Lucifer was cast into the bottomless pit." "God Himself had taught His lightning, thunderbolts, winds, waves, and earthquakes to strike," and men, too, would strike, "with bullets or ballots," until they walked "the earth free men." "Angels" had "transplanted" "sympathy," one of the "perennial flowers of the Celestial City" and the mainspring of human compassion for Debs, "in Eden for the happiness of Adam and Eve," and then "the winds had scattered the seed throughout the earth." Without sympathy, Debs concluded, there could be "no humanity, no elevating, refining, ennobling influences." [62]

The most eloquent Gilded Age labor reformer, George E. McNeill, was an abolitionist turned staunch American Federation of Labor trade unionist and Christian socialist. He was also an essential link between preindustrial American reform and the Gilded Age labor movement. McNeill rarely spoke or wrote without imparting a deep Christian fervor.[63] In 1876 he com-

61. *Labor Leader*, October 12, 1895.

62. *Union* (Indianapolis), January 17, 1896.

63. Arthur Mann, *Yankee Reformers in the Urban Age* (Cambridge, Mass., 1954), 178–84, contains perceptive comments on the career and importance of McNeill, but most labor historians have minimized his importance.

plained in the socialist *Labor Standard*: "It is the old, old story.
. . . Have the Pharaoh's descendants nothing to learn from
Pharaoh's fate?" [64] At a meeting eleven years later to condemn
the hanging of Albert Parsons, McNeill announced: "I believe
in the passive force of non-resistance as 'Him of old.' . . . I
come here tonight as a Christian." [65] In 1890 he once again tied
labor reform to Christian ethics:

> The Pilgrim leaven still works, true to the fundamental
> principles of the great Leader of men. . . . The influence of
> the teachings of the Carpenter's Son still tends to counteract
> the influence of Mammon. In this movement of the laborers
> toward equity, we will find a new revelation of the Old
> Gospel, when the Golden Rule of Christ shall measure the
> relations of men in all their duties toward their fellows. . . .
> Though the Mammon-worshippers may cry, "Crucify Him!
> Crucify Him!", the promise of the prophet and the poet
> shall be fulfilled . . . by the free acceptance of the Gospel
> that all men are of one blood. Then the new Pentecost will
> come, when every man shall have according to his needs.[66]

Three years later, McNeill found "the religious life" of the labor
movement nothing less than "a protest against the mammoniz-
ing interpretation of religious truth." He wanted "the kingdom
of Heaven (of equity and righteousness) to come on earth," but,
more importantly, argued that "religious truth," adapted to the
realities of industrial society, had meaning for his America. "A
new interpretation of the old truth, 'That the chief end of man is
to glorify God and to enjoy him forever,' reads that the
glorification of God is the reinstatement of man in the likeness
of God; that to enjoy God forever all things must be directed
toward the securing for all the largest measure of happiness." [67]

---

64. *Labor Standard*, November–December 1876.
65. *Labor Enquirer*, November 27, 1887.
66. *Labor Leader*, February–March 1890.
67. George E. McNeill, *The Philosophy of the Labor Movement* (Chicago,
1893), unpaged pamphlet.

McNeill never changed. In 1902, sixty-five years old, he reaffirmed his continued faith in the supremacy of "moral power," but nevertheless warned: "Submission is good, but the order of God may light the torch of Revolution." [68]

Evangelical Protestantism that emphasized the possibility of perfect holiness in this world found expression among trade unionists of less importance than McNeill and other national leaders. Negro activists in the early United Mine Workers of America (1890–1900) reveal such an influence.[69] A preacher and coal miner, William Riley won election in 1892 as secretary-treasurer of the Tennessee district and importuned fellow Negroes to join the union because "God Himself will bless you." [70] The tensions between an active, just God and the day-to-day realities of a Negro coal miner's life strained William E. Clark, a Rendville, Ohio, miner, who asked . . . "was this world of ours the hell we read about in the good book? If it is not, how can a man stand the punishment twice, and then live through eternity? They burn men alive, skin them, lynch them, shoot them, and torture them. . . ." [71] The most important early UMW Negro leader, Richard L. Davis, elected to the National Executive Board in 1896 and 1897, penned many letters that suggested the influence of evangelical imperatives. Miners who threatened to quit the UMW heard from him the words of Paul in the New Testament.[72] A common religious rhetoric helped Davis war against factionalism. Davis's evangelical fervor was not otherworldly.[73] "The Holy Writ" taught "that in unity there is strength." [74] "The miner has no rights that the coal barons are

68. *American Federationist*, 9 (September 1902), 479–80.

69. Further details on the role of Negroes in the early United Mine Workers of America are found in Herbert G. Gutman, "The Negro and the United Mine Workers. The Career and Letters of Richard L. Davis and Something of Their Meaning: 1890–1900," in *The Negro and the American Labor Movement*, ed. Julius Jacobson, 49–127.

70. Riley to the editor, *United Mine Workers' Journal*, September 8, 1892.

71. Clark to the editor, *ibid.,* August 9, 1894.

72. Davis to the editor, *ibid.,* August 15, 1895.

73. Davis to the editor, *ibid.,* April 18, 1892.

74. Davis to the editor, *ibid.,* February 11, 1897.

bound to respect," Davis said another time. "Surely, oh Heaven, this condition of things will not last forever." [75]

Just as Christianity motivated so many labor leaders who organized the reaction against the radical transition from preindustrial to industrial America, so, too, did it serve to condemn particular aspects of that new society and its ideology. A few examples illustrate. The *United Mine Workers' Journal* felt that legal convict leasing of coal miners proved "the laws of Tennessee . . . in conflict with Christianity, civilization and government." [76] Exploitative child factory labor caused the Chicago *Knights of Labor* to explode: "When Jesus said, 'Suffer little children to come unto me,' He did not have a shirt or cloak factory, nor a planing mill, that He wanted to put them into at 40 cents per day. He wanted to bless them and show them the light." [77] The San Francisco Manufacturer's and Employer's Association defense of "free contract" led Andrew Furuseth, secretary of the Sailors' Union of the Pacific, to exclaim indignantly: "If the present system be right, then Christianity is a lie; if the present system be right, then Robert Ingersoll is not a censer-boy in the Temple of Mammon, but the prophet of a new dispensation." [78] Critics of Labor Day learned that "Labor Day is one of the signs of the millennium." [79]

Those who saw in Christianity justification for industrial laissez faire especially felt the sting of labor critics. The *Locomotive Firemen's Magazine* declared the "theory" that "God assigns anyone a station in life . . . preposterous, repulsive, and degrading to God and man." [80] Men who argued that "labor, like flour or cotton cloth, should always be bought in the cheapest market" did so because "an All-wise God, for some inscrutable purpose, has created them" so that workers could see "to what viciousness the antagonism to labor has arrived" and

75. Davis to the editor, *ibid.*, March 3, 10, 1898.
76. *Ibid.*, December 8, 1892.
77. *Knights of Labor*, September 25, 1886.
78. *Coast Seaman's Journal*, June 29, 1892.
79. *Railway Times*, June 1, 1895.
80. *Locomotive Firemen's Magazine*, 11 (April 1887), 207–208.

then "beat back to its native hell the theory that . . . laborers
. . . are merchandise to be bought and sold as any other
commodity—as cattle, mules, swine. . . ." [81] Clergymen who
upheld the competitive system learned: "The church which
allows the competitive system of each for himself, without a
never-silent protest, is not a living Christian church; for 'each
for himself' is a gospel of lies. That never was God's decree." [82]
And the argument that poverty enjoyed God's blessings met the
retort: "Do you think it is anything short of insulting to God to
pretend to believe He makes of ninety-nine paving material for
the one to walk into Heaven over?" [83] Paul's directive to Titus to
"obey magistrates" was rejected. If followed "by the patriots of
'76," explained the *Locomotive Firemen's Magazine*, "a new
nation would not have been born." [84]

Christian example and religious exaltation proved especially
important in times of severe discontent and defeat and in
challenging dominant Gilded Age "myths." Two examples
suffice. After the Pullman strike and boycott and Debs's
imprisonment, a Portland, Oregon, railroad worker drew inferences and analogies only from sacred history:

Were Moses now living, and the Almighty should send him
to a General Manager's office to protest against corporation
robberies, he would be forthwith arrested and thrown into
jail, and if Moses should appeal to the Supreme Court, the
infamous proceedings would be sustained and declared
constitutional; and therefore, the way I look at it, the
corporation slaves of the United States are in a worse
condition than were the slaves of Pharaoh. But in the case of

81. *Ibid.,* 10 (September 1886), 519–20. See also Hermit of the Hills to the
editor, *National Labor Tribune,* January 1, 1876, who wrote: "No happiness can
come to men or nations—no Kingdom of Heaven can descend upon earth—as
long as this false system of antagonism—of working each against the other—
continues."
82. *Journal of United Labor,* September 13, 1888.
83. *Ibid.,* September 20, 1888.
84. *Locomotive Firemen's Magazine,* 18 (September 1894), 877–79.

Pharaoh, God put a curse upon him. The corporation
Pharaohs are not to have their way always. There may be a
Red Sea just ahead—but beyond it is the promised land.

Egypt had only one Pharaoh at a time on the throne. Here
we have probably a hundred of the abnormal monsters, all
engaged in enslaving working people. . . . The Egyptian
Pharaoh did not send Moses to prison. . . . He could have
done it. He had absolute power. He was a despot with a big
D. . . . Here a labor leader is condemned and thrown into
prison by a decree of one small contemptible Pharaoh at the
suggestion of a General Manager Pharaoh . . . and there is
no appeal except to the Buzzards Bay Pharaoh [Grover
Cleveland's Summer White House was in Buzzards Bay],
which would be like appealing from a pig stealing coyote to
a grizzly bear.[85]

The second example concerns Andrew Carnegie and his belief
in the "Gospel of Wealth," the notion of "stewardship." At the
time of its enunciation, the *Locomotive Firemen's Magazine*
scorned the "Gospel of Wealth" as "flapdoodle" and "slush." Of
Carnegie, it said: "While asserting that the ' "Gospel of Wealth"
but echoes Christ's words,' [he] endeavors to wriggle out of the
tight place in which Christ's words place him." It required
"patience" to read about "the 'right modes of using immense
fortunes' known to be the product of cool, Christless rob-
bery." [86] The Homestead conflict in 1892 caused the same
journal to call Carnegie and Henry Clay Frick "brazen pirates
[who] prate . . . of the 'spirit of Christ' [and] who plunder labor
that they may build churches, endow universities and found
libraries." [87] In 1894 the conservative *National Labor Tribune*
joined in mocking Carnegie's professions:

Oh, Almighty Andrew Philanthropist Library Carnegie, who
are in America when not in Europe spending the money of

85. *Railway Times*, August 15, 1895.

86. *Locomotive Firemen's Magazine*, 14 (February 1890), 104–106.

87. *Ibid.*, 16 (August 1892), reprinted in *Writings and Speeches of Eugene V.
Debs*, ed. Schlesinger, 378–82.

your slaves and serfs, thou are a good father to the people of Pittsburgh, Homestead and Beaver Falls. . . . Oh, most adorable Carnegie, we love thee, because thou are the almighty iron and steel king of the world; thou who so much resembles the pharisee. . . . We thank thee and thy combines for the hungry men, women and children of the land. We thank thee and thy combines for the low price of iron and steel and the low price paid in iron and steel works. . . . Oh, master, we thank thee for all the free gifts you have given the public at the expense of your slaves. . . . Oh, master, we need no protection, we need no liberty so long as we are under thy care. So we commend ourselves to thy mercy and forevermore sing thy praise. Amen! [88]

Such language could not be misunderstood.

Although the evidence emphasized in these pages indicates the existence of a working-class social Christianity and suggests that Protestantism had a particular meaning for discontented Gilded Age labor leaders, social radicals, and even ordinary workers, it is hazardous to infer too much from it alone about the working class. Too little is yet known about nineteenth-century American Protestant workers. Evidence on church affiliation, for example, is contradictory. While many contemporaries like D. O. Kellogg, general secretary of the Charity Organization of Philadelphia, frequently worried over the "widespread skepticism and alienation from Christianity prevalent among the

---

88. *National Labor Tribune*, n.d., reprinted in *Coming Age*, February 10, 1894. Such satiric use of traditional religious forms recurred in these years. See, for example, "A Miner's Prayer . . . ," *United Mine Workers' Journal*, May 16, 1895: "Oh! Almighty and allwise and powerful coal barons who art living in great and glorious palaces, when thou art not in secret meeting working for our interest and welfare, we hail thy blessed name as the great philanthropist of our commercial world to-day. We bow before thee in humble submission. . . . We are Americans of the modern type, not like Jefferson, Hancock and Washington. . . . We are your fools, liars, suckers; spit in our faces and rub it in. We have no business to want an education for our children or ourselves. We ain't got any sense. We don't want any; it don't take any sense to load coal for thee. . . . Did Dred Scott ever serve his master better? . . . Amen."

workingmen" and complained that institutional Protestantism often was "out of the poor man's reach," inadequate but significant statistics for church affiliation among the general population, not just workers, show an increase from 16 percent in 1850 to 36 percent in 1900.[89] Until more is known about particular groups of workers and their relations to institutional and noninstitutional religious sentiment and belief, however, it remains impossible to reconcile such seemingly contradictory evidence. Scattered but still inconclusive evidence hints at an apparent close connection between youthful religious conversion and subsequent labor militancy among certain workers.[90]

89. D. O. Kellogg, "Some Causes of Pauperism and Their Cure," *Penn Monthly*, 11 (April 1878), 275–76, 281–82; Olmstead, *op. cit.*, 447.

90. Of the British experience, Hobsbawm writes: "The sect and the labour movement were—especially among the cadres and leaders of the movement—connected . . . by the process of conversion: that is to say, by the sudden, emotionally overpowering realizing of sin and the finding of grace. . . . Conversion indicated, reflected, or perhaps stimulated the kind of unselfish activity which labour militancy inevitably implied. . . . Conversion of some kind is, of course, a commonplace in labour movements." (Hobsbawm, *Social Bandits and Primitive Rebels, op. cit.*, 140.) Too little is known about this phenomenon among American trade unionists and social reformers. But Gabriel perceptively points out that Henry George's beginning awareness of the "social problem" in New York in 1869 came to him as a "conversion after the pattern of evangelical Protestantism." George himself wrote: "Once, in daylight, and in a city street, there came to me a thought, a vision, a call—give it what name you please. But every nerve quivered. And there and then I made a vow." (Gabriel, *op. cit.*, 208–11.) There is also the case of Samuel Fielden, one of the anarchists convicted in the aftermath of the Haymarket bombing. As a Lancashire youth and factory worker, Fielden was converted to Primitive Methodism and became an active lay preacher. Years later, he wrote: "I felt that that religion . . . which I thought was calculated to better the world was something that was worth while for me to use my energies in propagating, and I did it. I could not help it. . . . So intense and earnest was I at that time that I was at one and the same time the Sunday school superintendent of a little Sunday school, a class teacher, a local preacher, and what was called an exhorter. . . ." Fielden came to the United States in 1868. Some years later he came into contact with secular radical ideology. His description of his "conversion" to socialism suggests a close parallel to evangelical conversion and the process Hobsbawm describes. Fielden explains his growing discontent with industrial America and goes on: "My ideas did not become settled as to what was the remedy, but when they did, I carried the same energy and the same determination to bring about that remedy that I

The considerable but as yet largely neglected variations in the experience and outlook of factory workers and skilled craftsmen and of self-educated artisans and casual day laborers as well as the different social environments of small, semirural factory and mining villages, industrial cities, and large urban centers suggest other important analytic problems in exploring the relationship between Protestantism and the "working class." [91] And there are additional complexities. It is risky to assume too close a relationship between religious sentiment and rhetoric and every-day behavior, and it is equally perilous to view church attend-ance and affiliation as proof of religious belief or not attending church as presumptive evidence of the opposite. An example of the confusion that might result was the response of an uniden-tified worker when asked in 1898: "Why are so many intelligent workingmen non-church goers?" "Jesus Christ," he replied, "is with us outside the church, and we shall prevail with God." [92]

Despite these many difficulties, a perspective over more than one or two generations suggests tentative connections between the religious mode of expression of many Gilded Age trade unionists and labor radicals and the behavior of larger numbers of disaffected Gilded Age Protestant workers. Except for those unions that drew support primarily from workers living in small towns and semirural or other isolated areas, the language of labor leaders and social radicals and the tone of their press after

had applied to ideas which I had possessed years before. There is always a period in every individual's life when some sympathetic chord is touched by some other person. There is the open sesame that carries conviction. The ground may have all been prepared. The evidence may have all been accumulated but it has not formed in any shape; in fact, the child has not been born. The new idea has not impressed itself thoroughly when that sympathetic chord is touched, and the person is thoroughly convinced of the idea. It was so in my investigation of political economy. . . . A person said to me Socialism meant equal opportuni-ties—and that was the touch. From that time on I became a Socialist. . . . I knew that I had found the right thing; and I had found the medicine that was calculated to cure the ills of society." (*The Accused, the Accusers*, 36–39.)

91. Asa Briggs, *The Making of Modern England, 1784–1867* (New York, 1965), 287.

92. H. Francis Perry, "The Workingman's Alienation from the Church," *American Journal of Sociology*, 4 (March 1899), 626.

1900 displayed a marked decline in religious emphasis when compared to the labor speeches, editorials, and letters penned between 1860 and 1900. In part this difference suggests the growing secularization of the national culture, but it also makes possible a particular view of Gilded Age workers, seeing them as a transitional generation that bridged two distinct social structures and was the first to encounter fully the profound strains accompanying the shift to an urban and industrial social order. Not separated emotionally or historically from a different past, they lived through an era of extreme social change and social disorder, but carried with them meaningful and deeply felt traditions and values rooted in the immediate and even more distant past. This process was not unique to the United States, but occurred at different times in other rapidly changing societies and greatly explains the behavior of the "first generation" to have contact with a radically different economic and social structure.[93] Although it is an exaggeration to argue that the violent and often disorganized protest characteristic of so much Gilded Age labor agitation resulted only from the tension between the outlook the worker brought to the Gilded Age and that era's rapidly changing economic and social structure, it is not too much to suggest that the thought and the behavior of Gilded Age workers were particular to that generation.

93. Hobsbawm, *Social Bandits and Primitive Rebels, op. cit.,* 1–12, 126–49, but especially 3 when he writes of this generation: "They do not as yet grow with or into modern society: they are broken into it. . . . Their problem is how to adapt themselves to its life and struggles." See also Max Weber's compelling observation that "whenever modern capitalism has begun its work of increasing the productivity of human labor by increasing its intensity, it has encountered the immensely stubborn resistance of . . . pre-capitalistic labor" and the extensive comments on it in Thompson, *op. cit.,* 356 ff. Perceptive argument for a "generational" analysis by social historians is found in Marc Bloch, *The Historian's Craft* (New York, 1964), 185–87: "Men who are born into the same social environment about the same time necessarily come under analogous influences, particularly in their formative years. Experience proves that, by comparison with either considerably older or considerably younger groups, their behavior reveals certain distinctive characteristics which are ordinarily very clear. This is true even of their bitterest disagreements. To be excited by the same dispute even on opposing sides is still to be alike. This common stamp, deriving from a common age, is what makes a generation."

Vital in both pre-Civil War reform movements and evangelical crusades, perfectionist Christianity carried over into the Gilded Age and offered the uprooted but discontented Protestant worker ties with the certainties of his past and reasons for his disaffection with the present by denying for him the premises of Gilded Age America and the not yet "conventional wisdom" of that day. In 1874 the secretary of the Miners' Protective and Progressive Association of Western Pennsylvania, George Archbold, called the trade union a "God-given right" and warned fellow unionists of employer opposition: "The Philistines are upon you, and the fair Delilah would rob you of your locks and shear you of your power." [94] Twenty-three years later and not in entirely dissimilar language, West Coast labor organizer and sailor Andrew Furuseth celebrated the twelfth anniversary of the Sailors' Union of the Pacific:

> Congress may rob us of our rights as men, and may make us bondsmen. The Judiciary may say "Well done" and uphold them. Yet we have our manhood from nature's God, and being true to our best interests we shall yet as free men turn our faces to the sun. . . . We must organize ourselves and align ourselves with the forces which in our country are making for that brotherhood for which Jesus died. So we must as individuals forget home, self and life if need be, to reconquer our liberty, to preserve the sacredness of our bodies, which by Paul were called "the temples of the living God." [95]

Such an emphasis was common to men who disagreed on other matters such as trade-union strategy and the long-range purposes of labor organization and reform. That it is found among "business" unionists, Knights of Labor, and socialist and anarchist radicals and is as prevalent in the 1890s as in the 1860s suggests that it characterized no particular segment of organized

94. *National Labor Tribune*, January 31, 1874.
95. *Coast Seaman's Journal*, March 17, 1897.

labor, but was common to a generation of disaffected workers. Even the German Marxist immigrant Adolph Douai revealed its influence. Although he worried that "enthusiasm without reason engenders fanaticism and thus baffles the noblest purposes," Douai nevertheless pleaded in 1887: "Our age needs religious enthusiasm for the sake of common brotherhood, because infidelity is rampant and hypocrisy prevails in all churches—an infidelity of a peculiar kind, being a disbelief in the destiny of men to be brothers and sisters, in their common quality [sic] and rights." Douai depicted the Gilded Age labor movement as "*the religion of common brotherhood.*" [96]

Preindustrial Christian perfectionism offered Gilded Age labor reformers absolute values in a time of rapid social change and allowed the labor reformer or radical to identify with "timeless truths" that legitimized his attack on the absolutes of Gilded Age social thought—the determinism of Spencerian dogma, the sanctity of property rights and freedom of contract, and the rigidity of political laissez faire.[97] "Conditions" had changed, but the "issues" remained as of old, wrote the *Printer's*

---

96. *Workmen's Advocate* (New Haven, Conn.), May 14, 1887.

97. Vittorio Lanterari, *The Religion of the Oppressed: A Study of Modern Messianic Cults* (New York, 1965), x. "Although each history has its own teleology," Lanterari writes, "the important fact is that the drive which motivates man's practical choices and causes him to struggle and suffer for a better future is common to all and rises out of a faith that is absolute. Thus, even while man is aware of the relativity of human values and goals, nonetheless he behaves 'as if' the goal were a final one *(eschaton)* and 'as if' the values he defends were absolute values." In this connection, an editorial in *Railway Times* (November 1, 1895) is of great interest. The official journal of the American Railway Union worried why, although "truth" is "one of the attributes of deity, . . . the disciples of error, the devotees of lies, professing to be champions of truth, have betrayed it and placed it on a thousand scaffolds, from Calvary to Woodstock." The *Times* explained: "There is an intimate relation between truth and freedom. Christ said, 'Ye shall know the truth, and the truth shall make you free.' It is this declaration that solves the problem. If men are free, they will have found the truth, but they will be free only while they cling to it, maintain it, defend it, hold it aloft, swear by it, and fight for it on every battle field where its enemies appear; and if need be, die for it. . . ." But this labor newspaper worried that in the United States "error has erected its golden god and commands the nation to fall down and worship it."

Labor Tribune, immediate forerunner to the important Pittsburgh *National Labor Tribune*, in arguing that "the war between capital and labor" was being "fought all the time, and [was] . . . identical with civilization itself." Privilege and monopoly were not new. "When Adam commenced business as a farmer, he enjoyed a monopoly, and the same might be said of Noah, but this could not continue," wrote the *Tribune* in 1873. Industrialism merely altered the terms of a historic conflict. "The age of steam, electricity and progress generally shows up a new phase of this old war. We have to fight against the old enemy of the masses, only under a new shape." [98] Coal miner and union organizer W. H. Haskins could declare: "Brothers, the principles of organized labor are as old as the old gray rocks and sand of Mt. Sinai." [99] And Knights of Labor leader Charles Litchman could promise:

> If you ask me to say how this system is to be changed, when the emancipation of the toiling millions on earth is to come, I can only say, "I know not *when* it will come, but I know it will come," because in the sight of God and God's angels the wrongs of the toiling millions on earth are a curse and a crime, and that as God is mercy and God is love, in His own good time the toiler will be free. [100]

Although the labor press frequently complained that institutional Protestantism had "come down to the level of merchandise, and our modern Levites worship the golden calf and offer their wares, like fakirs, to the highest bidder," [101] the *United*

---

98. *Printer's Labor Tribune* (Pittsburgh), November 27, 1873. See also the editorial in the Providence *Sun*, April 14, 1875, a Rhode Island labor weekly, which insisted: "From the Old Testament times the Almighty has had a controversy with those who have robbed the laborer of his wages."

99. *United Mine Workers' Journal*, January 17, 1895.

100. *Journal of United Labor* (Philadelphia), August 27, 1888.

101. *Coast Seaman's Journal*, October 18, 1893. Earlier examples of this critical attitude toward the clergy's dominant social conservatism are found in reviews of Washington Gladden's *Working People and Their Employers* (Boston, 1876) in the *Workingman's Advocate* (Chicago), August 26, 1876, and the

Mine Workers' Journal printed on its first page a sermon by Baptist minister J. Thalmus Morgan for good reason. Morgan warned from his Ohio mining village pulpit:

> God's laws of right and wrong are ever the same and cannot be changed until God and man's moral nature shall be changed. Opinions may change, but truth never. Truth is truth to the end of all reckoning. What was right in the time of Moses, Mordecai and Ehud will be right forever. . . . God shall judge the poor of the people; He shall save the children of the needy, and shall break into pieces the oppressor. Yes, He will do the poor justice, for He will delight in doing them good. . . . And [He] shall break into pieces oppression. He is strong to smite the foes of His people. Oppressors have been great breakers, but their time of retribution shall come, and they shall be broken themselves.[102]

National Labor Tribune, September 16, 1876. The *Tribune* was especially hard on Gladden: "He is a shallow thinker and writer. Had his book never been written nothing would have been lost. Preachers, as a class, are not able to deal with the Labor problem, and Mr. Gladden is no exception."

102. *United Mine Workers' Journal*, June 28, 1894. What Morgan's sermon typified cannot be known because the ideas and social outlook of local clergymen, particularly those in industrial towns and cities and those with predominantly working-class congregations, have not yet been studied, and it is not helpful to infer their thoughts and behavior from national religious periodicals. Scattered but inconclusive evidence suggests that an unexplored dimension of the clerical social gospel may be uncovered by studying the clergy in such communities. A few examples suffice. After discontented and unpaid Erie Railroad shopworkers and repair mechanics stopped trains and took control of the repair shops in March 1874, eighteen hundred state militia went to Susquehanna Depot, Pennsylvania, to restore order. But a local minister preached a severe Sunday sermon against the railroad company. (H. G. Gutman, "Trouble on the Railroads in 1873–1874," *Labor History*, 2 [Spring 1961], 228.) In 1880 a socialist newspaper editor, Irish immigrant Joseph P. McDonnell, served time in a Passaic County, New Jersey, jail for libeling a brickyard owner by publishing a letter that exposed conditions in a Paterson brickyard. Two Paterson clergymen, one a Baptist and the other a Methodist, publicly supported McDonnell and sided with the workers. (*Id.,* "Industrial Invasion of the Village Green," *Trans-action,* 3 [May-June 1966], 19–24.) After the fierce violence in

The transcendent values that organized labor found in such postmillennial Christian exhortation helped steel it in a transitional era of deep crisis. "The mandate, 'Thou shalt glorify me in thy works,' is Labor's first article of faith," concluded the *Coast Seaman's Journal.*[103]

Although trade unionists and labor radicals were not the only critics of Gilded Age industrial America, the social Christianity they espoused was different from the more widely known and well-studied social gospel put forth by middle- and upper-class religious critics of that society. Both groups reacted against the early disintegrating consequences of rapid industrialization and drew from the same broad religious tradition. But parallel developments are not necessarily synonymous even though they occur at the same time and share a common mode of expression. The available evidence suggests few formal connections between the two "movements" and for several reasons. Before the 1890s,

1892 between strikers and Pinkerton police that resulted in more than thirty deaths, a Homestead, Pennsylvania, Methodist preacher said of Henry Clay Frick at the funeral services for three dead strikers: "This town is bathed in tears today, and it is all brought about by one man, who is less respected by the laboring people than any other employer in the world. There is no more sensibility in that man than in a toad." (Leon Woolf, *Lockout. The Story of the Homestead Strike of 1892: A Study of Violence, Unionism, and the Carnegie Steel Empire* [New York, 1965], 133.) At the time of the 1894 Pullman strike and boycott, William Carwardine, pastor of the First Methodist Church of Pullman, bitterly attacked George Pullman and called his model town "a hollow mockery, a sham, an institution girdled with red tape, and as a solution to the labor problem most unsatisfactory." Carwardine supported the strikers and was joined by Morris L. Wickman, pastor of the Pullman Swedish Methodist Church, who sharply criticized the firm before the United States Strike Commission. (Almont Lindsay, *The Pullman Strike* [Chicago, 1942], 73, 103; May, *op. cit.,* 109–11.) Although he frequently criticized the social orthodoxy of most institutional Protestant churches and was himself without religious sentiment, Gompers nevertheless interestingly wrote in 1898 that not all clergymen deserved his condemnation: "The men who preach from their pulpits and breathe with every word their sympathy with the great struggling masses of humanity; . . . these ministers you will find always interesting, and not only interesting, but the churches filled with workers who go to hear them." (Perry, "Workingman's Alienation from the Church," 623.)

103. *Coast Seaman's Journal*, August 29, 1894.

the two groups, so different in their social composition and in
the way industrial and social change affected them, rarely
addressed each other and usually spoke to different audiences.
Despite many diversities (its "radical" and "conservative"
fringes), the essential attributes of the early social gospel
movement are characterized by Henry May in a way that makes
it possible to distinguish it from its working-class counterpart:

> The Social Gospel of the American nineteenth century . . .
> did not grow out of actual suffering but rather out of moral
> and intellectual dissatisfaction with the suffering of others.
> It originated not with the "disinherited" but rather with the
> educated and pious middle class. It grew through argument,
> not through agitation; it pleaded for conversion, not revolt
> or withdrawal.[104]

Critical of business behavior and the individualist ethic of their
time and anxious to infuse all social classes with a meaningful
Christian ethic, few early advocates of the social gospel identified closely with organized labor and its particular forms of
collective organization and protest. Few shared Henry George's
belief that "the revolt everywhere" against the "hard conditions
of modern society is really the religious spirit." [105] They sought

104. May, *op. cit.,* 235.
105. *Labor: Its Rights and Wrongs,* 261–68. George linked all contemporary
protest movements, even the most radical, and compared them to early Christian
history: "Who are these men, the Socialists, the Anarchists, the Nihilists, and
what is it they seek? . . . Is it not for a state of greater equality, for a state of
more perfect peace, for a condition where no one will want and no one will suffer
for the material needs of existence? That is the ideal those men have before
them, blind and wrong their methods though they be. And what is that ideal? Is
it not the kingdom of God on earth? What was the reason that a doctrine
preached by a humble Jewish carpenter, who was crucified between two thieves,
propagated by slaves and fugitives meeting in caverns, overran the world and
overthrew the might of legions and the tortures of the amphitheatre and
dungeon? Was it for theological distinction that Rome, the tolerant Rome, that
welcomed all Gods to her Pantheon, persecuted the adherents of this new
Galilean superstition? No. . . . It was because they sought the kingdom of God
on earth. It was because they hoped to bring it about there and then. . . . That

first to mediate between the competing classes and frequently failed to understand the "immediacy" of labor discontent. Only a small number, May finds, arranged "a successful working relation between their ultimate confidence in the new social spirit and the drab realities of day-to-day struggle." [106] Even the young Richard T. Ely and Washington Gladden, both so typical of the mainstream social gospel movement and both profoundly at odds with the materialism of their times, found it difficult at the start to associate themselves with working-class organizations and their methods and objectives.[107] Of the early social gospel movement, Charles H. Hopkins concludes that its "inclusive panacea" was "Christianity itself." Quoting Gladden, he adds: " 'the power of Christian love' was declared to be strong enough 'to smooth and sweeten all relations of capitalists and labor.' " Society would change mainly "through the converted individual whose changed character would produce a social transformation." [108] Such thought and argument stimulated numerous middle- and upper-class reformers in late nineteenth-century America, but what May calls its "facile optimism" and its "fatal tendency to underestimate difficulties and to neglect mechanism" cut it off from working-class critics of industrial society.[109]

doctrine of the fatherhood of a common Creator and the brotherhood of men struck at the roots of tyranny; struck at the privileges of those who were living in luxury on the toil and the blood and the sweat of the worker. . . ."

106. May, *op. cit.*, 231–35.

107. In 1886 Ely, for example, defended trade unions and attacked employer abuses in his significant *The Labor Movement in America*, but nevertheless urged discontented workers to "cast aside envy" and told them: "While the Bible is a good armory from which you may draw weapons of attack, it at the same time points out the right course for you to take. . . . It discourages no good effort; but even James followed his awful condemnation of the oppressor with these wise words, 'Be ye also patient.' " (R. T. Ely, *The Labor Movement in America* [New York, 1886], v–xiii.) Gladden early attacked the industrial abuses of his time, but still found labor unions "often unwise and unprofitable" and argued that "as a general thing" unions "result in more loss than gain to the laboring classes." (Quoted in John L. Shover, "Washington Gladden and the Labor Question," *Ohio Historical Quarterly*, 68 [October 1959], 335–52.)

108. Hopkins, *op. cit.*, 70, 89, 325.

109. May, *op. cit.*, 233.

Protestantism in Gilded Age America permeated the social structure and the value system of the nation more deeply and in different ways than heretofore emphasized by that era's historians. The careers and writings of Henry Ward Beecher, Dwight Moody, Mary Baker Eddy, Washington Gladden, and the trade unionists and labor radicals described in these pages illustrate the complexity of the relationship between religious belief and organization and the component parts of a particular social structure. Although what has been written here must not be interpreted as a single explanation for the little-studied subject of nineteenth-century working-class thought and behavior, it should be clear that the social gospel early found expression among those who professed to speak for the discontented lower classes and that the behavior of these critics of industrial capitalism cannot be understood without first exploring the religious (and secular) dimensions of their thought. For some workers and their leaders, including some of the most prominent Gilded Age trade unionists and radicals, a particular strand of Protestantism offered what Hobsbawm calls "a passion and morality in which the most ignorant can compete on equal terms" and what Liston Pope describes as a religion "intimately related to the everyday struggles and vicissitudes of an insecure life" and "useful for interpretation and succor." [110] In 1893 one American pondered existential questions:

While man is nothing more than a human, he has feeling. . . . While I am not a preacher nor one among the best of men, I am one who believes in Christ and His teachings and endeavor each day to live the life of a Christian. . . . My way is not everybody's way, and it would be wrong to even suppose it should be. . . . Now, what is my motive? . . . My reasoning is after this manner: Can man within himself accomplish as much while self exists as when he considers, Am I the only being that lives? and finds in answer, no. But

110. Hobsbawm, *Social Bandits and Primitive Rebels, op. cit.*, 132; Liston Pope, *Millhands and Preachers* (New Haven, Conn., 1942), 86.

I am one among millions, a pitiful drop in the bucket he thinks at once. . . . Am I right? Man wants everything but that which is best for him and his brother.[111]

These were not the words of Henry Ward Beecher, Russell Conwell, Mary Baker Eddy, Dwight Moody, William Lawrence, Lyman Atwater, John D. Rockefeller, Andrew Carnegie, or even Washington Gladden; they were penned by an unidentified but troubled Belleville, Illinois, coal miner.

111. *United Mine Workers' Journal*, June 29, 1893.

PART II

---

*Black Coal Miners
and the
American Labor
Movement*

3

The Negro and the
United Mine Workers of America

THE CAREER AND LETTERS OF RICHARD L. DAVIS AND
SOMETHING OF THEIR MEANING: 1890–1900

I

IN APRIL 1877, fifteen hundred Braidwood, Illinois, coal
miners struck against the Chicago, Wilmington & Vermillion
Coal Company to protest a third wage cut in less than a year
and a resulting 33 percent drop in wages. Two months later the
company imported Kentucky and West Virginia Negroes to
replace the stubborn strikers, and its superintendent contentedly
reported the Negroes as saying they had "found the Land of
Promise." But in July the strikers chased four hundred Negroes
and their families from Braidwood, and only a couple of Illinois
militia regiments brought them back. When winter approached,
the defeated strikers returned to work. The violence accompanying the great 1877 railroad strikes drew national attention
away from Braidwood, but in that small town only the coming
of the Negroes mattered, not the faraway riots in Pittsburgh and

---

The author is indebted to the State University of New York at Buffalo for
making available research funds to gather the materials for this essay. Critical
comments by Professor C. Vann Woodward of Yale University resulted in
significant changes in the tone of the concluding section of this essay. The
Center for Advanced Study in the Behavioral Sciences, Stanford, California,
made it possible for me to read portions of this essay at the annual meetings of
the Association for the Study of Negro Life and History in Baltimore, Maryland,
in October 1966.

other railroad centers. John Mitchell, then a seven-year-old orphan, lived in Braidwood and witnessed these events.[1] No record exists of young Mitchell's feelings at that time, but twenty-two years later an older Mitchell, now the newly elected president of the nine-year-old United Mine Workers of America, gave testimony before the Industrial Commission (set up by Congress in 1898) that might suggest to the innocent only that history repeats itself. Relations between Negroes and whites in the coal-mining industry troubled Mitchell and other UMW leaders. In 1898 and 1899 violence and death had followed the coming of Negro strikebreakers and armed white police to the Illinois towns of Pana, Virden, and Carterville. "I might say, gentlemen," Mitchell advised the Commission in 1899, "that the colored laborers have probably been used more to decrease the earnings in the mines . . . than in any other industry." To this fact Mitchell attributed much unrest. "I know of no element," he continued, "that is doing more to create disturbances than is the system of importing colored labor to take white men's places and to take colored men's places." [2]

Mitchell and the other UMW witnesses before the Commission did not draw the conclusion that such Negro strikebreaking justified the exclusion of Negroes from trade unions. They said the opposite and took pride in their interracial union. Although Mitchell personally believed that the Negro "standard of morality" was "not as high as that of white people," he nevertheless berated only those operators who used Negroes against the union and, insisting that the UMW constitution did not bar Negroes from membership, told the Commission: "Our obligation provides that we must not discriminate against any man on account of creed, color or nationality." [3] Even more explicitly than Mitchell, UMW Secretary-Treasurer W. C. Pearce insisted before the Commission:

1. Robert V. Bruce, *1877: Year of Violence* (Indianapolis, 1959), 292–94; Andrew Roy, *A History of the Coal Miners of the United States* (Columbus, 1906), 353.

2. "Testimony of John Mitchell, April 11, 1899," *Report of the Industrial Commission*, VII (Washington, D.C., 1901), 51–53.

3. *Ibid.*, 31–32, 51–53.

As far as we are concerned as miners, the colored men are with us in the mines. They work side by side with us. They are members of our organization; [and] can receive as much consideration from the officials of the organization as any other members, no matter what color. We treat them that way. They are in the mines, many of them good men.

Pearce objected to Negroes only when they became strikebreakers, but he blamed this condition on "their ignorance of the labor movement and the labor world" and on the frequent deceptions practiced against Negroes by operators. "When they get to a certain place," he said of these Negroes, "why, they are there, and some of them, I know, many times are sorry for it." [4]

These pages consider certain aspects of the early contact between the United Mine Workers and Negro miners. Too little is yet known for that story to be told fully, much less clearly understood. By 1900, when the UMW was only ten years old, Mitchell and Pearce estimated that between 10 and 15 percent of the nation's four hundred thousand coal miners were Negroes.[5] They almost all worked as bituminous miners, and their number varied between regions. Few labored in Western Pennsylvania, and many concentrated in the Border South (West Virginia, Kentucky, and Tennessee) and Alabama. The older bituminous areas of the Middle West all had smaller numbers of Negro miners than the South—and Negro miners spread through other states, too.[6] Some first came as strikebreakers, but most Negroes became miners in a more normal fashion—seeking work as unskilled or semiskilled laborers in a rapidly expanding industry. At the same time as the mining population increased in the 1890s, its ethnic composition changed radically. Traditional dominance of native whites and

4. "Testimony of W. C. Pearce," *ibid.,* 101.

5. *Ibid.,* 30–58, 101, 136, 149.

6. See the tables and other statistical materials in Sterling D. Spero and Abram L. Harris, *The Black Worker: The Negro and the Labor Movement* (New York, 1931), 209, 215; and in Herbert R. Northrup, "The Negro and the United Mine Workers of America," *Southern Economic Journal* (April 1943), 314.

British and Irish immigrants began to decline as East and South European Catholic immigrants and American Negroes settled into the industry. So heterogeneous a population posed vexatious problems for early UMW leaders. "With all of these differences," existing in industries like the mining industry, the Industrial Commission concluded in 1901, "it is an easy matter for employers and foremen to play race, religion, and faction one against the other." Even where employers made no such efforts, nationality and ethnic differences separated men in a common predicament. But although early UMW bituminous locals were based on nationalities, by 1900 they had given way to mostly "mixed" locals. In many mining districts the union "mixed" recent immigrants with "old" immigrants and native miners—and Negroes with whites.[7] Negro support explained part of the union's early successes among bituminous miners. By 1900, Negroes had contributed significantly to the building of that union, and twenty thousand Negroes belonged to it. Here we give attention mainly to the role and the ideas of one early UMW Negro leader.

7. *Report of the Immigration Commission. Immigrants in Industries,* VI and VII (Washington, D.C., 1911), *passim; Report of the Industrial Commission,* XV (Washington, D.C., 1901), 405–7 and *passim;* Frank Julian Warne, *The Coal Mine Workers: A Study in Labor Organization* (New York, 1905), *passim,* and *The Slav Invasion and the Mine Workers: A Study in Immigration* (Philadelphia, 1904), *passim.* The Industrial Commission made interesting but as yet unexplored observations about the impact of ethnic diversity on American trade-union organization. "This problem of mixed nationalities," it concluded, "results in at least one novelty in the method of organization of American labor unions compared with those of other countries, namely, branch organization based on race." The Commission found that this pattern tended to disappear as "the races assimilate or the needs of the industry dictate." In the UMW, it found disappearance of this form of organization by 1900. Whether or not this "principle" affected unions that organized Negroes into separate locals before 1900 has not yet been studied fully. But the Commission found, for example, that in 1886 the Chicago hod-carriers first formed an ineffective "mixed" union of all nationalities. In 1896 it set up a "council" that included representatives from four locals: a German-speaking local with a few Negro members, a Bohemian local, a Polish local, and an English-speaking local that included Italians and Swedes along with 250 to 300 Negroes. (*Report of the Industrial Commission, op. cit.,* 313, 426–28.)

I I

THE MOST IMPORTANT of these Negro miners, Richard L. Davis, twice won election to the National Executive Board of the United Mine Workers, in 1896 and 1897, but it is the way his entire career challenges traditional explanations of the relationships between Negro workers and organized labor in the 1890s and not alone his high office that forces attention on him. Biographical material so essential to fully knowing Davis and other Negro UMW officers is scant, and in Davis's case comes mainly from his printed letters and scattered references to him in the *United Mine Workers' Journal*. Such limited information allows only the piecing together of the barest outlines of his life. Much must be inferred and much is unknown, even his status at birth. Davis was born in Roanoke, Virginia, in 1864, the day before Christmas and only a few months before the Civil War ended, but there is not even a hint that he came of either slave or free Negro parents. The *Journal* called him "a full-blooded colored man" but said nothing else about his forebears. For several years Davis attended the Roanoke schools during the winter months. At eight, he took employment at a local tobacco factory and remained with that job for nine years when, "disgusted with the very low wage rate and other unfavorable conditions of a Southern tobacco factory," he started work as a coal miner in West Virginia's Kanawha and New River regions. In 1882 Davis moved to Rendville, Ohio, a mining village in the Hocking Valley region and southeast of Columbus. He married, supported a family of unknown size, and lived and labored there the rest of his brief life. Apparently only union duties took him away from Rendville and then but for brief periods. Davis died there in 1900. Of his life other than his work as a miner and his union career, nothing else is known.[8]

Life as a miner allowed Davis few amenities. Unsteady work made him, like other miners, complain frequently of recurrent

8. Brief biographical sketches of Davis are found in the *United Mine Workers' Journal*, April 23, 1896 and January 25, 1900 (hereafter cited as *UMWJ*).

unemployment. The depression in the mid-1890s hit Ohio miners hard. "Times in our little village remain the same . . . —no work and much destitution with no visible signs of anything better," Davis reported in February 1895.[9] More than a year later he wrote again: "Work here is a thing of the past. I don't know what we are going to do. We can't earn a living, and if we steal it we will be prosecuted."[10] The year 1897 proved little better. One week Davis's mine worked only half a day.[11]

His commitment to trade unionism added difficulties ordinary miners did not face. In August 1896, after certain Negro miners blamed Davis and another miner for organizing a strike to restore a wage scale, Davis went without work. "Just how they could stoop so low I am unable to tell," an angered Davis wrote of these Negroes, "and some of them, if not all, call themselves Christians or children of the most High God, but in reality they are children of his satanic majesty." Some Negro co-workers he called "as true as can be found anywhere" but his betrayers were "as mean men as ever breathed."[12] The *Journal* defended Davis and reminded Ohio readers he deserved their "respect and moral support" because of "his devotion to the cause of unionism."[13] But nearly four months later Davis, still without work, feelingly complained: "Others can get all the work they want; but I, who have never harmed anyone to my knowledge, must take chances with winter and its chilly blasts without the privilege of a job so as to earn a morsel of bread for my wife and little ones."[14] Two years afterward, in 1898, and for reasons unknown, Davis lived in a pitiful condition—this time, blacklisted. A letter dated May 16, 1898, poured forth a pained despair:

I have as yet never boasted of what I have done in the interest of organized labor, but will venture to say that I

9. Richard L. Davis to the editor, *UMWJ*, February 28, 1895 (hereafter cited as RLD).

10. RLD to the editor, *UMWJ*, April 30, 1896.

11. RLD to the editor, *ibid.*, February 11, 1897.

12. RLD to the editor, *ibid.*, September 10, 1896.

13. "Editorial Note," *ibid.*, September 10, 1896.

14. RLD to the editor, *ibid.*, December 17, 1896.

have done all I could and am proud that I am alive today, for I think I have had the unpleasant privilege of going into the most dangerous places in this country to organize, or in other words, to do the almost impossible. I have been threatened; I have been sandbagged; I have been stoned, and last of all, deprived of the right to earn a livelihood for myself and family.

I do not care so much for myself, but it is my innocent children that I care for most, and heaven knows that it makes me almost crazy to think of it. I have spent time and money in the labor movement during the past sixteen years, and to-day I am worse off than ever, for I have no money, nor no work. I will not beg, and I am not inclined to steal, nor will I unless compelled through dire necessity, which I hope the good God of the universe will spare me. . . . I can not think of my present circumstances and write [more], for I fear I might say too much. Wishing success to the miners of this country, I remain, as ever, a lover of labor's cause.[15,*]

---

15. RLD to the editor, *ibid.*, May 19, 1898.

* "Old Dog," a Congo, Ohio, Negro miner, took up Davis's complaint. "He can't get work in the mines, and he says he can't get work to do as an organizer." Old Dog called Davis "a staunch union man" and reminded *Journal* readers that Davis had "done more" than any single person to bring Ohio Negroes into the union. "I think he should be provided for in some way," he went on. "You do not often meet up with colored men like Dick. . . . He has a family to keep and I think we owe him something. He nor *[sic]* his children can not live on wind, and further, if he was a white man he would not be where he is—mark that—but being a negro he does not get the recognition he should have . . . such treatment will not tend to advance the interest of our union, but will retard its progress and cause colored men to look with suspicion upon it. . . . Give us an equal show. Dick deserves better usage. . . . He feels sorely disappointed. . . . For my part, I think if we would do right he could either go in mines to work or we should see to it that he was started up in a small business or given field work. I want President [Michael] Ratchford to show all colored men that he values a man irrespective of his color and he can best do this by giving Dick a helping hand. I hope you will excuse my bad writing and language and also method of speaking, but I believe in calling a spade a spade. I am sure we are not being treated just as we should." In 1909, William Scaife, British-born, an Illinois miner and then retired editor of the *United Mine Workers' Journal*, remembered the troubled last years of Davis. Scaife gave no details but noted: "R. L. Davis, by his devotion to

In December of that year Davis still sought work. "I am still a miner," he remarked, "but cannot secure work as a miner. Yet I love the old principles I have always advocated. Even though a negro, I feel that which is good for the white man is good for me, provided, however, it is administered in the right way. I want to see the negro have an equal show with the white man, and especially when he deserves it. I want it in the local, in the district, and in the national." [17] Little time remained for the fulfillment of Davis's wishes. Thirteen months later, one month after his thirty-fifth birthday and while the UMW met in convention in another city, Davis died of "lung fever." [18]

Learning of his death, the UMW convention delegates paused to pay special tribute to their deceased Negro brother. Davis deserved their attention. Enduring many difficulties, he had been one of the founders and pioneer organizers of the United Mine Workers during the 1890s, its first and perhaps most difficult decade. The delegates called attention to the "many years of his life . . . devoted to advancing the interests of his craft" and lamented that the union had "lost a staunch advocate of the rights of those who toil, and his race a loyal friend and advocate." [19] The particular experiences that drew Davis toward organized labor are unknown, and only scant evidence links him to the Ohio miners' unions that preceded the UMW in the 1880s and to the Knights of Labor. But there is no doubt of his

---

the miners' union, deserved better treatment than that accorded him in the last few years of his life." He scorned those who criticized Davis as a "has been" and "a barnacle," calling them "some of the mushroom growth of latter-day leaders" who were "unmanly and unremindful of the past." Davis had worked for the union when it "took sand, pluck, and grit to do it." Scaife lamented: "I sometimes think the poet of nature was hitting the right head with a ten-pound hammer when he said, 'Man's inhumanity to man makes countless thousand mourn.' . . . Our ignorance has often led us to injure, abuse and crucify our best friends." [16]

16. "Old Dog" to the editor, *ibid.*, May 12, 1898. (Old Timer [William Scaife], "Forty Years a Miner and Men I Have Known," *United Mine Workers' Journal*, November 19, 1909.)

17. RLD to the editor, *ibid.*, December 8, 1898.

18. *Ibid.*, January 25, 1900.

19. *Ibid.*, January 25, 1900.

importance to the UMW after 1890. The evidence is overwhelming. Many of his letters appeared in the weekly *Journal* and related quite fully his role in the Ohio unions, his career as a local and national organizer, and his feelings and ideas about the Negro, organized labor, and the changing structure of American industrial society.

Davis's formal role in the UMW can be described simply. In 1890 he attended its founding convention as delegate and also won election to Ohio's District 6 Executive Board. Another year he spurned efforts to nominate him for the vice presidency of District 6. But until 1895, when he ran for the National Executive Board and lost by only a small vote, Davis won annual re-election to the District 6 office. His close defeat for national office in 1895 proved* "very clearly" to him that the "question of color in our miners' organization will soon be a thing of the past," and he predicted that "the next time some good man of my race will be successful." [20] The year 1896 found Davis right. He and fourteen others stood for the National Executive Board at the annual UMW convention and Davis got the highest vote, 166. The next largest vote, 149, went to a white Illinois miner, James O'Connor. [21] A year later, Davis won re-election and ranked second among those vying for that high office.† The *Journal* celebrated Davis's first election in its customary fashion by printing brief biographical sketches of all new officers. It called Davis ("Dick") a man of "very fair" education, "a good reader," and the author of a "very good letter." It boasted that he gained election because UMW members found him "a good representative of his race because

* Twenty-eight men stood for the office; six were elected; Davis ran seventh and got 173 votes.

20. *Ibid.*, February 21, 1895 and April 23, 1896, and RLD to the editor, February 28, 1895.

21. *Ibid.*, April 23, 1896.

† Although renominated in 1898, he failed to win a third term. For unknown reasons, his popularity among convention delegates fell dramatically, and he got only ninety-four votes. [22]

22. In 1897 Davis got 124 votes and the candidate ahead of him netted 156 votes (*ibid.*, January 21, 1897). Details on the 1898 election appear in *ibid.*, December 22, 1897 and January 20, 1898.

the miners believe the colored men of the country should be recognized and given a representative on the [the executive] board." The *Journal* made much of the fact that he was Negro:

> He will in a special way be able to appear before our colored miners and preach the gospel of trade unions and at the same time will be able to prove to our white craftsmen how much progress may be made with very limited opportunities. . . . If it be a good principle to recognize races or nationalities on the board in preference to individuals, per se, the convention has done well to elect Dick, for he has certainly merited this recognition. In fact, he has merited it from either standpoint, for as a man, and more especially as a union man, he has deserved well of the miners of the country.[23]

The weekly wished Davis "success," and Davis took his charge with great seriousness, enthusiastic over "this manifestation of kindness in recognizing my people." He felt his election to be of great importance to all Negro miners:

> Not only am I proud but my people also. I know that a great deal has not been said publicly, but I do know that our people are very sensitive, and upon many occasions I have heard them make vigorous kicks against taxation without representation. Now, then, they cannot kick this year, for although the representative himself may be a poor one, it is representation just the same.

He promised to "try to so act that those who elected me shall not be made to feel ashamed." [24]

23. *Ibid.*, April 23, 1896.
24. RLD to the editor, *ibid.*, April 30, 1896.

III

THE PARTICULAR LANGUAGE and mode of expression found in so many of Davis's letters strongly suggests the influence of evangelical Protestantism on his thoughts and feelings. This strain of postmillennial Christianity was common among many self-educated late-nineteenth-century American reformers and radicals bred in a rural or semirural world. Davis, then, was not different from them. Religious images recurred often in his writings. Urging compact organization, he commanded: "Let us resolve to do better. We are taught by the teachings of the Holy Writ that in unity there is strength." [25] The acquittal of a Pennsylvania sheriff involved in the shooting of several Polish anthracite miners in 1898 caused the lament: "It is as we expected. . . . The miner has no rights that the coal barons are bound to respect. Surely, oh Heaven, this condition of things will not last forever." [26] Davis found in the United Mine Workers a secular church that promised redemption from an evil social order, and he gave his work all the zeal and devotion expected of a dedicated missionary. When Massillon, Ohio, miners threatened to quit the UMW, he reminded them of Paul's words in the New Testament: "Except those abide in the ship, ye cannot be saved." Preachers designated the "ship as a church," but Davis saw matters differently. He called the UMW "the ship" and explained: "I now exhort you that except ye abide in the ship ye cannot be saved. . . . If her crew will only remain at their posts and not mutiny, I think she will make the harbor safely." [27] Thus did Davis war against factionalism by drawing from and reinterpreting a common religious language. Another time, addressing nonunion Negroes, he dismissed their frequent complaint that the UMW was "a white man's organization."

> Now, my dear people, I, as a colored man, would ask of you to dispel all such ideas as they are not only false but foolish

25. RLD to the editor, *ibid.*, February 11, 1897.
26. RLD to the editor, *ibid.*, March 3, 10, 1898.
27. RLD to the editor, *ibid.*, August 15, 1895.

and unwise. Think a moment and see if you cannot come to the conclusion that you yourselves are men, and that you have the same interest at stake as your white brother, because I believe that to be the proper phrase; inasmuch as I believe in the principle of the fatherhood of God and the brotherhood of all mankind no matter what the color of his skin may be.

Davis castigated those who saw religious salvation only in otherworldly terms. He reminded nonunion Negroes that "labor organizations have done more to eliminate the color line than all other organizations, the church not even excepted," and called otherworldly aspirations inadequate:

I know that in former days you used to sing "Give me Jesus, give me Jesus, you may have all the world, just give me Jesus." But the day has now come that we want a little money along with our Jesus, so we want to change that old song and ask for a little of the world as well. Don't you think so friends?

Davis admitted he had been "thinking so for some time." [28]

IV

DAVIS'S MAIN INFLUENCE as a union organizer and labor stalwart was felt where he lived and worked—in Southeastern Ohio. Mining villages and towns dotted the landscape in Hocking, Athens, and Perry counties. Davis worked there under many disadvantages. Not the least important was the fact that Negroes had first been brought there in large numbers from Border-State cities and even the Deep South in 1874 and 1875 to break a bitter strike by Hocking Valley members of the Miners National

28. RLD to the editor, *ibid.*, April 18, 1892.

Association. The strikers had been mostly native whites and British and Irish immigrants. On arrival, some Negroes had refused their assigned role and left, but most did their job and remained on after the strikers surrendered.[29] Racial friction and ethnic mistrust inevitably followed, and coal operators often exploited tensions between Negro and white miners.

Although the history of that region has not yet been carefully studied, certain facts are known about the Negro and white miners. Southeastern Ohio felt deeply the influence of the Knights of Labor and its brand of evangelical democratic trade unionism. Local miners' unions, independent of or affiliated with the Knights, rose and fell before 1890, too.[30] Of the Negro miners little is yet known except from the letters Davis penned in the 1890s. Before the Knights exerted influence, Negro miners suffered severe disciminatory disabilities. Sunday Valley Creek Negroes (Davis lived in that valley) found themselves excluded from all but one mine, and that mine hired only Negroes. A few other mines employed occasional Negroes, but the pattern remained fixed and Negroes suffered. In the "Negro mine," Mine 3 where Davis worked, the screens on which the coal was separated from dirt and rock permitted more wastage of coal than those in the other mines, and its men got no pay for dead work. This meant a lower weekly wage for the same quantity of work that whites performed. The disadvantage lasted through the mid-1880s when Negro miners and the Knights abolished it. The Negroes in Mine 3 protested first to the operator and learned that their screens would be altered to conform with "white" screens but only if whites worked in "their" mine. The men told the operator, Davis remembered, "to put white men in, as they wanted the screens changed. So the screens were changed, and this was the advent of the white men in mine No. 3." At about the same time, the local Knights, including Davis and other Negroes among their members, agitated for wider

29. Herbert G. Gutman, "Reconstruction in Ohio: Negroes in the Hocking Valley Coal Mines in 1873 and 1874," *Labor History*, 3 (Fall 1962), 244–64.

30. Some clues about the union life of Ohio miners in the 1880s are found in Roy, *op. cit.*, 221–32.

Negro job opportunity in the entire valley and succeeded in gaining entry for Negroes in other valley mines. Davis recollected these victories and how the Knights had forced "the breaking of the ice." He remembered, too, the anger of certain operators, including one who warned the complaining Negroes that "whenever . . . the colored men demanded the same and caused as much trouble as the whites" the operators would have "no further use" for them.[31]

Integration and improvement in the Negro condition in Southeastern Ohio's mines did not end ethnic discord and employer exploitation of that feeling. In the summer of 1892, certain difficulties in Davis's town told much about lingering hostilities between Negroes and whites and employer attitudes toward both groups. The United Mine Workers, only a few years old, already had made substantial progress in that region, and Davis served as elected member of the District 6 Executive Board. His behavior told much about his attitude toward the race and labor questions and showed how he, an elected union official, could display much courage by challenging the attitudes of rank-and-file Negro and white miners, not to mention the power of local coal operators.

The trouble that threatened the survival of the union started after a white mine boss quit in July 1892 and was replaced by a Negro. Angered and unwilling to work under these conditions, the white miners left the pit. Davis called a union meeting and tried to soothe "very incendiary remarks" by both white and Negro union men. Though he thought he had successfully quieted the men, some disturbed Negroes talked of starting a separate Negro union. Davis pleaded with both the Negro and white miners:

> We have some men among us who are members of our organization only because they are forced to be. These men will naturally take any advantage that they can get to squirm out of it. Don't think that these are colored men

31. RLD to the editor, *UMWJ*, August 4, 1892.

alone. . . . Some few of our colored men say they will never do any good until they organize to themselves; that is, withdraw from our present form of organization and get up an organization of their own.

Well, when I hear stuff as that, no matter from whose lips it comes, it makes me nervous [mad], because I think that we are far too advanced in civilization to even entertain such foolish notions. I have got it fixed up in my brain that a man is a man, no matter what the color of his skin is, and I don't care who thinks different. I think myself just as good as anybody else, although the color of my skin is dark. I had nothing to do with the making of myself, probably if I had [,] the result would be somewhat different.

To those Negroes incensed by the white walkout, Davis reflected on his own mistreatment: "I have had men call me a nigger, but I always call him *[sic]* a fool, so we can keep even on that score." But he warned that the future of the union was at issue and even suggested that ethnic pride be put aside. At the same time, he also urged that white miners abolish all forms of job discrimination:

It is high time for the color line to be dropped in all branches of industry, for until then there will be no peace. The negro has a right in this country; those of today were born here, they didn't have to emigrate here. They are here and to stay. They are competitors in the labor market and they have to live, and I think were we, as workingmen, to turn our attention to fighting monopoly in land and money, we would accomplish a great deal more than we will by fighting among ourselves on account of race, creed, color or nationality.[32]

Despite his plea, a number of Negroes, particularly the younger men, remained dissatisfied and expressed continued

32. RLD to the editor, *ibid.*, July 21 and 28, 1892.

resentment. At this moment the owners of Mine 3, the William Rend family, long identified with the region and among its most powerful operators, offered to fill Mine 3 once again entirely with Negroes and give them eight or nine months of work each year. Davis still worked in Mine 3, serving as its elected checkweighman. He also sat on its elected union "mine committee." A number of Negroes immediately supported Rend's offer in spite of opposition from F. H. Jackson, another Rendville Negro miner, who explained Rend's strategy: "Of course, I understand this gentleman's idea. The organization is getting too respectable for him, and he probably deems a split in our ranks a very convenient thing. I wish all my race could see through this as I do." [33] Davis made the same point and reminded his Negro adversaries of their condition when they worked separately in the mid-1880s:

> Now, what does this move mean? It means simply this, to get up the race fighting among us and finally the disruption of our organization. . . . I would not be so much against this thing if men were hired irrespective of color, but colored men to be hired exclusively and whites to be turned away I don't like; and it is not right.

Davis pointed out that the national union opposed all such arrangements and scornfully commented on Rend's promise of more work for Negroes:

> This is the business view of it. Does it stand to reason that he thinks any more of you or me because of our color? Not much. He is like the balance; he will get his coal where he can get it cheapest, no matter whether it be from white or black. Now, then, do you mean to say that you can produce this coal cheaper under this plan?

Instead, Davis urged that Negroes be spread among all the mines. "It does not matter if there are not more than two or

33. F. H. Jackson to the editor, *ibid.*, August 11, 1892.

three in a mine; it will go to show that we can work together." [34]

His forthright defense of interracial trade unionism and his attack on Rend's proposal caused Davis much difficulty. Negro critics called him a "traitor" and promised not to re-elect him to local union office. "I have been given to understand that my time is not very long at Mine 3," Davis reported. Not all Negroes opposed him ("We have some colored men here who are as true as steel, who are as good union men as ever breathed the breath of life," Davis insisted), but the choice he had made endangered his local position. Davis nevertheless did not back away and struck again at his Negro critics, accusing them of believing that "capital has a right to the reins of supremacy and that labor should bow submissively to the bidding of capital." "I know you don't like me because I tell you of your wicked ways," he addressed them. "I can't help it, boys." Of the threat to "down me off the tipple" and force him to "tramp the ties," Davis responded calmly: "Well, boys, there is a providence that rules the destiny of nations, and I think I can make it and my friends, too." Some months later Davis reported much improved conditions and wrote of the spirit of "unanimity" among the men. But he offered no details on the pit election. He still defended his earlier actions: "It doesn't hurt . . . to keep up a little agitation now and then and to keep the men in mind of their duty and the reforms needed for the emancipation of the wage slaves. . . . It is our fight, and no one can fight it but ourselves." [35] That year Davis was once again re-elected to the District 6 Executive Board and held that office until he won national office in 1896.

Work as a union organizer took Davis to other bituminous regions, but he did not neglect mining conditions in Ohio valleys nearby. In 1892 he exposed the policies of mine operators in Congo, Ohio, a new mining enterprise one and a half miles from Rendville. "Not the Congo we have so much read of in Stanley's work, but Congo, O[hio]," he first noted. The operators planned

---

34. RLD to the editor, *ibid.*, August 4, 1892.
35. RLD to the editor, *ibid.*, August 11 and October 2, 1892.

to "make a model town of it," and what Davis found there upset him. The company was establishing methods no longer "in vogue" throughout the region. Its house-lease arrangement meant that only men living in company-owned houses could work there, and they had to vacate within five days if they quit work or struck. Davis called the new village "the O.M.P.," the Ohio miners' prison:

> . . . The place is fenced in all around, with two gates, one at either side, and at each of these gates, so I am informed, they are going to have gate-keepers . . . to keep out all wagons or teams except those belonging to the company. Do you see the point? to keep peddling wagons out. You see they don't want the honest farmer to come in and sell his produce to the miners; no, for that would be competition and the company would not reap the profits accruing to it. . . . Yet this is a free country, eh! Well, if it is, I don't want any of it. . . . I believe in a man having freedom of speech, freedom of thought and freedom of action, and if the present state of things are [sic] allowed to exist he [the Congo miner] will have freedom of neither [sic]. . . .

He found especially wrong the company's separation of Negro from white miners:

> Congo, unlike one of our ancient cities, sits on two hills or ridges with a deep ravine between, access being to either side by means of a bridge. On one of these ridges or hills the white miners' houses are built. I don't know what they call this ridge, but on the other ridge the colored miners' houses are built; they call it Nigger Ridge, see? A distinction is made by the company, and if a colored man goes there seeking a house he is very courteously conducted over on the other ridge, you know. If he wants one on the white folks' ridge, why he is told that he can't get it, and if he insists he is called saucy, and is told that he can get neither house nor work; that's freedom, you know.

Now, I will leave the houses alone and go down into the mine. Here we have another distinction. On one side all the white men work, on the other all the colored men work. This is called "over in Africa," how is that, eh? Don't suit me.

Such conditions convinced him that "employers . . . keep up a distinction between men for the purpose of breeding strife and dissension in our ranks." Ethnic and religious differences had to be put aside. "Just even horse sense" made it clear that only the operators benefitted from such divisions. "While we are fighting among ourselves, they wag away with the spoils, and what do we get—only the dregs." [36]

Union men soon filtered into Congo ("There are missionaries going there most every day," Davis noted), but it took some time for conditions to improve. The exact causes are unknown, but in 1897 Davis, Congo's most severe critic, called it "the best mining camp in this part of the valley." There, the union had been fully recognized and the men "treated civilly and gentlemanly." A miners' committee adjusted grievances, and the company offered certain primitive welfare benefits. "I say these things," Davis explained, revealing much about himself, too, "in justice to the company because of what I have said in years gone by." [37]

V

ALL THROUGH THE DIFFICULT 1890s, as a member first of the Ohio Executive Board and then of the National Executive Board, Davis worked as a roving UMW organizer and helped establish new locals, strengthen existing ones, and counsel miners engaged in bitter industrial disputes. Although most of his organizing was done in Ohio, special assignments and particularly severe crises brought him to Western Pennsylvania,

36. Davis wrote four letters about the Congo mines in *ibid.*, September 15 and 22 and October 6 and 20, 1892.
37. RLD to the editor, *ibid.*, March 11, 1897.

Virginia, West Virginia, and Alabama. On certain occasions he went only because an organizer was needed, but at times he was sent to an area where the national officers felt a Negro could best appeal to nonunion Negro miners. Organizing nonunion miners was not easy in the 1890s. Employer opposition and miner apathy, fear, or ethnic division hampered Davis and his associates. In the summer of 1897, for example, Davis and other UMW organizers aided by national union leaders such as Samuel Gompers and Eugene V. Debs poured into West Virginia to urge unsuccessfully that its miners join the nation-wide bituminous strike.[38] Some West Virginia miners quit work. But the overwhelming majority did not, and of them Davis wrote: "To call them slaves is putting it mildly." Injunctions limited Debs and others. Davis faced other problems. "It was like taking one's life in his hands at times," he wrote afterward. "While we never had any injunctions issued against us, we had men and Winchesters against us which were in most cases just as effective." [39]

That Davis was Negro added to his difficulties as an organizer. In May and June 1892 he worked through the southern West Virginia New River region, an area almost entirely hostile to labor organization. His color exposed him to severe hardship. Davis detailed his trip:

> . . . A word about the traveling accommodations in this part of the country for one of my race. . . . Had it not been for Brother E. E. Page, traveling salesman of the West Virginia Cut and Dry Tobacco Co., of Wheeling, and Brother Moran [a UMW organizer] this boy could have seen a hard time of it. . . . We . . . arrived at Peterstown at about six o'clock, in time for supper. After washing and getting ready for eating as I thought, the colored man who worked there came to me and told me that he would show

38. See, e.g., Chris Evans, *History of the United Mine Workers of America* (Indianapolis, 1918), 2: 464–69, 492–95.

39. RLD to the editor, *UMWJ*, September 9, 1897.

me my room. . . . Well, I went with him, and where do you suppose he took me? Away, away from the main building, out in the wood yard, to an old dilapidated log cabin. I looked in and saw the bed. I turned to the man and asked him if it was intended that I should sleep there. He said yes, that he slept there. I told him that he might sleep there but I wouldn't, that I would walk to Lowell, 30 miles away, that night first.

Page, a white, intervened and convinced the proprietor to give Davis "the best bed in the house." "I would not be afraid to bet that I am the first negro to eat at a table in that man's dining room," Davis remarked. The next day Davis and the others stopped at a Red Sulphur Springs eating place where Davis encountered more personal insults:

I was told that I could not eat in that house. My dinner was prepared outside. I lost my appetite . . . I didn't want anything to eat. We started from there a little after two o'clock and arrived at Lowell at about 8 o'clock. Brother Moran asked the proprietor, could I get supper there, and his answer was, oh, yes, but, lo, when the bell rang and I was to enter the dining room he caught me by the shoulder and told me to wait awhile. Brother Page turned around to him and told him I was with them. He looked as though he was thunderstruck and of course I got my supper.

Davis applauded Moran and Page. "Had it not been for those two white brothers," he believed, "I don't know but that I would have been by this time behind bars." [40]

On another occasion Davis actually feared for his life. In 1894, recent immigrants threatened to replace disaffected native white and Negro miners in Pocahontas, Virginia. Davis went to bolster the Negroes and secretly organized them into "a good little local." But "spy" reports exposed these Negroes, and the

---

40. RLD to the editor, *ibid.*, June 9, 1892.

operators fired and evicted them. Davis's role became known, too, and made his situation precarious:

> I . . . [was] sitting or standing at different places when maybe two or three strange fellows would come along accompanied by one of the sucks ["spies"?]. . . . When they would get to where I was I would hear one say, there he is, or there is the s—— b——. Not only that, but I have heard myself spoken of in the same way by business men when walking along the streets; besides I have heard threats made as to what they would do to me if I did not leave.

Union adversaries also talked of "doing up" George Harris, a white union organizer, and Davis hastily left Pocahontas, explaining to his critics:

> Boys, I am not yet ready to become a martyr to the cause, and I am confident that had I remained there much longer that would have been the result. . . . Now, you might say, oh, he left because he was scared, but boys, let me say to you that I was then south of Mason's and Dixon's line, and there is but little justice for the black man anywhere, and none at all down there, and for safety I thought it would be best for me to leave and even in doing this I had to be escorted to the station . . . the threats being openly made about doing me up. . . .

The gestures against Harris made Davis even more fearful. "Now, I was born in the State of Virginia, and I know that when they threaten a white man it is an absolute certainty about the negro and he had better make himself scarce, that is, if he values his life any." [41]
Physical discomfort and personal danger were not the only troubles Davis encountered. Other obstacles frustrated or made more difficult his organizing efforts. In March 1892, for example,

41. RLD to the editor, *ibid.*, May 24, 1894.

two local Negro leaders, one a church deacon and the other a Republican Party stalwart, stymied his attempt to convert nonunion McDonnell, Pennsylvania, Negro miners. They condemned interracial organizations, and the deacon explained:

. . . While I speak bear in mind that I am speaking in defense of my people. Join that thing and you will rue the day you ever thought of it. Don't you know that if you join that thing you can't get nothing out of the store. I tell you you will starve, you and your little children. I tell you I know just how you people are fixed; you are just like me. I 'aint got but one pitiful dollar and you 'aint got that. Some of you are a long way from home, in a strange land, away from North Carolina. . . . I know what I am talking about. If you don't want to sup sorrow, don't join this 'ere organization.[42]

That same year, racial mistrust blocked Davis's work in West Virginia's New River region ("the whites say they are afraid of the colored men and the colored men say they are afraid of the whites"). But in West Virginia employer hostility, the apathy of the miners toward the union, and their fear of the operators hampered him even more. Davis got permission from the Claremont school trustees to hold an organizing meeting in a schoolhouse, but local operators convinced the trustees to "shut the house up." Unable to buoy the spirit of the men ("They were that badly scared that I could get them to do nothing"), Davis left town. Although the school superintendent in nearby Alaska closed his building to him, Davis planned an open-air meeting. His description of what followed is almost a classic account of the difficulties union organizers faced when confronted with hostile employers and apathetic or frightened workers:

I notified every man on the place and . . . had them at the meeting. In fact it seemed to be my brightest meeting that I had ever gotten up in the district. We were about to open

42. RLD to the editor, *ibid.*, March 24, 1892.

the meeting and were trying to select a chairman. Nobody would serve. Some of the men were upon box cars and some were upon the ice house. I heard some fellow in the crowd say, "Here comes a chairman; Brown will serve." I didn't know what he was talking about, but I soon learned that he was one of the head pushers of the place. Well, he came right up in the crowd and ordered the men to get down off the ice house. They didn't move fast enough and he picked up a stone and pretended that he was going to throw it and I tell you they rolled off, all except one colored boy, who remained perfectly still and who had the manhood to tell him that he had better not strike him. After this he went away, so we resumed our efforts in trying to get a chairman and seeing they were afraid, I opened the meeting, starting my talk with [the] boys.

Everything was going lovely. I suppose I had talked about twenty minutes or a half hour when that gentleman returned. I had noticed some of the men shying away, but thought nothing of it; well, he walked right up in front of me with stone in hand, and addressed me thus: "Say, look here, you ―― ―― black scamp, I want you to get off of these premises right away, move along or I'll knock ―― out of you in a minute." I had not very far to go; I just stepped down on the railroad track and told the boys to come on with me, and we would have our meeting anyhow. That wasn't enough, he came again and says: "―― ―― your black soul, I want you to move either up or down this track and ―― quick." I then gave him to understand that I was not his property, and would not go any further. I tried to get the boys to follow me, but to no avail. They were afraid, and so when I left there I left for home, and that night too.

"Flowery speeches and enthusiasm" would not bring the UMW to West Virginia. Davis argued after this trip that only a permanent resident organizer together with "time and money" might assure some success.[43]

43. RLD to the editor, *ibid.*, June 30, 1892.

Birmingham, Alabama, tested Davis even more than his work in the Northern bituminous fields and in West Virginia. Alabama coal mining boomed in the 1890s. At the start of the decade, the state counted 8,000 miners of whom 3,600 were Negroes. When the new century began, the total had increased to nearly 18,000, including 9,700 Negroes. Early efforts to build successful Alabama miners' unions had failed, and in 1894 the United Mine Workers of Alabama, an interracial statewide union, had fallen to pieces after a bitter four-month strike against the Tennessee Coal, Iron, & Railroad Company and lesser operators. A pliant Bourbon governor used state militia freely against the new union, and substantial numbers of Negro strikebreakers weakened and defeated the white and Negro union miners.[44] Davis visited Alabama, the "so-called Eldorado of the South," in December 1897 and January 1898, and saw little to please him. He found much sentiment for the UMW among the miners but also formidable obstacles to successful organization. "Everything is cheap here but a living," he reported. "Labor is cheap, human life is cheap, but the necessities of life are out of sight, and yet it seems that many of these people are perfectly contented." The reasons were many. The failure of earlier local unions made many miners suspicious of the UMW. Convict labor in competing coal mines nearby weakened the bargaining position of free miners. Widespread illiteracy also added difficulties. Fear among the miners was ever present. Even men Davis had known in Ohio, who now worked in Alabama and retained strong union feeling, remained silent. "All of them are in close touch with us," Davis found. "Of course they can not express themselves here as if they were in the North. Oh, no, to do this would be to discriminate against themselves, and in consequence they do not say very much."

The "race question"—many aspects of it—most hindered Davis. Although he found "a number of good men both white and colored," relations between whites and Negroes caused him

---

44. Spero and Harris, *op. cit.*, 215; and Robert D. Ward and William W. Rogers, *Labor Revolt in Alabama. The Great Strike of 1894* (University of Alabama, 1965), *passim.*

to despair. "The one great drawback is the division between white and colored. I do not mean to say all are this way, but a very large number are." The reasons for such division were not simple, and their complexity did not escape him. He focused particular attention on three causes of racial mistrust and conflict. The fact that most Negroes worked as "laborers" for white miners (and some more fortunate Negroes) but not directly for an operator gave Davis a clue to the slow progress of Southern labor organization. A variant of the traditional English subcontract system, this relationship had racial overtones, dividing Negroes from whites as well as "laborers" from "miners." Davis explained it:

I have often heard the question asked, why is it that the miners of the South will not organize? To me the reasons are plain, and the answer is simply this: For the colored men there has *[sic]* been no inducements, and for the white to organize and be honest he would simply be giving away a good thing. Understand I am now speaking of the past. In the first place, the white miners, when they went into the Southern coal fields, saw an opportunity to make money by hiring colored men to work for them; these people being ignorant of course allowed themselves to become the servant of a servant, working for from 75 cents to $1 per day, and doing all the work thereby making for his servant employer fairly good wages, while he himself only earned a pittance. This custom continued to grow until today not only the whites do this, but the colored gentlemen have adopted the system and they feel proud to stand up and tell you they made say $15 or $25 this week. But ask him, if you please, did he earn it himself, and he will answer, oh, no, I have so and so many laborers. Right here let me say that he honestly does not, for a moment, realize that he has robbed the other poor devil.

Davis found this system at all the Alabama mining camps with one exception, and there the men got rid of it "only . . . recently by giving the company 2½ cents [a ton?] to do it."

Opposition to the UMW by certain Birmingham Negroes also impeded Davis's work. A Negro minister, W. M. Storrs ("one of the most intelligent young colored men we have in the South"), publicly encouraged Davis's organizing efforts, but Davis and the UMW were bitterly condemned by the *Southern Sentinel*, a Birmingham Negro newspaper, which urged Negro miners to form their own separate labor union. Davis pleaded with the *Sentinel*'s editor:

. . . If you continue to follow along the lines that you are now following, then your headlines should be changed to read as follows: "Devoted to the interests of the coal and iron monopolies of the south," for you could not possibly serve them better than you are now doing. You say that you believe in "The Unity of Man," and yet you teach disintegration. I cannot understand your philosophy. Of workingmen in this country we have two races—the white and the black. Of the two the negro constitutes a very small minority. Now I want to know how he can separate himself from the white laborer and live? I am sure that you have intelligence enough to know that an employer of labor cares not what the color of a man's skin may be; he will employ the fellow who will work the cheaper.

The United Mine Workers of America seeks to better the condition of the miners, be they white or black; we seek to place all men on a common level. For heaven's sake, don't seek to further oppress the miner, but rather seek to help him elevate himself. Do this and you will be doing right.

The *Sentinel* printed Davis's criticisms but curtly dismissed them and their author. Davis found in this newspaper another example of "what we have to contend with down here." Not all opposition to interracial trade unionism came from Southern whites.

Yet it was the "color line" in Alabama—the tradition of deeply felt racial prejudice against Negroes together with the hardening of legally enforced separation—that cast an even grimmer shadow over Davis and other advocates of biracial unionism in the South of the 1890s. Exceptions to the "rule" encouraged Davis but also proved the "rule," and he explained:

> In matters of this kind I think it best to be truthful. I found in the South that while white and colored miners worked in the same mines, and maybe in adjoining rooms, they will not ride even on a work-train with their dirty mining clothes on together, nor will they meet in a miners' meeting together in a hall without the whites going to one side of the hall, while the colored occupy the other side. You may even go to the post office at Pratt City, and the white man and the colored man can not get his [sic] mail from the same window. Oh, no, the line is drawn; the whites go to the right and the colored to the left.
>
> Now I do not say this is encouraged by all of the whites, for I met quite a number who made it their special business to point out these things to me, and at the same time express their disgust at such a state of affairs, yet they could not help it, though the practice might be ever so distasteful.

Davis hoped for a breakthrough among the Alabama miners and predicted that "in a short while we will get the ball rolling good and strong." But the obstacles to such an advance were too real to be ignored. He ended his January 1, 1898, Birmingham letter sadly convinced of need for dramatic changes in Albama. "As our people [the Negroes] are celebrating the emancipation proclamation, we will stop now and go out to listen awhile. But we need another proclamation of equal importance, and that one is to emancipate the wage slaves, both white and black." [45]
Davis had frequent difficulties and disappointments as an organizer, and coupled with his frustrations in finding employment, these made his life a troubled one. But the sum of these experiences added up to a deeper commitment to the UMW and to his belief in the redemptive role of biracial industrial

45. Davis wrote three letters from Alabama and another from Rendville about his Alabama experiences, and they appear in *UMWJ*, December 16 and 23, 1897, and January 6 and February 10, 1898.

unionism. At all times the union commanded his support. Suggestions poured forth to strengthen it. The use of East European immigrant strikebreakers in Virginia convinced him that "a Hungarian organizer . . . be sent there as soon as possible." [46],* Factionalism he called "suicide." [48] Letter after letter urged readers to gather a large defense fund and to "attend your local meetings [and] pay your dues." [49] A visit to a mining camp meant an opportunity to canvass for new subscribers to the weekly *Journal*.[50] He found holidays and national crises the occasion to prod the inactive. The Spanish-American War, for example, caused Davis to exclaim: "We are all talking of going over to free Cuba. I would like to see poor Cuba freed, but would like better to free myself, the same with every other American coal miner. Boys, get a move on yourselves, for if you don't the day may soon come when it will be almost too late." [51]

46. RLD to the editor, *ibid.*, May 24, 1894.

* Davis took pleasure in 1892 in his successes among East European miners. That year he and another organizer went among these recent immigrants, and he reported of one meeting: "Another feature of the meeting was the large number of foreigners present and what I mean by that is the Polanders, Hungarians, Bohemians, Slavs, etc. One thing that I would like to say about these people is that they were very attentive to the business of the meeting and especially when one of their own number was speaking. I will just here make this plainer. The checkweighman at this mine is a Polander, but can speak the English language quite fluently. After Vice President Miller and myself got through speaking, this gentleman got up and interpreted it to the Polanders, Huns and Slavs in a very able manner. It was quite interesting to notice how they would flock around him while he was talking. . . . Although the meeting was an out-door one, one could almost hear a pin fall while he was talking. After he was through a motion was made that they would join in a body; the vote was taken by the raising of the hands and the motion was unanimously carried, with loud cheers from the foreign-speaking element. At this juncture a secretary was elected from each nationality to take their names as members of the organization. . . . Of the officers chosen, among them were one Hungarian, one negro, one Polander, one Slav and one white, so you can readily see that these people mean business and have started about it in the right way. . . ." [47]

47. RLD to the editor, *ibid.*, March 3, 1892.

48. RLD to the editor, *ibid.*, March 14, 1894.

49. See, e.g., RLD to the editor, *ibid.*, November 22, 1894 and March 3, 10, and 24, 1898.

50. RLD to the editor, *ibid.*, June 23, 1898.

51. RLD to the editor, *ibid.*, March 24, 1898. A year earlier Davis had urged the celebration of yet another holiday: "You forget the day I love most, and that

VI

ORGANIZING NONUNION miners, particularly Negroes, consumed
much of Richard Davis's time in the 1890s, but there was more
to his work than just that. If Negroes had often to learn the
gospel of trade unionism and labor reform from union partisans
like Davis, so, too, white unionists and their leaders needed
frequent prodding from self-conscious Negroes like Davis when
they rejected the "religion of brotherhood" and displayed
insensitivity, prejudice, or open hostility toward Negroes. In one
sense, then, Davis simultaneously inhabited two worlds: the one
shaped by his experiences as a coal miner and the other as a
Negro. His life as a trade unionist and organizer exposed him to
frequent frustration and even personal danger. But his life as a
Negro exposed Davis's white fellow unionists to his recurrent
anger over the "color line" and to his zeal for racial democracy
within the United Mine Workers. In letter after letter Davis
emphasized the need for full integration of Negro miners while
the union was still young.

Davis was not a utopian optimist. Personal experience taught
him that certain operators used Negro strikebreakers effectively,
and thereby increased white hostility toward Negroes. His
appeals to white miners therefore frequently emphasized their
own "self-interest." And those who viewed Negroes negatively
learned from Davis:

. . . In this country it must be agreed there are a goodly
number of miners who belong to the negro race. These men
are certainly following that avocation for the sole purpose of
earning a livelihood. . . . In a great many instances the
negro has been used as a means of accomplishing the ends
desired by capital. . . . Have we been asleep all of this time,
instead of educating ourselves upon the necessities of the
times? Well, I don't think that all of us have been asleep; no,

---

is emancipation day. By all means let us celebrate the day when the shackles
were cut loose and 4,000,000 of black men were liberated from the galling yoke
of chattel slavery." (RLD to the editor, *ibid.*, March 11, 1897.)

not by half. Some of us have learned to know that we are men and have certain rights that must be respected, and we are willing to fight for these rights, too.

Self-interest required that white and Negro miners "lay aside petty prejudices and get together, as men." Otherwise, strife and dissension would allow the operators to "wag away with the cream." [52]

Because so many Negroes worked as miners, Davis insistently called for the election of Negro union officers. His arguments varied, but he often remarked that nonunion Negroes found the absence of Negro leadership "proof" that unions benefitted "whites only." After learning that no Negroes had been nominated for national office, Davis exploded in December 1891:

> . . . These things should not be left for the colored man to mention, but you white men should see that one colored man is elected. Some fellow might say that we can do without that; I wish to say that it is impossible, for take the negro out of our organization, and you have a vast army against you, one that is strong enough to be felt and feared. . . . Let us have one of them and put him to work. Give the poor negro a chance. Its [sic] high time this was being done. Remember the white people of this country in 1776 cried out no taxation without representation. I hear that cry today among negroes of this country, and I as a negro say take warning and heed the cry.[53]

Davis continued this appeal. Two years later he urged high office for competent Negro trade unionists. They deserved the prestige and status—as well as the income—that went with national union election:

> Will you admit that you need us in your unions? If so, why should we not hold offices, also? Are we not men? Have we

52. RLD to the editor, *ibid.*, August 25, 1892.
53. RLD to the editor, *ibid.*, December 24, 1891.

not the same ambitions as you people have? Are we not in many instances as competent as you? Then why should we not hold office? Not office in name, but office in deed; something there is money in that we may cope with our white brothers as an equal.

Davis denied personal interest: "I am speaking in defense of a people who have been down long enough. The day has passed and gone that we, as a people, shall . . . be content with small things." [54] That his plea was answered affirmatively is known. Davis's election to national office and that of other Negroes to lesser offices are a matter of record.

Davis's concern for the place of the Negro worker in the trade-union movement extended beyond the mining industry. The rapid growth of Eugene V. Debs's American Railway Union, the fact that like the UMW it was an industrial union, and its bitter controversy with the railroads during the 1894 "Pullman Boycott" made it attractive to UMW leaders, who vigorously supported it. Davis found the ARU "best for railway men in this country" and hoped it would "grow and prosper." But Debs's union, like the railroad brotherhoods, excluded Negroes from membership, and this Davis called a "sad mistake." In July 1894, during the Pullman crisis and after some railroads had used Negroes as strikebreakers, he urged ARU leaders to admit Negro members:

Surely, gentlemen, you have sense enough to know that we were born here and intend to remain here. We are American citizens and should be treated as such. But what can you expect of the negro with this kind of treatment? Remember that he is as sensitive as any other nationality or race of people. We find that the Hungarian, Polander, Italian, Chinaman, and even the lazy, shiftless Indian can be a member, but an intelligent negro who was born in this country and who has helped to make the country what it is, is considered as naught, and is debarred.

54. RLD to the editor, *ibid.*, June 1, 1893.

It is just such treatment as this that has caused the negro to take your places when you were striking. Now, if there is anything that I do despise it is a blackleg, but in places in this country that they will not allow the negro to work simply because of his black skin, then I say boldly that he is not a blackleg in taking your places. He is only doing his plain duty in taking chances with the world. We ask no one to give us anything. All we want is the chance to work and we assure you we want just as much wages as the whites. . . .[55]

A year afterward Davis again criticized the ARU. Condemning Debs's imprisonment, he nevertheless rejected UMW affiliation with the ARU. "I will never be a party to the agreement, nor will any other colored man who has a sense of respect or pride of his race, nor will he if I can bring any influence to bear upon him." "Just think of it . . ." Davis angrily concluded, "I, an American citizen by birth, and many of them are not yet dry from crossing the salt water pond, and yet they have the unlimited gall to say that an American citizen shall not take part in an American institution because of the color of his skin. . . . Away with such rottenness." [56,*]

Not a socialist, Davis was nevertheless radical by the standards of his time and believed deeply that the present and future

---

55. RLD to the editor, *ibid.*, July 19, 1894.

56. RLD to the editor, *ibid.*, August 1, 1895. Davis appears later to have sympathized with or respected Debs. In 1899 he visited Princeton, Indiana, to help its miners celebrate the need for an eight-hour day. A speech by a local minister impressed Davis, who noted: "In fact, Debs could hardly have handled his subject better." (RLD to the editor, *ibid.*, April 13, 1899)

* Daniel Wallace, a white Ohio mine leader who favored affiliation with the ARU, answered Davis. He condemned mistreatment of Negroes and urged that the ARU alter its constitution and admit Negro workers. "This is my country," Wallace explained, "every man is my brother and to do good is my religion. . . . I was a member [of the Knights of Labor] when that grand old man Uriah S. Stevens was general master workman . . . and would still be a member if R. L. Davis was general master workman." Wallace condemned all forms of racial injustice, but urged Davis to favor closer ties with the ARU, "put aside nonsensical quarreling," and "stand by our unions." [57]

57. Daniel Wallace to the editor, *ibid.*, August 15, 1895.

welfare of Negroes depended on the strength and character of the "labor movement." In 1893 an article entitled "The Colored Race and Labor Organization" offered his most explicit statement on the "race problem." "What . . . should be done with the negro" troubled "the minds of a great number of the American people," so Davis decided to analyze the Negro "condition":

. . . It seems . . . plainly evident that he is a citizen of this country and should be treated as such. This, in my mind, is the only solution to the supposedly knotty problem. Less than thirty years ago he was given his freedom, and turned loose to the cold charities of the world without a dollar or an acre of land. Turned loose as he was, is there any nation of people who has made such rapid progress as the negro has made? Search all history and we find them not. During all these years in a said-to-be Christian and civilized country, notwithstanding the rapid strides he has made, he has been looked down upon by both the church and party politics both of which should have been his best friends.

Since most nonrural Negroes labored as wage-earners, Davis next considered the relationship between the Negro worker and the trade unions:

Being poor and used to it, he had to obey the divine injunction, viz.: To earn his bread by the sweat of his brow. In so doing we find him a great competitor with American white labor. It is at this period that we find that the labor organizations, or rather some of them, did that which no other organization had done, the church not even excepted, [and] threw open their doors and admitted him as a full member with the same rights and privileges as his white brother. This, in our opinion, was the first or initiative step toward the equality of mankind, and we are sorry to say that until the present day the labor organizations are the only ones that recognize the negro as an equal and as a man.

He then confronted the suspicion of so many Negroes toward the predominantly white trade unions:

> . . . It is also true that some of our people have not yet gained enough confidence in his *[sic]* white brother as to trust him very far. And yet, is this strange? When we notice the fact that in our midst we have some as bitter enemies as anywhere else. While we admit that our labor organizations are our best friends, it would be well to teach some of our white brothers that a man is a man no matter what the color of his skin may be. We have nothing but the best of words for labor organizations, and hope they may continue in the same line of actions, and we are confident that they will not only better the conditions of the working classes, but will also wipe out all class and race distinctions, and in the meantime the negro will be found as loyal to labor organizations as his white brother.

Davis looked ahead to those "better days for organized labor with the Negro in the ranks doing his share in the way of emancipating labor." "Confidence" between Negro and white workers was essential because "reform" could come only through "the medium of organized labor." Reform meant changes that would "solve the race problem, better the condition of the toiling millions, and also make our country what it should be, a government of the people, for the people, and by the people." [58]

VII

RICHARD DAVIS'S ELECTION to the National Executive Board of the UMW in 1896 and 1897 was not an isolated example of Negro participation in that union's leadership. Although Davis

---

58. RLD, "The Colored Race and Labor Organization," *ibid.*, May 26, 1893.

won the highest position a Negro held in the UMW's early history (and, probably, in any national union before 1900), other Negro miners held elected local, state, and regional offices in the 1890s.* John Mitchell advised the Industrial Commission in 1899 that native Alabama white and Negro miners cooperated in the union. Mitchell admitted that ethnic tensions existed but explained:

> I will say there is no difference as far as our organization is concerned. They [the miners] recognize—as a matter of necessity they were forced to recognize—the identity of interest. I suppose among miners, the same as other white men in the South, there is [sic] the same class differences, but they have been forced down, so they must raise the colored man up or they go down, and they consequently have mixed together in their organization. There are cases where a colored man will be the officer of a local union— president of a local union.

A surprised commission investigator asked Mitchell: "With white members?" And Mitchell replied: "With white people in the union." [59] It was the same in other bituminous districts. Negro William Riley served as secretary-treasurer of the Tennessee district in the early 1890s and in those years F. A. Bannister was vice president in West Virginia.[60] In the competitive fields stretching west from Pittsburgh, Davis was only one of a good number of Negroes in office. Although the exact number cannot be determined, it is clear that Negro leadership was not simply a case of Negro miners electing Negro officers. A Grape Creek, Illinois, Negro miner, S. C. Armstrong, found less than

---

* Writing in 1909, William Scaife remembered that a Negro miner named Warner held national UMW office before the election of Davis in 1896. I have not uncovered further references to Warner. (*United Mine Workers' Journal*, November 19, 1909.)

59. *Report of the Industrial Commission*, VII, *op. cit.*, 53.

60. William Riley to the editor, *UMWJ*, September 29, 1892, and Henry Stephenson to the editor, *ibid.*, August 3, 1899.

one-fourth of his district's men Negroes, yet observed: "I think this one [district] very fair from the fact that our district vice-president, Henry Rector, is colored, and very deeply colored. . . . Not a local in the district is there but has colored local officers. As for myself, I have had more offices than I know what to do with." Armstrong served as elected checkweighman in his mine, but only three of the three hundred men there were Negroes.[61] In Mystic, Iowa, Negro miner O. H. Underwood boasted that "the chasm of prejudice has been bridged with the plank of common sense." "Visit the different locals with me if you will," Underwood insisted, "and [see] all the colored men presidents, secretaries, and members of the executive boards." [62] Milton Reed vigorously led the Kansas miners, and the *Journal* sadly and affectionately noted his premature death in 1901.[63] Two years earlier Thomas H. Rollins, born in Virginia in 1857 and a miner from the age of eleven, gained unanimous election as vice president of the new Saginaw, Michigan, district, and white Michigan miners boasted that Rollins had done much to dispel local racial mistrust.[64]

Such widespread Negro participation resulted partly from the union's efforts to counter employer use of Negro strikebreakers. Some Negro miners urged even more Negro organizers, especially in West Virginia, Tennessee, and Alabama. An Indiana Negro, A. H. Harris, pleaded: "In time of trouble, we can . . . get to see them much quicker. . . . If they would put a colored man in each field and let him preach this great organization . . . when trouble arose between any company and its men they would know better than to go." "By doing do," Harris believed, "we can save money, trouble and also lives." [65] The practical self-interest of white unionists, however, only partially explains the active role Negroes played in a predominantly white union. White unionists could have perhaps protected themselves by

61. S. C. Armstrong to the editor, *ibid.*, November 10, 1898.
62. O. H. Underwood to the editor, *ibid.*, July 20, 1899.
63. "In Praise of Milton Reed, Negro Organizer," *ibid.*, July 25, 1901.
64. *Ibid.*, June 8, 1899.
65. A. H. Harris to the editor, *ibid.*, September 21, 1899.

excluding Negroes entirely. Certain craft unions had adopted this policy by the 1890s. But two considerations, among others, worked against such a strategy. The fact that the United Mine Workers was an industrial union from its start made the notion of exclusion difficult to justify. In addition, early local and especially national leaders of the union deeply believed in the principle of human solidarity and in a kind of evangelical egalitarianism. This mixture of industrial unionism and reform ideology made it hard to exclude Negroes. Anti-Negro diatribes, common in the press and journals of the 1890s, were rare in UMW publications despite the difficulties in organizing Negro miners fresh from rural areas and despite the use of Negro strikebreakers.[66] The older ideology of evangelical reform trade unionism smothered smoldering racial antagonisms and the heat generated by job competition. A byproduct, despite much racial friction and even violence, was the active participation of Negroes in union leadership. Difficulties and disagreements frequently arose between Negro and white miners, but Negro activists displayed a deep, fierce union loyalty. The same union, well in advance of other unions, also gave particular attention to the "new" Catholic immigrants and even printed part of its weekly newspaper in Polish. But the Negro miners concern us, and it is sufficient to note only that UMW attitudes toward Negroes probably reflected still deeper attitudes toward the varied ethnic groups that made up the mining population.

The particular importance of the UMW position toward Negroes must also be measured against national developments in the 1890s. C. Vann Woodward and other historians of the "New South" have made clear that the 1890s witnessed the rapid and widespread deterioration of the Negro's political, economic, and social status. Segregation and disfranchisement became more rigid in those years. Violence against Southern Negroes increased, and Northern interest in the Negro condition all but vanished. Few were the whites who felt a deep concern for the

66. Rayford W. Logan, *The Negro in American Life and Thought. The Nadir 1877–1901* (New York, 1954), 159–69, 239–74.

increasing plight of black Americans after the Populist debacle.[67] In this setting, the firm (although at times inconsistent) adherence of the UMW to interracial unionism assumes its proper historical significance. Not all white unionists drifted with their "times." Instead, the *United Mine Workers' Journal* saw a close relationship between the deteriorating status of Southern Negroes in the 1890s and the unwillingness of many Negroes to identify with organized labor. In May 1892, for example, the *Journal* pointed to the "unmistakeable pathos pervading the letters of our colored friends" and blamed it, in part, on their condition in the South. Edited by Irish immigrant Martin Kane in its first years, the *Journal* avowed "a feeling of shame and disgust at the frequency" with which Negroes "as a class are outraged and wronged by the barbarous deeds perpetrated on their compatriots by the myrmidons and minions of that fiendishly blind autocrat, Judge Lynch," and found in the growing violence practiced against Negroes sufficient reason for "the tardy and restive progression" of the Negro "to the advances of his palefaced friends." But it urged Negroes to put aside their distrust of white unionists:

Point out to us the true member of our United Mine Workers' organization and we will vouch for it that he is a detestor of the things we complain of. We can safely go further and say that the influence of the members of organized labor with those whom they come in daily contact is such that even they are not to be found in the rabble who cling to the coat tails of the remorseless judge. This in itself should indicate to our colored friends where their interest lies.

Labor unions favored the suppression of "monstrous outrages" against Negroes and wanted Negroes to share in "all the things which go to make up a higher civilization." For these reasons,

67. C. Vann Woodward, *Origins of the New South 1877–1913* (Baton Rouge, 1951), 321–95.

the *Journal* welcomed Negroes into the UMW: "Try it, remain with it, and we have no misgivings as to your decision." [68]

If a significant test of the depth and sincerity of a belief is its relationship to behavior, the UMW's early national officers scored well in this regard. They did more than offer criticism of distant outrages and admonish Negroes to support organized labor. Two incidents involving Richard Davis revealed much about their conception of union power and their attitudes toward race prejudice and discriminatory practices. In June 1892, Davis visited the West Virginia mining fields on an organizing trip and, as seen, encountered much difficulty because of his color so that only the intervention of two sympathetic whites allowed him to manage the trip. The *Journal* noted the "many inconveniences" Davis suffered "on account of his sable complexion *[sic]*" and reminded its white readers: "It doesn't take a very great wrench of the imagination to picture him winding the hills of the Little Mountain state and wondering whether or not he will have to lie in a ditch when he arrives at his destination." Commending those whites who aided Davis, the *Journal* also applauded the Ohio Negro for "compelling some of the insularly inclined hotel proprietors to take the barriers down, if it is only for once." [69]

Three years later, a few months before Davis won election to the National Executive Board, an incident occurred that demonstrated even more convincingly the hostility of white UMW officers to racial discrimination. Davis arranged a miners' mass meeting in Corning in Perry County, Ohio, and on August 22, 1895, national and state officers came to address it. President Philip Penna and Secretary-Treasurer W. C. Pearce, both from England originally and active in Indiana and Ohio union affairs before taking national office, arrived on the forenoon train. So did Michael Ratchford, a Clare County Irishman, then an Ohio union leader and soon to be national president. Other Ohio officials, co-workers with Davis and all of them white, came, too,

68. *UMWJ*, May 5, 1892.
69. *Ibid.*, June 9, 1892.

and Davis met the group at the Corning train depot. They went
to the town hotel for dinner. Davis registered at the hotel but
quickly learned from a clerk that Negroes could not eat there
because certain West Virginia patrons "would get insulted." By
that time, Penna, Pearce, Ratchford, and the others had taken
their seats and awaited their host. The clerk explained his
absence to them. What followed is of great interest. "It was
then," wrote D. H. Sullivan, a white Rendville miner, "that our
officers showed the true union principle that should characterize
all true members of our craft, for they refused to eat dinner and
went elsewhere." The incident did not end with this gesture.
After consulting a lawyer, Davis entered suit against the
Corning hotelkeeper. More than six months later the case came
to trial and Penna, Pearce, and Ratchford, together with a few
other Ohio white union leaders, testified in Davis's behalf.[70] The
results of this litigation remain unknown, but the entire set of
circumstances, particularly the involvement of the national
leaders, offers telling evidence for the loyalty Davis and other
Negroes felt toward their union and for the UMW's successes
(despite so many obstacles) in gaining early significant support
from Negro miners.

VIII

OTHER NEGRO MINERS joined Davis in filling the *Journal* with
letters that explored and exposed their condition and pleaded
with Negro and white miners for biracial cooperation. One of
them, William Camack, worked in Jellico, Tennessee. Camack
was not without humor and asked of those who emphasized
racial differences: "I would like for some one to tell me the
difference between a negro who has seven-eighths of white blood
in him and a white man with one-eighth of negro blood?" Six
years before Negroes in large numbers left Jellico for the Illinois
coal fields as strikebreakers, Camack explained the difficulties

70. D. H. Sullivan to the editor, *ibid.*, March 12, 1896.

his people faced and fixed the main cause on slavery. "When Uncle Sam was a very small boy and did not know as much as he does at present," Camack wrote in 1892, "he allowed the 'negro' to be brought into his domain, not as the other nationalities came, free, but in shackles." Enslaved because they "happened to resemble Ham a little more . . . than Japeth," Negro labor "built up an aristocracy" in the South. Although in error, Camack's explanation of emancipation was unusual for its time and not without interest to later readers. His argument hinted at a deep sense of betrayal by the party of Lincoln and drained the Civil War of any moral meaning:

> . . . The North had its manufacturing establishments and the South grew cotton. The Southern planter controlled the labor of the black man and the planter could charge whatever price he pleased for his product, and, as the Northern manufacturer was at the mercy of the South, he became mad and jealous and said to himself, "If these black men were free we could control their product and these Southern gentlemen would have to come down a notch." And so the North became very philanthropic and set to work and secured the colored man a nominal freedom.

What followed emancipation did not please Camack either:

> So after centuries of primeval existence and years of chattel slavery, we find him turned loose in 1865 without a dollar; ignorant, credulous, yet full of gratitude, and easy prey to the cupidity and avarice of a far worse set of Shylocks than the ones the Nazarene carpenter drove out of the temple of Jerusalem.

Like so many other nineteenth-century American workers, Camack reflected on the past mainly to draw lessons for the present. His conclusion was quite simple: white miners had to understand that "there is no color line but simply the slave line." Drawing from personal experiences, he went on:

I have known men and women of other nationalities who were nearly as black, a great deal more ignorant, and four-fold more degraded than the very meanest "nigger" I ever saw[,] and they were received by some of the kickers against the black with open arms as their social equals. "Oh, consistency, thou art a jewel."

Camack meant to convince white miners "who do not like to sit down in the same [local] assembly as the colored" that slavery, not race, explained the Negro condition. Reminding hesitant white readers of the constitution of the multiracial Knights of Labor, he advised them: "The man who can't stand that kind of doctrine, let him jest get up and git." [71]

Negro union miners did not blame racial friction and union weakness entirely on their white brothers; they found difficulty with nonunion Negroes as well. The frustrations they often encountered in convincing fellow Negroes of the union cause deeply angered them. Soon after Davis faced attack from Rendville Negroes for fiercely condemning their support of employer-sponsored "colored mines" in 1892, the *Journal* published over several issues a lively and revealing exchange among Negro miners on this and other questions. Its tone was sharp and explicit, at times perhaps embarrassing, never defensive, and always deeply committed to biracial trade unionism. An Indiana Negro miner took time out to commend the *Journal* for opening its columns to such a discussion by "colored correspondents." He called that action "a step in advance of any white journal, except those who *[sic]* have done so for selfish gain, and even then it has been only the leaders of the race." [72]

Like Davis's letters, these were the writings of self-educated nineteenth-century workers. Such men were given to flashes of deep insight but not to subtle distinctions or carefully logical and analytic arguments. Their language was often grammatically imperfect: tenses were confused, punctuation misused, and

---

71. William Camack to the editor, *ibid.*, May 5, 1892.
72. "Willing Hands" to the editor, *ibid.*, September 29, 1892.

colloquialisms abounded. An argument most often took the form of a series of explicit and blunt statements. Even though the emphasis was this-worldly, evangelical Protestantism reinforced this style and provided a common and deeply felt set of images, analogies, and metaphors. In all of this, the Negro miner sounded no different from the white worker. A well-rounded education, after all, was not a prerequisite for laboring in a nineteenth-century American coal mine. Miners and other workers used the language at hand, and the Bible together with popular political clichés served them well. For the Negro an additional influence shaped his perception—the imponderable and still unexplained effects of slavery. How that experience or the Negro miners' memories of it particularly shaped their views of industrial America cannot be answered on the basis of the evidence examined in these pages. Their letters and other writings nevertheless offer clues to this significant relationship and to an understanding of them as workers and as Negroes groping with their condition, that of their fellow men, and that of a society filled with inequities and in the midst of profound economic and social transformation.

Davis's Negro critics got their sharpest rebuke from William Riley, who opened the 1892 exchange. A minister and a coal miner, Riley had been elected secretary-treasurer of Tennessee District 19 earlier that year and had won the votes of all whites and all but a few Negro miners there. A Negro, Riley nevertheless minced no words in attacking Davis's Negro adversaries:

> Did you not know that the worst enemies we have to contend with are among our own race? Did you not know that they will seek more undue advantage over you than anyone else? What? A nigger! He is the worst animal living against his race, and when I say nigger I mean nigger and not colored people.

Riley made much of this distinction and urged Davis to "press forward," make all the "colored and white friends" he could, and not "worry over the niggers and dogs." [73] Another time Riley again complained that "the negro is the worse *[sic]* enemy to one another that *[sic]* they have on top of dirt," but he made clear that his words applied only to those opposing unions:

> Now, let me say to the colored people who are trying to be men second to no man, continue to battle on for the right, seek wisdom and be wise, act honest men and by so doing both white and colored men will love to respect you, and God Himself will bless you. . . . Yes, my people, wake up and ask yourselves these questions: How long am I to live in ignorance? How long am I to be a pullback to my race? How long am I to be a stumbling block for the cause of labor, justice and humanity? Say as the prodigal did: I will arise and join the labor unions and rally for its *[sic]* rights, defend its *[sic]* cause and be known among my own craftsmen as a man among men.[74]

Riley did not back away from his criticism of recalcitrant fellow Negro miners. Accused of being "wrathy at the negroes," he answered: "I do think I made a clean distinction in spelling out those two words. I never wrote any harm about the negro at all, for I have no fight to make against them *[sic]*. But I wrote and will continue to write against the niggers and dogs." His frustration and disappointment spilled out when he explained: "We have tried petting, coaxing and soft words with these curs for years, and we have gained nothing from them[,] only hard names." "My brother," Riley advised a friendly critic, "I live in the South, among these people and know whereof I speak. Of course, there are some good people in the South as there is *[sic]* elsewhere, and again there are some of the worst curs that ever lived." [75]

73. William Riley to the editor, *ibid.,* August 28, 1892.
74. William Riley to the editor, *ibid.,* September 8, 1892.
75. William Riley to the editor, *ibid.,* September 29, 1892.

The Brazil, Indiana, Negro miner identified only as "Willing Hands" found Riley's judgments somewhat harsh and reminded him of the difficulties Southern Negro miners encountered. "I have never seen a white and colored man work together around the mine anywhere in the South as buddies unless it was by the company's order." And then "some hoodlum would be up in arms about social rights." Parts of Indiana offered little more to Negroes; in Clay County, "Willing Hands" found "nothing but ignorance and petty-prejudice among them all, both white and colored." But he had only good words for the whites in his mining village:

> . . . Let me say there are not many colored people here but what are treated white by the whites. I am working with a white man of his own accord and have seen several others go buddies[;] also a few respectable families live in double houses together[,] and the closest neighbor I have is white; also where the colored people here merit good treatment from the whites they get it from most all, both men and women of all colors.

The same miner nevertheless expressed deep concern for the generally deteriorating condition of American Negroes and criticized the Knights of Labor and the American Federation of Labor for participating in the Chicago Columbian Exposition which had rejected Negro appeals that it recognize the achievements of their race. Such requests had been "buried so deep that Gabriel's trump" would not disturb them. The South agitated "Willing Hands" even more than the Columbian Exposition. The murder of certain People's Party leaders in Mississippi and Georgia and the electoral successes of the "Bourbon element" that year convinced him that the Bourbons had "about wiped out the negroes" in those states and he asked: "Is the white South civilized? and . . . would it not be wise to emigrate some Christian missionaries there in those fields of labor." [76]

76. "Willing Hands" to the editor, *ibid.*, September 29 and December 22, 1892.

Davis did not remain silent during this exchange but commended Riley and "Willing Hands," urging them to go ahead because "our people will begin to think," and then added some observations of his own. He made less allusion to the Negro than the others, choosing instead the general condition of the "laboring classes" as his text. Workers needed "a few more students," for if they studied their "interests as workingmen more" they soon would be "in a better condition." Davis denied "any pretences *[sic]* of scholarship," but the contrasts between industrial realities, working-class life, and the American Dream tortured him and demanded comment:

> We claim we have a new country, a new age[,] and that we need new thoughts and a new method by which to bring about much needed reforms. Well, these things cannot be brought about unless the people awaken themselves to the full sense of their duties. We cannot expect others to do that that we do not do ourselves.

Davis brought together two widely held and popular nineteenth-century American ideas—the theme that knowledge was power and the notion of "self-help"—in defense of effective labor organization. The "monied kings" would never "soften their hearts to give us better wages, better homes or anything else unless we . . . demand and enforce the demands when made."

> Too many men run away with the idea that capital must rule, [but] for the life of me I cannot conceive why or how a man can be so ignorant. . . . We are too indolent to try to better ourselves.

American workers had "the power of freemen" but permitted the "enslavement of themselves."

> We boast of this being the home of the brave and the land of the free, but can you not see the deception of the thing? Now, let us have the truth. Is this not the land of the rich

and the home of the slave? Truth doesn't hurt anyone, and I ask is this not true?

Davis offered these words less than three years before Booker T. Washington urged upon Negroes at the Atlanta Exposition a path of improvement derived from eighteenth-century individualist thought and devoid of a clear assessment of the realities shaped by a maturing industrial society. Like Washington, Davis took the American Dream seriously but saw its fulfillment only through "thorough and compact organization." Unwilling to accept the permanence of racial conflict and ethnic division, Davis urged miners to "cast aside petty prejudices and work together as men." The mean mixture of race and class that depressed the condition of most Negroes and weakened trade-union effectiveness could be overcome only in a collective fashion. "Let us learn," Davis concluded in language alien to Washington and his numerous admirers, "that an injury to one is the concern of all. Until we do learn this, we can hope for no better." [77]

Except for Davis's frequent letters, the flow of correspondence from Negro miners to the *Journal* slowed up after 1892 and did not pick up again until 1898 and 1899, when the use of Negro strikebreakers in Illinois and the ensuing racial violence caused much comment. An exception to this pattern was W. E. Clark, who lived in Davis's town, Rendville, and penned three unusually interesting letters in 1893–94 that told a good bit about the disquiet of certain Negroes concerning their status. Clark first eloquently condemned racial prejudice and advised white miners:

. . . Prejudice on account of color is not a natural sentiment. There is a natural prejudice among the civilized nations to certain conditions in life incident to a state of barbarism; there is a natural prejudice to those who are given to immorality . . . but there is not a natural prejudice

77. RLD to the editor, *ibid.*, October 27, 1892.

to a man simply because he is black, brown or yellow. The influence of a man's complexion is not greater than that of his moral and intellectual culture.

Very much of the nineteenth century, Clark insisted that "virtue is the highest influence that move[s] the heart of man, and though it may be clothed in ebony or Parian marble it will command honor, love, obedience and respect in every quarter of the civilized world." But Clark was not an innocent Victorian optimist. Although he believed that prejudice against an individual could be effaced easily, the "removal of prejudice attached to the entire race, incident to a state of slavery," was "a labor of centuries and centuries." However, he unqualifiedly rejected all Negro efforts to form their own voluntary associations:

> There should be no desire to keep up race distinction in this country or in the organization of labor when all have a common interest in it. No benefit can come to the Afro-American by withholding himself apart from the white people, [and forming] a distinctive negro community, a distinctive negro civilization, distinctive negro organization and social orders. . . . These are not only not desirable, but indeed are reprehensible, for they create class distinction and foster the race prejudices of which we desire to free ourselves.

Immigrants quickly shed their ethnic identity on coming to America and Negroes were advised to follow their examples. Except for "the one black spot on its escutcheon, which has impressed itself upon the heart of the negro, as a hot branding iron," Clark argued, "the Anglo-Saxon civilization . . . by its grandeur and majesty, commands our highest admiration. We desire to live, act and move with such a civilization." Urging racial amalgamation, Clark reminded whites that Ruth had said to Naomi: "Thy people shall be my people, and thy God my God." [78]

78. William E. Clark to the editor, *ibid.*, November 9, 1893.

Seven weeks later Clark turned his thoughts to the "labor question . . . the supreme question of the hour" and tried bolstering the despair of Negro readers. "We see it often," he admitted, "with horror and alarm, and men, women and even children grapple with it, amidst the progress and poverty of our crowded centers of civilization." The "love of money" was "sucking the very life blood of modern society, impairing its vitality, destroying its better, nobler instincts." But those who despaired were advised to view the condition of the workers, particularly Negro workers, in the light of evolutionary theory. Whites, too, once had been slaves, "helpless slaves," and Clark quoted Tacitus as his authority. The Negro now was adjusting to the status of free labor:

> Methinks, I see the negro rising like the white laborer out of the depths in which slavery left him. . . . If we have been slaves, they have been slaves; if we have been beaten, they have been beaten, if we have at times been cruelly murdered, they have also [been] without judge and jury. They have risen; we are rising.

Pessimists were advised of the sacrifices made by Wat Tyler, Robert Emmett, Toussaint L'Ouverture, and John Brown. Clark saw better times ahead. As the Negro improved his social status and found industrial employment, he would soon learn "the value of co-operation and . . . make it a practical part of his varied life." [79]

When Clark wrote again after a silence of nearly eight months, his tone was quite different. "I have been asleep so long," he started. The year 1894 was a bad year for the nation, and Rendville was not different. A nationwide depression cut deeply through the entire society. "Dissatisfaction seems to be the ruling power here now," Clark reported. Personal failure to prevent labor agents for the Northern Pacific Coal Company in the state of Washington from hiring away Rendville Negroes

79. William E. Clark to the editor, *ibid.,* December 29, 1893.

angered him. Only the talk of a new political party by certain national union officials buoyed Clark's spirit. The optimism of his earlier letters was gone:

> My mind has wandered from world to world. My first wonder was, I wonder if the other worlds were inhabited? Did they have the same kind of law and government that we have? and my next wonder was, was this world of ours the hell we read about in the good book? If it is not, how can a man stand the punishment twice, and then live through eternity? They burn men alive, skin them, lynch them, shoot them and torture them. . . .

These outrages convinced Clark that Negroes did not owe existing political parties "a debt of gratitude." But he saw no clear alternative. He urged Negroes to join a new multiracial party if it "pledged itself to them or adopted a plank in the platform for the protection of its citizens" and would see they were "not discriminated against." But in the same breath, Clark, who some months earlier had favored racial amalgamation and attacked Negro voluntary associations, now wanted "the black man of America [to] form a party of his own." "If you do that," he admonished Negro readers, "you will be recognized as citizens, as it has been said [that] in a body we can elect or defeat." [80] Clark's confusion and despair were not without cause. The South (not to speak of the United Mine Workers) was in profound crisis in those years, and the Negro fell victim in the cruel defeat of Southern Populism and the vindication of Bourbon power.

Of Negro miners like Clark little is known. But during a bitter West Virginia strike, nine years after he penned these letters, three Negroes, one of them named William Clark and probably the same man, were shot to death while sleeping by local police officials. Chris Evans, a union stalwart as far back as the 1870s, the leader of the great Hocking Valley 1884–85 strike, and for

80. William E. Clark to the editor, *ibid.,* August 9, 1894.

some time secretary of the American Federation of Labor, investigated the shootings and found "this slaughtering of miners, simply because they are forced to struggle for a just cause . . . a sad commentary on our boasted Republic." [81]

IX

IN ITS EARLY YEARS the United Mine Workers faced serious obstacles in building a multiracial industrial union. Its early leaders, mostly British and Irish immigrants and native whites, had rich trade-union experience and high expectations but limited financial resources and a powerful opposition. Not the least of their difficulties was the hostility of most coal operators, particularly large corporate firms such as the Philadelphia & Reading Coal Company, to effective national unions. The diverse ethnic composition of the mining population added other troubles. By 1890 its traditional native white and North European composition had already started to change radically. In Pennsylvania, where most Eastern and Southern European immigrant miners worked, 58,000 of 235,000 coal diggers were of Slavic and Italian origin. Alabama miners counted 2,787 native whites, 1,492 immigrants, and 3,687 Negroes, while the West Virginia coal mines employed 6,314 native whites, 1,375 immigrants, and 2,016 Negroes. These ethnic groups in the coal fields have been inadequately studied, but profound historical imagination is not essential to grasping the difficulties of building a permanent labor organization composed of so heterogeneous and changing a population.

For Negro and white miners to work together was made harder by several additional considerations. Widespread belief in Negro racial inferiority, itself the continuing influence of the historic master-slave relationship, together with the rapid general deterioration of the Negro's social and political status in the 1890s, explained some of the obstacles faced by white and

81. Chris Evans to the editor, *ibid.*, March 5, 1903.

Negro trade unionists. The Southern rural background of most Negroes laboring in late nineteenth-century industry and mining complicated the difficulty. Education was limited for Negroes in the rural South, and deference and dependence more normal in a rural than an urban environment. Although little is known of the early Negro miners, it is possible that their aspirations differed from those of native white miners. They may have viewed their status as workers as a temporary one. In parts of West Virginia, for example, North Carolina, and Virginia Negro farmers worked as miners only in the winter months to accrue income to pay farm mortgages.[82] To such workers, unions often seemed unnecessary. Viewing their industrial work as a means to another way of life, they must have thought the danger of union affiliation unnecessarily risky.* Finally, Negroes, although often ignorant of their mission at its start, were used as strikebreakers on numerous occasions.

Only a romantic or tendentious interpretation of American labor history dares ignore the friction between competing ethnic groups; so much of working-class history between 1890 and 1920 was shaped by that factor. Part of this conflict was inherent in the changing composition of the labor force, but opposition to trade unions often led coal operators to exploit ethnic differences in order to weaken potential trade-union solidarity. No ethnic group, including native whites, was free from this role, although recent immigrants and Negroes seem to have served such a purpose more regularly. In 1892, for example, two carloads of Negroes were imported to northern West Virginia from the Carolinas and Virginia. When they proved unsatisfactory a year or two later, employers brought in Italian and Polish

82. Charles W. Simmons, John H. Rankin, and U. G. Carter, "Negro Coal Miners in West Virginia, 1875–1925," *Midwest Journal* (Spring 1954), 64. This article contains much information on the West Virginia coal fields, but its authors failed to consult the *United Mine Workers' Journal* and their findings are quite limited.

* This also was true of certain white miners. For the years 1886–1893, the Industrial Commission blamed the absence of trade unionism among Southern Illinois coal miners, mostly native whites, on the fact that they were "farm laborers who had turned to the mines as a source of ready cash."

workers from Northeastern cities. In 1895 Virginia Governor Charles T. O'Ferrall sent militia to protect four hundred Italians who were replacing striking native miners.[83] But the Negro concerns us in these pages, and his use as a strikebreaker merits attention in assessing the early role of Negroes in the United Mine Workers.

Negroes had been used as strikebreakers in the bituminous fields before the 1890s. In the 1870s Southern Negroes protected by white armed guards came for this purpose to bituminous mining villages in Indiana, Ohio, and Illinois. Not all Negroes arrived as strikebreakers, but their entry in this fashion drew widespread attention to them. The dramatic events surrounding their coming have been recorded for the Ohio Hocking Valley in 1874 and 1875 and for Braidwood, Illinois, in 1877.[84] But little else is known of these early years. In 1880, imported Negroes apparently broke a nine-month strike in the Ohio Tuscarawas Valley, and that year fifty Negroes went to Pittsburgh mines, too.[85] Employer use of Negroes increased in the 1890s as the United Mine Workers gained strength in the bituminous fields. The Henry Clay Frick Coal & Coke Company first imported Negroes as early as 1892 and then again in 1895.[86] In the Southwestern coal district (Arkansas, Kansas, and Oklahoma) Negroes came before 1890 but after the union's early successes arrived in larger numbers. In 1896–97 during a Kansas strike recruiting agents distributed a typical handbill among Birmingham, Alabama, Negroes:

WANTED! COLORED coal-miners for Weir City, Kan., district, the paradise for colored people. Ninety-seven cents per ton, September 1 to March 1; 87½ cents per ton March 1 to September 1, for screened coal over seven-eighths opening. Special train will leave Birmingham the 13th.

83. Woodward, op. cit., 267–68.
84. Bruce, loc. cit., and Gutman, loc. cit.
85. Spero and Harris, op. cit., 210.
86. Ibid., 210, 212.

Transportation advanced. Get ready and go to the land of promise.[87]

The Missouri Pacific Railroad carried 175 Southern Negroes to the struck Kansas mines. As they were unloaded near a stockade white strikers convinced 125 of them not to enter the mines. Some joined the strikers, but most wanted to return to Alabama, and the union paid their way. A federal injunction against the union weakened its further efforts and made it easier to bring in Negroes.[88] In the same years numbers of Southern Negroes went under contract to the Colorado Fuel & Iron Company, too.[89]

But it was in Illinois in 1898 and 1899 that the confrontation with employers using Negroes to weaken the UMW was most severe, and Victor Hicken has told part of that story well.[90] Illinois miners took part in the UMW general bituminous strike that started on July 4, 1897, and as a result the Illinois operators agreed to negotiate with the district union. A joint conference in Chicago in January 1898 led to significant improvements in miners' wages, hours, and working conditions. Wages fixed at forty cents a ton meant an increase of almost fifteen cents a day for ordinary pit workers. Later that year, however, the operators along the Chicago and Alton Railroad south of Springfield protested the wage increase. The Chicago-Virden Company, the state's largest coal company with mines that returned 348,000 tons a year, headed the group. Their complaint was submitted to the National Executive Board of the United Mine Workers, as provided in the earlier agreement. According to it, the signers promised to accept the Board's decision. But the Board rejected the operators' complaints, and four companies, Hicken finds, "set about to operate their mines with nonunion labor."

Trouble broke out first in Pana. Early efforts to bring in

87. *Ibid.,* 210–11.
88. *Ibid.,* 211.
89. *Ibid.,* 213.
90. The details in this and the following three paragraphs draw largely from Victor Hicken, "The Virden and Pana Wars," *Journal of the Illinois State Historical Society,* 51 (Spring 1959), 263–78.

nonunion whites failed, and, after threatening to import Chinese laborers from the Far West, the Pana operators turned south and sent agents to recruit among Alabama Negro miners. Opposition from the Birmingham branch of the Afro-American Labor and Protective Association did not hinder the agents. Two Birmingham Negro miners testified of their experiences:

> Benj. Lynch and Jack Anderson being duly sworn, upon their oath say they are residents of Birmingham, Ala., resided at Birmingham for 11 years; occupation coal miners; say that on Monday, Aug. 22, 1898, they were approached by two white men and one colored man who represented that they were from Pana, Ill.; that most of the miners had gone to the [Spanish-American] war for two years; that there was a new mine opening there and a great demand for labor, and they wanted 150 men; and there was no trouble there; said about eight or nine months ago there had been a little trouble but that all was settled; affiants said they were working . . . but on being told that they could make from $3 to $5 per day were induced to give up their jobs and go to Pana.

The Pana miners protested the coming of nonunion workers and sent men to meet a trainload of Negroes in Centralia. Some Negroes left but most stayed on the train and headed for Pana—protected by special white police. White Pana businessmen and merchants protested against the Negroes to Republican Governor John R. Tanner, and local Republican and Democratic politicians condemned the operators. But the Alabama Negroes were brought in and housed in a stockade.* A

* According to *The Public*, a Chicago reform weekly edited by Louis Post, the Negroes first learned of the strike on arriving in Pana. They "complained that they had been deceived by the operators, and most of them refused to go to work," *The Public* reported. But, the same source added, deputies at the mines "are charged with threatening to shoot negroes who attempted to leave." (Quoted in Ray Ginger, "Were Negroes Strikebreakers?" *Negro History Bulletin* [January 1952], 73–74.)

few weeks later violence and even shooting broke out when angry miners attacked two operators. By the end of September the Illinois national guard was patrolling Pana and had restored order.

Happenings in Virden were even more violent, and numerous deaths and injuries resulted. The Chicago-Virden Company hoped to execute its plan flawlessly. It first constructed a stockade around the mines, and then imported fifty armed white police, mostly ex-Chicago policemen and detectives from a private agency in St. Louis. The miners responded in kind. They set up patrols, some armed, along the railroad tracks into the city and in September prevented a trainload of Negroes from disembarking there. The engineer drove on to Springfield, where district UMW President J. M. Hunter convinced many Negro families to quit. Soon after, Negroes were persuaded to leave trains in other Illinois towns. The company then made a second major effort to bring Negroes to Virden. An appeal to the governor for military protection failed, but the company went ahead and paid off a number of resident white miners. On October 13 a train filled with Southern Negroes and white guards approached the town. As it stopped near the stockade heavy gunfire broke out between the white guards and the miners. A St. Louis detective found it "hotter than San Juan Hill." The train pulled away without unloading, but the dead remained still on the battlefield. Five guards were wounded and four dead. About thirty miners lay wounded and seven gave their lives. Not a single Negro died, but some suffered wounds. The angered miners destroyed the company store; then the violence abated. No Negroes worked the Virden mines, but at a cost that cannot be measured. As in Pana, the national guard came and stayed in Virden. The Negroes, Hicken found, reached Springfield "in a pitiful condition—frightened, tired, and shamefully disillusioned." They were kept as virtual prisoners aboard the train. District union President Hunter sought to talk with them but was thrown from the train by white guards and badly injured. His second effort proved more successful, and some Negroes left the train. Most went later to St. Louis to find work, and still others returned to Birmingham. The Virden operators had suffered a severe setback, and even though a temporary injunction held back the Pana white miners from "preventing the mines from operating with Negroes" the Pana operators, too, failed in the end. By 1899 the Pana and Virden operators were employing their old hands at the fixed wage rate and under the old contract.

But the tragic violence accompanying the defeat of the Illinois operators strained relations between Negro and white union members. A good number had deserted the operators and all had suffered, but the fact that Negroes had been used and violence and death had resulted shook many white miners. Letters in the *Journal* condemned the Negroes and often slurred their race. Negro unionists also complained of what had happened but tried explaining to white miners the causes of Negro involvement in the Pana and Virden happenings and to both white and Negro miners the benefits of interracial union cooperation.

Three days before the outbreak of the bloody violence in Virden, Richard Davis penned his thoughts on the Illinois crisis. Davis was himself in difficulty. He was blacklisted and without work for some time during 1898. "I am indeed sorry to see the state of affairs as it exists there," Davis wrote of the Illinois events, "and yet it teaches us that one lesson seemingly so hard to learn by a great many of us, viz., to organize." The hostility of white union men toward Negroes especially dismayed him:

> I do not mean to organize against the black man, as they are now doing, for that will do no good nor will there any good results accrue from it, and fight it as you may the result will be the same. I have watched it in the past and have never known it to fail. I would advise that we organize against corporate greed, organize against the fellow who, through trickery and corrupt legislation, seeks to live and grow fat from the sweat and blood of his fellow man. It is these human parasites that we should strive to exterminate, not by blood or bullets, but by the ballot, and try as you may it is the only way.

Those whites who attacked the Negro heard sharp words from Davis. "You can't do it by trying to exterminate the negro or 'big black buck niggers,' as they were referred to a few weeks ago through the columns of *The Journal.*" His anger was unrelenting. "I assure anyone that I have more respect for a scab than I have for a person who refers to the negro in such a way, and God knows the scab I utterly despise." Davis, who had been in Birmingham in 1897 and seen firsthand the condition of Southern Negroes, attributed to their depressed and exploited status their willingness to serve employer objectives in Northern mines. So long as the South remained a source of cheap labor, just so long would Southern Negroes play that role:

> The negro North has no excuse, or very few excuses, for scabbing, but the negro South has lots of them, and while I give the North a great deal of credit, I fear that I made a mistake, for in many places even in the North, no matter how good a union man he may be, he can not get work [but] only as a blackleg. And in the South he can work almost anywhere provided he is willing to be the other fellow's dog, and I don't mean the employer alone, but the white laborer as well.

"The negro," Davis insisted, "like the mining machine, is here to stay, and you may as well make up your minds to treat them *[sic]* right." Where Negroes and whites worked together "you seldom or never hear of negroes being brought in . . . to break a strike." He drew only one conclusion: "I say treat the negro right and he will treat you right." But Davis was too strong a union partisan to dismiss the substantive complaints of the white Illinois miners and added, "I earnestly hope to see the miners of Illinois win their battle, for I suppose they are like miners elsewhere. Their pittance is already too small." [91,*]

91. RLD to the editor, *UMWJ,* October 13, 1898.
* The conclusions drawn by Davis should be contrasted with those of certain other contemporaries concerned with the relations between Negro and white

Although Pana and Virden attracted national attention in 1898 and 1899, the neglected importation of Southern Negro miners to Carterville, Illinois, in the same years sheds additional light on the Negro miner and, in particular, on George Durden, a Negro leader of the Illinois miners. Paul Angle has written fully of the Carterville troubles in *Bloody Williamson*, and here we sketch only an outline to make sense of important letters written by Durden.[92] Financed largely by St. Louis and Cincinnati capital, in 1890 Sam T. Brush organized the St. Louis and Big Muddy Coal Company, located near Carterville in southern Illinois, and soon managed one of the Midwest's great mines. In 1897, it produced more coal than any other single Illinois mine. Brush bitterly opposed the still young UMW, and, at first, fought it with skill. That year, he raised wages and successfully convinced his men not to join a statewide strike. In 1898, he rejected joint efforts made by the UMW and other operators to persuade him to accept the statewide wage scale. On April 1, 80 percent of his men quit work, and six weeks later Brush replaced them with 178 Jellico and Coal Creek, Tennessee, Negro miners. Some loyal whites worked with the Negroes. Much bitterness followed Brush's first victory. A Negro later complained that Brush had "dumped unwelcome people in Illinois" to "rob honest men of all that is dear to human existence." After the

---

workers. The Chicago *Public*, for example, found the Virden tragedy "not a race fight at all, but a labor fight." It insisted: "The fact is noticeable that trades unions, instead of being controlled by race prejudice against negroes, harbor very little of that prejudice. The anti-negro spirit must be looked for higher up." And a Chicago Negro clergyman (who founded the Institutional Church and Social Settlement, a "Negro Hull House"), Reverdy C. Ramson, hoped that white workers would learn from Virden and Pana that "the degradation, by industrial and political serfdom, of the millions of black toilers of this land" menaced "their own industrial independence and prosperity, as well as their political liberty." (Quoted in Ray Ginger, "Were Negroes Strikebreakers?" *Negro History Bulletin* [January 1952], 73–74.)

92. Full detail on the Carterville strikes, the violence, and trials that followed is found in Paul Angle, *Bloody Williamson, A Chapter in American Lawlessness* (New York, 1952), 89–116, 281–83. Angle exhausted local sources but did not use labor sources, and important additional information is found in unsigned letters, probably written by George Durden in *UMWJ*, July 20 and October 9, 1899.

Tennessee Negroes arrived Brush "deliberately entered the union miners' homes (white) and bundled their bedding, wives and children together and cast them out in the rain and mud." Brush's success made his the only large Illinois mining company unaffected by the UMW, but his triumph lasted for less than a year. In March 1899, Brush instituted an eight-hour day and raised wages above the UMW scale but rejected a request from some whites and Negroes that a UMW local be recognized. On May 15, a strike started: between 150 and 175 men quit (about half of his force; all the whites and some Tennessee Negroes). Brush decided to replace them with new Negroes. He sent a Negro minister to get more Tennessee Negroes and then hired forty Negroes let go by the Pana operators after they settled with the union. The Pana Negroes added fuel to the fire and especially angered the Negro and white Carterville strikers. When they arrived on June 30 in special Illinois Central Railroad cars, rifle shots wounded twenty and caused the death of the wife of a nonunion Pana Negro miner. Brush's loyal hands retaliated that night. Near the Brush mines was Union City—some frame shacks built by the UMW to house evicted miners and mostly inhabited by Negro UMW supporters. Brush's men attacked the encampment and burned it to the ground. A few days later state militia arrived, to remain for nearly two and a half months. Brush brought in more Negroes and was once assaulted by two men, but the region quieted down and the soldiers left on September 11. Only six days passed before bitter violence again erupted and resulted in the death of six loyal Brush Negroes, who with others had marched armed into Carterville and confronted armed white miners. The militia returned to restore order. Two trials followed.

Negro UMW miner George Durden figured prominently in the first of these two trials. Durden, six other Negroes, and two whites were indicted for the June 30 murder of Anna Kerr, and twelve whites were indicted for the September shootings. Durden's group came to trial in early December 1899. Six weeks later the second trial started. Moved to a county nearby, the first trial attracted much attention, as two batteries of lawyers (including a former Missouri lieutenant governor who defended

Durden and the union miners) tried to sway an all-white jury of farmers. A white miner, Thomas Jeremiah, and Durden were named as ringleaders in the June 30 shooting, and the dead woman's husband accused Durden of firing the fatal shot. But the jury freed Durden and the others. The second trial also failed to convict the union miners. In 1906, Brush, who had kept his mines under heavy guard (even using a Gatling gun) in the intervening years, sold out to the Madison Coal Company, and then the UMW won recognition quickly. But it is Durden's letters written while in prison and soon after his acquittal that most interest us.

A testament to his abilities as a trade unionist and an incisive observer of contemporary events, Durden's prison letters exposed the fact that the Negro strikers were held incommunicado in the county jail and eloquently pleaded the cause of increased trade-union power. ("The calloused handed miner is a conspicuous figure in the land of civilization. Living and sculptured monuments of heroes dead and gone have no parallel to the tribute paid the miner.") But it is a letter Durden wrote soon after leaving his jail cell that is most important. The union was engaged in a bitter debate over whether to accumulate a "National Defense Fund." Concerned over the increasing use of Southern Negroes to weaken the UMW in the Northern bituminous fields and with the Illinois experience still fresh in his mind, Durden argued for such funds to support striking union men and also to educate "disorganized, pauper, and other labor." He referred here mainly to Southern Negroes. "I am sorry to say that the greater part of this disorganized labor is the man of color." And he favored using funds to "send educators to these dangerous regions [the South] and instill into the hearts of these men the principles of our order." Durden then pleaded the particular case of the Southern Negro and appealed to his white brothers:

. . . Ask your conscience why it is that this class of labor fails so absolutely to see their interest. This question answers itself when you take into consideration the life, past and present, of the 8,000,000 Afro-Americans. In the year 1626 *[sic]* the negro was contented roaming the sunny jungles of Africa. There he was kidnapped and in chains and fetters he landed in America, and here he entered a life of shame and death. . . . The man of color had taken on this yoke of slavery and thus burdened he toiled 250 long years in serfdom educating the children of his master and having his own family in ignorance and want. The evident value of the negro can be seen from Virginia even to the Gulf of Mexico. The gigantic oak that once seemed to defy time has not a root left . . . where the wild animal once roamed at will is now the play grounds of the school children. Even statesmen today . . . owe their education to the labor of the sons of toil that was *[sic]* never paid. There were hundreds of thousands of these unfortunates who have been driven to their untimely grave with nothing left to mark their own existence, but a sacred mound of clay. Fathers and mothers have watched their first born sons and daughters sold and borne away from the mother's care, to meet again only on judgment day. The dark secret vaults have been filled with the blood-stained dollars derived from their labor, for which the toiler has never received or asked recompense.

With the tears from their eyes, they have watered the crops, and with the blood from their backs, they have enriched the soil. Thus the public can see and understand why he can toil so earnestly and for so small a sum uncomplainingly. Hence education, labor education, a union education, aided by and with Defense Funds will show my people the pathways of justice. Backed by the independence of the greatest order known to civilization . . . the Southern colored miners will cease to be a factor or a yoke upon the neck of organized labor. The public with our union must remember that the negro is yet a child to our civilization. . . . Educate him to your ways and note the results . . . the heart is as true as steel and his efforts are untiring.[93]

93. G. A. Durden to the editor, *ibid.,* October 9 and especially November 25, 1909.

At a time when few Americans thought in such terms and probably as a result of his own experiences as a Negro and a trade unionist, Durden grasped the significant interplay between race and class that would shape so much of twentieth-century American social history.

The tension between Illinois Negro and white union miners did not end after Pana, Virden, and Carterville. That would have been expecting too much from both groups. In July 1899, Danville UMW Negro miners and mine laborers publicly demanded "the right of being employed in any capacity in or about the mines . . . which we are capable of filling without discrimination by either our white brothers or employers." [94] At the Illinois State Miners' Convention in 1900, similar questions arose. Springfield Negro miners complained that five local mines managed by good union men refused to employ Negroes. Cal Robinson, a Negro delegate from Spring Valley, demanded action from the convention and explained, "If you do what is right in this matter, gentlemen, you will have none of your Virden and Carterville riots, and no blood will be spilled. . . . We want to abolish all of those evils, and then we shall not have to get out our Gatling guns; we will have no fights along these lines, and we will have no riots. I hope you will help to abolish this thing here and now." G. W. Williams, a white Grape Creek miner and an Illinois union stalwart since the Civil War, joined Robinson in urging an end to discriminatory employment practices:

I have been in the union since 1866, and am one of the oldest members. Back in those dark days there were times when black men could not and dared not meet with white men or even attempt to express themselves as being willing to meet. He [the Negro] would have been annihilated by the operators for daring to think of it. But in this progressive age I am astonished. . . . Gentlemen, the time for this is past. I do not expect to hear of such things from young and

94. *Ibid.,* July 6, 1899.

intelligent men. Those things belong to the time of your fathers, and I hope that you will see this evil is eradicated.

Others spoke, too, and then Durden rose for his turn.

Durden faced a difficult task, one that other Negro union officials had confronted on similar occasions. His sense of the plight and the need of the Negro was without question. Virden, Pana, and Carterville were still fresh in his mind and those of other Illinois miners. So, too, at least for the Negro miners and especially those committed to the union, was the gnawing reality of discriminatory practices against black miners. There may also have been the possibility that frontal attacks on the discrimination a few local unions practiced against Negroes (contrary to explicit national policy) would split the union. What particular ideas turned about in Durden's mind cannot be reconstructed, but he emphasized the benefits Negroes enjoyed as UMW members and not the isolated acts of discrimination they often suffered. His was a plea for a powerful and multiracial union:

. . . We have made applications to organizations to help us time and again. You know how even the Masons and Odd Fellows have discriminated against us. There has been no organization that has come to our assistance with such outstretched arms as has the United Mine Workers of America. We are sensitive, it is true. There is a certain class of men in some localities who will not allow the black to work side by side with his white brothers. No such discrimination is made by the Constitution of our organization. There are many places in this State where no color is known when it comes to work. I have seen this organization reach out its arms for my race. They have given them homes and friends; they have helped them when they most needed help. This organization has extended to us more help than we received from any other organization in America. There are places in this State where colored men have been told that they could not stay at all, where when we were without friends, almost without clothes, where the moment we presented our union cards we were taken in and helped and given work. . . . Let us have no break between the white and the black. Your constitution has not made any discrimination against anyone. The organization is strong; and we love it and we know that it is only individuals who make objection to our working, and we should not get sensitive over this and attack the union.[95]

Such was the loyalty that the UMW commanded from an Illinois Negro who had suffered in prison, lived still in the shadow of Virden and Pana, and nevertheless pushed aside what he detested in the interest of an organization that had proven itself to him.

X

THE EVIDENCE GATHERED in these pages reveals much about the early history of the United Mine Workers of America and, in particular, about that union's attitudes toward Negro workers and the important role Negro miners like Richard L. Davis and George Durden played in its formative years. But the unfortunate absence of a detailed and comprehensive history of the UMW's early decades makes it perilous to claim too much beyond these facts.[96] And yet these are hard truths filled with considerable meaning. Any authoritative history of the UMW surely will tell of the endless and formidable difficulties and frustrations that accompanied early efforts to build this interracial industrial union. It will include grimly detailed pages about

95. Parts of speeches by Robinson, Williams, and Durden appear in the "Official Proceedings of the Illinois Miners' Convention," *ibid.,* March 18, 1900.

96. The works of Evans, Roy, and Warne, previously cited, are entirely unsatisfactory accounts of the early UMW history. Additional information can be found in Norman Ware, *The Labor Movement in the United States, 1860–1895* (New York, 1929), 214–22; Philip Taft, *The A.F. of L. in the Time of Gompers* (New York, 1957), 137–40; and McAlister Coleman, *Men and Coal* (New York, 1943), *passim.* There remains a serious need for a full, scholarly history of the UMW.

racial and ethnic quarrels and even death and violence. But it will also make much of the successful early confrontation between the UMW, its predominantly white leaders and members, and Negro workers. And it will explain why—in a decade that saw the general deterioration of the Negro's condition, North and South, and in which C. Vann Woodward argues "the Mississippi Plan" became "the American Way"—why enormous sacrifices by white and Negro miners made this union a reality.[97]

Even though the available statistics are meager and somewhat suspect, their symbolic value so far as the Negro's direct role and primary importance in building the UMW between 1890 and 1900 is crystal-clear. The essential fact is that about 20,000 Negroes belonged to the UMW in 1900.[98] In its first decade the UMW grew fitfully and mostly among bituminous miners. At its start it had almost 17,000 members and increased rapidly, but before the 1897 nationwide bituminous strike membership had fallen to less than 11,000. Rapid growth followed that strike. In 1900, just before it made its commanding advances among anthracite miners, 91,019 miners paid UMW dues, and John Mitchell embarrassingly chided Samuel Gompers, "We are seriously contemplating the absorption of the American Federation of Labor." Mitchell's amiable jest was not without meaning.[99] The UMW was far and away the largest AFL union in 1900. The Federation counted only 548,000 workers in all of its affiliated unions that year, so that no less than $16\frac{1}{2}$ percent of its members were miners. And Negroes made up an unusually large proportion of UMW membership.[100] Of its 91,019 members, the

97. Woodward, *op. cit.,* 321–49.

98. This figure is quoted widely in the standard sources. See, for examples, Spero and Harris, *op. cit.,* 76–78; and Ira DeA. Reid, *Negro Membership in American Labor Unions* (New York, 1930), 101–3. It seems originally to come from W. E. B. Du Bois, ed., *The Negro Artisan* (Atlanta, 1902), 158. Du Bois wrote that "the figures as to Negro membership [in 1900] are reported to us by the unions." Efforts by this writer to secure independent sources that verify this important fact have not been successful.

99. *Report of the Industrial Commission,* XVII, *op. cit.,* 184–85; John Mitchell to Samuel Gompers, April 12, 1900, as cited in Philip Foner, *History of the Labor Movement in the United States* (New York, 1955), 2: 345. See also Ware, *op. cit.,* 214–22.

100. Taft, *op. cit.,* 233.

UMW included only 8,893 anthracite miners and since few, if any, were Negroes, a measure of the Negro's consequence to the UMW should count only bituminous miners.[101] If 20,000 Negro bituminous miners belonged to the UMW in 1900, then 24 percent of the union's bituminous members were Negroes. Mitchell and other union officials figured in 1899 that Negroes made up between 10 and 15 percent of the mining population. Leaving aside again the anthracite miners, about 30 percent of all bituminous miners were UMW members, but between 36 and 50 percent of Negro bituminous miners belonged to the union. And not without additional interest is the fact that 3½ percent of the AFL's members in 1900 were Negro coal miners. Further research undoubtedly will adjust these statistics but should not appreciably alter their meaning—a meaning that affects Negro history as well as labor history.

Despite formidable hindrances, particularly in Alabama and West Virginia, the UMW's efforts to organize and to hold Negro members did not end in 1900. Take Alabama as an example. Davis had been overwhelmed and depressed by the "color line" there in 1897 and 1898. But in 1899, 23 percent of its miners belonged to the UMW, and by 1902 the union claimed 65 percent of them, a majority being Negroes. In 1904 certain large operators repudiated the Alabama union and caused a strike that lasted two years—"the longest strike on record." Court injunctions held back union officers but not union funds. Through its national treasury and its districts and locals, the UMW sent more than $1,000,000 to the Alabama strikers. The Illinois District (where Pana, Virden, and Carterville still remained living memories) alone gave $100,000. The strike failed, but the UMW held on until 1908 when operators refused to renew expired contracts and also cut wages. A second and larger strike then started and lasted nearly two months. Eighteen thousand miners—all except the convict coal diggers—quit work. Violence and shootings were common; hundreds of union

101. For a reasonable explanation of the absence of Negro anthracite miners, see Spero and Harris, *op. cit.*, 207.

men, Negro and white, suffered. The UMW spent an additional $407,500 to hold the men together but without success. The power of a hostile governor, himself a former lessee of convict labor who banned public meetings, a state militia that broke up interracial "tent villages" of evicted miners, and a committee of leading Alabama citizens that argued that "the people of Alabama" never would "tolerate the organization and striking of Negroes along with white men" finally ended the strike—and severely impaired the union. A year later the UMW counted 700, not 18,000, Alabama members, and effective trade unionism did not return there until the First World War and then only for a brief time. But that is another story.[102] What matters here is that despite the Alabama setback and the loss of so many Negro members, national UMW Negro membership probably did not decline precipitously between 1900 and 1910 and the union made a vigorous and costly effort to hold districts with large Negro membership.

What, finally, is the import of the successful participation by large numbers of Negroes in the early UMW so far as the general practices and attitudes of organized labor before 1910 are concerned?

Although the subject has been inadequately studied and much misunderstood, it appears that nothing about Negro workers more agitated and angered many white trade unionists between 1890 and 1910 than the frequent use of Negroes as strikebreakers and the "threat" of "Negro competition." The Pana and Virden violence, for example, "proved" to the *Locomotive Firemen's Magazine* (its union excluded Negroes) that "the entire social fabric of the Northern states may crumble before the invasion of hordes of cheap negro labor from the South." [103] In 1900, the year Richard Davis died, Samuel Gompers's annual report to the American Federation of Labor emphasized that unorganized Negroes would be "forced down in the economic

102. Woodward, *op. cit.*, 362–65; Spero and Harris, *op. cit.*, 352–57; Northrup, *op. cit.*, 319–21; Roy, *op. cit.*, 430–32.

103. *Locomotive Firemen's Magazine*, 25 (October 1898), 378–79.

scale and used against any effort made by us for our economic
and social advancement." He warned that "race prejudice"
would become more "bitter" to "the injury of all." [104] Confronted with complaints from Booker T. Washington and other
Negro leaders that numerous affiliated unions formally or
informally excluded Negroes from membership and therefore
jobs, the AFL Executive Council in 1901 did not claim
"perfection" for the labor movement but defended its efforts
among Negro workers. It criticized Washington for his belief
that "the economic, social, and moral progress and advancement of the negro is dependent upon the philanthropic and
humane consideration of their [sic] employers" but most
severely censured Negro strikebreaking as the main cause of
"economic bitterness and antagonism between the races":

> The real difficulty in the matter is that the colored workers
> have allowed themselves to be used with too frequently
> telling effect by their employers as to injure the cause and
> interests of themselves as well as of white workers. They
> have too often allowed themselves to be regarded as "cheap
> men," and all realize that "cheap men" are not only an
> impediment to the attainment of the worker's just rights,
> and the progress of civilization, but will tie themselves to the
> slough of despond and despair. The antipathy that we know
> some union workers have against the colored man is not
> because of his color, but because of the fact that generally
> he is a "cheap man." It is the constant aim of our movement
> to relieve all workers, white and black, from such an
> unprofitable and unenviable condition. [105]

104. *Proceedings of the Twentieth Annual Convention of the American Federation of Labor . . . 1900*, 22–23. See also Gompers's testimony before the
Industrial Commission in 1899 (*Report of the Industrial Commission*, VII, *op. cit.*,
647–49) and his early recognition that exclusion of Negroes would encourage
strikebreaking in Taft, *op. cit.*, 308–12, and Bernard Mandel, *Samuel Gompers*
(Yellow Springs, Ohio, 1963), 142–45.

105. "Trade Union Attitude Toward Colored Workers," *American Federationist*, 8 (April 1901), 118–19. See also Logan, *op. cit.*, 149–50.

Four years later Gompers harped on the same theme but with a new twist. He argued that the labor movement sought no conflict with Negroes but warned: "If the colored man continues to lend himself to the work of tearing down what the white man has built up, a race hatred far worse than any ever known will result. Caucasian civilization will serve notice that its uplifting process is not to be interfered with in any way." [106] At that moment the UMW was pouring hundreds of thousands of dollars into Alabama to preserve its early advances among Negro and white miners.

Negro strikebreaking and the existence of much racial prejudice among white workers and their leaders were hard realities, but these conditions alone were insufficient causes for the exclusion of Negroes from many organized trades between 1890 and 1910—and even earlier in certain unions. The early history of the United Mine Workers belies such an explanation. It is impossible to measure racial prejudice among white coal miners seventy years ago, but few would deny its existence. "Negro competition" constituted a recurrent threat to the status of established white miners. Negro strikebreakers probably were used with greater frequency in the bituminous mining industry than in any other between 1890 and 1910. And yet (even though Negro strikebreaking surely intensified anti-Negro feeling among white miners in the short run and may even have displaced white unionists) an all-white or racially segregated union did not result. Overwhelmingly white and many of them self-educated British and Irish immigrants, the early UMW leaders, not without formidable difficulties, welcomed Negro members and drew them actively into the union. As a result, an unknown but significant number of Negroes held local and district offices, helped organize both white and Negro miners, diminished some of the racial prejudice and mistrust between Negro and white miners, and stabilized their union in a time of repeated crisis. Rank-and-file Negroes consequently were not to

106. Quoted by Ray Marshall, *The Negro and Organized Labor* (New York, 1965), 19.

be spotted occasionally throughout the union but added greatly to its strength by their sheer numbers. And after only ten years the UMW functioned as a viable, integrated trade union and quite possibly ranked as the most thoroughly integrated voluntary association in the United States of 1900. Good reason led Negro miner O. H. Underwood to insist in 1899: "I believe that the United Mine Workers has done more to erase the word white from the Constitution than the Fourteenth Amendment." [107]

XI

WAS THE UMW'S EXPERIENCE with Negro workers repeated in one fashion or another by other unions before 1910? Could it have been? Or was the UMW's conspicuous success the result of "conditions" peculiar to the mining industry and its population? The particular preoccupation of most labor historians and others studying relations between Negro and white workers and their unions at that time allows for easy but meaningless answers to these and even more pertinent questions. Critics and defenders of Samuel Gompers and the early American Federation of Labor have studied this subject in a one-dimensional manner and focused almost exclusively at the top level—giving needed attention to the restrictive membership clauses and practices of numerous craft unions and the policy decisions affecting Negro workers by the AFL Executive Council after 1894. From different viewpoints, their findings concur and tell much.[108] The

107. O. H. Underwood to the editor, *UMWJ*, July 20, 1899.

108. See, for examples of widely different explanations of national craft-union behavior and especially policy decisions by the AFL Executive Council, Taft, *op. cit.*, 308–17; Philip Taft, *Organized Labor in American History* (New York, 1964), 665–70; Marshall, *op. cit.*, 14–33; Foner, *op. cit.*, 2: 347–61, and 3: (New York, 1964), 233–55; Mandel, *op. cit.*, 142–45 and 234–39; B. Mandel, "Samuel Gompers and the Negro Workers, 1886–1914," *Journal of Negro History*, 40 (January 1955), 34–60; Gerald Grob, "Organized Labor and the Negro Worker, 1865–1900," *Labor History*, 1 (Spring 1960), 164–76; Herbert Hill, "In the Age of Gompers and After. Racial Practices of Organized Labor," *New Politics*, 4

Railroad Brotherhoods and other unions such as the Brotherhood of Boilermakers and Iron Shipbuilders, the International Brotherhood of Electrical Workers, and the International Association of Machinists explicitly excluded Negroes. Certain other craft unions barred them indirectly through narrow apprenticeship regulations, racial "rituals," and other informal but nevertheless effective devices. Some unions, particularly in the South, admitted them but only to separate locals. After 1900 the AFL Executive Council sanctioned separate Negro locals and even central organizations where affiliated unions would not accept Negroes. And from that time the AFL leadership retreated from its earlier declaration that "the working people must unite and organize irrespective of creed, color, sex, nationality, or politics," and from its earlier efforts to uproot racial practices by member unions. By 1910 or so, just before the start of the great Negro migration to Northern cities and industry, the most recent survey of American trade-union history concludes: "The labor movement was not only neglecting to organize Negro

(Spring 1965), 26–46; Herman D. Bloch, "Labor and the Negro, 1866–1910," *Journal of Negro History*, 50 (July 1965), 163–84. Taft finds that the Federation "retreated from its earlier position" concerning Negro workers and stresses the importance of craft autonomy and the widespread opposition to integrated unions in the South. The policy of separation, he finds, was "the only one which would make possible the retention of unions in the South." Grob calls the AFL shift "simply a part of a larger development that came to characterize all areas of American life." Foner finds in these years "proof" of a "deliberate conspiracy between employers and the craft unions" to exclude Negro workers and uses this explanation (a "conspiracy") seven times in less than two pages (Foner, *op. cit.*, 2: 353–55). Hill argues from scattered evidence that "at the turn of the century the AFL had fully capitulated to a policy of chauvinism and overt discrimination." Bloch stresses that "local" interaction between Negro and white workers shaped discriminatory patterns more than national decisions but infers this without examining much local source material. Much of this dispute is tendentious since these writings generally ignore what E. P. Thompson calls "the goings-on 'in the provinces'" and view local labor history "as shadowy incidents or unaccountable upheavals on the periphery of the national scene" (Asa Briggs and John Saville, eds., *Essays in Labour History* [London, 1907], 276–77). Until the national and local pictures are put together—and this only after yeomanlike digging in Northern and Southern sources—little more can be written of the relations between the Negro and organized labor, 1890–1910.

workers, but it was following a deliberate policy of exclusion of Negroes from many jobs." [109]

And yet while much is known about the racial practices of certain unions and the "impotence" of or "betrayal" by the Federation when challenged by them, a great deal is misunderstood and lost by an exclusive emphasis on *national* policy and on the *intent* of national leaders. The controversy on this matter carried on by certain labor historians and tendentious publicists generates much heat but sheds little light on the relations between Negro and white workers. In another connection, British historian Edward P. Thompson has perceptively criticized such a perspective because it neglects "the tensions and lines of growth in movements which . . . have always been exceptionally responsive to problems of local social and industrial context." [110] Thompson's observation bears directly on our inability to assess fully the UMW experience. The stress in most labor histories means that little is known of the interaction between Negro and white workers, North and South, in particular communities between 1890 and 1910 so that too much is inferred solely from national policies and mere rhetoric. The tradition of Negro craftsmanship that carried over from slavery in many Southern communities, particularly in the building trades, is hardly explored. [111] In addition, although most Negroes lived in rural areas in 1900, seventy-two cities each had more than 5,000 Negroes and of them Baltimore, Memphis, New Orleans, New York, Philadelphia, and Washington more than 50,000. In Southern cities such as Baton Rouge, Charleston, Jacksonville, Montgomery, Savannah, Shreveport, and Vicksburg, Negroes outnumbered whites. The largely nonunion manufacturing industries counted 146,000 Negroes in 1890 and nearly 350,000 twenty years later. [112] Most urban Negroes

109. Taft, *Organized Labor in American History*, op. cit., 670.

110. E. P. Thompson, "Homage to Tom Maguire," in Briggs and Saville, eds., *op. cit.*, 276–77.

111. Woodward, *op. cit.*, 360–61.

112. Du Bois, ed., *op. cit.*, 91, and John Hope Franklin, *From Slavery to Freedom* (New York, 1947), 393, 429.

labored as unskilled and semiskilled wage-earners. But modern scholarship tells inconsequentially little about urban working-class Negroes between 1890 and 1910—about their community life and collective aspirations as well as their interaction with white workers and employers.[113] Where most urban Negro and white workers confronted each other, more than the edicts of national unions affected their behavior. The story was simple if a particular national or local union explicitly excluded Negroes. But where no such barrier was found, local "traditions," particular notions of "self-interest," the conflict between racial attitudes and the egalitarian emphasis of much trade-union ideology, and numerous other influences as yet unstudied shaped the behavior and the attitudes of Negro and white workers.[114]

The absence of detailed knowledge of the "local world" inhabited by white and Negro workers between 1890 and 1910 leaves only an obscure and tangled reality—filled with scattered and contradictory but suggestive bits of information. The available evidence deals mostly with craft unions and reveals precious little about the "mass" of unskilled and semiskilled Negro and white factory workers. Some facts confirm deep economic and racial fear of Negroes and their exclusion from local trade unions. But other significant information tells a quite different story, one that can only be hinted at in these pages.

In 1902 the International Longshoremen's Association counted 20,000 members, 6,000 of them Negroes, and a Great Lakes officer commented: "We have many colored members in our Association, and some of them are among our leading officials of our local branches. In one of our locals . . . there are

113. An exception is the standard work: W. E. B. Du Bois, *The Philadelphia Negro* (Philadelphia, 1899).

114. Much can be learned about methods for approaching this subject from the recent work of British labor and social historians. See, e.g., "Conference Report," Society for the Study of Labour History, Bulletin IX (Autumn 1964), 4–9; Eric Hobsbawm, *Labouring Men* (London, 1964), *passim;* and in particular E. P. Thompson, *The Making of the English Working Class* (London, 1963), *passim.*

over 300 members, of which *[sic]* five are colored; of these, two hold the office of President and Secretary." A New Orleans Negro longshoreman boasted: "I believe that we are the only craft in that city who *[sic]* have succeeded in wiping out the color question. Our members meet jointly in the same hall and are the highest paid workmen in New Orleans." [115]

A major citywide building trades strike affected Chicago through most of 1900, and the employment of nonunion Negroes caused some racial strife and even violence.[116] But the Chicago Federation of Labor favored another solution and appealed to these nonunion Negroes:

> The frequency with which unscrupulous employers of labor are of late supplanting white men by their colored brethren in times of industrial troubles is a question of most serious moment to the wage earners of this country. In calling attention to this question it is not our intention to arouse sentiment which might lead to race prejudice, or a race war, which would be deplorable in its results, but rather in a friendly spirit to lay before our colored brethren a statement of facts which we hope may convince them of their error. . . . We do not condemn them, believing they are most justly entitled to our sympathy and support. In the slavery days, now happily gone by, when the traffic in human flesh and blood remained a blot on our civilization, the Negro was unable to free himself from the bondage. His white brother rose in arms and declared that the slave should be free. Today the Negro is being used to keep the white man in industrial slavery. The colored man, more simple in his

115. Du Bois, ed., *The Negro Artisan, op. cit.,* 158, 160–61. In 1899, however, trouble developed between Negro and white longshoremen in Newport News, Va. ILA locals there were entirely Negro. White workers refused to join them, and only after some time did the Negro unionists agree to separate locals for the whites.

116. This important strike is discussed at length in Ernest L. Bogart, "The Chicago Building Trades Dispute of 1900," in John R. Commons, ed., *Trade Unionism and Labor Problems* (New York, 1906), 87–96.

ways, with fewer wants and these more easily satisfied, is contented to work under conditions which are irksome to the white workman, and he is today, perhaps unconsciously, being used to try to drag the white man down to a level lower than was the Negro before he was freed from slavery. . . .

It is to remedy this that we appeal to him, to welcome him into our fold, to elevate him to our standard and to better his condition as well as our own. The trades-union movement knows no race or color. Its aims are the bettering of the condition of the wage earner, whatever his color or creed. In this spirit we appeal to the colored workmen to join us in our work. Come into our trades unions, give us your assistance and in return, receive our support, so that race hatred may be forever buried, and the workers of the country united in a solid phalanx to demand what we are justly entitled to—a fair share of the fruits of our industry.

This appeal did not fail. Many Negroes quit as strikebreakers and became "zealous for the cause of unionism." Although the strike was lost and the unions weakened, more Negroes than ever before, particularly the hod-carriers, joined these unions.[117]

In 1906, Negro trade unionist and New Yorker James S. Wallace reported that in his city "many unions, viz., plasterers, carpenters, printers, teamsters, pavers, engineers, drillers, longshoremen, cigarmakers, etc. . . . have a large Negro membership, and they are treated as men." Wallace then served as elected third vice president of the International Union of Pavers and Rammersmen. That union had among its members a substantial number of recent Italian immigrants.[118]

117. The Chicago Federation of Trades appeal appears in R. R. Wright, "The Negro in Chicago," *Charities*, 15 (October 7, 1905), 69–73. Much else of interest about Negro workers in the meat-packing industry and Negro teamsters is found in Wright's article which is reprinted, in part, in Herbert Aptheker, ed., *A Documentary History of the Negro People in the United States* (New York, 1951), 838–42.

118. James S. Wallace to the editor, *New York Age*, July 12 and August 30, 1906, reprinted in *ibid.*, 843–44.

In 1902, responding to pressure (which came mainly from delegates representing white Southern locals at the 1901 and 1902 national conventions) that Southern Negro carpenters be organized, the United Brotherhood of Carpenters and Joiners President appointed a South Carolina-born Negro, then President of a Savannah local, as a Southern organizer.[119] Much controversy followed, and many Southern white members complained of the "threat" of social equality, said "this is a white man's country," and insisted that whites "revolt voluntarily and involuntarily from a close and intimate association with the negro." One argued that this feeling toward Negroes was "a part of the bone, flesh, and blood of every southern man regardless of his social stratum." [120] Yet the union leadership held firm, and *The Carpenter*'s editor instructed critics that "prejudice on these lines has no standing in the labor movement." A white Savannah business agent supported the union President:

> In Georgia they [Negroes] must be organized. I was born and raised among them; my father once owned some of them, and I know them. . . . We are always in competition with them. The contractors prefer them because they can get them cheap. . . . We have 300 white carpenters and 500 negro carpenters [here], and the latter have less unemployed than the whites. The reason is that they are not well organized and can be hired for less wages. So I say we must organize them; for if we can afford to work all day on a scaffold beside them, then we can surely afford to meet them in the hall for an hour or so once in a while. . . . The mere fact that all of the boss builders in the South are advocating leaving the negroes out of the unions is a good reason why we should organize them. . . . Let the good work go on, and let us hope for the day when there will be equal rights to all and special privileges to none. . . .[121]

119. "Editorial," *The Carpenter*, 23 (January 1903), 3–4.

120. Critical letters from Southern white union carpenters appear in *ibid.* (April 1903), 6–7.

121. Savannah, Georgia, carpenter to the editor, *ibid.* (September 1903), 3, 6.

The white president of Atlanta's District Council, who had lived in the South for fourteen years, also favored the effort and urged his white Southern brothers: "Let us lay aside all our prejudice (I have as much as any southern born white man) and look the question fair and square in the face." He had few doubts. "We want that organizer here in Atlanta for about three months. I believe he can do us more good than anything else." [122] The union did not rescind its appointment.[123]

Reliable information tells us that in 1902 Negroes in Florida unions included 2,000 cigarmakers, 1,200 building trades laborers, 1,000 carpenters, 800 longshoremen, 300 plasterers, 200 painters, and 200 bricklayers. Some Negro women belonged to Florida unions, too. One of that state's Negro union stalwarts wrote of his city's unions:

> The Negroes in this city have no need to complain, as white men work, smoke, eat, and drink together with them, meet in a Central Union, and hold office together. I organized and installed the Central Union as General Secretary, and I am a Negro, and have held the same [office] for two elections and was elected by whites who are in the majority. I have presided over the same body, but do not visit their daughters and have no wish [to do so]. The white painters do in a way draw the [color] line, but not openly; the boiler makers also, but none others.[124]

A year later the state AFL started a weekly newspaper in Jacksonville called *The Florida Labor Journal* and an early issue featured a long defense of militant trade unionism by regular local columnist Lynn C. Doyle. Doyle also gave much attention to the Southern Negro and blamed all of the South's racial troubles on Northerners—"the sanctified scum of the earth who

122. H. B. Adolphus, President, Fenton County, Georgia, District Council, to the editor, *ibid.*

123. Spero and Harris, *op. cit.,* 66.

124. Du Bois, ed., *The Negro Artisan, op. cit.,* 111–12, 177.

first put hell—yes, hell—into the negro of the south . . . and
incidently skinned the poor ignoramuses out of all their
earnings." Approving lynching and terror against "violent"
Negroes and the "use of the gun to suppress riot," Doyle made it
clear that "we cannot now, nor ever will, for one moment make
them our social equals." And yet even Doyle was not without
the contradictory tensions flowing from a commitment to a
belief in trade-union egalitarianism and a feeling of racial
exclusiveness and superiority:

> . . . Right here in our city the spirit of the laws of the A. F.
> of L. are carried out, even admitting, in some instances, the
> negro to the white locals. The olive branch was long ago
> extended, and across the bloody chasm (made by the
> agitator of the north and the political parasite) the white
> man and the black clasped hands as brothers in the battle of
> life. Their foe is a common one—the enemy of all man-
> kind.[125]

Although the *Labor Journal* printed little news about local
Jacksonville Negroes in its first two years, what it reported
reflected creditably on Negro trade unionists. In January 1903 it
urged strengthening three weakened Negro unions, supported
extensive organization among Negro workers by white and
Negro AFL Florida organizers, and saw in such developments
the promise of "a tidal wave of the old union spirit" that would
"shake the foundations of autocracy and plutocracy as . . .
never before . . . in Florida." A local of Negro women,
apparently clothing workers, and the city's largest union, invited
the *Journal*'s editor to a meeting chaired by its woman
president. He found it "well regulated" and commended it to
white and Negro readers:

> It is to the shame of some unions in Jacksonville that they
> sit back and knock their brethren while these women, who

125. Lynn C. Doyle, "Education That Don't Educate," *The Florida Labor
Journal*, 1 (February 6, 1903), 1–4.

on an average draw less than $3 per week, attend their meetings, keep in good standing, and pay a sick benefit of $2 per week. Too much credit cannot be given to those good women. . . .[126]

A Democratic Party supporter, the *Journal* nevertheless printed a Jacksonville Socialist Party advertisement addressed "To the Colored Voters of Jacksonville" during a June 1903 municipal election campaign. The Socialists appealed to Jacksonville Negroes: "The Democratic Party excluded you (by direct prohibition) from voting in the late primary. . . . There is now no place for SELF-RESPECTING MEMBERS of your race to go in the city election except into the Socialist Party. . . . VOTE FOR YOUR OWN INTERESTS. . . ." [127] Six weeks later, without comment the *Journal* reprinted on its front page a commentary on W. E. B. Du Bois's *The Souls of Black Folk*, which first appeared in *Boyce's Weekly*. "This negro question," the Northern labor journal (about which no information has been found) said, ". . . is, in its essentials, a working class question."

A certain proportion of the white people of the United States are determined that a man with a black skin must be ever and always a hewer of wood or drawer of water. His brain may have the genius of a Dumas or a Frederick Douglass, but if in its veins flows a trace of black blood he is condemned to occupations that stunt and dwarf his mentality.

North and south alike this condition exists. If the problem seems more acute in the old slave states it is only because its proportions are more commanding. The spirit which condemns the black man to his own restricted sphere, industrially as well as socially, exists quite as much among the whites north as south of Mason and Dixon's line.

126. *Ibid.* (January 30, 1903), 14–15.
127. *Ibid.* (June 12, 1903), 9.

What support Negroes found, *Boyce's Weekly* believed, came mostly from white men "outside . . . the laboring class" and this was "a grave blunder."

> Race prejudice is easily transformed into class prejudice. The spirit that says the negro may not hope to become a lawyer, teacher, educator or banker—save for the service of his own race—will soon say the same of the Russian, the Hungarian, the Jew. If a man of surpassing talents and earnest industry may not rise above the dead level of his race, we shall soon find it will be equally hard for him to surmount the boundaries of his class. Indeed, today class spirit no less than race prejudice is becoming characteristic of American society.

White workers therefore had much to learn from Du Bois's book.

> If you want to know what this means to the negro of trained intellect get Professor Du Bois' pathetic book "The Souls of Black Folk." To imagine what it may yet mean to working-men you have only to translate his stories into terms of your own class.

Boyce's Weekly commended those Southern whites in the labor movement who were "taking the negro into full communion" and called such involvement the possible "beginning of the most effective work for the correction of an evil that menaces the rights and liberties and the souls of white as well as black workingmen." [128]

What occurred in Jacksonville was not repeated in all Southern cities, but the few details available show that Negroes were not excluded or separated everywhere. In 1901 the Industrial Commission summed up its findings about Southern

128. "Black and White," *Boyce's Weekly*, n.d., reprinted in *ibid.* (July 24, 1903), 1–2.

unions: "As the unions have grown, separate locals have been demanded. . . . In some places the city central bodies have begun to reject colored delegates. *While there are still many places in the South where negroes and whites meet on an absolute plane of equality in the labor organizations,* there are others where not only separate local trade unions but separate city federations have become necessary." [129] (Italics added.) In Atlanta, where most Negro unionists apparently met in separate locals, the State Federation of Labor nevertheless refused to join the 1898 "peace jubilee parade" because Negro workers could not parade, too.[130] Respondents to W. E. B. Du Bois's inquiries that resulted in *The Negro Artisan* (1902), a neglected pioneering study, gave evidence of much discrimination against Negroes by Southern unions, but their replies also showed contrary trends. In Atlanta, Birmingham, Danville, Memphis, New Orleans, Richmond, and Savannah, Negro union plasterers outnumbered their white brothers and met in locals that were "often mixed." Masons and bricklayers also had "mixed" locals in parts of the South.[131] Some Asheville, Charlotte, and Winston-Salem unions admitted North Carolina Negroes. In Georgia, Athens Negroes combined with whites in certain unions, while Savannah and Augusta had several Negro unions. Savannah counted seven separate Negro locals among the building trades laborers, carpenters, coopers, lathers, painters, and tinners.[132] New Orleans had the greatest number of Negro trade unionists in any

129. *Report of the Industrial Commission*, XVII, *op. cit.*, xxviii–xxix.

130. *Ibid.*, 36–37. See also the testimony of Du Bois, *ibid.*, XV, 175. Asked what he knew about the extent of Negro labor organization in the South, Du Bois remarked: "Not very much. I simply know that in most building trades the negroes can join, and considerable numbers have joined. They sometimes meet in the same hall, the whites on one side and the colored on the other." Useful information about Negro union bricklayers and their different status in various parts of the country is found in the testimony of John Healey, *ibid.*, VII, 162–63. Data on the complex relations between Negro workers and organized labor in Georgia, which can only be evaluated after additional research in local Georgia materials, are found in *ibid.*, 236–38, 242, 542, 547–48, 554–55, 560, 564–68.

131. Du Bois, ed., *The Negro Artisan, op. cit.*, 162–63.

132. *Ibid.*, 114–15, 137.

Southern city, almost four thousand. The Crescent City had many unions that admitted Negroes and six powerful all-Negro unions in the docking and transport industries. The much-impressed Negro secretary of the New Orleans Central Labor Union reported to Du Bois: "By amalgamation of organizations and through International connections, we expect to have the color line in work removed." [133] Du Bois's study was not nearly as optimistic. His survey of contemporary trade-union practices found much that deserved criticism. And yet, paradoxically, he could write: "At the same time, there are today [1902] probably a larger number of effective Negro members in the trade unions than ever before, there is evidence of renewed inspiration toward mechanical trades, and a better comprehension of the labor movement." [134]

XII

NOTHING WRITTEN in these final pages should be taken to suggest that Negro workers had an easy time in Northern and Southern crafts and factories between 1890 and 1910. This evidence means merely to indicate the difficulties involved in judging the "uniqueness" of the UMW experience and to hint that the full story of the confrontation between Negro workers and organized (as well as unorganized white) labor at that time has yet to be written—and that when examined it must be from "the bottom up." Surely, however, the evidence in these pages tells us that Booker T. Washington (himself a member of the Knights of Labor as a young man) exaggerated when he boasted that "the Negro is not given to 'strikes'" and that trade unionism was "that form of slavery which prevents a man from selling his labor to whom he pleases on account of his color." [135] William Hooper Councill, the Negro head of the Agricultural

133. *Ibid.*, 127–28.

134. *Ibid.*, 158. Du Bois's observation must not be exaggerated and must be read in the context of his detailed criticisms of trade-union discriminatory practices (*ibid.*, 153–78). Yet labor historians have frequently ignored the evidence of Negro participation in Southern trade unions that the Du Bois study brought to light.

135. Quoted in Woodward, *op. cit.*, 364.

and Mechanical College for Negroes at Normal, Alabama, and very much a prophet of a subordinate role for Negroes in the "New South," was also wrong in arguing that Southern labor unions "will bring into the South the disorders that will exceed the disturbances of 'reconstruction days'" and that trade unionism would chase the Negro from the South so that "Communism [will] drive the white man's coach, Nihilism cook and serve his food, Agrarianism plow his fields, and the red flag of Anarchy float over every Southern industry." [136] Equally

---

136. W. H. Councill, "Negro Labor and Labor Organizations," *The Tradesman* (Chattanooga), January 1900, reprinted in the *Locomotive Firemen's Magazine*, 28 (March 1900), 197–98. A vivid sketch of Councill is found in August Meier, *Negro Thought in America, 1880–1915* (Ann Arbor, 1963), 209–10. Councill's paper appeared in *The Tradesman*, a leading Southern commercial publication, as a part of a symposium on "the South and its future." Other contributors included the secretary of Huntsville Chamber of Commerce and Southern Industrial Convention, N. F. Thompson, and a former Georgia governor who found in the Negro "one of the South's best undeveloped resources . . . if properly trained." He urged Northern capital to come into the South whose "labor" made that section "a stranger to riots, strikes and ugly uprisings among the people. . . ." Thompson argued for legislation that would "make it a crime to inaugurate a strike that in any way affected the general public." (*The Tradesman, loc. cit.,* 195–97.) That same year, Thompson, who had also spent five years in Johnstown, Pennsylvania, and been secretary of the Birmingham, Alabama, Commercial Club, at another time, warned the Industrial Commission that Birmingham Negroes "are being taken into the unions practically on the same basis as all others." Thompson complained of "a deficiency of collective education among the masses" and that "the educational influence of the labor organizations" had gone unchallenged in the South for twenty-five years. He even favored the use of violence against outspoken union activists (*Report of the Industrial Commission*, VII, *op. cit.,* 755–59). John P. Coffin, vice president of the Southern Industrial Council, urged that Negroes be used as "a reserve force in case of strikes." "I believe," he told the Commission, "that in the negro labor of the South lies the panacea for the wrongs frequently committed by organized labor, and a reserve force from which can be supplied any needed number of workers when the time shall come that they will be needed." Before they would "submit to unjust domination by unions," Coffin predicted, the "Southern people" would "negroize their industries." An amazed Commission investigator pressed Coffin on this point and only the Mad Hatter could entangle what followed:
"*Q.:* That would bring negro domination in industry then, would it not? *A.:* It will bring negro domination of the labor market if labor is unjust.

erroneous was Samuel Gompers, who in 1910 could insist that
Negroes just did not "understand the philosophy of human
rights." [137]

In all of this, it is the problem of perspective and the lack of
detailed knowledge that plague us. Much has been written about
the trade unions and their national leaders and about their petty
and significant quarrels as well as their larger successes and
frequent failures, but little is yet known of the quality of life
and the complexity of thought and feeling of ordinary white and
Negro workers in the early modern era. August Meier has
explored painstakingly and well the world of Booker T. Washington and his Negro critics and defenders,[138] but the world of
men like Richard Davis awaits its historian. How difficult it is
therefore to grasp the response of a Negro worker to the racial
sentiment of the older Gompers or to imagine the feelings of a
white trade unionist confronted with the antilabor imprecations
of Washington and Councill. When the United Brotherhood of
Carpenters and Joiners disturbed so many of its Southern white
members by appointing a Negro organizer, the St. Louis
Advance, a labor weekly, applauded its action and urged further
organization of Negro workers:

It is useless to read homilies on thrift and morality to
under-paid labor. . . . More and more the Brotherhoods are

"*Q.:* And the white man will dominate the social and political conditions of the
South, and the negro will dominate the labor market of the South? . . . If they
dominated white labor, white labor would be suppressed? *A.:* No; they would
never dominate white labor. He *[sic]* will take their places, but domination will
rest with the whites. There is no fear of negro domination in the South.
"*Q.:* I do not mean domination over the employer, but domination over the
white labor. They would be eliminated, would they not? *A.:* No; the employer
would dominate the labor, not the negro. The negro will never dominate the
Anglo-Saxon. He may take his place in work under certain conditions; but the
Anglo-Saxon was not created to be dominated. . . .
"*Q.:* Is it not really, then, to be held up as a menace over the white labor to make
them understand that they must not make unjust demands, but that they must
submit to the employer in all things? *A.:* . . . I believe in white labor as far as
possible; but I also believe in justice." (*ibid.,* 790–91.)
137. Quoted in Woodward, *op. cit.,* 361.
138. Meier, *op. cit., passim.*

opening their doors to him [the Negro], telling him to step in. The labor leaders know that without the Negro their organizations are lop-sided and their movements necessarily failures, and the Negro can see that as a laborer he must ally himself with his brother, or remain as he is now in the South, the poorest paid laborer in the world.[139]

The *Advance* was wrong in its prediction. Although Richard Davis and the early white leaders of the United Mine Workers of America were among those to make such a connection, theirs was not the dominant influence between 1890 and 1910. Davis died in 1900. By 1910 surely only those coal miners, Negro and white workers, who had felt his presence and benefitted from his experience and courageous leadership remembered his name.*

139. St. Louis *Advance*, n.d., reprinted in *The Carpenter*, 23 (April 1903), 6–7. See also the letter of a Texas trade unionist, probably white, who wrote to Du Bois: "The Negro question is the one drawback to the success of the labor movement today [1900–1], especially is this true in the South. The Negro has always been the stumbling block in the way of success in many cases; this, however, is not the fault of the Negro, but until the white men realize that it is with the organization and assistance of the Negro, that they can and must win, the labor movement will not be as successful as we hope for." He went on: "They are laborers, in a larger percentage, than their white brothers; they are the ones used to whip the white men into line when striking for their rights or demanding recognition from their employers, whereas, if they were organized, no inducement could be made to cause them to falter in their duty to mankind" (unidentified letter from Texas, quoted in Du Bois, ed., *The Negro Artisan, op. cit.*, 178).

* In 1909, William Scaife recorded his memories of the early UMW years. Scaife devoted an entire article to Richard Davis and called him "a heroic fighter." Scaife scorned those who neglected the pioneering efforts of the Ohio Negro miner and reminded his readers of his "unflagging zeal . . . against trials and tribulations that would have daunted and discouraged the best of them." "If he was black," Scaife said of Davis, "he had a heart as white as any man, and a devotion to union principles that was second to no man in the movement. His color he could not help, and I don't know that it matters a great deal anyhow." Scaife found in men like Davis reason not to "erect in the miners' organization a 'color standard,' but one of manhood." "We need more colored men like Dick Davis," he concluded, "and we white men want to treat them right for the common good of all of us." (Old Timer [William Scaife], "Forty Years a Miner and Men I Have Known," *United Mine Workers' Journal*, November 19, 1909.)

Historians often characterize an era by a dominant personality, a figure who looms large over a period of time and leaves more than a momentary impression or in his person symbolizes significant changes. In this sense, the years between 1890 and 1910 did not belong to men like Richard Davis. This was indeed "The Age of Samuel Gompers" and "The Age of Booker T. Washington." Men like Davis were not asked to serve as presidential advisors or as members of federal commissions. *The New York Times* did not query them for their opinions on the "race" and "labor" questions. Instead, their long-range vision and concrete aspirations for democratic interracial trade unionism were stifled by the defensive strategy of organized labor and middle-class Negro leadership as well as the rising tide of racism within the labor movement and throughout the country.

The American people have journeyed far from the Age of Washington and Gompers. One measure of the distance traveled and the losses incurred is that so little is known about working-class Negroes like Richard Davis who displayed so full an awareness of their plight and that of their brothers and who retained and exemplified older traditions of pride and hope and militancy. We know a great deal about the world of Washington and Gompers. But until we know more fully the world of men like Davis, we shall not clearly comprehend the tragedy and the hope embedded in recent American history.

PART III

The Industrial City

4

The Reality of the
Rags–to–Riches "Myth"

THE CASE OF THE PATERSON, NEW JERSEY,
LOCOMOTIVE, IRON, AND MACHINERY MANUFACTURERS,
1830–1880

IN RECENT DECADES, historians have vigorously disputed the validity of the belief that nineteenth-century American industrialists rose from "rags to riches." A popular literature has been subjected to critical textual analysis, and the promises of popular ideology have been measured by empirical head-counting that involves the collection of data about the social origins of "business leaders." These studies share a common conclusion: very few workers—day laborers, unskilled workers, and skilled artisans—became successful manufacturers. After studying nearly two hundred leaders of the largest early twentieth-century corporations, William Miller convincingly concluded that to look for men of "working class or foreign origins" among the most powerful financiers, public utility and railroad executives, and mining and manufacturing corporation officials was "to look almost in vain." Fully 95 percent came from families of upper- or middle-class status. Not more than 3 percent started as poor immigrant boys or even as poor American farm boys. Andrew Carnegie was an important American in 1900, but hardly any men of his economic class or social position shared with him a common career pattern.[1]

1. William Miller, "American Historians and the Business Elite," in William

Other studies, not as careful in their selection of a representative sample of manufacturers, have tended to validate Miller's findings about the 1900–1910 elite for earlier periods of industrialization. Miller's study carefully explained its limits: his data described " 'career men'—bureaucrats that is . . . all office-holders, many of them [having] *never* organized a business of any kind." The work of C. Wright Mills and his critics Reinhard Bendix and Frank W. Howton ranged over all of American history in an effort to define the changing composition of the "American business elite." Mills drew evidence from biographical sketches of business leaders in the *Dictionary of American Biography*.[2] Bendix and Howton worked primarily from biographical sketches in the *National Cyclopedia of American Biography* to challenge—provocatively but not convincingly—Mills's conclusion that "in the nineteenth century the business elite was composed of significantly more men from the lower classes than was the case previously or than has been the case since."[3] Both Mills and his critics agreed, however, that the "American business elite" always drew its membership predominantly from men born with high status and sired by well-to-do fathers. But Mills and his critics quarreled about the changing social composition of the "business elite" over time. Overall, for the *DAB* entries examined on business leaders born before 1907, Mills found that 9.8 percent were the sons of skilled craftsmen or semiskilled and unskilled workers. The percentage varied from generation to generation but was highest (13.2 percent) among those industrialists, merchants, and financiers born between 1820 and 1849. Using mostly *NCAB* biographies, Bendix and Howton found little change over time in the

Miller, ed., *Men in Business. Essays on the Historical Role of the Entrepreneur* (New York, 1962), 309–28.

2. C. Wright Mills, "The American Business Elite: A Collective Portrait," in Irving Horowitz, ed., *Power, Politics and People. The Collected Essays of C. Wright Mills* (New York, 1962), 110–39.

3. Reinhard Bendix and Frank W. Howton, "Social Mobility and the American Business Elite," in Reinhard Bendix and Seymour Martin Lipset, eds., *Social Mobility in Industrial Society* (Berkeley, Calif., 1959), 114–43.

percentage of those industrialists who came from working-class families. The *rates* were consistently low: 2 percent for those born between 1801 and 1830, 1 percent for those born between 1831 and 1860, and 2 percent for those born between 1861 and 1890.

Percentages may be useful for comparative purposes over time, but they are dangerous statistical abstractions and may tell little about a particular moment in history. How representative, for example, was the Bendix and Howton sample for the pre-Civil War generations? They found information about only fifty-six fathers of "business leaders" born between 1801 and 1830 and 225 born between 1831 and 1860. Translating their findings into absolute numbers, we learn from this sample that only three out of 281 business leaders born between 1801 and 1860 came from working-class families.[4] Even cursory knowledge of the history of American manufacturing before 1890 should raise numerous questions about a sampling technique that yields so narrow a base for a historical generalization.

The most detailed study of the early post-Civil War "industrial elite" has been conducted by Frances W. Gregory and Irene D. Neu, who generally confirmed the earlier findings.[5] Gregory and Neu examined the careers of 303 leaders of the railroad, textile (mostly cotton), and steel industries in the 1870s by studying the place of birth, the occupation of the father, the religious affiliation, the educational level attained, and the age on first starting work of the executives of seventy-seven large firms. These included the treasurer and agent of thirty textile mills mostly capitalized at more than one million dollars; the president, vice president, and general manager (or superintendent) of thirty steel mills; and the president, vice president, and

4. Bendix and Howton also report the findings of Susanne Keller in her unpublished dissertation, "The Social Origins and Career Lines of Three Generations of American Business Leaders." Of 254 business leaders born about 1820, Keller found that only eight (3 percent) had fathers who labored as "wage earners and office workers [clerks?]."

5. Frances W. Gregory and Irene D. Neu, "The American Industrial Elite in the 1870's: Their Social Origins," in Miller, ed., *op. cit.*, 193-211.

general manager of the seventeen largest railroads. Their careful findings about the occupations of 194 fathers showed that 8 percent (sixteen men) were the sons of "workers." Not one railroad leader rose from the "lower depths"; 15 percent of the textile manufacturers (ten of sixty-seven) did, along with 11 percent of the steel manufacturers (six of fifty-seven). In contrast, 64 percent of the entire group came from business or professional backgrounds; one of every four was born on a farm; 3 percent were the sons of "public officials." The authors asked and answered a critical question: "Was the typical industrial leader of the 1870s, then, a 'new man,' an escapee from the slums of Europe or from the paternal farm? Did he rise by his own efforts from a boyhood of poverty? Was he as innocent of education and of formal training as has often been alleged? He seems to have been none of these things." Combining variables, they described the archetypal industrial leader of the 1870s. He was American by birth, of a New England father, a Protestant in his religion, and distinctly upper class in origin:

> Urban in early environment, he was . . . born and bred in an atmosphere in which business and a relatively high social standing were intimately associated with his family life. Only at about eighteen did he take his first regular job, preparing to rise from it, moreover, not by a rigorous apprenticeship begun when he was virtually a child, but by an academic education well above the average for the times.

For the men they studied, Gregory and Neu found little evidence that "the top-level businessman" of the 1870s was "but a generation removed from poverty and anonymity." [6]

More recently, Stephan Thernstrom has brought significant and original insight to the patterns of social mobility in mid-nineteenth-century industrializing America. *Poverty and Progress: Social Mobility in a Nineteenth Century City* breaks with older studies of social mobility by focusing in close detail

6. See Miller, ed., *op. cit.*, 149.

on one community: it treats the career patterns of nearly three hundred unskilled day laborers in Newburyport, Massachusetts, between 1850 and 1880.[7] Thernstrom finds among them a good deal of geographic mobility out of the city, but for those immigrant and native workers and their sons who remained, substantial material improvement ("property mobility" or the acquisition of personal and real estate) and occupational mobility (from unskilled to semiskilled and skilled work). Their most common form of social advancement was "upward mobility *within* the working class." Thernstrom finds no evidence of spectacular upward mobility: "In the substantial sample of workers and their sons studied for the 1850–1880 period not a single instance of mobility into the ranks of management or even into a foremanship position was discovered." Many workers and their sons improved in these thirty years, some even as small shopkeepers and white-collar workers. But not one met the test of the rags-to-riches ideology. "Few of these men and few of their children," Thernstrom concludes, "rose very far on the social scale; most of the upward occupational shifts they made left them manual workers still, and their property mobility, though strikingly widespread, rarely involved the accumulation of anything approaching real wealth."

The findings of Thernstrom, Gregory and Neu, and Miller, among others, are the work of serious scholars, careful in their methods, deep in their research, and modest in their conclusions. But there is question about the larger inferences to be drawn from these studies about the social origins of the industrial manufacturing class in the decades of prime American industrialization. Hundreds, even thousands, of successful manufacturers—often members of particular elites in their particular communities but rarely memorialized on the national level—did not meet the criteria for admission to the *Dictionary of American Biography* or the *National Cyclopedia of American Biography*.

7. Stephan Thernstrom, *Poverty and Progress: Social Mobility in a Nineteenth Century City* (Cambridge, Mass., 1964), *passim* but especially 114, 161–65, 213, 223.

Gregory and Neu reveal in detail the social origins of "the industrial elite" of the 1870s, but draw heavily in their narrow sample on a well-developed industry (cotton textile manufacturing) and an industry that attracted as its leaders lawyers, merchants, and financiers (the railroads). Thernstrom tells much that is new and significant about the life-style and aspirations of mid-nineteenth-century workers, but Newburyport had developed as a manufacturing city before 1850; and although the composition of its population changed between 1855 and 1880, the city underwent little development in the years studied.

What of the manufacturers who founded new firms that involved small outlays of capital at the start? What of the workers, skilled as well as unskilled, who lived in rapidly expanding cities? In these pages, we shall examine a select group of successful local manufacturers in one such city—the locomotive, machinery, tool, and iron manufacturers of Paterson, New Jersey, between 1830 and 1880. Were they as a group a lesser mirror image of the archetypal industrialist described by Gregory and Neu? If there were workers among them, were they unusual and atypical? Information is available only on their occupational careers and their places of birth, but it is sufficient to test the reality of the promise of rags to riches in one important industrial city.

In explaining why Paterson, New Jersey, became a prime nineteenth-century American industrial city, economic and social historians usually have stressed its development as a center of textile, particularly silk, manufacture. And with good reason. By 1890, Paterson was the Lyons of America. But the silk industry came quite late in the city's development: not until the Civil War and the decade following did the silk mills and the city become so closely entwined. Yet Paterson had been an industrial city of importance before that time. Its magnificent waterfalls promised potential water power, and it early attracted the attention of Alexander Hamilton and other industrial enthusiasts. The story of the ill-fated Society for Establishing Useful Manufactures in the 1790s is well known. But after it failed, irregular and usually unsuccessful efforts at cotton manufacture shaped the city's industrial history until 1837 and remained important (although not essential) after that time. However, such uneven enterprise (only one of nearly twenty cotton "mills" survived intact the depression in the late 1830s) did not explain Paterson's solid growth as an industrial city between 1830 and 1880. Early textile manufacturing mattered mainly because it attracted machinists to the city to repair and build cotton and other textile machinery. These men and others who followed them after 1840 were in the city at the start of a great boom in the manufacture of transportation equipment, machinery, and ironware of all kinds. Between 1830 and 1880, they sparked the development of Paterson's locomotive, iron goods, machinery, and machine-tool industries—changes that in turn spurred the city's growth. In 1850, 11,000 persons lived in Paterson, and about 1,450 worked in these industries. Ten years later, the city counted nearly 20,000 residents, and one of every ten was an "iron worker." A great industrial spurt occurred between 1860 and 1873, partly the result of the rapid rise of large silk and other textile mills but also a consequence of the expansion of older industries. By 1870, the population had risen to 33,581, and the locomotive, iron, and machinery industries employed 5,300 workers on the eve of the 1873 depression. About 15 percent of the city's entire population worked in these industries. The invigorated and new textile mills recruited large numbers of women and children to their factories so that adult male workers in the Paterson manufacturing industries after the Civil War found jobs primarily as ironworkers and machine, tool, and locomotive makers.

Although the Paterson iron and machine industries have not yet found their historian, a quick glance suggests their importance to the city's development and even to the national economy. In the mid-1850s, Paterson had four locomotive factories: Rogers, Ketchum & Grosvenor (probably the second largest such factory in the country, outdistanced only by the Philadelphia Baldwin Locomotive Works); the New Jersey Locomotive and Machine Company; the Danforth Locomotive and Machine Works; and William Swinburne's Locomotive

Works. Swinburne's enterprise failed in 1857–58, but the three that survived had an annual capacity of 135 locomotives in 1859. Eighteen years later, their combined capacity had risen to 554, sixty-four more than the Baldwin Works. In 1837–38, Rogers, Ketchum & Grosvenor (renamed the Rogers Locomotive Works in 1858 after Rogers's death) completed its first five locomotives. In the great burst of railroad construction between 1869 and 1873, the factories filled orders for no less than 1,683 locomotives. Overall, between 1837 and 1879, Paterson locomotive workers built 5,167 locomotives and contributed much to the "transportation revolution."

The growth of the Paterson iron, tool, and machinery manufacturers may have been less spectacular than the locomotive manufacture but was just as substantial in different ways. Textile machinery and tools formed an important part of the local manufactured product. The market for Paterson firms after 1850 reached across the continent and even stretched around the globe. The J. C. Todd Machine Works (later Todd & Rafferty) marketed its hemp and twine machinery as far away as England and even in Russia, Latin America, and Asia in the late 1850s. After 1857, the Paterson Iron Works, which specialized in rolling large bars of iron, built heavy forgings used by transoceanic steamships and even sent iron shafts across the continent on order to the Pacific Mail Steamship Company. The Watson Manufacturing Company exported its millwright work and machinery to Mexico and South America, and gained wide attention for its turbine wheels and Corliss steam engines. The huge bevel wheels it constructed helped make the Higgins Carpet Factory one of New York City's great manufacturing establishments. The manufacture of structural iron later allowed the Watson firm to contract to build iron bridges in and near New York City, and its finished iron found place in the city's Museum of Natural History, Metropolitan Museum of Art, Equitable Building, and Lenox Library. In the 1870s and 1880s, the Passaic Rolling Mill also found important customers in the great metropolis nearby: the iron beams that built New York's first elevated trains came from it as did the iron for such projects as the Harlem River bridge, the New York *Post* building, and the massive Seventh Regiment Armory. Finished iron from the Passaic Rolling Mill also helped build the new state capitol in Albany, a widely acclaimed drawbridge over the Mississippi River at St. Paul, an elevated cable car in Hoboken, and the 1876 Centennial Exposition buildings in Philadelphia. These examples are cited merely to illustrate the importance of the Paterson locomotive, iron, and machine factories in the development of industry and transportation and in the building of Victorian American cities.

What were the social origins and career patterns of the men who founded and developed these particular firms between 1830 and 1880? These men or their firms persevered in the turbulent early decades of industrialization. In 1880, some of the pioneer manufacturers were dead, others at the height of their careers, and a few still relatively new to enterprise. Many had failed in comparison to the number that succeeded. Although the printed sources tell little about those who started unsuccessful manufacturing enterprises, there is no reason to think that most of them differed in social origin from their more favored contemporaries. For the group that succeeded, useful biographical information has been found for nearly all of them. What follows therefore is *not a sample* but a description of the social origins of the most successful Paterson iron, locomotive, and machinery manufacturers.[8]

8. Several sources supply the salient data, but the most important is L. R. Trumbull, *A History of Industrial Paterson, Being a Compendium of the Establishment, Growth, and Present Status in Paterson, N.J., of the Silk, Cotton, Flax, Locomotive, Iron and Miscellaneous Industries; Together with Outlines of State, County and Local History, Corporate Records, Biographical Sketches, Incidents of Manufacture, Interesting Facts and Valuable Statistics.* Published in Paterson in 1882, the Trumbull volume is just what its title suggests: an ill-digested but rich and invaluable collection of local firm histories interspersed with biographical accounts of early Paterson industrialists. Supplementary biographical information is found in Charles Shriner, *Paterson, New Jersey. Its Advantages for Manufacturing and Residence: Its Industries, Prominent Men, Banks, Schools, Churches, etc.,* Published Under the Auspices of the [Paterson] Board of Trade (Paterson, 1890); Edward B. Haines, ed., *Paterson, New Jersey,*

Scientific American, groping for a simple sociological generalization about these men, praised Paterson's early enterprisers in these words: "In the eastern States [New England], flourishing cites have been built up by corporations of wealthy capitalists. . . . In Paterson, it was different. With few exceptions, almost every manufacturer started, financially, at zero, enlarging his establishment as the quicksilver expanded in his purse." *Scientific American* was not guilty of mouthing abstract rhetoric or just putting forth a paean of traditional tribute to an invisible hero, the "self-made man." Instead, it accurately described the successful locomotive, iron, and machinery manufacturers of the era, and what it wrote applied as well to the group in 1840 and 1880 as in 1859.

One Paterson manufacturer started as a clerk. A second, the son of a farmer, made his way first in railroad construction before turning to iron manufacture. Two others had fathers who were manufacturers. George Van Riper took over a bobbin-pin factory in 1866 that had been started by his grandfather in 1795 as a small shop and then run by his father for thirty-five years. Patrick Maguinnis was the son of an Irish cotton manufacturer who left Dublin after the failure of revolutionary anti-British agitation and manufactured cotton and velveteen first in Baltimore and then in Hudson, New York.

But the social origin of these four manufacturers was not characteristic of the thirty-odd men studied. The typical successful Paterson manufacturer arrived in the city as a skilled ironworker or a skilled craftsman or as a young man who

---

1792–1892. [The] Centennial Edition of the Paterson Evening News (Paterson, 1892); William Nelson and Charles Shriner, *History of Paterson and Its Environs. The Silk City* (New York and Chicago, 1920). These books share a common weakness in celebrating uncritically the triumphs of local enterprise, but it is unwise to dismiss them as no more than primitive public relations works. Buried among adjectives of pious praise are rich morsels of data that tell much about these local "heroes" and their firms. Additional information has been culled from Paterson city directories published in 1859, 1871–72, and 1880–81, and from a detailed survey of Paterson manufactures that appeared in the first volume of *Scientific American* in 1859 under the dates October 29 and November 5, 12, and 19.

learned his skill by apprenticing in a Paterson machinery works. Individual proprietorship or co-partnership allowed him to escape from dependence and start his own firm. Only a small number of Paterson apprentices became manufacturers between 1830 and 1880, but most successful Paterson iron, machinery, and locomotive manufacturers started their careers as workers, apprenticed to learn a skill, and then opened small shops or factories of their own.

With only a few important exceptions, the men who were either Paterson-born or migrants to Paterson before 1830 played an insignificant role in the subsequent development of these industries. In 1825, the Rev. Dr. Samuel Fischer counted seventy-seven ironworkers in eleven blacksmith shops, two millwright shops, and a single iron foundry. Some repaired and built textile machinery. Trumbull lists at least ten machine shops that lasted only a few years. Biographical information is lacking for the men who started these faulted firms, but information is available for four men who pioneered in the development of the Paterson machinery and locomotive industries: John Clark, his son John Clark, Jr., Thomas Rogers, and Charles Danforth. Not one was native to the city. John Clark, Sr., settled there first. Born in Paisley, Scotland, the elder Clark, then aged twenty-one, migrated to Paterson in 1794 with his wife and two children to build machinery for the Society for Establishing Useful Manufactures. After the Society failed, Clark, first with his partner and then alone, used a portion of the idle mill to manufacture textile machinery. One son, John, Jr., followed in his footsteps, and in the early 1820s took two partners, Abram Godwin (a local resident, Godwin's father had served on George Washington's military staff) and Thomas Rogers. A hotel and store-keeper and the father of Parke Godwin, noted later as a journalist and as editor of the New York *Evening Post*, Abram Godwin supplied Clark with capital. Rogers's contribution was of another order.

Born in 1792 in Groton, Connecticut, and, according to Trumbull, descended from a Mayflower pilgrim, Thomas Rogers apprenticed himself at the age of sixteen to a Connecticut house carpenter. He settled in Paterson as a journeyman house carpenter and built several dwelling houses before a cotton-duck manufacturer hired him to construct wooden loom patterns. Soon Rogers was building wooden looms for John Clark, Sr. After the elder Clark retired, Rogers joined with Godwin and young Clark to expand the firm. The three partners bought an empty cotton mill, purchased a small foundry and a molding shop, and managed, for the first time in Paterson, a machine shop with all branches of the trade under "one roof." The partners prospered in the 1820s, but in 1831 Rogers left the firm to start his own machine works, the Jefferson Works, and to spin cotton yarn. Rogers's early triumphs as a machine builder attracted the attention of Morris Ketchum and Jasper Grosvenor, two New York City merchant capitalists and financiers active as railroad developers. A partnership was founded, called Rogers, Ketchum & Grosvenor. A house carpenter turned skilled machinist and then machine manufacturer thus had as business associates two men whom *Scientific American* called "men of abundant means and decided financial ability."

Charles Danforth replaced Rogers in the machine works of Clark and Godwin. The evidence concerning Danforth's background is unclear. Trumbull records that his father was a Norton, Massachusetts, "cotton manufacturer," but a more detailed biographical sketch in *The History of Bergen and Passaic Counties* notes that Danforth's father was "engaged in agricultural pursuits" and that in 1811, then fourteen, Danforth worked as a throstle-piercer before engaging as an ordinary seaman. After the War of 1812, he taught school near Rochester, New York, and in 1824 superintended a cotton carding room in a Matteawan, New York, factory. Hired to help set up a new cotton mill in Hohokus, New Jersey, he invented an improved spinning frame and settled in Paterson in 1828 to manufacture it as a partner with Godwin and Clark. Financial troubles in the late 1830s caused the dissolution of the partnership, and in 1840 Danforth bought out the entire machine-shop interest and in 1848 formed Charles Danforth and Company. His partner was John Edwards, his foreman. Born in England, Edwards moved to Paterson as a young man and worked in a hotel; he later apprenticed to John Clark and became his foreman, keeping the same supervisory position under Rogers and Danforth. Danforth so valued Edwards's abilities that he gave him a one-tenth interest in the firm.

The career of another workman, William Swinburne, illustrates this same mobility through the possession of technological skills. Born in Brooklyn in 1805, Swinburne first worked as a carpenter before moving to Matteawan as a machine patternmaker. Swinburne then came to Paterson to work as a patternmaker for Rogers and soon found himself draftsman, patternmaker, and superintendent of the new locomotive shops. Here he worked with Watts Cooke, Sr., from County Armagh, Ireland. By trade, Watts Cooke also was a carpenter. He migrated to Montreal in 1822, helped construct Notre Dame Cathedral there, moved to Albany, New York, stayed five years to learn the skill of patternmaking at an Albany furnace, worked for the Matteawan Machine Company, and settled finally in Paterson in 1839. When Swinburne took over the locomotive shops, he hired as his assistant one of Cooke's four sons—the seventeen-year-old John Cooke, an apprentice patternmaker.

In 1845, both Swinburne and young Cooke left Rogers, Ketchum & Grosvenor to become its competitors. Swinburne first joined former ironmolder Samuel Smith and cotton manufacturers Patrick Maguinnis and James Jackson to make textile machinery and cotton cloth, but the completion of the Erie Railroad's eastern division directed their attention to locomotives. In 1851–52, when it incorporated as the New Jersey Locomotive and Machine Company (later renamed the Grant Locomotive Works), Swinburne quit for unexplained reasons and started his own company, the Swinburne Locomotive Works. It was the first large Paterson manufacturer to depend entirely on steam power, and Swinburne soon employed between two and three hundred hands. He prospered until the 1857 depression caused severe financial difficulties that persuaded him to sell this plant to the Bank of New Jersey. Soon his factory was nothing more than an Erie Railroad repair shop.

John Cooke found more fortune than Swinburne. In 1852, Edwin Prall, Danforth's chief bookkeeper, urged his employer to add locomotive manufacturing to his enterprise and suggested John Cooke, then earning $1,800 a year as superintendent of the Rogers locomotive shops, as a partner. When the Danforth works was incorporated in 1865, Danforth, Cooke, and Prall became the principal stockholders. Prall's background differed from that of Cooke, Rogers, Swinburne, and even Danforth. He was born on Staten Island ("of good Knickerbocker-Moravian stock," noted Trumbull) and although orphaned as a child, grew up in a family immersed in entrepreneurial aspirations, surrounded by enterprising relatives. He worked first for a New York City cousin who imported drugs, then for an uncle who manufactured cotton in Haverstraw, New York, and finally for another uncle who was Danforth's bookkeeper. Prall took over when his uncle died.

John Cooke and his brothers, the sons of an immigrant patternmaker, assumed important roles in the Danforth locomotive shops. Brother William Cooke became chief draftsman, and Watts, Jr., joined the firm under unusual circumstances. Then nineteen years old, he was a bound apprentice to Thomas Rogers and was in Cincinnati installing three engines when John Cooke shifted from Rogers to Danforth. Rogers let him buy the "balance" of this time as an apprentice, and young Cooke became foreman of the Danforth locomotive erecting shops— aged nineteen. Two years later (1854), a customer, the Delaware, Lackawanna & Western Railroad, hired him as Master Mechanic, and Watts Cooke did not return to Paterson until 1868. Significantly, a fellow apprentice at Rogers, James Ayres, took Cooke's place as foreman of the Danforth locomotive erecting shops and held that position for nearly thirty years.

As a group, the developers of the Paterson locomotive industry, except for Ketchum and Grosvenor (and they lived in New York City), experienced enormous occupational mobility in their lives. In one generation—often in a few years—men jumped class lines and rose rapidly in prestige and status. One can argue about Danforth, but Prall had been an orphan and a clerk as a boy, and the others—Clark, Rogers, Swinburne, Watts Cooke, Sr., his sons William, John, and Watts, Jr.—had all started in life as skilled artisans and risen to become factory foremen or superintendents and owners of large, new manufacturing enterprises. The triumphs of these men were only part of the Paterson story. Their locomotive factories became workshops that trained machinists and other skilled ironworkers. Most did not stay within the firm. They struck out on their own as small manufacturers to be swept up and tested by the surge of industrial development after 1843. A few became manufacturers of great wealth; most succeeded in a more modest fashion. All were closely identified with the development of Paterson's iron and machinery and tool industries between 1843 and 1880—a process shaped by the efforts of self-made men entirely different in social origin from the archetypal members of Gregory and Neu's "industrial elite" in the 1870s. None came from professional, mercantile, or manufacturing backgrounds. Only one was born in New England, and almost all of them were British immigrants. These were not "princes" prepared by training and education to become "kings" of industry. Instead, they rose from the lower classes and achieved substantial material rewards in their lifetimes. For those of their contemporaries who sought "proof" about the promise of rags to riches, these men served as model, day-to-day evidence.

Paterson's two most successful machinery works were started by apprentice machinists, one who labored as a child in a cotton factory and the other who grew up on a farm and worked first as a carpenter. William Watson and Joseph Todd learned their machinist skills in the Paterson machine and locomotive shops. In 1844, Joseph Todd and a partner opened a small machine shop in the rear of a cotton mill, a common practice. They started with two lathes (one borrowed), and a few years later one Phillip Rafferty joined them. (The sources tell only that Rafferty was employed to build a blacksmith shop in an early textile mill in 1837.) Senior partner Joseph Todd was born on a New Jersey farm and at sixteen apprenticed as a carpenter to his uncle. Three years later, he left for New York City, and then went to Paterson to help construct a Methodist church. He stayed on to work at Godwin, Clark & Company and Rogers, Ketchum & Grosvenor as a machine patternmaker. His successful development of a hemp spinning machine led him, at twenty-seven, to start his own small machine shop. In 1860, the firm employed 135 workers, and a decade later as many as 350 hands. Its successes rested on the manufacture of the twine machinery, but it also made steam engines and boilers and later manufactured jute bagging.

William Watson was even more successful than Todd. Watson and his younger brother spent their childhood in Lancashire, England, and followed their father to Belleville, New Jersey. At the age of ten he helped his father in a print works. When the family moved to Paterson, the young Watson brothers labored in textile mills. Then William Watson apprenticed to a machinist, studied draftsmanship, and became a foreman. After a few years, Watson left Paterson, worked in a Newburgh mill, and helped run a New York City screw factory. In 1845, then twenty-six, he opened his own Paterson machine shop, employing ten men in millwrighting work, tool manufacture, and later in structural iron. The firm counted sixty employees in 1860 and no less than eleven hundred men and boys in 1873.

Few other manufacturers were as successful as Todd and Watson between 1840 and 1880, but the career patterns of eight lesser manufacturers and the seven machinists who formed a co-partnership called the Machinists' Association paralleled the paths followed by Todd and Watson. Examples from among them show a quite distinct pattern. Samuel Smith left Ireland as a youth and worked for a time for a Nova Scotia clergyman before settling with his family in Paterson and apprenticing as a molder at Rogers, Ketchum & Grosvenor. In later years, he and a co-partner started a foundry, opened a machine shop, and manufactured steam boilers.

Benjamin Buckley and a partner began manufacturing spindles and flyers for textile machinery in 1844. Born in Oldham,

England, in 1808, Buckley came to the United States in 1831, first worked in a Paterson cotton mill, then for Rogers and finally for Danforth. When he opened a small factory of his own he employed six hands. Buckley later failed as a cotton manufacturer, but his spindle works survived more than forty years. He employed twenty workers in 1859 and ran the enterprise with the help of his sons. Buckley also was president of the Passaic County National Bank in the early 1870s.

Three years after Buckley settled in Paterson, John Daggers arrived from Lancashire, England. Born in 1819, he apprenticed at the Rogers factory and then traveled south to construct cotton machinery in Alabama and Georgia. Later he returned to Paterson to manufacture bobbin pins. George Addy and Robert Atherton arrived in Paterson in the late 1840s. Addy, a third-generation Yorkshire blacksmith, borrowed passage fare to cross the Atlantic in 1849, worked two years for Danforth, then for Rogers, and in 1851 started manufacturing bolts and screws. Addy's firm expanded over the years, and in the 1880s made bolts and screws, smut machines, moving machines, and straw cutters. He also earned income from successful urban real estate investment. Robert Atherton did not rise as rapidly as Addy. Atherton grew up in Westchester County, New York, finished primary school there, moved to New York City, and settled in Paterson in 1848. He labored first in a cotton mill, apprenticed to a roller manufacturer and then to Buckley, failed in a partnership with Samuel Watson (William Watson's son), worked a number of years as a "general machinist," superintended a silk-machinery manufactory, and in 1878 started a machine works with his sons that soon occupied about seven thousand square feet in a cotton mill and employed nearly fifty workers in the manufacture of silk machinery.

Atherton's later success depended in good part on the development of the Paterson silk industry after the Civil War. So did the fortunes of some other Paterson machinists. Among the first to benefit were seven machinists (the *Scientific American* called them "practical mechanics"), most of them former Danforth employees, who formed the co-partnership in 1851 called the Machinists' Association. Nothing is known of them as individuals except that each contributed two hundred dollars to start the firm. By 1859, with most of their orders coming from southern textile mills, the firm was assessed at $25,000, clear of all obligations. The Machinists' Association shifted from the manufacture of general textile machinery to silk machinery and soon thereafter employed more than one hundred men. By 1876, its machinery had been bought by more than two hundred manufacturers.

When he started, Benjamin Eastwood had no partners. In 1872–73, with an investment of $1,500 and three employees, he began manufacturing silk machinery. Two years later he moved to larger quarters in the rear of a silk mill and hired ten or twelve workers. In 1878, he built his own mill, employed between fifty and sixty men, and was ready to become the city's major manufacturer of silk machinery. Eastwood's career illustrates extensive geographic and occupational mobility. Born in Lancashire, Eastwood benefitted from a "common school education" and training in a machine shop before his departure for the United States in 1863. He worked for a time in Paterson, then briefly in Milwaukee, and again in Paterson. A gold-mining venture in Mecklenberg County, North Carolina, took him south to build engines and machinery and to serve as a mine superintendent for two and a half years. The company failed, and Eastwood returned to Paterson to work again as a machinist. He started a small shop but left it to travel to Venezuela as a "mechanical engineer." Illness ("fever") sent him back to Paterson for the fourth time but only to spend a year in a locomotive shop. He then went to a New York City "experimental shop" that hoped to develop ways to use motive power more efficiently on canals. Eastwood remained in New York City for eighteen months. He returned to Paterson again, worked for a year in a sewing machine factory that soon left the city, and in 1872 or 1873, ten years after he arrived in the country and after having traveled to Milwaukee, North Carolina, Venezuela, and New York City, opened his small silk machinery factory.

Two other British-born machinists, John Royle and James Jackson, also manufactured textile machinery, but they started at it quite late in life. Royle was born in Chester, England, migrated to Paterson with his parents in 1830, worked in a cotton mill as a ten-year-old, and became an apprentice machinist. Illness forced an early retirement, but he later supervised the construction of turbine water wheels manufactured by Watson. He remained with Watson until 1860, rented a small machine shop that failed quickly, worked again for Watson manufacturing flax machinery for two years, left to wander through the West for a time seeking "opportunity," and finally returned to Paterson in 1863 and started manufacturing textile machinery "on a very limited scale." Royle developed a quality high-speed routing machine and other valued textile machinery, and the firm expanded rapidly after 1878. Jackson's career was somewhat different. Born in Caton, England, he was the son of a silk dresser and the grandson of a master carder. He did not migrate to the United States until he was forty. At thirteen, he apprenticed to a machinist, and at twenty-one he started a ten-year stint as master mechanic and superintendent of a Caton cotton mill; then he superintended another twelve years at an Oldham mill. Migrating to the United States in 1869, he spent several months in Philadelphia before settling in Paterson to work as a machinist at the Rogers Locomotive Works. In 1873 he started making Jacquard silk machinery. A year later, he expanded to a larger mill and, like Royle, took his sons into the manufacturing business.

Machine and tool shops owned by men like Eastwood, Royle, and Jackson depended on one or another branch of the textile industry for customers, but Paterson's two large ironworks resulted from sparks set off by the railroad boom after 1840. Neither the Paterson Iron Works nor the Passaic Rolling Mill Company was started by apprentices or artisans, but men who had begun their careers as workers soon controlled them. The Paterson Iron Works began in 1853 because of the efforts of two

New Hampshire capitalists, cotton manufacturers in the Granite State drawn to Paterson by the developing locomotive industry. They hoped to manufacture axles, tires, and shapes for locomotives and heavy engines. A year later, Franklin Beckwith, a railroad contractor, bought an interest in the firm, and by 1861 he had purchased the interest of the New Hampshire men and a local manufacturer. Beckwith dominated the firm until his death in 1875, when his sons took over the enterprise. Beckwith's career differed from those who ran successful machine shops. Born in Saratoga, New York, one of nine sons of a farmer, he worked on the family farm until age nineteen and received, at best, a common-school education. An older brother who had become chief engineer and contractor in building the Boston & Albany Railroad hired him as a foreman. Beckwith soon became a contractor himself. He settled in Troy, but in 1845 was drawn to Pennsylvania to try iron smelting. Five years later, he was principal contractor on the Delaware division of the Erie Railroad. When the Erie Railroad acquired the old Paterson & Hudson River road, Beckwith went to New Jersey to rebuild its track and its railroad bridges. Paterson attracted his attention, and this farmer turned railroad construction foreman and contractor became an iron manufacturer. In 1860, his firm employed forty workers and built seven thousand railroad tires and forgings for seventeen hundred locomotives.

Sherman Jaqua, one of the men from whom Beckwith purchased an interest in the Paterson Iron Works in 1861 for about $20,000, did not then rest quietly. Soon after, Jaqua received a charter for a new Paterson ironworks that would specialize in making rolled bar iron from scrap. Called the Idaho Iron Company, it failed, and Jaqua sold his machinery to a California company. In 1868, the Cooke brothers, spurred by Watts Cooke, Jr., who returned from Scranton and brought with him some investment capital supplied by the Delaware, Lackawanna & Western Railroad, purchased what remained of the Jaqua property, renamed the firm the Passaic Rolling Mill Company, and in three months turned out rolled iron bar. The firm specialized in making structural iron beams, angles, and teels, and shifted to bridge iron in 1876. William Cooke quit his brothers in 1873 to work in New York City, but W. O. Fayerweather purchased his interest. Watts Cooke, Jr., who had purchased his apprentice contract from Thomas Rogers in 1852, came back to Paterson sixteen years later as president of the Passaic Rolling Mill Company. W. O. Fayerweather, who had left Paterson as a young man to work as an errand boy in the great metropolis nearby, returned in 1873 as treasurer and partner of one of the Northeast's most important iron factories. Like Watts Cooke, Jr., Fayerweather had returned home. Both men traveled different routes, but they followed tracks that moved steadily upward.

Pertinent biographical information to complete this collective portrait is lacking for a number of other Paterson manufacturers of machinery, tools, and textile supplies. Similarly, the social origins of certain small manufacturers of wire hoop, copper and brass castings, files, and weaver's supplies are not recorded. Nevertheless, scattered evidence tells that some of these men and other small manufacturers had careers no different from the dominant pattern uncovered for most Paterson manufacturers. C. C. E. Van Alstine's unusual success resulted from his inventive genius. Van Alstine started as a machinist in Paterson in 1872, worked for a company for a year, took odd jobs repairing optical glasses and sewing machines, and finally invented a machine press that punched "the eye of a lingo" (an important weaving implement) and shaped its head at the same time. Van Alstine became a manufacturer and quickly improved his position. Starting in the mid-seventies with four workers, he employed between 175 and 200 in a few years. Other skilled workers and craftsmen began the trek upward in less spectacular ways. When James Walder started manufacturing reeds and heddles in 1866, he hired two men and rented factory floor space. He moved several times (always to rented premises) before purchasing a small building and enlarging it to a 20-by-200-foot plant. In the early 1880s, Walder was Paterson's most important reed and heddle manufacturer. Eight other firms followed Walder's path between 1855 and 1880, and the evidence suggests that all were started and developed by skilled workers who opened small shops as individuals or with a partner. Although the data about these men (Charles Moseley, Christian Kohlhaus, James Dunkerley, Robert Brooks, Robert Taylor, Robert McCullough, and Thomas Wrigley and his brother John) is slight, there is enough information to tell that all started as skilled workers, usually machinists, and rose to become manufacturers in a single generation.

Much remains to be written about the Paterson iron, locomotive, and machinery manufacturers who started in life as workers, and their social status, their political role (many held public office), and their labor policies cannot be briefly summarized.[9] What matters for purposes of this study is the fact that the rags-to-riches promise was not a mere myth in Paterson, New Jersey, between 1830 and 1880. So many successful manufacturers who had begun as workers walked the streets of that city then that it is not hard to believe that others less successful or just starting out on the lower rungs of the occupational mobility ladder could be convinced by personal knowledge that "hard work" resulted in spectacular material and social improvement. Thernstrom has argued convincingly that small improvements in material circumstances counted for much in explaining the social stability of Newburyport between 1850 and 1880. What role did the frequent examples of spectacular upward mobility in developing industrial Paterson play vis-à-vis its social structure? Whether the social origin of the Paterson manufacturers was typical of other manufacturers of that era cannot yet be known, but their career pattern was quite different from the one uncovered by other students of the nineteenth-century American "business elite."

9. Some evidence of the social and political role played by the Paterson manufacturers in the 1870s is found in H. G. Gutman, "Class, Status, and Community Power in Nineteenth-Century American Industrial Cities—Paterson, New Jersey: A Case Study," in Frederic C. Jaher, ed., *The Age of Industrialism in America: Essays in Social Structure and Cultural Values* (New York, 1968), 263–87.

Detailed research, however, has not yet been done on the manufacturers of other new industrial cities such as Buffalo, Pittsburgh, Cincinnati, and Chicago. Developing industrial cities and new manufacturing industries offered unusual opportunities to skilled craftsmen and mechanics in the early phases of American industrialization. Such was the case in Paterson, and surely such opportunities existed in other cities. Who took advantage of such opportunities, however, is still a subject for careful inquiry. The detailed examination of other local industrial "elites" will make it possible to learn whether the Paterson manufacturers were a mutant group or mere examples of a pattern of occupational mobility common to early industrializing America. Whatever the final findings, such community-oriented studies will shed unusually important light on one of the many dark corners of the mid-nineteenth-century American economic and social structure.

5

Class, Status, and Community Power in Nineteenth–Century American Industrial Cities

PATERSON, NEW JERSEY: A
CASE STUDY

Muᴄʜ ɪꜱ ᴋɴᴏᴡɴ about the early history of New England textile towns, but too much is inferred from this single source about the nineteenth-century American industrial city. Although little is known about the development of the industrial city, urban historians as well as labor and business historians have generalized much about it. Unwarranted assumptions about the social and economic structure of the early industrial city, however, have distorted significant patterns in its early development. Paterson, New Jersey, an industrial city that attracted the attention of men as diverse as Alexander Hamilton, William Haywood, and William Carlos Williams and that had as its official motto *Spe et labore* (With Hope and Labor), serves as a case study to test some of the generalizations and assumptions.

A version of this paper was read at the December 1964 meetings of the American Historical Association, Washington, D.C., and appeared in an abbreviated form as "Industrial Invasion of the Village Green," *Trans-action*, 3 (May/June, 1966), 19–24. The author expresses his gratitude to the Social Science Research Council and the State University of New York at Buffalo for research grants that made possible the gathering of much source material presented herein.

I

LITTLE IS KNOWN of the inner history of the nineteenth-century American industrial city. Historians have detoured around Paterson and other nineteenth-century industrial cities for many reasons. Perhaps the landscape seemed unattractive. Perhaps the roadways into and out of the city seemed simple and one-dimensional. Whatever the cause, specialists have built roadblocks that deny access to a rich and hitherto untapped social history. The urban historian apparently finds the large, complex metropolis a greater challenge and a more accessible source for information than the simpler, intensely specialized, and grim factory town. The labor historian learns quickly that industrial cities lacked permanent labor organizations, and since he is by tradition little more than the chronicler of trade-union history he just ignores the factory town. And the business historian, anxious to trace the detailed internal development of a particular firm or industry, all too often takes for granted its external relationships to the larger community. These attitudes, among others, have focused attention away from the industrial city as a legitimate subject for detailed and careful inquiry.[1]

Only two events in Paterson's history, for example, have attracted detailed attention: Alexander Hamilton's ill-fated effort to start "the Society for Establishing Useful Manufactures" in the 1790s and William Haywood's equally troubled effort to organize the immigrant silk workers into the Industrial Workers of the World, in 1913. No less than 120 years separates these two incidents—a period of time that sheds light on the transition

1. A pioneer study on this subject is Robert K. Lamb, "The Entrepreneur and the Community," in William Miller, ed., *Men in Business* (New York, 1952), 91–117. The examples drawn upon in Blake McKelvey's study *The Urbanization of America* (New Brunswick, N.J., 1963) show how little attention historians have given to the industrial city. Vera Shlakman's *An Economic History of a Factory Town* (Northampton, Mass., 1936) is the classic in the field but devotes little attention to the factory and the community at large. Any of the numerous labor histories can be consulted for any period of time to notice quickly how little attention labor historians have given to the industrial city.

from Hamilton to Haywood. But historians have not filled in the void between these two men in ways that make the transition meaningful. Instead, they have too often relied on crude and utterly misleading generalizations about the industrial city, its social order, and its power structure. Here one of these misleading generalizations, perhaps the most important, is subjected to close and critical examination: the widely held view that from the start, industrialists had the social and political power and prestige to match their economic force, and that they controlled the towns. This generalization has several corollaries: industrialists faced ineffective opposition; town politics reflected their interests; other property owners—particularly small businessmen and professionals—identified with industrialists and applauded their innovations and pecuniary successes. Factory workers enter this version of history only as passive, ineffective, and alienated victims, practically helpless before their all-powerful employers. Stated in another fashion, it is the proposition that from the beginning there existed a close relationship between economic class, social status, and power and that control over "things"—especially industrial property and machinery—was quickly and easily transformed into authority and legitimized so that industrialists could do little wrong and, better still, quoting Max Weber, "realize their own will in communal action even against the resistance of others who are participating in the action." [2] In place of this common view, another is argued. Through its early years, for at least a generation, the factory and its disciplines, the large impersonal corporation, and the propertyless wage-earners remained unusual and even alien elements in the industrial town. They disrupted tradition, competed against an established social structure and status hierarchy, and challenged traditional modes of thought. In these years, therefore, the factory owner symbolized innovation and a radical departure from an older way of life. His power was not yet legitimized and "taken for granted." Surely powerful be-

---

2. Max Weber, *Max Weber: Essays in Sociology*, trans. and ed. by H. H. Gerth and C. Wright Mills (New York, 1946), 180.

cause of his control over "things," the factory owner neverthe-less found it difficult to enforce noneconomic decisions essential to his economic welfare. He met with unexpected opposition from nonindustrial property owners, did not dominate the local political structure, and learned that the middle and professional classes did not automatically accept his leadership and idolize his achievements. Moreover, the new working class, not entirely detached from the larger community, had significant ties to that community which strengthened its power at critical moments and allowed it, despite the absence of strong permanent labor organizations, often to influence events at the expense of the factory owner.

Men hold authority in a particular setting, Robert M. MacIver has observed, when they possess "the established right to determine policies, to pronounce judgments on relevant issues, or, more broadly, to act as the leaders or guide to other men." [3] The industrial town was too new at the start for the industrialist to command this kind of prestige and to hold this kind of authority. Class position and social status were closely related. But as a new class, the industrialists had not yet achieved high social status. In fact, the absence of the kind of authority described by MacIver shaped much of the dramatic early history of the industrial city. The owners of disruptive and radical innovations—power-driven machinery, the factory, and the large corporation—sought to legitimize their economic power in these years. And Paterson is a good illustration of the frustrating search by the industrialist for status and unchal-lenged authority.

II

BY THE EARLY 1870S, Paterson ranked as a major American industrial city. Located fourteen miles from New York City, its factories manufactured mainly locomotives, machinery, iron

3. Robert M. MacIver, *The Web of Government* (New York, 1947), 83.

goods of all kinds, and silks and other textiles. Its three locomotive firms contained 25 percent of the nation's locomotive capacity. Paterson also stood as America's pre-eminent silk manufacturing center, and its separate jute, flax, and mosquito net mills were each the largest of their kind in the nation. With a few exceptions, most of the mills came to Paterson after 1850 so that their owners ranked as relative newcomers to the city twenty years later. Older Patersonians saw their small city change radically between 1850 and 1870.[4]

Before 1850 Paterson had grown fitfully. Early in the nineteenth century, small cotton factories started there to take advantage of available water power and the New York market and port nearby. Although the city had twenty cotton mills in 1832, inability to compete with more efficient New England firms caused them to stagnate in the 1840s and 1850s. According to its official industrial historian, as late as 1838 most New Yorkers regarded Paterson as "an upcountry hamlet, chiefly noted for its fine waterfall and valuable waterpower."[5]

But the cotton mills attracted machinists to repair and build textile machinery, and the start of the railroad era in the 1830s led one of them, aided by New York capital, to begin locomotive manufacturing in 1836. His pioneer factory grew slowly before 1850, as did a number of smaller machine and iron shops. The great increase in the demand for railroad equipment, iron, and machinery after 1850 stimulated the rapid growth of these industries. Two more locomotive factories opened, and between 1850 and 1873 the three together produced 4,437 locomotives and sold them over the entire nation. In 1873, 3,000 men worked in the locomotive shops. Other ironworks grew as quickly. Two

4. Data on the growth of Paterson's manufacturing industries comes from the 1850, 1860, and 1870 unpublished schedules for manufactures of the U.S. Census deposited in the New Jersey State Library, Trenton, New Jersey, and the following works: L. R. Trumbull, *A History of Industrial Paterson* (Paterson, 1882); Charles Shriner, *Paterson, New Jersey: Its Advantages for Manufacturing and Residences* (Paterson, 1892).

5. Details on the Paterson cotton industry are found in Trumbull, *op. cit.*, 50–69.

Lancashire millwrights, for example, started a machine works in 1845 with ten hands and employed 1,100 in 1873.[6]

The silk industry grew even more quickly and spectacularly than the iron and locomotive industries. The pattern was quite simple. A declining cotton industry made available water power, cheap mills, and a resident labor force. These first attracted English silk manufacturer John Ryle to Paterson in 1839, after a successful start as a New York silk importer. Small spinning and weaving shops began in the 1840s and 1850s. But the great stimulus came from outside the city in the 1860s, when New York and Boston silk and textile manufacturers and importers moved their mills to Paterson or built new ones there. A few examples suffice. A Coventry Englishman brought his silk mill from New York in 1860. In the next two years, the nation's leading importer of tailor trimmings left Boston for Paterson, as did another Bostonian, a pioneer American silk manufacturer. In 1868, one of New York's great silk importers became a Paterson manufacturer. From the start, these men of wealth constructed large mills and introduced power machinery, and other innovations. One imported a whole English factory. These men transformed the industry. In 1860 four silk mills employed 590 workers. In 1876, eight silk ribbon and six broad silk factories gave work to 8,000 persons, two-thirds of them women. One of every four silk workers was under sixteen years of age. Outside capital also financed other large textile mills in these years. A mosquito net factory came from New York, and Scottish money built the nation's largest jute mill. Eighty-one years after its founding in Northern Ireland, in 1865, Barbour Brothers opened a linen factory that quickly became one of Paterson's great mills. Smaller workshops continued, but by the 1870s the large mills dominated the local economy.[7]

6. The locomotive, machinery, and tool and iron industries of Paterson are described in detail in Trumbull, *op. cit.*, 72–148. But see also the *Annual Reports* of the Paterson Board of Trade (Paterson) that started to appear in 1873.

7. Especially useful information on the early development of the Paterson silk industry is in Trumbull, *op. cit.*, 149–57, 176–253; Shriner, *op. cit.*, 196–206; William Wycoff, "Report on the Silk Manufacturing Industry," *Tenth Census of*

Older Paterson residents in 1873 lived in a different city than they had known in 1850. The coming of the large mills, particularly from outside the city, transformed Paterson in many ways. The mill owners, a new industrial leadership mostly alien to the older city, represented a power unknown in earlier years. More than this, their factories drew in increasing numbers of immigrant and native workers and the city boomed. In 1846 Paterson had only 11,000 inhabitants. In the next twenty-four years, its population increased to 33,000. Immigrants made up more than a third of its residents. French and German skilled silk workers, but especially English skilled hands and an increasing number of unskilled Irish laborers, found work in the rapidly expanding factories. Built on two major industries, iron and textiles, the Paterson economy offered employment to whole families: the iron factories hired only men and textile mills relied mainly on female and child labor. Rapid growth in the 1850s and 1860s illustrated in Paterson all the severe social dislocations incident to quick industrialization and urbanization everywhere, but it also opened new opportunities for small retail businesses. Between 1859 and 1870, for example, the number of grocers rose from 105 to 230 and the number of saloonkeepers from 46 to 270. Paterson's industrial leaders in the early 1870s, mostly new to the city, had innovated boldly and caused a city to change radically in less than twenty years from one characterized by small workshops to one typified by large factories. Between 1873 and 1878 a severe depression temporarily halted this process.[8]

------

the United States, 1880. Statistics of Manufacture (Washington, D.C., 1883), 905-35; Victor S. Clark, History of Manufactures in the United States, 1860-1893 (New York, 1929), 2: 449-58. The reports of the New Jersey Bureau of Labor Statistics also are filled with much useful but scattered information on the silk manufacture. The 1878-1880 reports have been especially useful in this study.

8. Population data is found in Tenth Census, 1880, Statistics of the Population (Washington, D.C., 1883), 452, 671, 855-59. Information on retail enterprise comes from the 1859 and 1870 Paterson City Directory (Paterson).

III

IT IS SUFFICIENT TO REPORT briefly that this first of modern
industrial crises, 1873–1878, crippled the Paterson economy and
strained the city's total resources and all its citizens. "Among all
classes," it was noted as early as October 31, 1873, "there is a
feeling of gloom and intense anxiety in regard to the future."
Nearly three years later, a silk worker reported with good reason
that "Paterson is in a deplorable condition." The unemployed
regularly overtaxed limited public and private charities and
occasionally paraded the streets demanding public works. The
locomotive workers especially felt the diminished demand for
labor. From 1871 to 1873 the three locomotive factories
produced 1,185 engines; in 1875, 1876, and 1877 the figure
totalled only 195. The 1873 wage bill for 3,172 locomotive
workers came to $1,850,000; four years later (1877) the same
firms paid 325 workers only $165,000. The silk and other textile
workers apparently suffered less unemployment, but recurrent
wage cuts between 1873 and 1877 ranged from 10 to 30 percent
and meant exceedingly hard times for nearly 10,000 textile
workers. Sporadic silk strikes, particularly in 1876, illustrated the
workers' reactions to these deplorable conditions. Despair
permeated the city. Its population fell almost 10 percent
between 1875 and 1878. With good reason, a New York *Sun*
reporter in September 1876 called Paterson an industrial ghost
town comparable to a Southern city after Lee's surrender.[9]

In analyzing the consequences of the 1873–1878 depression,
historians have argued that the hardship resulting from extensive
unemployment and lowered wages shattered labor organizations
and immeasurably strengthened employers. But this exclusively
economic interpretation ignores the fact that the same cyclical

9. The severity of the depression in Paterson is described in Chicago *Times*,
October 31, 1873; New York *Sun*, September 3, 1876; *The Socialist* (N.Y.), April
29, 1876; Chicago *Tribune*, August 4, 1877; New York *World*, February 23,
1877; Paterson Board of Trade, *Annual Report, 1877* (Paterson, 1878), 13–17 and
Annual Report, 1880 (Paterson, 1881), 18–19; L. R. Trumbull, *op. cit.,* 147–48.

crisis, coming after two decades of radical economic and social change, also tested the status and power of Paterson's new industrialists and workers within the community. The depression created grave economic difficulties for the entire population, and, in trying to solve certain of their problems, the Paterson industrialists sought support and sanction at critical moments from the local community and its leaders. Their successes, but more importantly their failures, revealed much about their status and power in the city, measured the stability and legitimacy of the new industrial order, and gauged the attitudes of shopkeepers and merchants, professionals, politicians, and other prestigious persons in the precorporate city toward the new order and its leaders.

Four incidents between 1877 and 1880 involving Paterson's "public"—two textile strikes and two libel suits against a socialist newspaper editor—will be examined briefly in order to explore the early relationship between economic class, social status, and power.

IV

THE FIRST INCIDENT illustrated the inability of the new large manufacturers to commit the city government to their interests. It occurred between June and August 1877 and was an unprecedented general strike of ribbon weavers, mostly English, French, and German immigrants, against the biggest silk manufacturers. They protested a 20 percent wage cut and an irksome labor contract and demanded a 10 percent wage increase and a board of arbitration modeled on English and French precedent. At its peak, the strike—the greatest in Paterson to that time—idled 2,000 workers and closed the mills. After ten weeks, a compromise including restoration of the wage cut took place. What allowed the workers to effect this compromise in the absence of permanent labor organization and after forty-four months of depression? Why did the silk manufacturers fail? In part, the staying power of the weavers frustrated the manufacturers, but even more serious obstacles denied them success.[10]

Important and powerful groups in the community refused to sanction and support the mill owners. Nonstrikers and elected city officials either supported the strikers or, more significantly, rejected pressure and commands from the mill owners. Small shopkeepers extended credit and subscribed relief funds to the strikers. A weekly German-language newspaper also supported them. Although critical of the strikers, the two daily newspapers did not cheer the manufacturers and they even lectured the mill owners to "put conscience as well as capital" into their enterprises. The local courts displayed their independence of the manufacturers and on several occasions weavers charged with disorderly conduct went free or suffered, at best, nominal fines. After manufacturer William Strange successfully prosecuted two weavers for violating written contracts, pressure from city officials, including the mayor, convinced a local judge to postpone indefinitely forty additional trials.[11]

The Republican mayor, Benjamin Buckley, and the Democratic-controlled Board of Aldermen gave the manufacturers their greatest trouble. The aldermen were mostly self-made men: skilled workmen of independent means and retail shopkeepers. Their number included neither factory workers nor manufacturers. Mayor Buckley personified the precorporate American dream. Born in England in 1808, he had come to Paterson as a young man, worked first in a cotton factory, and then achieved wealth and high status. By 1877, he owned a small spindle factory, headed a local bank, and looked back on a successful

10. Background information on the 1877 ribbon weavers' strike is found in *Labor Standard* (N.Y.), January 20–June 16, 1877; *The New York Times*, May 15, June 20–23, 1877; Paterson *Guardian*, June 11, 19, 21, 25, July 10, 14, 1877; Paterson *Weekly Press*, June 21, 1877; Silk Association of America, *Sixth Annual Report, 1878* (New York, 1878), 15–17.

11. Pertinent editorial comment is in Paterson *Guardian*, June 21, 25, July 10, 14, 25, 30, 1877, and Paterson *Press*, July 5, 11, 12, 21, 1877. Full details on court action against the strikers and the postponement of trials is in Paterson *Guardian*, July 14, 17, 21, 25, 26, 27, 28, 31, 1877; Paterson *Press*, July 14, 16, 20, 1877; Chicago *Tribune*, August 4, 1877.

career in Republican politics including several terms in the state legislature and the presidency of the state senate. He started the first of his several terms as Paterson's Republican mayor in 1875. Because he viewed his role as maintaining the public peace and little more, Buckley infuriated the silk manufacturers. During the dispute, he used his powers, especially the small police force, with great skill and tact to suppress overt disorders only. This angered the mill owners. They insisted that inadequate civic authority allowed a few agitators to intimidate hundreds of loyal workers. In the strike's seventh week, therefore, the Paterson Board of Trade, dominated by the largest silk and iron manufacturers, called a special meeting to pressure the city authorities to enlarge the police force and also to declare a state of emergency limiting the strikers' use of the streets and their freedom of action. The Board publicly charged that "the laws of the land are treated with contempt and trampled upon by a despotic mob" led by immigrant radicals and "communists." A silk manufacturer warned that unless the authorities put down these troublemakers Paterson soon would be "a city without manufactories . . . with nothing . . . but the insignificant industries of an unimportant town." Other manufacturers expressed even graver anxieties: one urged that strike leaders be "taken out and shot" and another offered to finance a private militia. Iron manufacturer Watts Cooke admitted their deepest fear—the absence of sufficient status and respect in the city. "All the classes of the community," Cooke lamented, "are coming to lean towards and sympathize with the men rather than the employers." He and the others demanded the protection of the city authorities.[12] But Mayor Buckley and the Board of Aldermen turned a deaf ear toward the complaints and demands of the large manufacturers. Buckley did not issue a proclamation,

12. Biographical information on Benjamin Buckley is in E. H. Haines, ed., *Paterson, New Jersey, 1792–1892. Centennial Edition of the Evening News* (Paterson, 1892), 63; the composition of the Paterson Board of Trade is detailed in its *Third Annual Report, 1876* (Paterson, 1877), 88–90; the role of the Board of Trade is described in Paterson *Guardian*, July 31, August 1, 2, 3, 4, 1877; Paterson *Press*, July 31, August 1, 2, 1877.

defended his use of civic authority, and advised the aldermen that the Board of Trade did "great injury to the credit of the city." He especially commended "the good sense of the working people." The Democratic Board of Aldermen upheld the Republican mayor. It unanimously passed three resolutions: the first tabled without discussion the request for a larger police force; the second applauded Buckley's "wise and judicious course"; and the third, as if to reiterate the independence of the city government from the manufacturers, urged immediate prosecution of mill owners who violated local fire escape ordinances. The manufacturers were unable to alter public policies during the strike. City officials—all property owners—maintained an independence of judgment and explicitly rejected iron manufacturer Watts Cooke's insistence that the Board of Trade was "best able to judge what the city needed to protect it." [13]

After the strike, although the Paterson *Guardian* advised the Board of Trade to get into local politics and "pay the proper attention to the men . . . elected to the city council," the large manufacturers turned away from politics and to the private militia. The Board listened approvingly to a member who found "more virtue in one well drilled soldier than in ten policemen or in one bullet than in ten clubs in putting down a riot." Silk manufacturer Strange led the group that subscribed the first $4,500 for arms and equipment. And of the 120 militiamen signed up by January 1880 at least 50 percent were manufacturers, merchants, clerks, salespeople, and professionals. It proved easier to subscribe funds for a militia than to "reform" the city government. The manufacturers had more than enough wealth to finance a private militia but inadequate prestige and power to dominate the city government. In 1877, Paterson had one police officer for every 1,666 residents; ten years later, it had a militia

13. Buckley's response to the Board of Trade is in Paterson *Guardian*, July 28, August 2, 3, 4, 5, 1877; Paterson *Press*, August 7, 8, 15, 1877. The action of the aldermen is in Paterson *Guardian*, August 7, 8, 1877, and Paterson *Press*, August 7, 8, 1877. Biographical information about the aldermen is in the *Paterson City Directory*, 1871–1872, 1877–1878, 1880–1881, 1887–1888.

company but the ratio of police to population remained the same. The manufacturers' use of private power indicated weakness, not strength, vis-à-vis the body politic and the city government.[14]

V

A YEAR AFTER the ribbon weavers' strike, a second dispute involving textile workers again illustrated the limited power of the Paterson manufacturers. A third wage cut in less than a year convinced 550 unorganized workers, mostly women and children, to quit the textile mills owned by two brothers, Robert and Henry Adams. One of the East's great textile mills, R. & H. Adams and Company symbolized the rapid rise of the new industrialism in Paterson. It had moved a small factory there from New York City in 1857 and had thrived in the next twenty years, adding several large and efficient mills to its original plant. By far the largest of its kind in the country and perhaps in the world, the firm exported huge quantities of mosquito netting overseas, especially to Africa and Asia. Two more unequal adversaries than the unorganized Adams strikers and their employer hardly could be found. Yet, after a strike lasting nine months, the company conceded defeat in March 1879, and its senior partner, Robert Adams, who vigorously and publicly combatted the strikers, quit the firm and left Paterson.[15]

Once again, community attitudes toward the dispute shaped its outcome, and Robert Adams, not the striking women, had no allies in this battle. The Board of Trade kept silent. No one

14. Editorial comment on failure of the Board of Trade is in Paterson *Guardian*, August 16, 1877. Manufacturer talk about a city militia is found in Paterson *Press*, August 15, 1877, and the early history of the Paterson militia is detailed in John Hilton, "Paterson's Militia," in Shriner, *op. cit.*, 89–97. Failure by the manufacturers to enlarge the police force can be traced in the *Annual Reports of the City Government for* 1877, 1878, 1879, 1880, and 1886 (Paterson).

15. A detailed history of the R. & H. Adams firm is found in Trumbull, *op. cit.*, 208–12, and an obituary of Henry Adams appears in *American Silk Journal* (June 1890), 137–38.

publicly protested Adams's recurrent threat to move the mills. The press remained neutral. With one exception noted below, Adams got no overt encouragement from other manufacturers, retail businessmen, or politicians. He even had trouble with his foremen and had to fire a few who defended the strikers. Unlike Adams, the strikers found strength in the community. Many took jobs in other local textile mills. Strike funds gathered mainly from local workers, shopkeepers, and merchants fed the others. Concerts and picnics buoyed their spirits and added to their funds. At least one of every eight Patersonians signed a petition attacking Adams. Frequent street demonstrations indicated additional support. Soon after the trouble began, an outspoken Irish socialist, Joseph P. McDonnell, came to Paterson from nearby New York to encourage the strikers. He organized them into the International Labor Union, an industrial union for unskilled factory workers led by immigrant socialists and Yankee eight-hour reformers. McDonnell stayed on and soon started a socialist weekly newspaper, the Paterson *Labor Standard.* Although its masthead quoted Karl Marx and its columns heaped abuse on local mill owners and called Adams "Lucifer" and his mills "a penitentiary," its back pages contained numerous local business advertisements. Forty-five retail enterprises, mostly saloons, groceries, and clothing, dry-goods, and boot and shoe shops sustained the paper as it railed against manufacturer Adams.[16]

Adams's power against the workers was limited to his firm's income. He sent special agents to Fall River and other New England towns to recruit new workers. Adams hired many new hands but retained few because the strikers made full use of the streets. The strikers and their sympathizers, at one time as many

16. Much information on the strike and community attitudes toward it are found in *Labor Standard* (N.Y.), July 7, 14, 21, 28, August 4, 11, 18, 25, September 7, 14, 1878; Paterson *Guardian*, July 23, August 22, September 3, 5, 9, 14, 1878; Paterson *Press*, August 16, 17, 21, 22, 1878; *Irish World* (N.Y.), September 21, 1878. Early issues of the Paterson *Labor Standard* that illustrate support for McDonnell from retail storekeepers are dated November 23, December 7, 1878.

as 2,000 persons, met the new workers at the rail depot or in the streets, urged them to quit Adams, and even financed their way home. This tactic worked: the first time jeers, taunts, and ordinary discourse convinced twenty-two of twenty-five Fall River workers to leave immediately. Although the city authorities arrested a few workers when tempers flared, they quickly released them and made no effort to restrain strikers using the streets peacefully. By carefully separating "peaceful coercion" from "violence," the authorities effectively if unintentionally strengthened the strikers and Adams's wealth gained him no advantage. The freedom to use the streets to persuade outsiders from taking their jobs together with support from shopkeepers allowed the otherwise weak strikers to check Adams's power, thereby revealing his impotence and finally forcing him to surrender and to leave the city.[17]

VI

THE THIRD AND FOURTH EVENTS centered on Joseph McDonnell and his socialist newspaper, the *Labor Standard*. Dublin-born McDonnell had crowded much radical experience into his thirty-two years before coming to Paterson in 1878 to aid the Adams strikers. He had edited several Dublin and London Irish nationalist journals, engaged in Fenian "conspiracies," represented Ireland at the 1872 Hague Congress of the First International and sided with the Marxists, organized several huge London labor free-speech demonstrations, and served

17. The failure of the effort to bring in Fall River workers is found in Paterson *Guardian*, September 9, 10, 11, 12, 1878; Paterson *Press*, September 13, 1878; New York *Sun*, n.d., reprinted in *Labor Standard*, September 14, 21, 1878. The role of city officials and courts is in Paterson *Guardian*, August 14, September 9, 24, October 1, 1878; Paterson *Press*, October 1, 2, 3, 1878; *Labor Standard*, August 18, October 5, 1878. The end of the strike and the defeat of Adams can be traced in *Irish World* (N.Y.), September 28, October 5, 19, 1878; Paterson *Labor Standard*, November 23, December 7, 1878; Fall River *Labor Standard*, October 30, December 14, 1878; Paterson *Press*, October 27, November 22, 1878.

three prison terms before coming to the United States in January 1873. Soon after his arrival, McDonnell exposed steerage conditions in indignant letters, edited a New York socialist weekly, and traveled all over the East condemning capitalism, advocating socialism, and organizing weak socialist trade unions. According to traditional historical stereotypes, McDonnell should have been a pariah to all but a few Patersonians and therefore easy game for his opponents. But even though the Irish socialist had serious legal troubles and went to prison, he and his newspaper soon won acceptance as legitimate and useful critics of the new industrial order.[18]

McDonnell's difficulties began in October 1878, before the ink had dried on the *Labor Standard*'s first issue, and continued unabated for eighteen months. The formal complaint of a few loyal Adams workers whom the *Labor Standard* attacked as "scabs" convinced the county grand jury to indict McDonnell for libel. A petit jury found him guilty and a judge fined him $500 and court costs. A few months later, McDonnell apparently averted a second libel indictment. But in the fall of 1879, a second grand jury indictment did come, for McDonnell had printed a bitter letter by a young worker, Michael Menton, exposing inadequate working and living conditions in a Passaic River brickyard, where Menton had labored and become severely ill. In February 1880 a jury found McDonnell and

18. Details on McDonnell's career are found in obituaries reprinted in Paterson *Labor Standard*, January 20, 1906, and "Interview with Mrs. J. P. McDonnell, 1908," McDonnell Mss., Wisconsin State Historical Society. Useful background material on the London milieu from which McDonnell came to the United States is found in Royden Harrison, *Before the Socialists. Studies in Labour and Politics, 1861 to 1881* (London, 1965), 210–45. The Wisconsin Historical Society holds two manuscript lectures that McDonnell delivered in 1873–1875 and other useful information about his career before coming to Paterson is found in *The New York Times*, February 17, 1874, and August 8, 1877; *National Labor Tribune*, May 8, August 7, September 28, October 16, 23, 1875, and March 4, 1876; *The Socialist*, April 15, June 19, 1876; *Labor Standard*, August 12, November 11, 1876, January 27, August 4, 1877; New York *Commercial Advertiser*, n.d., reprinted in *Labor Standard*, August 19, 1876; Utica *Observer*, n.d., reprinted in *Labor Standard*, March 3, 1877.

Menton guilty of libel and a judge sent them to the Passaic County jail for three months. Viewed only in these narrow terms, McDonnell's difficulties prove to traditional labor historians only the repressive power of "capital" and the pliancy of the judiciary. Actually, McDonnell's difficulties strengthened him. If these legal troubles were intended to drive him from Paterson, the opposite resulted. Support from workers, mostly nonsocialists, and from other persons prominent in the community assured his survival.[19]

Although new to Paterson, McDonnell was not a complete outcast during his first trial. His lawyer, an old Patersonian, had grown wealthy as a real estate speculator, fathered the state's first ten-hour law and important banking reforms, organized the city's waterworks, and been a prominent Republican for twenty years before becoming Greenback candidate for New Jersey governor. Despite the county prosecutor's plea to convict McDonnell as a "woman libeler," a "threat" to established order, and a "foreign emissary" sent by English manufacturers to "breed discontent" in America, the jury, composed mostly of storekeepers and skilled workmen, remained deadlocked for three days and three nights. Only unusual pressure by the presiding judge finally brought conviction. The $500 fine, substantially less than the maximum $2,000 fine and two-year prison term, told much. A second judge in the case, himself originally a Lancashire worker and then the owner of a small bobbin pin factory, convinced the presiding judge to go easy on McDonnell. After the conviction, storekeepers and merchants contributed handsomely to McDonnell's "defense fund." [20]

19. The author possesses a microfilm copy of McDonnell's 1878 grand jury indictment; the original is in the Passaic County courthouse, Paterson, New Jersey. Detailed reports on his first trial appear in Paterson *Guardian*, Paterson *Press*, and Paterson *Labor Standard*, October 20–November 10, 1878. The same newspapers contain materials on the 1880 trial in issues published between January 1 and April 5, 1880.

20. A biographical sketch of McDonnell's lawyer, Thomas Hoxsey, appears in Shriner, *op. cit.,* 312. See also *Irish World*, November 3, 1877. Occupational information on the jury is found in *Paterson City Directory*, 1877–1878 and 1880–1881. John Daggers, the manufacturer and lay judge, who urged leniency

McDonnell's lower-class supporters made known their displeasure with the trial and used the threat of their potential political power. They crowded the courtroom to cheer McDonnell and after the conviction, raised the fine and court costs quickly and carried their hero through the streets. More important, the trial occurred during the bitter 1878 congressional election, and they humiliated the county prosecutor, a Democratic politician. Workers joined by sympathetic storekeepers crowded the annual Democratic election meeting and in a raucous demonstration refused to let it start until the prosecutor left the hall. The meeting ended quickly. McDonnell's supporters then jammed a second meeting and hundreds silently walked out when the prosecutor rose to speak. Politicians competing for labor votes got the point. A Republican argued that only free speech and a free press could preserve American liberty. Fearing the loss of labor votes, the Democrats publicly defended the right to strike and one Democrat declaimed: "Away with the government of the aristocracy! Away with legislators only from the wealthy classes! We have had enough of them!" A nearby newspaper sympathetic to McDonnell concluded: "In Paterson, he [McDonnell] is stronger than his accusers. Today he has the sympathy of the people, and his paper from this time forth is deeply rooted in Paterson." [21]

The second trial and subsequent imprisonment of McDonnell attracted national attention but only its local significance concerns us. The support McDonnell received this time revealed

in sentencing McDonnell, had the details of his life recorded in Shriner, *op. cit.,* 209–10, and McDonnell later wrote warmly about him in Paterson *Labor Standard*, November 27, 1897, and November 3, 1898. Details on the payment of McDonnell's fine are found in Henry Rose to the editor, Indianapolis *Times*, November 2, 1878; Paterson *Labor Standard*, n.d., reprinted in *The Socialist* (Chicago), November 23, 1878; Paterson *Guardian*, October 26, 1878; Paterson *Press*, October 26, 1878.

21. The political tumult that followed McDonnell's trial is fully described (but in a partisan fashion) in Paterson *Guardian*, October 27, 28, 29, 30, November 1, 4, 5, 1878; Paterson *Press*, October 27, November 2, 4, 5, 1878; Paterson *Labor Standard*, November 23, December 7, 1878; Passaic *City Herald*, n.d., reprinted in *The Socialist* (Chicago), November 23, 1878.

his growing local prestige and power. Except for the litigants, no one publicly attacked him. His competitor, the Democratic Paterson *Guardian*, found the verdict "to say the least, a great surprise to those who heard or read the testimony." The judge justified sending McDonnell to prison only because he feared that others again would pay a fine. This time, McDonnell's lawyers were the son of a former Democratic mayor and Socrates Tuttle, Paterson's most respected attorney, who had been Republican mayor some years before. Ably defending his client, Tuttle warned that a conviction would endanger the free press and mean that the working classes would "henceforth never be allowed to complain." Three Northern New Jersey nonlabor weeklies emphasized the same point. McDonnell's sympathizers were led by two former silk factory foremen, one German and the other English, and both now successful entrepreneurs. Two clergymen, one a Baptist and the other a Methodist (both active in Republican politics and Paterson's most popular clergymen) condemned McDonnell's treatment and counseled the socialist. Several aldermen, former aldermen, and county freeholders visited him in prison. Garrett A. Hobart, a Paterson corporation lawyer, president of the state senate and that year elected chairman of the Republican State Committee, sent McDonnell ten dollars for his defense, offered "to do his best" and sought to amend the state libel law. Even the son of Henry Adams and nephew of Robert Adams, McDonnell's 1878 adversary, gave the socialist twenty dollars and visited him in jail.[22]

McDonnell's jail experience, surely one of the most unusual in

22. McDonnell's prison diary is the most useful source for judging his support while in prison, and the manuscript copy is deposited in the Wisconsin State Historical Society. The names of his visitors have been checked to the *City Directory* for 1880–1881. Much additional information is found in Paterson *Labor Standard*, January 3, 24, 31, March 13, 20, 27, 1880; Paterson *Guardian*, January 30, 31, February 2, 3, 1880; Paterson *Press*, January 30, 31, February 2, 3, 1880; Fall River *Labor Standard*, February 28, 1880; *Irish World*, March 6, 13, 1880; *The Trades* (Philadelphia), March 13, 1880. Details on McDonnell's lawyer, former Republican Mayor Socrates Tuttle, appear in Shriner, *op. cit.*, 319–20.

American penal history, depended upon John Buckley, the former mayor's son. He had been a locomotive worker as a young man, a prominent Republican, and warden of the county prison. Apparently distressed over the conviction, Warden Buckley did his best to assure McDonnell's comfort and his freedom while in prison. McDonnell kept a prison diary, and its entries record many surprising amenities. The warden let him edit his newspaper and organize a national and local protest campaign against his imprisonment. McDonnell's supporters visited him daily and often brought their children along. Buckley allowed them to meet in his office. One day as many as twenty-one persons called on McDonnell. Every day his meals arrived from outside, and saloon- and boardinghouse-keepers kept him overstocked with cigars, wines, and liquors. Others brought fresh fruits, cakes, and puddings. On St. Patrick's Day shamrocks came, and on his birthday, two fancy dinners. The day of his release, Warden Buckley publicly commended the good behavior of prisoner Joseph P. McDonnell.[23]

Let out ten days early, McDonnell benefitted from a demonstration of popular support unprecedented in Paterson's history. Organized by a committee of seventy-five that was dominated by workers but included twelve saloon- and innkeepers and five grocers, the demonstration counted between 15,000 and 20,000 persons. After that, few Patersonians doubted the labor agitator's place and power in their city. McDonnell's *Labor Standard* survived until his death in 1908. He founded the New Jersey Federation of Trades and Labor Unions and pioneered in pushing protective labor legislation. Several clues indicate his rapid acceptance as a radical critic. Soon after his imprisonment, the Democratic prosecutor who had called him a "woman libeler" and a "foreign emissary" sent by British manufacturers began advertising his legal services in the *Labor Standard*. The city government regularly bought space to print legal public

---

23. Here, again, McDonnell's prison diary offers the most evidence on his jail experiences. But see also the biographical sketch of Warden John Buckley in Haines, ed., *op. cit.,* 146.

notices. In 1884, less than six years after he had come to Paterson and four years after his release from jail, socialist McDonnell was appointed New Jersey's first deputy inspector of factories and workshops.[24]

McDonnell never lost feeling for those who helped in the early days. In 1896, although the *Labor Standard* still carried Karl Marx's words on its masthead, McDonnell printed kind words about Garrett Hobart, then running with William McKinley against William Jennings Bryan. He called Hobart "a rare specimen of manhood in the class in which he moves" and, remembering Hobart's aid in 1880, concluded that "to know him is to like him whether you agree with his opinions or not." [25]

VII

WHAT GENERAL MEANING can be inferred from these Paterson events? If they are unique to that city, then only the local historian profits from them. In fact, they typified obstacles encountered by industrialists in other post-Civil War industrial towns and cities during crises similar to the 1877 and 1878 Paterson textile disputes. Time and again, the industrialist found his freedom of action confined by particular local "circumstances." Several examples illustrate his difficulties. A Western Pennsylvania jury convicted a mine operator when violence resulted after he brought Italians there. The merchant mayor of an Illinois mining town disarmed Chicago Pinkerton police sent to guard an operator's properties. A sheriff raised a posse to chase special New York police sent to protect railroad repair shops in Eastern Pennsylvania. Ohio Valley newspapers con-

24. McDonnell's release from prison and the celebration that followed are detailed in his manuscript diary, *Irish World*, April 17, 1880; Paterson *Press*, April 2, 1880; and Fall River *Labor Standard*, April 10, 1880. McDonnell's role in the New Jersey Federation of Trades and Labor Unions is detailed in its annual reports, and his work as deputy factory inspector is noted in the *Annual Reports* of the factory inspector that appeared between 1884 and 1886.

25. Paterson *Labor Standard*, October 31, 1896.

demned iron manufacturers for arming strikebreakers. Northern Pennsylvania merchants housed striking evicted coal miners. A pronounced pattern emerges from these and similar events.[26] Unorganized or poorly organized workers displayed surprising strength and staying power and found sympathy from other groups in the community. Local political officials often rejected or modified the pressures of industrialists. Nonindustrial capitalists—persons with power and prestige locally and persons committed to competitive private enterprise and the acquisitive spirit in their own dealings—responded equivocally or critically to the practices of the new industrialists. Such behavior is quite different from that usually characterized as typical of early industrial America. And yet it occurred frequently in the first decades of the industrial city. How can this pattern of behavior be explained?

Unless two misleading and erroneous conceptions are disregarded, this pattern of response seems anomalous and even meaningless. The first is the idea that the industrialist achieved status and legitimized his power quickly and easily in his local community. The second is the belief that urban property owners as a group shared a common ideology in responding to the severe dislocations resulting from rapid industrialization and in reacting to the frequent disputes between workers and factory owners. Because Congress gave huge land grants to railroads, and state governors frequently supplied militia to "settle" industrial disputes, it does not follow that the industrialists in Paterson and other cities so dominated the local political and social structure that their freedom of action remained unchecked. Because a grocer owned his business and a mayor presided over a bank, it does not mean they sympathized with

26. Herbert G. Gutman, "The Buena Vista Affair," *The Pennsylvania Magazine of History and Biography*, 88 (July 1964), 251–93; "The Workers' Search for Power," in H. Wayne Morgan, ed., *The Gilded Age; A Reappraisal* (Syracuse, N.Y., 1963), 38–68; "The Braidwood Lockout of 1874," Illinois State Historical Society, *Journal*, 53 (1960), 5–28; "An Iron Workers' Strike in the Ohio Valley," *The Ohio Historical Quarterly*, 58 (1959), 353–70; "Trouble on the Railroads in 1873–1874," *Labor History*, 2 (1961), 215–35.

the social policies of a large factory owner. Because Andrew
Carnegie applauded Herbert Spencer, it does not mean that
jungle ethics reigned supreme in the industrial city. If we are free
of these distorting generalizations, it is possible to look afresh at
social behavior and conflict in Gilded Age America. Take the
example of the use of state troops in industrial disputes. Such
action may have resulted from the low status and power the
industrialist had in his local community. Unable to gain support
from locally elected officials and law enforcement groups and
unable to exercise coercive power in the community, he reached
upward to the state level, where direct local pressures were felt
less strongly. If, as E. D. Baltzell writes, "power which is not
legitimized tends to be either coercive or manipulative," much is
explained by the low status of the new industrialists. Careful
examination of particular local industrial conflicts that involved
the use of state as opposed to local police might help explain the
widespread violence and corruption so often condemned by
Gilded Age historians and yet so little understood.

In nineteenth-century America, power and status had meaning on several levels of society. Here the focus is a particular
community. If the industrialist is viewed as an innovator in a
local context, the Paterson events take on broader meaning. The
new industrialist—especially if he came from elsewhere—was a
disruptive outsider. He did not create an entirely new social
structure, but he confronted an existing one. He found a more or
less static city, which thrived on small and personal workshops
and an intimate and personal way of life. It was hardly ideal, but
it was settled and familiar. Making goods and employing people
differently, the industrialist abruptly disrupted this "traditional"
way of work and life and, as a person, symbolized severe local
dislocations. The older residents and the newer workers responded to these changes in many ways. But if the industrialist,
in cutting costs and rationalizing production, violated traditional community norms or made unusually new demands upon
the citizenry—such as the special use of a police force or the
suppression of a newspaper—his decision often provoked opposition.

The size of the industrial city and the particular composition of its population made the industrialist's innovations more visible and his power more vulnerable there than in the larger complex metropolis. Residents of the early factory town had a more direct relationship with one another and with the innovations. Even persons indirectly affected by industrialism could hardly avoid close contact with the large factory, the corporation, and the propertyless wage-earners. The closeness of the middle class and the old resident population to the new industrialism gave such persons the opportunity to judge the industrial city's social dislocations and social conflicts by personal experience, and not simply through the opaque filter of ideologies such as laissez-faire liberalism and Darwinism. In addition, the worker had more power as a consumer and as a voter and could express particular needs more effectively in the factory town than in the metropolis. Street demonstrations had a greater impact in Paterson than in New York or Chicago. In the industrial city, the retail merchant depended heavily on a narrow class of consumers (mostly workers) and the politicians appealed to more homogeneous voting groups. All of these considerations contributed to the industrialists' difficulties. So, too, did the rapid growth of the mill town itself weaken their chances for civic and police control. A number of studies of the mobility patterns of Paterson men (three thousand fathers and sons between 1870 and 1890) show that the more ambitious and able workers found expanding opportunities outside the factories in small retail business, politics, and city employment (including the police force)—the very areas in which the industrialists demanded cooperation or control.[27] Conservative

27. Drawing from all fathers and sons in three wards as listed in the unpublished 1870 manuscript census, this study traces occupational mobility over a twenty-year period. Males listed in the 1870 census are searched for in the *Paterson City Directory 1887–1888*. Comparisons in the occupation of the father over this period as well as between the fathers and the sons are made. More than 30 percent of the males listed in 1870 census have been traced and located in the later directory. Careful comparison of the *Paterson City Directory* between 1865 and 1885 makes it possible to trace the social origins of Paterson policemen,

in many ways, these men had a stake in the new society. Some identified entirely with their new class and repressed their origins. But others—a large number in the early years—still had memories and roots and relatives among the workers. Some had even suffered from the same employers they were now called on to protect. In crisis situations such as those that occurred in the 1870s, their social origins and older community ties may have created a conflict between their fellow-feeling and even family sentiment and their material achievements. The evidence does not make explicit such conflict, but it makes clear that during strikes and other crises the industrialists could not expect and did not get unswerving loyalty or approval from them.

VIII

HISTORIANS HAVE NOT EMPHASIZED SUFFICIENTLY the subtle and complex patterns of response to social change in nineteenth-century America—particularly to the coming of industrial capitalism. Much has been omitted in these pages: no judgment is passed on working conditions or standards of comfort in the industrial city; nothing is said of the important but little-studied working-class subculture that thrived in the industrial city, and no attempt is made to measure precisely the strength of the opposing forces of workers and industrialists. The conclusions stated here are that economic power was not easily translated into social and political power, and that the changes resulting from rapid industrialization stimulated sufficient opposition to the industrialist to deprive him of the status and the authority he sought and needed. The theme in this essay illustrates Dorothy George's (*England in Transition*, 1953) view that "social history is local history" but local history in a larger context that permits

---

politicians, and small businessmen. In 1877-78, for example, the city had twenty patrolmen. Eight had been policemen in 1870. Six others had been workers in 1870. In 1877-78, at least five policemen, all different from the six who had been workers in 1870, had close female and male relatives who worked in the Paterson factories. Similar patterns occur for small retail businessmen.

the careful examination of grand and sweeping hypotheses. It is finally suggested, indirectly, that knowledge of the early history of American industrialization and urban growth tells much about modern society and the contemporary city: its social structure, its power relationships, and its decision-making process. The nineteenth-century city differed from its twentieth-century counterpart; so much of what "makes" a city has changed in the past seventy years. In *Victorian Cities* (1963), Asa Briggs wisely argued for historical specificity and interdisciplinary approaches to the study of nineteenth-century cities. Free of the nostalgia of those historians who compare the "city" only to the "country" but sensitive to the acute social disorganization that accompanied rapid industrialization and urban development, Briggs showed that different British cities each had a distinct history (shaped by particular inner social patterns) and also that their histories should not be confused with the later city so powerfully affected by radical innovations such as the automobile, the national corporation, and the revolution in communications. All too often, however, social scientists and even historians view the contemporary city in exceedingly ahistorical terms or only study its past by projecting present "trends" backward. For them, as Barrington Moore notes, the past becomes "merely a storehouse of samples," and "facts" are "drawn upon as if they were colored balls from an urn." Stephan Thernstrom's pioneering study of nineteenth-century Newburyport, Massachusetts, *Poverty and Progress* (1964), splendidly illustrates the grave pitfalls of an ahistorical view of urban social mobility. It further shows that however carefully the present is studied and however refined the techniques of analysis, the present is not fully comprehended if the past is ignored or distorted.

Class and status altered as the industrial city matured. The industrialist's power became legitimized. The factories and their owners dug deeper into the lives of the mill towns and became more accepted and powerful. The old middle class, and those who revered the old, precorporate town, lost influence and disappeared. They were replaced by others who identified more fully with the corporate community. The city government became more bureaucratic and less responsive to popular pressures. Why and how these changes occurred remain important subjects for study. But in order to grasp the magnitude of these changes it is necessary to discard the notion that the nineteenth-century factory owners moved into control of the industrial town overnight. This myth masks reality and prevents us from focusing on the differences between the nineteenth-century city and the contemporary city. If these differences are located and analyzed, "trends" no longer seem timeless, and the "modern condition"—so often tied to the "urban condition"—assumes a meaningful historical dimension because it is rooted in an understandable past.

5a

A Brief Postscript

CLASS, STATUS, AND THE
GILDED AGE RADICAL: A RECONSIDERATION

IF THE STATUS of the Gilded Age industrialist in factory towns differed greatly from that emphasized by conventional historians married to a crude economic model of social behavior, it is not surprising that the status of labor radicals and trade unionists also differed from that stressed in conventional studies. The career of the Irish-American labor editor Joseph P. McDonnell illustrates the importance of putting aside that conventional approach. McDonnell spent his adult years in Paterson, New Jersey, and experienced many of the same social and economic crises as the silk mill owners discussed in the last essay. I have extracted portions of another previously published essay below in order to illustrate how a different view of Gilded Age America puts McDonnell in a more accurate perspective and, more importantly, suggests new ways of seeing how the so-called "welfare state" had its origins in the discontent organized by men like McDonnell rather than in the pressures mounted by middle- and upper-class critics of industrial capitalism.

This essay considers a single individual in order to assess his career but more important to re-examine certain general views of the Gilded Age American radical and of the Gilded Age itself. An Irish immigrant, Joseph Patrick McDonnell was a socialist, a trade-union organizer, a lobbyist for protective and reform legislation, and a New Jersey newspaper editor. Orthodox labor history relates these facts and little more. Standard historical works of a broader sort entirely ignore men like McDonnell. Yet he was a figure of some importance between 1873 and 1893 and typified an entire generation of Gilded Age labor radicals. Men like McDonnell played dominant roles in the labor and radical movements of that time. They were harsh critics of the emerging industrial society. They pioneered in early legislative efforts to humanize a changing and an insensitive social order.

These are significant facts. Why, then, is so little known about radical and working-class leaders like J. P. McDonnell? Re-creating the past is an ongoing and a selective process. But the principles that guide such selection are not objective and are often shaped by a particular overview (a general interpretation) of a past era. The dominant view of Gilded Age America allows little room for radicals like McDonnell and much else of importance. At best, such men are counted as nagging and ineffective reminders that conscience and moral purpose did not entirely wilt in that American Dark Age. At worst, such men exist beyond the fringe or simply are forgotten by a collective memory cramped by certain crude and misleading stereotypes that give conceptual shape to the Gilded Age. Men like McDonnell are misunderstood, minimized, or entirely neglected. Their role as critic escapes the historian. Their successes and failures confuse the historian. The Gilded Age radical lives outside the mainstream of his times. Even his own historians emphasize this fact and often study the radical and his movements as little more than exercises in exposure. Historians of the working class accept this larger view, too, and their writing records mainly bitter industrial conflicts as well as the tiresome inner struggles between working-class leaders over principles of organization as well as strategy and tactics. Together with the more general historians, they concede that the age belonged to Andrew Carnegie. Disaffected workers, moralists like Henry George, Edward Bellamy, and Henry Demarest Lloyd, agrarians like the Populists, and scattered mugwump intellectuals were eloquent but powerless censors. Displaced craftsmen, rural folk, and utopian intellectuals, they were overwhelmed by a national ethos that thrived on an ugly materialism, deified the dollar, and worshipped in the marketplace. There is some truth in this perspective, and much has been learned from it. But it is defective in essential ways.

In examining McDonnell's role and influence, we do more than just study a single man. We reconsider the status of the Gilded Age radical and the character of the Gilded Age itself. The reason is important: careful assessment of his radical efforts challenges some of the comfortable clichés about the Gilded Age that saturate our historiography and obscure our past.

I

WE FIRST CONSIDER the dominant view of the Gilded Age more closely. Historians correctly emphasize indisputably significant themes such as industrialization, urbanization, and immigration and see the post-Civil War decades as a time (in Sigmund Diamond's words) when the "nation" was "transformed." Certain widely held assumptions affect their treatment of these themes and should be summarized (perhaps too simply, but this is a short paper). Industrialism was still new to most Gilded Age Americans—new as a way of work and new as a way of life. Its norms were not yet internalized, institutionalized, or legitimized. Yet the Gilded Age is described as a time when industrialization generated new kinds of economic power which, in turn, immediately altered the older social and political structure. Much follows from this flawed assumption. In another connection, I have summarized some of its implications. Studying Gilded Age social conflict as reported by most historians is to learn

> that the worker was isolated from the rest of society; that the employer had an easy time and relatively free hand in imposing [new] disciplines; that the spirit of the times, the ethic of the Gilded Age, worked to the advantage of the owner of industrial property; that workers found little if any sympathy from nonworkers; that the quest for wealth obliterated nonpecuniary values; and that industrialists swept aside countless obstacles with great ease. The usual picture of these years portrays the absolute power of the employer over his workers and emphasizes his ability to manipulate a sympathetic public opinion as well as various political, legal, and social institutions to his advantage.

No one has expressed this view more cogently than Louis Hacker. Writing in 1966, he insisted:

> The end of the Civil War . . . cleared the way for the triumph of American industrial capitalism. . . . Far from being sharply critical of the capitalist processes of private accumulation, investment, and decision-making, Americans, *almost to a man*, veered to the opposite position; what before had been rejection now became assent. This new climate produced new institutions (values and attitudes) to support

and strengthen industrial capitalism; in the law-text writers . . . ; in the writers of economy texts; . . . in the
acceptance by the clergy of a market economy with its
unequal distributive shares; in the programs and formula-
tions of the labor organizations. *Americans, almost univer-
sally, during 1865–1900, when industrial capitalism made its
swiftest progress in the United States, looked upon a market
economy founded on the rules of laissez-faire . . . as the
normal, more the right, way of life.* [Italics added.]

So bold a statement exaggerates what others often accept in
more quiet and subtle ways. J. P. McDonnell's career allows us
to examine this view.

I I

WHEN JOSEPH MCDONNELL crossed the Atlantic in December
1872 to settle permanently in the Great Republic of the West
(first in New York City and then in Paterson, New Jersey), he
already was a radical. Then just twenty-five years old, he carried
unusual baggage with him. Four arrests and three prison terms
suggest that he was not typical of the immigrant millions
pouring into post-Civil War America. Militant Irish nationalism
and socialism had shaped his formative years. Never a worker,
he was born to a middle-class Dublin family in 1847, attended
Dublin's schools and its university, and prepared for the
priesthood. Irish nationalism ended his formal education. He
refused to take the Maynooth Oath, joined the National
Brotherhood (the Fenians), helped edit Irish nationalist newspapers, and soon spent ten months in Dublin's Mount Joy Prison.
Just twenty-one, he quit Ireland in 1868 to live in London for
five years. Lectures and impressive public demonstrations that
he organized urged amnesty for Irish political prisoners and
independence for Ireland. In 1869, to cite one example, he led
several thousand persons in a July 4 march from London to
Gravesend. They carried Irish and American flags. London
street demonstrations twice resulted in his arrest.

More than the cause of Ireland attracted McDonnell's concern and support during his London years. Working-class social movements won his allegiance. In 1869, the *Sheffield Journal* called McDonnell "a full-fledged Republican—disloyal but highly talented." He went to Geneva to an International Peace Congress, stayed in London for an International Prison Congress, and helped organize the Anglo-Irish Agricultural Union. The Franco-Prussian War caused yet another arrest after McDonnell formed an "Irish Brigade" that hoped to leave England illegally to support the French Republicans against their German enemies. McDonnell publicly endorsed the Paris Commune, won nomination to Parliament from London, and organized massive street parades and demonstrations to test the right of public assembly and free speech. He also joined the International Working Men's Association, associated with Karl Marx, became a socialist, and served as Irish secretary of the International's General Council. McDonnell brought these experiences and values with him to the United States. Few other immigrants carried to industrializing America so full and so complete a set of radical credentials.

His five years in New York City followed a predictable pattern. Socialist and labor agitation consumed his time. On his arrival, McDonnell's bitter letters filled long columns in the New York *Herald* as he exposed steerage conditions on immigrant vessels. "Better accommodation is provided for cattle . . . than . . . for human beings," fumed the new immigrant. Challenged in print by a less angry passenger, socialist McDonnell exploded:

He evidently has more money than heart and belongs to that intelligent class of Englishmen who delight in discussing the qualities of dogs and horses over their punch and pipes. It is a well known fact that such men are very humane when horses or dogs are concerned, but their eyes are blind and their ears deaf to the miseries of the poor and toiling.

McDonnell told American readers he had "allied" himself "permanently with the great proletarian movement throughout Europe," and that steerage abuses of immigrants proved once more "that there is one law for the poor and another for the rich, even on the ocean."

Between 1873 and 1878, McDonnell involved himself deeply in the faction-ridden, tiny New York City socialist movement. These were busy but not fruitful years. Calling himself a "journalist and orator," McDonnell lectured widely and traveled the East Coast to spread socialism and to strengthen existing craft unions and build collective strength among the unskilled factory workers. After 1876, he gave much time to editing the New York *Labor Standard*, a Marxist weekly. His public lectures revealed a large but not total debt to Marx: "The modern State has given them [the workers] perfect freedom to go whither they list and die when they please. It is that system which has turned earth into a Hell for the toiler and a Heaven for the idle monopolist." A second lecture told that the promise of America remained unfulfilled: "The despot Poverty seizes our noblest intellect by the throat and stifles out its genius. . . . Law which the founders of the Republic meant to be Justice is now only a farce when invoked for the protection of innocence or humanity." Although the *Labor Standard* survived a difficult birth, factionalism aborted the socialist movement that had given it life. McDonnell himself attracted little notice outside radical and labor circles. During the 1877 railroad strikes and riots (which McDonnell called a "a sort of guerilla warfare" by workers "for their rights"), he pleaded with New York City workers: "The laziest hog can grunt; if we are Men we shall not grunt any more, we shall act. . . . We must organize; unorganized we are a mob and a rabble; organized in one compact body we are a power to be respected. . . . Union is your shepherd." A similar speech in Baltimore (the scene of much bloodshed and industrial violence) finally caused *The New York Times* to notice McDonnell but only to warn that he preached "disorganizing doctrines" and "the unadulterated gospel of communism" to "loafers and ruffians." That was in August of 1877. A year later,

McDonnell moved himself and his newspaper from New York City to Paterson and settled permanently in that New Jersey industrial city.

Failure and factionalism pushed the radical McDonnell from New York City. But the condition of the silk and other textile workers (the largest number of them women and children) together with his desire to organize them into the International Labor Union pulled McDonnell to Paterson. By then, he and a few other socialists had made common cause with New England labor radicals like Ira Steward and George McNeill hoping to organize unskilled factory workers and to spark a movement among them for shorter hours that would end by abolishing the "wages-system." Before that time, McDonnell had occasionally lectured to the Paterson workers. In 1876, he had helped some Paterson radicals celebrate bitterly the nation's centennial at an open air meeting at the Passaic Falls. A general strike by Paterson silk ribbon weavers in 1877 had commanded sympathetic attention in his New York newspaper. A year later, a nine-month strike by unorganized women and girls against the nation's largest cotton mosquito net manufacturer convinced McDonnell that Paterson was fertile ground to plant his radicalism. He moved there, helped organize the cotton strikers, and renamed his newspaper the Paterson *Labor Standard*. Across its masthead, he emblazoned the words of Karl Marx: "The Emancipation of the Working Classes Must be Achieved by the Working Classes Themselves." In its columns, he defended the Paterson workers and scorned their employers. McDonnell addressed the cotton strikers:

All hail! Your struggle is the struggle of humanity for humanity. Your warfare is the warfare of human hearts against a heart of stone. Your contest is that of human flesh against the Dagon of gold. . . . Those who serve a lordly autocrat to cut down the living of full grown human beings without a word do sell themselves for slaves. . . . Whoever holds his food at the will of another, he is the other man's slave.

McDonnell minced no words in demeaning the factory owner:

> Sir, you are a man born to the image and likeness of your
> Creator. . . . You ought to remember that you have sprung
> from poverty, that you are nothing, and that in the natural
> order of events, death will close your eyes in a few more
> years. What will all your ill-gotten wealth then avail you?
> Your mills will stand as monuments of your cruelty. . . .
> The greatness that is won by shattering the health and
> happiness of thousands, driving young men to crime and
> young women to prostitution is the greatness of Lucifer. Be
> just and fear not. . . . Descend from the pedestal of your
> sinful pride, and wipe away some of the stains from your
> past life.

Paterson residents got a different message. In its first issue, the
Labor Standard warned:

> After a century of Political independence, we find that our
> social system is not better than that of Europe and that
> labor in this Republic is not better than that of Europe, and
> that labor in this Republic, as in the European monarchies,
> is the slave of capitalism, instead of being the master of its
> own products.

McDonnell argued that to save "the Republic . . . from
monarchy and ruin"—even from "a dreadful revolution"—
"steps" had "to be taken and at once to prevent the march of
poverty and the growth of industrial despotism."

Such severe printed words were new to Paterson and shocked
and worried otherwise uneasy manufacturers and their supporters. From his start, therefore, McDonnell faced critics who
wanted to stamp out the growth that he and his newspaper
nurtured. Soon after his arrival, in October 1878, loyal nonstrikers convinced a county grand jury to indict McDonnell because
the *Labor Standard* had called them "scabs." A citizens' jury
found McDonnell guilty of libel, and a judge fined him $500. A

year later, McDonnell angered a local brick manufacturer. His newspaper published a letter from Michael Menton, a young, itinerant common laborer, which exposed working and living conditions in his Passaic River brickyard. The manufacturer charged McDonnell and Menton with libel. A court found them guilty. They were fined, and in early 1880 McDonnell and Menton spent nearly three months in the Passaic County jail.

III

NOTHING YET in McDonnell's career challenges the general view sketched earlier of Gilded Age America. Quite the contrary. His two trials and his imprisonment illustrate and strengthen that view. But these few facts are not the full story. McDonnell left prison in 1880. Despite much difficulty, his newspaper survived its early troubled years and remained a weekly labor paper until McDonnell's death in 1908. More important, less than four years after his release from prison a New Jersey governor appointed McDonnell as the state's first deputy inspector of factories and workshops. Although he held that position for less than a year, in 1892 he was chosen to head New Jersey's short-lived State Board of Arbitration.

Even these appointments lose significance beside other information about McDonnell's post-1880 career. McDonnell and a few other trade unionists, labor reformers, and radicals founded the New Jersey Labor Congress in 1879 and a few years later changed its name to the Federation of Organized Trades and Labor Unions of the State of New Jersey. Between 1883 and 1897, McDonnell headed the Federation's Legislative Committee. The Federation never was a powerful body. Its constituent organizations never represented more than 65,000 workers and less than a third of that number in the 1890s. For a few years, the dispute between the craft unions and the Knights of Labor severely weakened it. Its annual expenditures rarely exceeded $250 before 1900.

And yet, between 1883 and 1892, much of the spirit and

pressure that resulted in remedial laws to check the freedom of the industrialist and to improve the condition of working people and other citizens came from this small group. Each year, McDonnell and other members of the Federation's Legislative Committee drew up laws and organized campaigns to prod Trenton legislators for their support. Not all of their efforts were successful. A factory inspector and several deputies were empowered to enforce these laws, but some laws were badly written. Few of these laws passed without bitter legislative battles, and some became statutes only after amendments had weakened them. But their range was impressive and their intent clear. McDonnell believed that the state's major duty was to satisfy "the wants of those who by their toil are the architects of the State's greatness," and the laws satisfied that objective. The list of laws passed after 1883 is too long to be catalogued fully but deserves brief summary. In 1883 and 1884, the state checked contract convict labor and child labor for the first time. A year later, the first of eight general factory laws passed between 1885 and 1893 took effect. These laws began civilizing primitive factory working conditions. Some provided for fire escapes and adequate factory ventilation; others required protective covering on dangerous machinery, belts, and gearing. Another limited the employment of children in dangerous occupations; factories were required to provide seats and suitable dressing rooms for women. Other laws incorporated trade unions, cooperatives, and working-class building and loan associations. Archaic conspiracy legislation was repealed. Nonresidents, often Pinkerton police, were prohibited from serving as public officers. Labor Day became a legal holiday first in New Jersey. So did the fifty-five-hour week for workers engaged in manufacturing. McDonnell and the Federation drew up and won even broader social reforms including ballot reform, the protection of tenants from landlords, the founding of public libraries, and, most important, the state's first comprehensive compulsory education law. "No better measure ever passed a legislative body," argued McDonnell, "and no state in the United States can boast of having a better system of compulsory education." Reviewing this law and others like it enacted between 1883 and 1892, McDonnell concluded: "The interests of the wage earners have been promoted through legislation. . . . No other state in the United States can show greater accomplishments by legislation for the welfare of the wage class during a like period."

After 1892, McDonnell's efforts were much less successful and he and others like him despaired greatly, but McDonnell deserved much credit for the earlier successes. "Every labor law on the state statute books of New Jersey owes its birth to the fostering care and indefatigable work of McDonnell," said the Boston *Post* in 1897. "Not a tithe can be told of all he has done for the betterment of mankind." But to say only this is to miss the larger significance of McDonnell's career. He could not have done this much alone. And it is here that we return to the larger view of Gilded Age America. McDonnell survived despite his Paterson critics; he won two state-appointed offices; he engineered significant legislative victories that industrialists bitterly opposed. Why was this possible? Why was this radical critic able to affect the political system in ways that promoted pioneering reform legislation? Answers to these questions require that we examine neglected but important aspects of the Gilded Age social, economic, and political structure.

IV

So BRIEF A PAPER cannot entirely alter the larger view of Gilded Age America, but it can suggest new ways of looking at that world so that McDonnell's career and much else fall into place better. We must first put aside the view that the industrialist had authority as well as power because his ownership of "things" (machinery and a new technology) together with a widely shared set of beliefs that sanctified property, entrepreneurship, and social mobility gave him unexampled social prestige and exceedingly high status.

Many persons new to the urban-industrial world did not settle easily into a factory-centered civilization. McDonnell was one of them. More significant, however, is the fact that McDonnell's survival, much less his success, depended on such tension and conflict. Certain elements in the preindustrial American social structure and in older patterns of popular ideology persisted strongly into the post-Civil War urban world, profoundly affected behavior, and served as a source of recurrent opposition to the power and status of the new industrialist. At times, they narrowed the industrialist's freedom of action and widened McDonnell's opportunities. Four such "factors" deserve brief note and then illustration:

First: Not all urban property owners and professionals shared common values with the industrialist. Older patterns of thought and social ties persisted among such persons and often alienated them from the new industrialist. Some became his severe critics. Others supported men like McDonnell.

Second: Vital subcultures among the immigrant and native-born poor as well as among the more substantial craftsmen and artisans thrived in Gilded Age America and were sustained by particular norms that shared little with the industrialist and his culture.

Third: Such subcultures were especially important in the Gilded Age industrial town and city and gave its social structure a particular shape and its quality of life a special tone.

Fourth: Politics in the industrial city was affected by these subcultures and an awareness of a potential (and, at times, active) working-class political presence. Many industrial city politicians had special ties to working-class and immigrant voters that usually filtered through a political machine but nevertheless affected the style of politics.

McDonnell's status and power rested on this world. Without support from it, his efforts would have failed, and he would have earned the anonymity that historians undeservedly have assigned to him.

V

IT IS UNFORTUNATE that so little is yet known about the Gilded Age industrial city because most of the significant changes that altered traditional American society occurred in such places. Tensions between the old and the new social structure were sharpest there. Immigrant and working-class subculture was most vital there. To say this is not to minimize all else but to locate just where the factory, the worker, and the immigrant intersected. New Jersey was the nation's sixth largest industrial state in 1880. Ten years later, five major manufacturing cities (Camden, Jersey City, Newark, Paterson, and Trenton) counted one-third of the state's population and more than half of its 150,000 factory workers. Immigrants (90 percent of them in 1890 still from Ireland, Germany, and Great Britain) settled overwhelmingly in these and smaller industrial towns. Because its main industries were diverse (especially boots and shoes, jewelry, thread, shirts, scissors, felt hats, and leather goods), Newark, the state's largest city, was untypical. One or two industries characterized the usual New Jersey industrial city. The dock and railroad workers of Bayonne, Hoboken, and Jersey City gave those towns a special character, but large sugar refineries and the huge Lorillard tobacco factory centered in Jersey City and the mammoth Standard Oil refineries towered over Bayonne. Iron miners and iron mill workers lived in the Sussex and Morris county towns. Trenton had important iron and steel works, and its potteries made it the center of the American whiteware (common table dishes) industry. Camden was best known for its iron factories and shipyards. Orange specialized in the manufacture of hats. Southern New Jersey towns such as Bridgeton, Minatola, Millville, and Glassboro made that region a major producer of varied glass products. Paterson's silk and other textile factories caused it to be called the Lyons of America, but its workers also labored in locomotive, iron, and machine shops. Although the social history of such towns has not yet been written, sufficient scattered evidence indicates the presence of vital clusters of urban working-class subculture, a diversity of attitudes among non-workers toward industrial power, and unique patterns of protest and politics essential to understand the larger developments of that time.

Let us turn first to McDonnell's trials and his imprisonment to see what it was that protected him from his early critics and allowed him to make Paterson his permanent home. It is necessary to repeat some of the evidence used in the preceding essay but to view it from a different perspective. Paterson was a model industrial city. Some of its nearly 50,000 inhabitants (in 1878) were radicals like McDonnell but only a few. Campbell Wilson had been a Scot radical before working as a Paterson silk weaver and then running a working-class boardinghouse and saloon. A Lancashire Chartist, Samuel Sigley had fled England in 1848 after a threatened treason trial. He made out nicely as a Paterson house painter. Another Lancashire worker, Simon Morgan, had settled in Paterson after being blacklisted for leading a Fall River cotton strike. Irish and German radicals also befriended McDonnell, but by themselves they lacked the power to protect the socialist editor against his local critics.

Others in the city sustained McDonnell, and their behavior reveals much about the industrial city's inner structure. We consider first his supporters among nonworkers. Twenty "agents," including nearly every stationer and newsdealer on the city's main thoroughfares, sold the *Labor Standard*, and early issues earned advertising revenue from forty-five retail shop-keepers and other vendors of goods and services (among them eleven clothing and drygoods stores, ten saloons, eight boot and shoe makers, and eight grocers). Ethnicity varied among these petty retailers: the group included German, Irish, French, Dutch, and ordinary "American" names as well as an Italian bootmaker and three Jewish clothing dealers. Such support may have been just good "business sense," but the sympathy McDonnell evoked during his first trial rested on other causes. His lawyer was a pioneer manufacturer who later grew wealthy as a real estate speculator. He had broken with the Whig Party over slavery and later quit the Republicans to protest the "money power." A jury of shopkeepers and successful independent artisans agreed that McDonnell was guilty but only after unusual pressure by a presiding judge. Even then, another judge, himself a poor Lancashire immigrant who then owned a small bobbin factory, convinced the presiding judge to fine McDonnell and not send him to prison. Some storekeepers and merchants helped McDonnell pay his fine. Aid also came from a prominent coppersmith and alderman as well as a third-generation Yorkshire blacksmith who then headed a small bolt and screw factory. Orrin Vanderhoven also cheered McDonnell. Vanderhoven had traveled a long route from Jacksonian Democracy to Greenback reform and soon would return to the Democracy. "A scab," Vanderhoven wrote in his own newspaper, "is a man who deserts his fellows. . . . The name of 'scab' is not degrading enough for such a person. It ought to be a 'villainous, shameless, sneakthief traitor'. . . . God bless the laboring classes. . . . May the God of fortune favor them through life. . . . May their beds be roses and their bolsters banknotes."

Others of local prominence joined editor Vanderhoven to side with McDonnell during his second trial. Two respected lawyers defended the troubled socialist. The son of a New Hampshire blacksmith, Socrates Tuttle was then sixty-one and Paterson's most revered Republican leader—a lawyer who had served as school commissioner, city clerk, state assemblyman, and mayor. William Prall, the son of a former Democratic mayor and cotton manufacturer, helped Tuttle defend McDonnell. A few years later, Prall went to the state assembly; after that, he gave up politics and became an Episcopal clergyman. Just before his trial, McDonnell had complained loudly that Paterson's clergy prayed to "that Trinity of Power, 'the Almighty Dollar, the Golden Eagle, and the Copper Cent,'" but two prominent clergymen protested publicly in his behalf. A Baptist, one of them worked among the Paterson poor and later played a significant role as a Midwestern antitrust propagandist. The other, John Robinson, was an Irish Protestant, a Primitive Methodist, for a time Republican state senator, and Paterson's most esteemed clergyman. Nor was this all. Two former silk factory foremen (one English and the other German) and soon to become prosperous businessmen organized McDonnell's sympathizers. Thomas Flynn, then a saloonkeeper and ten years later speaker of the state assembly, posted bond for Menton, and a contractor financed the young man in a well-drilling business. Several aldermen, former aldermen, and county freeholders visited McDonnell in prison. On McDonnell's release, a committee of seventy-five arranged a celebration. Not only workers organized the fete. The committee included a band leader, a contractor, a clothier, a doctor, five grocers, and twelve saloon- and hotelkeepers.

His first night in jail, McDonnell angrily confided in his diary: "Here in Jail for defending the poor in their Rights! Alas, for American Liberty." Yet his prison stay was made less harsh than expected by a county jail warden, John Buckley, who would himself soon head the county Republican organization. McDonnell's imprisonment apparently upset Buckley. He made his guest as comfortable as circumstances allowed. McDonnell spent some of his prison days writing letters for illiterate fellow prisoners and himself appealing to the New Jersey governor to enforce a moribund ten-hour law. Buckley also let him edit his newspaper and organize a national protest campaign from his cell. Visitors (twenty-one came on a single day, and children often called on McDonnell) met the editor in the warden's office. Meals came regularly from outside the prison. So did cigars, wines, and liquors supplied by friendly saloon- and hotelkeepers. Others brought fresh fruit, cakes, and puddings. Shamrocks came on St. Patrick's Day and two fancy dinners on McDonnell's birthday. On his release, Buckley commended McDonnell as a model prisoner.

Scores of ordinary working people supported McDonnell in their own way. They crowded the jail to console him and raised the money to pay his fines. But their support came in more significant ways. After his first trial, working-class sympathizers (and even some shopkeepers) jammed Democratic political rallies to humiliate the Democratic county prosecutor. On his release from prison eighteen months later, working people (organized mostly by skilled silk workers) arranged Paterson's greatest celebration to that time. Quite possibly more than half of the city's residents filled its streets and "almost mobbed" their hero. A band played; a carriage awaited him to carry McDonnell through the jammed streets; American flags decorated the parade route; a rally followed the street march; then came a festive banquet at which three young girls presented the socialist editor with a gold watch—a gift from "the ladies of Paterson." "No one ever purchased the title of martyr at so slight a cost," sneered a hostile Paterson newspaper. A sympathizer disagreed. "Paterson," he insisted, "is redeemed by the suffering of the innocent for the guilty." Such varied opinions did not matter as much as the fact that Paterson residents made it possible for McDonnell to survive in a social setting usually identified with little more than hopeless poverty, disorganized and ineffective protest, and God-like industrial power.

McDonnell's 1878–1880 Paterson experiences were never exactly repeated in other New Jersey Gilded Age industrial cities, but events like them occurred with sufficient frequency to suggest that the Gilded Age worker was more than "a factor of production," that he was the sum of a total culture that has been scarcely recognized and little studied. That culture differed between groups of workers. Ethnicity and levels of skill counted for much in explaining these diversities. Despite them, however, Gilded Age workers had distinct ways of work and leisure, habits, aspirations, conceptions of America and Christianity, notions of right and wrong, and traditions of protest and acquiescence that were linked together in neighborhoods by extensive voluntary associations and other community institutions. Not all of this entirely separated the industrial city's workers from the larger community, but these strands wove together in ways that shaped a particular subculture.

Evidence of convincing support from nonworkers is drawn from an Orange hatters' boycott (1885). Nearly two thousand men and women worked in more than twenty Orange hat factories. The Knights of Labor won much sympathy from them, but a single manufacturer named Berg discharged women employees who wanted to join the Knights, refused to negotiate, and brought in new hands. A citywide boycott followed, and a labor journalist reported the attitude of the boycotters and their supporters toward Berg and the nonstrikers ("the foul"):

> They will not trade with any person who has any dealings with the boycotted foul or with any one who furnishes goods or supplies to Berg himself. Brewers refuse to furnish beer to foul saloonkeepers; bakers refuse to furnish bread to the fouls; and the knights of the razor turn them out of doors. One fair manufacturer discharged a man because he lived with his brother who is a foul, and two female trimmers were refused admission to the roller-skating rink because they were foul. . . . The foul cannot even find lodging places, and are compelled to resort to adjacent localities at night for bed and board. . . . One beer seller who has been threatened says he may be forced to sell beer to a foul, but he cannot be prevented from charging him a dollar a glass for it.

Although this reporter's enthusiasm caused some exaggeration, he insisted that the boycott had "the sympathy of nearly everybody in Orange."

What, finally, was politics like in the industrial city? The ballot gave the industrial city worker a presence, if not a power, that has been little studied. Political machines often disciplined the worker-voter and narrowed his choices. Votes were even purchased by "bosses" for cash and favors. That is an old story, but it is not the full story. Working-class voting behavior took many forms as a protest device. Camden and Phillipsburg had workers as mayors in 1877 and 1878. Some Southern New Jersey counties sent glass blowers to the state legislature. Paterson elected two workers as state assemblymen in 1886 and two more in the early 1890s. A Paterson machinist and outspoken socialist twice served as city alderman. The direct election of workers on independent tickets, however, was not common. More typical was the elected official who was not a worker but nevertheless sympathized with the workers or feared alienating working-class electoral support. During the 1877 general silk strike, Paterson's Republican mayor (a Lancashire cotton worker who became a Paterson banker, manufacturer, and popular politician) and the Board of Aldermen publicly rebuked efforts by the Paterson Board of Trade to enlarge the police force and to deny strikers the use of the streets for their effective public demonstrations. Ten years later, Jersey City's Democratic mayor, a former Congressman and also a manufacturer named Orestes Cleveland, declined to deputize Pinkerton police during a violent coal handlers' strike. After *The New York Times* condemned Cleveland as "a demagogue," the mayor fired back: "It is not the business of Jersey City to interfere between the great monopolies and their workmen. . . . If it were proper for Jersey City to interfere at all, we should interfere to assist and protect the men who are fighting for the right to live, instead of for the protection of the great monopolies. . . ."

The Jersey City mayor may have been a "demagogue." It is also possible that he learned from the bitter experiences of other urban politicians who had sided with employers or broken promises to organized workers. Here a third pattern—punishment—emerged. During the 1877 potters' strike, Trenton's Republican mayor condemned the potters in the New York *World*. Their response was to vote him out of office that spring. Such flashes of independent political anger among urban workers recurred in the 1880s. A Camden Republican state assemblyman promised McDonnell's Federation his help but turned back on his pledge after the election. Aided by two Camden newspaper editors (one of them German), McDonnell organized Camden workers and prevented his re-election. The 1887 coal handlers' strike saw similar results. Bayonne aldermen and a Jersey City police official opposed the strikers and suffered defeat at the polls. These few examples suggest some of the ways in which working-class political presence affected industrial city politics. Such a presence also was felt on the state level and helped explain McDonnell's legislative victories.

VI

McDONNELL WON reform legislation between 1883 and 1892 by playing "pressure politics." Not enough is yet known to tell that story fully, but its outlines seem clear. For one thing, two state officials—one elected and the other appointed—supported McDonnell and eased his way in Trenton. One was Leon Abbett, twice-elected Democratic governor (1883–1886 and 1889–1892), and the other was Lawrence Fell, the chief factory inspector from 1883 until 1895 when a hostile state senate finally rejected his reappointment and began undoing his pioneering work. Fell's support was the more unusual, and Abbett's was the more important.

The available evidence allows us to say no more than that Leon Abbett supported the efforts of McDonnell and the Federation. Just why remains obscure and is entangled in bitter controversy over his motives and his career. But it is sufficient in these pages to know only that McDonnell had a powerful friend in Abbett, New Jersey's most significant nineteenth-century governor. During his two terms, Abbett gave much time battling the New Jersey railroads to tax them fairly, and in doing so he attacked the state's most well-organized private interest. Abbett won a public victory but twice lost a United States Senate seat as his reward. Abbett's methods aroused much public criticism. That he built "a machine" to fight "a machine" worried many as did his continued public appeal for electoral support from urban workers and immigrants. The son of a Philadelphia Quaker journeyman hatter, Abbett was a wealthy Jersey City lawyer and state legislator. Even then (in the late 1860s and the 1870s), his actions showed a concern for the lower-class vote. As president of the state senate (1877), he worked hard to abolish scrip money and company stores then common in the Southern and Western New Jersey iron and glass towns. That same year, he represented workers in a successful suit for back wages against a bankrupt railroad and also defended strikers arrested in the aftermath of the 1877 railroad riots. Abbett accepted no fees in these cases. As candidate in 1883 (his Republican opponent was the judge who had sentenced McDonnell to prison in 1880), Abbett appealed to immigrant and working-class voters. After his election, the governor proclaimed: "Every citizen of this State, whether he be high or low, whether he be rich or poor, can always see me personally without the intervention of any man." Abbett was not a John Peter Altgeld, but McDonnell and the Federation found him sympathetic to their proposals. Historians, incidentally, have credited his administration's labor legislation solely to Abbett and not realized that it first came from men like McDonnell. But Abbett's response should not be neglected.

Lawrence Fell is easier to explain than Abbett and is, in some ways, more interesting. His career suggests how new experiences remade even grown men. The 1883 legislature allowed the governor with the state senate's approval to pick a chief factory inspector to enforce the new laws. Fell was not the governor's first choice. Instead, a Newark hatter and outspoken trade unionist, Richard Dowdall, was nominated. But the senate turned him down because, according to *The New York Times*, it felt him "a labor extremist, a demagogue identified with the [Irish] Land League, and altogether an unfit person." An Orange hat manufacturer and real estate dealer, Fell was his replacement. If the conservative senate thought him a "safe" choice because of his background, Fell disappointed it. He became a vigorous proponent of enlarged and more effective labor legislation. He worked diligently under difficult circumstances to enforce the school and factory laws, and he cooperated openly with McDonnell and the Federation. When the opportunity existed, Fell urged the appointment of McDonnell and a Newark trade unionist as his deputies. After their appointment and work angered industrialists and caused their removal, Fell praised them: "The manner in which they have acted is sufficient proof that the advocates of labor interests are fitted to fill the highest [public] labor offices."

What Fell learned as chief factory inspector made him a reformer and an advocate of extensive remedial and protective legislation. "Old faces and dwarfed forms are the offspring of the Child Labor System," his first report concluded. "In a country where life is so intense as it is in this, where so much is expected in a little time, childhood and youth should be a time of free physical growth." Fell's second report detailed widespread illiteracy among "factory children." His description is a neglected classic of its kind. Fell told of his experiences with twelve- to fifteen-year-old boys and girls in the New Jersey factories:

Nearly all the children examined were naturally bright and intelligent, but neglect, years of work and their general surroundings had left sad traces upon their youthful forms and minds. It is not possible in this report to enter into the details of every case, either of factory or child examination; to do so would be to fill the largest volume that the State has ever published. . . . There is no exaggeration in saying that three-fourths of the work-children know absolutely nothing. The greatest ignorance exists on the most commonplace questions. Most of these children have never been inside of a schoolhouse, and the majority have either been at school for too short a period to learn anything or have forgotten the little instruction they received.

Not two percent know anything about grammar or have ever been taught any. One of the few children who professed to know something about grammar said that the word "boy" was "a comma," when asked what part of speech it was. The vast majority could not spell words of more than one syllable, and very many could not spell at all. About ten percent could answer questions in simple multiplication. Of the remaining ninety percent, the majority know absolutely nothing about simple geographical and historical questions. The number able to read and write, in a distinguishable way, was shockingly small, and very many could neither read nor write even their own names.

Fell illustrated his experiences concretely:

Very few of these children, the large majority of whom were born in the United States, ever heard of George Washington. Amongst the answers given about Washington, by those who heard of him, were the following: "He is a good man." "He chased the Indians away." "He died a few years ago." "He is President." "I saw his picture." "He is a high man in war." "He never told a lie." "He discovered America." "The best man who ever lived," and so forth. Over ninety-five percent never heard of the revolutionary war, Abraham Lincoln, the Civil War, Governor Abbett or President Arthur.

At least sixty percent never heard of the United States or of Europe. At least thirty percent could not name the city in which they lived, and quite a number only knew the name of the street where they housed. Many who had heard of the United States could not say where they were. Some said they were in Europe and others said they were in New Jersey. Many big girls and boys were unable to say whether New Jersey was in North or South America. Girls were found in Jersey City and Newark who never heard of New York City. In Newark and Jersey City this was, of course, the exception, but in other parts of the State it was the rule. Some who had heard of New York said it was in New Jersey, and others answered that Pennsylvania was the capital of New Jersey. Not ten percent could tell what an island was. Very few had heard of the city of Washington, and not three percent could locate it. A girl aged fourteen years said Europe was in the moon. A few were found who never heard of the sun, or moon, or earth, and a large number who could not tell where or when they were born. . . . Children who had been brought to this country before their sixth year, in some cases, never heard the name of their native country, and others could not locate them.

One finding especially concerned Fell:

Boys and girls who had been brought to this country from Great Britain, Ireland and Germany, between the ages of twelve and fifteen years, were better educated and knew more about the geography and history of America than children born and reared in the State. . . . This sad tale of illiteracy is not overdrawn in the slightest degree. It is, alas, too true. . . .

Such evidence caused legislative critics in 1885 and again in 1886 to try to abolish Fell's office. But McDonnell and the Federation frustrated such efforts, and Fell continued his work for another decade.

VII

ALTHOUGH FELL AND ABBETT provided important help, McDonnell's legislative success depended on more than their support. It came only when McDonnell and the Federation could make a majority of the state's elected officeholders conscious, if not fearful, of the presence and potential power of the industrial city's workers and immigrant poor. This was not an easy task. The New Jersey legislature was a jungle of competing special interest groups, the railroads king among them. In addition, the state senate increasingly underrepresented the growing industrial cities and became a choice nesting ground for well-organized interest groups opposed to the Federation and its legislative programs. McDonnell scorned the typical state legislator, advising workers: "Leave him to himself and his surroundings, and he will forget all about you and his promises." So harsh a judgement was not unfair. Despite the Federation's important legislative gains, in 1897 New Jersey spent $222,400 for its National Guard ("our tin soldiers," McDonnell called the militia), a sum that nearly equaled the state's educational expenditures and was almost ten times the amount allotted to the Bureau of Labor Statistics and the Bureau of Factory Inspection.

In such a world, a single belief informed McDonnell's legislative efforts. His radicalism together with his experiences convinced McDonnell that neither rhetoric nor "right" won legislation. Only pressure worked, and the worker's weapon was the organized but "independent" vote. McDonnell preached and practiced this point for twenty-five years. As early as 1878, he advised *Labor Standard* readers: "Heaven help the laborers who rely upon their public officers to legislate for the good of labor. But honest legislation can be forced by labor unions." He regularly published the names of antilabor legislators with the frequent admonition: "If there is courage, intelligence, and Manhood in the people, not one of these enemies will ever again be elected to a legislative position. Men of New Jersey, kick them out." McDonnell explained in 1882: "It is Power that men in office fear, and it is because the wage workers have not had organized Power that they have been treated with the grossest contempt." Legislative victories came because workers had "commenced to think and to act." "Politicians," he said in 1893, "are as a rule what we make them or what we permit them to be." Five years of decline in the Federation's influence (1893–1897) caused a similar outburst: "We should not forget that if we won't aid ourselves, no one else will, and that we shall get just as much as we fight for, *and no more*." Nothing, McDonnell insisted, "of importance will be obtained from our Legislature unless they hear the workingman's and workingwoman's growl. We can get anything we want *by growling loud enough*."

A "growl" unaccompanied by a "bite" was hardly enough, and that potential "bite" was the electoral power that rested in the industrial cities and their diverse but dense clusters of working-class subculture. McDonnell and men like him therefore cut the Federation loose from all formal political ties to enable it to apply nonpartisan local pressure. The Federation supported Abbett when he favored its program, but it also gave its blessings to sympathetic Republican legislators. "The political policy of the Federation," a spokesman said in 1884, "has been and is to identify itself with no party but to support men of all parties favorable to their objects." In this way, McDonnell hoped to create effective working-class pressure and cement "natural" alliances with its legislative representatives. The regular procedure was simple. Each year the Federation convention established legislative priorities. Just before the fall election, it circulated a pledge among all candidates for public office:

> I pledge my word of honor that if elected to the Legislature, I will support the bills introduced for the benefit of the wage class by the Legislative Committee of the New Jersey Federation of Trades and Labor Unions, whether said bills were approved or opposed by the political party to which I belong, provided that said bills are of a purely labor character; and I will support no measure, whether of a private or party nature, which may be introduced in opposition to labor measures and against the wishes of the organized wage-workers of New Jersey.

Approval of the pledge won Federation endorsement together with Federation scrutiny and pressure while the legislature met. For fifteen years, McDonnell spent the winter months largely in Trenton working this risky strategy. It depended for its success almost entirely on the Federation's ability to mount pressure from outside the party system. A Federation without close ties to the industrial city working class was weak and lacked such strength. Between 1883 and 1892, such connections were sufficiently strong to win significant legislative achievements. And so in this neglected fashion, social reform came from "below." Such successes angered conservatives and those who found comfort in the ever-increasing gross national product. These victories so upset the New York *Herald* that it accused many New Jersey legislators of lacking in "courage." "Fear of the loss of the labor vote," moaned the *Herald*, "drives public men and parties into concessions against which their consciences and better judgments often rebel. . . . The law of supply and demand is offended at every tack and turn. The philosophy of trade is set at defiance." McDonnell did not share the *Herald*'s rhetorical remorse.

Just what kind of industrial city legislators supported McDon-

nell and the Federation is difficult to tell. These men differed in
social background and seemed to share only the fact that their
constituents were mostly wage-earners. Take the cases of two
quite different Paterson legislators: Thomas Flynn, a Democrat
and for a time state assembly speaker, and Robert Williams, a
Republican state senator.

Tom Flynn was a model Gilded Age ward politician. He
started as a machinist, drove a horse car, fooled with firehouse
politics, studied for the law, opened a saloon, built a personal
political machine among the Paterson Irish, traded favors for
votes, and went to the assembly several times starting in 1881.
He became a Trenton power and critics identified him with
corruption and the "racetrack lobby." The New York *Tribune*
complained of his "unscrupulous conduct and aggressiveness."
"A product of the slums, endowed by nature with more than an
ordinary amount of acuteness, . . . and utterly without moral
scruple or finer feeling," the *Tribune* saw in "Flynn's life from
the first to the last . . . what any careful student of human
nature might have predicted." But Flynn supported the Federation's legislative program from the very start. McDonnell often
praised him and with good reason. He helped abolish an
antilabor conspiracy law and pushed the regulation of prison
labor. He tried to get the legislature to lower utility rates and
regulate insurance companies. Flynn worked so diligently for
the fifty-five-hour law that Paterson silk workers renamed him
"Fifty-five Hour Flynn." A candidate for re-election, he emphasized his ties to the workers and his efforts in their behalf.
Working-class voters learned that Flynn still "ranks among his
friends the men who were then his comrades at the bench." A
Democratic leader urged Paterson workers to re-elect Flynn:
"You have named him Fifty-five Hour Flynn, and he deserves
the title. He fought your battle and kept the faith."

A graduate of the Columbia College Law School and a
Republican newspaper publisher, Robert Williams was the
antithesis of Tom Flynn. Democratic opponents mocked his
upper-class style when Williams sought election to the state
senate:

Robby Williams. Nice boy, sweet little beard, dreamy way and langorous expression, long wavy hair. . . . Robby's a real nice fellow, but what does he know about labor? . . . He was born with a silver spoon in his mouth and never did anything but dandle it round his mouth. . . . Starvation has never stared him in the face. . . . and [he] cannot legislate for something of which he knows nothing.

Williams disappointed his political enemies: he knew his constituents well and regularly voted for Federation legislation. He even introduced bills drawn up by McDonnell. When Williams quit the senate, McDonnell had only words of praise: "This county has never had a Senator who more faithfully represented the interests of the common people." The real test for McDonnell was neither man nor party; only the issues counted. "Robby" Williams had also "kept the faith.".

Just how McDonnell and other Federation leaders worked with men like Abbett, Fell, Flynn, and Williams can be illustrated briefly in 1884 and 1893. A fairly complete record relates McDonnell's Trenton experiences in 1884. He and the Federation's Legislative Committee met twice in December 1883 to discuss proposed labor legislation with a sympathetic Newark assemblyman and Abbett. After that, McDonnell drew up the several laws. Between mid-January and late March, he spent thirty-four days in Trenton and conferred with, cajoled, and pressured Democratic and Republican legislators from such industrial cities as Paterson, Jersey City, and Newark. He and other Federation spokesmen testified before legislative committees and brought pressure to bear in other ways. "We had hard work getting the child-labor bill through the Senate," reported McDonnell, "as they were trying to kill it by amendments, but several Senators were brought to terms by delegations of workingmen waiting upon them in their respective districts." When the Assembly Committee on Revision of Laws held back a strengthened factory inspection law for two weeks and then allowed only a brief public hearing, McDonnell accused it of "discourtesy toward the labor organizations" to force it to hear him and Fell. The committee stalled again so Federation leaders conferred with Abbett. But the committee quickly won Assembly support for a badly amended bill. A labor journalist reported what followed:

> [McDonnell first] succeeded through Assemblyman Flynn. . . . in having the vote on the report reconsidered and the bill recommitted. The members of the Federation Legislative committee then went to work gallantly among the members, until they made things very unpleasant for the Committee on Revision of Laws. Mr. McDonnell at once telegraphed to the absent members in various parts of the State, urging them to come to Trenton at once, which they did early on Thursday morning. By this time, the aspect of things had changed. It was rumored among the Assemblymen that the labor men and their friends were swarming into Trenton like bees, and that their power was not to be made little of. The forenoon's work produced good results.

The factory inspection bill left the committee without its crippling amendments and soon became law. "What a change in twenty-four hours!" enthused McDonnell. "Would it have taken place if the labor men were not alive and doing?"

A different tactic prevented repeal of the fifty-five-hour law in 1893. It had passed the year before, the first of its kind in the United States. Inadequately enforced, manufacturers nevertheless bitterly opposed it. Some went to the courts to test its constitutionality. Others mounted a campaign for its repeal, and in 1893 sent such circulars together with instructions to factory superintendents to get the signatures of workers. McDonnell quickly responded. A public appeal to the state's legislators defended the law, and a circular (entitled "Danger Ahead") urged every New Jersey trade union to elect delegates to attend a special Trenton convention on twenty-four hours' notice. The response was gratifying. Nearly all picked delegates and flooded Trenton with resolutions favoring the law. The manufacturers backed away from full repeal, but their supporters pushed two bills to emasculate the law. McDonnell worked for their defeat. The night before final adjournment, the Senate passed one of them. Then, Tom Flynn and others from the industrial cities stepped in. "Thanks now and forever to Speaker Tom Flynn and other friends," McDonnell explained, "neither . . . bill went through."

VIII

THIS JOURNEY has taken us from Dublin, to London, to New York, to Paterson, and finally to Trenton. That was the route McDonnell traveled, and we have followed it to fit the Gilded Age labor radical into the mainstream of that era's history. To do so, several detours were necessary to avoid the roadblocks set up by certain misconceptions concerning the Gilded Age itself. Some of the larger implications of that trip through America's Dark Age deserve summary. For one thing, McDonnell's New Jersey career was not isolated and unique. Similar patterns of working-class political pressure for reform were found in such states as New York, Massachusetts, Pennsylvania, Ohio, Indiana, Michigan, Illinois, and Connecticut. Their success varied, but the men who led these movements shared a common moral purpose with radicals like McDonnell. "The foundation of the Republic," McDonnell insisted in 1882, "is men not things, and to attend to the welfare of man, knowing that things will take care of themselves is the true wisdom of statesmanship." McDonnell believed in the 1880s that strong trade unions and legislative reform would open the way to more radical changes, but a little-studied conservative political backlash in New Jersey after 1892 that made it a one-party state for more than a decade blocked such possibilities and began weakening the ties that had given power and status to men like McDonnell. After that McDonnell faded in significance, and his last fifteen years were filled with much personal and political disappointment. It remains to be said, however, that the modern "welfare state" was not just the child of concerned and sensitive early twentieth-century upper- and middle-class critics of industrial capitalism. A generation earlier, working-class leaders, including radicals like McDonnell, had helped give birth to a premature "welfare state." They had arranged a marriage between the industrial city's workers and immigrants and their political representatives. Such men, not the Progressive reformers of a later time, were the founding fathers of modern movements to humanize industrial society.

"What a comment upon our civilization it is that you who have given so much of yourself have received so little for yourself," George McNeill wrote of McDonnell in 1896. A worker who had matured in the world of the New England abolitionists, McNeill was McDonnell's counterpart in Massachusetts. His letter reassured his Irish friend by quoting a poem McNeill had written some years before when another neglected American radical, Ira Steward, had died:

Even now I see the coming day, the dawn appears,
The thoughtless brain will some day think
And at thy fountain pause and drink,
And praise thy name.

Although men like McDonnell deserved such recognition, it was not just because they gave so much and got so little. In 1873, McDonnell's first American letters had appeared in the new York *Herald.* The young socialist denounced steerage abuse of poor, powerless European immigrants. He explained his concern for them by quoting John Milton, not Karl Marx:

Not to know at large of things remote
From use, obscure and subtle, but to know
That which before us lies in daily life
Is the prime wisdom. What is more is fume
Or emptiness or fond impertinence,
And renders us in things that most concern
Unpracticed, unprepared and still to seek.

Milton's words belong in this final paragraph. As more is learned of the world and the culture that bred men like McDonnell, more is revealed about the larger "forces" that have shaped modern American society. And that reason, not mere sentiment, is why we look with care at the life and times of radicals as obscure as Joseph P. McDonnell.

PART IV

Local Behavior and Patterns of Labor Discontent in Gilded Age America

6

Trouble on the Railroads in 1873–1874

PRELUDE TO THE 1877 CRISIS?

Strikes," complained the New York *Railroad Gazette* in January 1874, "are no longer accidents but are as much a disease of the body politic as the measles or indigestion are of our physical organization." [1] Between November 1873 and July 1874, workers on the Pennsylvania system and at least seventeen other railroads struck.[2] Engineers, firemen, brakemen, and track hands as well as shopmen and ordinary laborers resisted wage cuts, demanded salary due them, and opposed such employer practices as blacklisting and the use of iron-clad contracts. None of these disputes was so dramatic or important as the general railroad strike in 1877, but together they prophetically etched the outlines of that violent outburst. The strikes also revealed certain explosive elements in the social structure of postbellum America. Seemingly pathetic and seldom lasting more than a week or two, the signficance of the strikes lay not in their success

1. "The Strike," *Railroad Gazette*, January 3, 1874, p. 4.
2. Between November 1873 and June 1874 workers struck on the following railroads: the East Tennessee, Virginia, and Georgia, the Philadelphia and Reading, the Pennsylvania Central, the New Jersey Southern, the New York and Oswego Midland, the various eastern divisions of the Erie Railroad system, the Boston and Worcester, the Delaware, Lackawanna, and Western, the Louisville Short Line, the Allegheny Valley, and the Chicago and Alton.

or failure but rather in the readiness of the strikers to express their grievances in a dramatic, direct, and frequently telling manner. Even though the workers were mostly without trade-union organization or experience, they often exerted a kind of raw power that made trouble for their employers. Most of the 1873–1874 disputes, furthermore, took place in small railroad towns and in isolated semirural regions where small numbers of workers often could marshal surprising strength. The social structure and ideology in these areas often worked to the advantage of the disaffected workers. Large numbers of non-strikers frequently sided with them. Though the railroad opera-tors put down almost all the strikes, they faced difficulties that they were unprepared for and that taxed their imaginations and their energies.

Even though the railroad industry was probably the largest single employer in the country when the 1873 depression started, most railroad workers were without unions of any kind.[3] The track hands, switchmen, firemen, and brakemen had no union. A small number of machinists employed in certain repair shops belonged to the Machinists' and Blacksmiths' International Union, but the large majority of shopmen and stationary hands were not union members. Most conductors also were free of union ties, for the Locomotive Conductors' Brotherhood was a weak union. Founded in 1868, it had only twenty-one locals five years later.[4] Only the engineers had an effective union in 1873,

3. The railroad system had grown enormously by 1873. Only 9,201 miles of track were used in 1850, but in the next ten years this figure had more than tripled. By 1873 slightly over 70,000 miles existed. In the four years between 1869 and 1873 more than 24,000 miles were built. Not counting clerks, Pennsylvania had about 18,000 railroad workers in 1870. Nearly 30,000 men worked for the Ohio roads in 1873. See, for examples, American Iron and Steel Association, *Annual Report to December 31, 1874* (Philadelphia, 1875), 75–77; Pennsylvania Bureau of Labor Statistics, *First Annual Report*, 1872–1873 (Harrisburg, 1874), 407–408; Ohio Bureau of Labor Statistics, *First Annual Report*, 1877 (Columbus, 1878), 281–83.

4. *Brotherhood of Locomotive Engineers' Monthly Journal*, 7 (December 1873), 598. Examples of the strength of the Machinists' and Blacksmiths' International Union in the Indianapolis repair shops appear in the Indianapolis *Daily Sentinel*, December, 27, 1873 to January 10, 1874.

the Brotherhood of Locomotive Engineers. Almost 10,000 engineers, employed on nearly every major trunk line, belonged to the Brotherhood. Led by Grand Chief Engineer Charles Wilson, the Brotherhood enforced written contracts on a number of lines, published a monthly magazine, and maintained a well-managed accident and insurance program.[5] At the same time, the absence of trade unions among most railroad workers was no proof of their satisfaction with their jobs and their employers, for they voiced numerous grievances.[6]

5. Charles Wilson, a conservative trade unionist, rejected labor reform and politics, did not allow union members to cooperate with other nonrailroad workers, opposed strikes, stressed matters such as sobriety, and believed that workers and employers shared a common interest. Under Wilson's leadership, the BLE worked closely with the American Railway Association, an organization of employers. Local lodges could not strike without his permission on pain of expulsion. Many engineers, especially in the West and the South, opposed his policies, but in 1873 his position seemed unassailable. See, for examples, *Brotherhood of Locomotive Engineers' Monthly Journal*, 7 (November 1873), 508; "List of Sub-divisions," *ibid.,* 7 (December 1873), 612–16. Wilson's views of other labor leaders such as Robert Schilling, John Fehrenbatch, and William Saffin are found in "The Missouri Strike," *ibid.,* 7 (September 1873), 408. See also George McNeil, ed., *The Labor Movement: The Problem of Today* (New York, 1891), 321–32 and John R. Commons and others, *History of Labour in the United States* (New York, 1918), 2: 63–66.

6. Railroad workers had numerous grievances. They often complained that employers withheld wages from them for several weeks or even months. Certain Wisconsin roads made them trade in company-owned stores. Pennsylvania workers at the large Susquehanna Depot repair shops of the Erie Railroad said that many of the "best and oldest" workers were discharged "without assigned cause" and that "utterly unskilled" laborers received the same wages as some skilled mechanics. Engineers and firemen on the Pennsylvania system charged that when engines were damaged the workers paid the repair cost regardless of the cause. "If you don't pay the damages," company officials reportedly told complaining engineers, "we'll discharge you." Many engineers lost as much as three months of work every year because company officials did not supply them with new engines when their cabs were in repair. After listing a number of grievances, one engineer declared, "If I fall sick and am even absent for an hour from the engine I am docked the time, while the company can throw me off just as many hours as they choose." "We get paid so much a day for every day we are on a run," said another engineer. "They pay us by the 'run' not by the day. . . . A day is 12 hours and from our point of view there are 14 days in the week." See *Workingman's Advocate*, February 21, 1874; "Resolutions of the Susquehanna

During the early months of the depression, many railroads hastily adjusted to the drop in freight and passenger traffic. The New York Central Railroad, for example, discharged 1,400 shopmen in New York City, and Jersey City, an important eastern rail terminus, listed thousands of unemployed workers by early November 1873. Railroads in every region—the Union Pacific, the Missouri, Kansas and Texas, the Louisville and Nashville, and the Lake Shore and Michigan Southern, to cite only a few examples—cut wages. A number of financially pressed roads also withheld wages.[7] In a number of instances, furthermore, the companies added insult to injury when they instituted their new wage policies. Knoxville officials of the East Tennessee, Virginia, and Georgia Railroad told their employees of a 20 percent wage cut the day before it went into effect.[8] On November 30, the various divisions of the Pennsylvania system announced that the wages of engineers and firemen would fall 10 percent the next day. The Pennsylvania violated a written agreement drawn up with the Brotherhood of Locomotive Engineers in 1872, for that contract fixed a wage scale that could not be altered by either side without prior notice or joint consultation. After the firm's announcement, therefore, the union sent a special committee to J. N. McCullough, the system's western superintendent. McCullough brushed the committee aside, fired its members, and issued an order that forbade leaves of absence to other engineers who sought to discuss the matter with him. When angered engineers threatened to strike,

---

Depot, Pa., Strikers," n.d., printed in *ibid.*, March 14, 1874; "Interviews with unidentified locomotive engineers," n.d., Chicago *Tribune*, December 29, 1873 and Chicago *Times*, December 31, 1873. See also the discussion of conditions of work in Robert V. Bruce, *1877: Year of Violence* (Indianapolis, 1959), 42–47.

7. Examples of the severe amount of unemployment among railroad workers are found in the *Workingman's Advocate*, October 11, 18, 25, November 22, 29, December 30, 1873; Chicago *Times*, October 31, November 10, December 3, 5, 24, 1873; Philadelphia *Inquirer*, November 5, 1873. The New Jersey Southern Railroad, a major link between Philadelphia and New York, in serious financial trouble, withheld $40,000 of back wages (*New York Times*, January 14, 15, 1874).

8. Knoxville dispatches, Cincinnati *Commercial*, November 5, 7, 1873; Chicago *Times*, November 6, 7, 1873.

McCullough, aware of the thousands of unemployed railroad men, announced, "Let them strike, I can't help it. If it is to be a strike, strike it must be." [9]

Most of the 1873–1874 strikes revealed the power of the railroad workers to disrupt traffic on many roads. Engineers, firemen, and machinists on the East Tennessee, Virginia, and Georgia Railroad demanded fewer hours in place of a wage cut in November 1873, but the Knoxville company turned them down. After the men left work, they removed coupling pins from many freight cars so that master mechanics, nonstriking engineers, and new hands could not move them. No serious violence occurred, but for several days only mail trains left Knoxville. [10] New Jersey Southern Railroad workers tore up sections of track, disabled locomotives, and cut telegraph wires. Where track was removed, they posted signals to prevent accidents. Anxious to collect $40,000 of back wages, the men publicly denied responsibility for these depredations. Still, conditions on the New Jersey line remained chaotic and trains did not run in mid-January and early February 1874. [11] Soon after, track hands on the New York and Oswego Midland Railroad, who wanted five months' back

9. J. D. Layng, Assistant General Manager, Pennsylvania Railroad Company, Pittsburgh, to A. J. Poole, Chairman, Committee of Locomotive Engineers, January 20, 1872, and AJP and nineteen representatives of the various divisions of the Pennsylvania Central Railroad, "Agreement with the Company," n.d., printed in the Indianapolis *Daily Sentinel*, December 28, 1873; Richmond, Indiana, dispatch, Chicago *Tribune*, December 31, 1873; A. J. Poole, "For the Indianapolis Engineers, Resolutions Unanimously Adopted on December 27, 1873," Indianapolis *Daily Sentinel*, December 28, 1873; Peter M. Arthur, "Speech . . . at the Atlanta Convention, 1874," *Brotherhood of Locomotive Engineers' Monthly Journal*, 8 (November, 1874), 584–85; "Interview with J. N. McCullough," Pittsburgh dispatch, Chicago *Times*, December 28, 1873.

10. R.A.B., Knoxville correspondent, Cincinnati *Gazette*, n.d., reported in Chicago *Tribune*, November 8, 1873; Cincinnati *Commercial*, November 5, 7, 1873; Chicago *Times*, November 6, 7, 1873; Manufacturer to the editor, n.d., Cincinnati *Commercial*, November 7, 1873; P. M. Arthur, "Address . . . to the Citizens of Knoxville . . . December 16, 1874"; *Brotherhood of Locomotive Engineers' Monthly Journal*, 9 (January 1875), 33–34.

11. *The New York Times*, January 14, 16, 1874; *Railroad Gazette*, January 24, 1874, p. 31; Philadelphia *Inquirer*, January 16, 1874.

pay, spiked switches and tore up sections of track near Middletown, New York.[12] In April 1874 two hundred and fifty section hands struck the Louisville and Nashville Railroad for the same reasons. Freight trains did not run for a time, and the company told of switches tampered with and water tanks ruined.[13] Brakemen, switchmen, and track hands on the Western New York division of the Erie Railroad also stopped trains. The strike centered in Hornellsville, where the Erie made important connections with other railroads. The workers allowed Erie trains to enter the town but would not let them leave. Within twenty-four hours, trains from three lines crowded the area. The strikers let mail trains pass but removed the brakes from passenger and freight cars. According to one report, seventy-five freight trains and five passenger trains with 1,000 persons were detained for two days.[14]

The Lehigh Valley Railroad's coal line from Pittston, Pennsylvania, to Waverley, New York, was in similar difficulty in March 1874. On the condition that wages would improve when rail traffic picked up, its workers had accepted a 10 percent wage cut in December 1873. The company, however, reneged, and two hundred and fifty men, all the employees except the engineers, struck. Congregating in Waverley, they set brakes, removed brake wheels, switched track, and allowed only mail trains to pass. They escorted stranded passengers to the depot and politely carried their baggage, moved into stalled railroad cars and raised an American flag over their new "home," and visited local hotels and taverns to prevent excessive drinking among the workers. For several days, the workers controlled local affairs.

---

12. *Railroad Gazette*, February 14, 1874, p. 48.

13. Cincinnati *Commercial*, April 18–26, 1874.

14. The brakemen protested after the railroad, in an economy move, dropped one of every four brakemen on a train crew, and the switchmen and track hands complained about a wage cut and a simultaneous order to pay rent "for the shanties in which many of them lived along the railroad line." Details are found in *Railroad Gazette*, March 7, 1874, p. 87; Hornellsville dispatch, Chicago *Tribune*, March 7, 1874; "Strikes—Riot—Revolution," *Woodhull and Claflin's Weekly*, March 14, 1874, pp. 8–9.

An observer noted, "No threats of violence are made—no disorderly conduct is feared—no drinks [are] allowed. . . . The property of the company is being guarded with as much care and zeal as if it were their own." Nevertheless, when officials ran a coal train over the Delaware, Lackawanna, and Western Railroad's tracks, strikers met it, unhooked its cars, and threw the coupling pins into a canal nearby.[15]

Shop workers and repair mechanics in the large Erie Railroad shops in Susquehanna Depot, a Northeastern Pennsylvania town, also struck in late March 1874. They had many grievances against the corporation but especially complained about its failure to pay regular wages. More than 1,000 of them left work on March 25, and they attracted nationwide attention. "Susquehanna is the subject of talk the country over," wrote the Scranton *Times*. The Chicago *Times* called the walkout "one of the most startling incidents that ever occurred in Pennsylvania." [16]

After electing a Workingmen's Committee to manage their affairs, the workers seized control of the repair shops. "Bells were rung" and "a mammoth steam whistle was blown." The men forced company officials from the shops, and within twenty minutes the entire works was cleared and "under the complete control of the men." Temperance committees visited tavern owners and asked them to close. For the moment, the strikers allowed trains through the city but warned Erie officials that

15. Philadelphia *Inquirer*, January 14, March 6, 1874; Philadelphia *Bulletin*, January 14, 1874; Scranton *Times*, March 5, 11, 1874; Chicago *Tribune*, March 5, 1874; *Railroad Gazette*, March 14, 1874, p. 94.

16. The Erie Railroad frequently waited six or eight weeks before paying its employees. Most of the shopmen had worked three-quarters time during the early months of the depression, and in early March they struck and demanded a regular pay date. The company agreed to pay them on the fifteenth of each month, and the strike quickly ended. When March 15 came, the men were put off until March 25, and on that day the Erie managers again announced a postponement. See *Workingman's Advocate*, March 14, 1874; Scranton *Republican*, March 30, 1874; Scranton *Times*, March 28, 1874; Chicago *Times*, April 2, 1874; Pennsylvania Bureau of Labor Statistics, *Ninth Annual Report, 1880–1881*, III (Harrisburg, 1882), 309–10.

they would halt traffic unless they were paid within twenty-four hours and the firm introduced a regular payday, time-and-a-half for overtime work, and a decent apprenticeship system. Instead of paying the men, the managers fired the strike leaders and said wages would be offered at a future unspecified time. On March 27, therefore, the workers made good their threat. "As fast as trains arrived," an Erie official wrote, strikers "proceeded to disable the locomotive by removing portions of the machinery." At least forty-five engines were switched into a roundhouse. Passenger and freight cars were left on track nearby, but mail cars were let through the town. For a few days, rail business remained stalled in Susquehanna Depot. Although a number of prominent citizens found the strikers "quiet and orderly," the agitated shopmen indisputably controlled the Erie Railroad's valuable properties.[17]

Disgruntled engineers and firemen on the western divisions of the Pennsylvania Central Railroad also stopped trains. Acting without the permission of Charles Wilson, western members of the Brotherhood of Locomotive Engineers secretly planned a general strike and invited the firemen to join them in December 1873. A surprise walkout started at noon on December 26. About 3,000 engineers and firemen simultaneously quit in many

17. The behavior of the strikers was quite revealing. When Erie officials refused to allow mail cars through alone, the strikers telegraphed postal authorities in Washington and lodged a complaint against the firm. The Assistant Postmaster-General thanked the strikers for "facilitating the transportation of the United States' mails." Another time, as an express train drew up toward the city, the Erie Division Superintendent met it and ordered the engineer to drive through Susquehanna Depot at full speed and "in spite of hell." Filled with three hundred passengers, the train dashed into the city at an excessive speed and stopped at the rail depot. Beyond the city to the west was a loose rail that could have derailed the entire train. "The Workingmen's Committee knew this," explained the Scranton *Republican*, "and . . . two of their [sic] number boarded the engine at the depot and in spite of the engineer and [Superintendent] Thomas stopped the train." Thomas drew a revolver on the strikers, but he was seized and disarmed, and a warrant was issued for his arrest. See Scranton *Republican*, March 30, 1874; "Statement of James C. Clarke," Third Vice President, Erie Railroad, New York *Tribune*, April 9, 1874; Adjutant General of Pennsylvania, *Annual Report*, 1874 (Harrisburg, 1875), 18–20, 23.

western cities. They struck in large cities such as Chicago, Pittsburgh, Cincinnati, Louisville, Columbus, and Indianapolis as well as smaller Ohio and Indiana towns such as Dennison, Alliance, Crestline, Logansport, and Richmond and affected almost the entire western division of the Pennsylvania system, including the Pittsburgh, Fort Wayne, and Chicago Railroad, the Little Miami Railroad, the Pittsburgh, Cincinnati, and St. Louis Railroad, and the Jeffersonville, Madison, and Indianapolis Railroad. Ohio's Portsmouth *Tribune* called the dispute "the greatest railroad strike" in the nation's history.[18]

The suddenness of the strike paralyzed traffic on most of the Pennsylvania's divisions for several days. Stranded passengers filled the Pittsburgh Union Depot and loaded freight cars piled up in yards nearby. Huge crowds gathered in depot yards in all the affected cities and, egged on by strikers, hooted at workers and company officials who tried to run the trains. In Indianapolis, for example, a noisy crowd jeered loudly as a superintendent manned the locomotive of a Vincennes-bound train. Cincinnati supervisory personnel found it hard to hire new engineers and firemen. Repair shops in many of these cities also closed.[19]

The most serious trouble occurred in Logansport, Indiana, a small rail terminal north of Indianapolis, where two hundred engineers, firemen, and train hostlers halted traffic on the Pittsburgh, Cincinnati, and St. Louis Railroad. The men gath-

18. The Indianapolis branch of the Brotherhood of Locomotive Engineers, for example, publicly criticized the Pennsylvania Railroad for its "oppressive and tyrannical" practices toward men who had "exerted themselves to work for the interest of the company." Though the engineers and firemen openly attacked the company, none publicly mentioned the strike before it actually began. See Portsmouth *Tribune*, December 27, 1873; Cincinnati *Commercial*, December 26–29, 1873; Chicago *Times*, December 26–29, 1873; Indianapolis *Daily Sentinel*, December 26–31, 1873; Charles Wilson, "To All Members of the Brotherhood," n.d., *Brotherhood of Locomotive Engineers' Monthly Journal*, 8 (January 1874), 28–30.

19. See, for many details on the early effects of the strike, Pittsburgh *Post*, December 27, 1873; Cincinnati *Commercial*, December 27, 28, 1873; Chicago *Tribune*, December 27, 28, 30, 1873; Indianapolis *Daily Sentinel*, December 26–31, 1873; Chicago *Times*, December 27, 28, 1873.

ered in the depot yards, uncoupled coaches and freight cars, pulled nonstrikers from their cabs, and tampered with engines and boilers. They fixed one engine so that it could run only backward. A nonstriking engineer was hit with a stone. Even though the sheriff swore in special deputies and arrested fifteen men and the mayor pleaded with the strikers to allow the trains through, company officials found it impossible to conduct their business. When an excited nonstriker drove an express train through the city at a hazardous speed and in violation of state and local law, furthermore, he was arrested. Crowds continued to jam the depot yards, and trains remained still.[20]

In most cities, the strike was less effective than in Logansport. Still, for at least two or three days only mail trains regularly traveled the 3,000 miles of struck road. Passenger trains manned by nonstrikers, company officials, and master mechanics occasionally left one or another of the struck depot yards but few freight trains moved. The engineers and firemen, however, had uneven strength. In some cities, such as Pittsburgh and Chicago, they were quickly put down. In Cincinnati, Louisville, and Columbus, they held out for a week or two. Indianapolis engineers appealed to the traveling public, "We are not ready to sell our labor . . . for a price that would virtually close the doors of our educational institutions against our children and compel them to begin a life of drudgery without the first rudiments of a common school education." Striking Cincinnati engineers explained, "We assure you that we intend to fight it out on this line if it takes all winter and summer, too." [21]

20. Indianapolis *Daily Sentinel*, December 27, 28, 29, 1873; Cincinnati *Commercial*, December 27, 29, 1873; Chicago *Times*, December 27, 1873; Chicago *Tribune*, December 29, 1873. The stoned engineer told a reporter that his assailant, a fireman named J. Hogan, "had no companionship with the Logansport strikers." (Interview with Charley Miller, Chicago *Times*, December 31, 1874.)

21. Division 11, B.L.E., "To the Public," n.d., Indianapolis *Daily Sentinel*, December 31, 1873; Little Miami Railroad Division Engineers, "To the Commuters on the Little Miami Division of the Pennyslvania Central Railroad and the Public in General," n.d., Cincinnati *Enquirer*, January 1, 1874. See also E. Price, First Assistant Engineer, Little Miami Division, B.L.E., Lodge 34, to

The strike was not without a number of violent incidents. Railroad officials everywhere accused the men of throwing switches, cutting telegraph lines, derailing trains, threatening and stoning nonstrikers, disengaging engines, and putting "soap or oil in water tanks to explode engines." In Cincinnati, they blamed the strikers after an express train jumped the track a few miles east of the city. After a former official of the Indianapolis branch of the Brotherhood of Locomotive Engineers shot a nonstriking engineer in the arm as the latter drove a train out of the city, the companies charged the union with fomenting violence. Company spokesmen also reported numerous threats against working engineers and said nonstrikers feared to return to work.[22]

Publicly counseling against violence, the striking engineers and firemen rejected the charges of the railroad companies. The Cincinnati strikers offered a reward for information concerning the derailment and then blamed it on a cowardly nonstriker, who jumped from the express engine after he erroneously threw an air brake. The strikers accused the railroads of hiring "immoral, drunken, rowdy, and incompetent" engineers, who had been discharged previously by the same firms, as strike-breakers. Indianapolis engineers offered a reward for the arrest of those who caused violence and even asked the permission of their employers to guard railroad property against possible destruction. The managers refused and instead armed those men who remained loyal. The strikers then offered to "stand or fall by the verdict of an impartial tribunal" and insisted that certain persons committed "unlawful depredations and charge the same to the engineers and firemen in the hope of turning public opinion against us and in favor of the railroad companies." [23]

Brother Committeemen, n.d., *loc. cit.* Price gave the *Enquirer* the names of "scab" engineers in his letter and urged his fellow-strikers to hang posters everywhere so that the public would learn of the incompetent skills of these "scabs."

22. See, for examples, Chicago *Times*, December 27, 1873; Chicago *Tribune*, December 30, 1873; Cincinnati *Commercial*, December 28, 29, 1873; Indianapolis *Daily Sentinel*, December 28, 29, 30, 1873.

23. The scant and often contradictory nature of the evidence makes it impossible to establish responsibility for the acts of violence. The Cincinnati

In each of these strikes, the workers disrupted traffic and made other kinds of trouble. The character of their behavior closely paralleled events that would take place in the summer of 1877. Commenting on the seizure of railroad property and the halting of trains in 1873-74, *Railroad Gazette* insisted that the workers were in "flat rebellion, not simply against the companies . . . but against the law of the land." Such behavior was "a defiance to every law-abiding citizen." The trade journal explained:

Imagine a servant girl disconnecting the water and gas, putting the range out of order . . . locking up the kitchen, and coolly declaring that there shall be no cooking in the kitchen till she gets her pay and the right to two "afternoons out" weekly.

Charging the strikers with criminal and violent acts, most urban newspapers supported the *Railroad Gazette* and advised "swift, decided, and exemplary" punishment.[24]

Enquirer, no friend to strikers, said that "a large amount of terrorism existed in the minds of [railroad] managers." (Cincinnati *Enquirer*, January 16, 1874. See also *Coopers' New Monthly*, 1 [January 1874], 13–14.) Jerry Bush, who shot the nonunion engineer in Indianapolis, was held in $3,000 bail, but no trial record has been found. (Indianapolis dispatch, Chicago *Tribune*, December 30, 1873.) Samuel Marchbanks was arrested for cutting down telegraph wires near Dennison, Ohio, but no information has been located about his occupation or his motive. (Cadiz, Ohio, dispatch, Cincinnati *Commercial*, February 23, 1874.) There is suggestive but incomplete data concerning the Cincinnati derailment. In mid-January 1874, the Cincinnati railroad companies announced that several private detectives had studied the incident and that seven firemen and an engineer from Zenia, Columbus, and Cincinnati were partners to the "crime." Accused of "conspiracy," planning to pour soap and lye into boilers and engines, and throwing the switch that derailed the express, the men faced jail sentences of from seven to twenty-one years if convicted. One of them, Daniel Harvey, a fireman, confessed and implicated the other six. Henry Lewis, the supposed ringleader, was defended by a prominent Ohio state senator, W. P. Reed. The railroad officials pleaded in Harvey's behalf and said the others had misled him. No record has been found of the outcome of the trial. (*Ibid.*, January 16, 1874; Cincinnati *Enquirer*, January 16, 21, March 14, 1874.)

24. "Railroads Seized by Strikers," *Railroad Gazette*, April 4, 1874, p. 122; "The Railroad Strike," Philadelphia *Bulletin*, December 27, 1873. See also the

Evidence of community support for the 1873-74 railroad strikers also suggested a parallel with the later 1877 events.[25] Engineers and firemen from the Alabama and Chattanooga Railroad refused to run idle Knoxville trains during the East Tennessee, Virginia, and Georgia Railroad strike.[26] The strikers on the New Jersey Southern Railroad found local support in and near Manchester, New Jersey, and even though the railroad pleaded for state and even federal intervention in its behalf, the New Jersey legislature made back wages a first lien on the receipts of railroads in receivership.[27] During the Lehigh Valley Railroad dispute, Erie Railroad workers brought the strikers provisions, and many Waverley citizens also supported them.[28]

editorials in Philadelphia *Inquirer*, December 27, 1873; Cincinnati *Commercial*, December 28, 1873; Chicago *Times*, December 30, 31, 1873; Chicago *Tribune*, December 28, 1873; extracts from editorials in Louisville *Courier and Journal*, n.d., Chicago *Inter-Ocean*, n.d., Cincinnati *Times*, n.d., and other Western and Southern newspapers reprinted in the Indianapolis *Daily Sentinel*, December 30 and 31, 1873. Certain newspapers such as *The New York Times* and the Chicago *Tribune*, however, took a more conciliatory approach and especially criticized those roads that failed to pay their workers on time. "Men who are starving for the want of wages," observed *The Times*, ". . . cannot be expected to be always reasonable." "They are dependent on their wages for bread," wrote the Chicago *Tribune* of the Susquehanna Depot strikers. "The remedy of a law-suit is a mockery to a starving man or, in this case, a starving community." While critical of the Erie Railroad, these same newspapers and others still supported the Pennsylvania governor when he sent militia to allow the trains to run again. See, for examples of this moderately critical attitude, *The New York Times*, March 29, 31, 1874; Chicago *Tribune*, March 30, 1874. See also Cleveland *Leader*, March 31, 1874; Philadelphia *Bulletin*, March 30, 1874.

25. Evidence of the character of community support for workers during other industrial disputes at the start of the 1873 depression can be found in Herbert G. Gutman, "Two Lockouts in Pennsylvania, 1873–1874," *The Pennsylvania Magazine of History and Biography*, 83 (July 1959), 322–25 and "An Iron Workers' Strike in the Ohio Valley," *The Ohio Historical Quarterly*, 68 (October 1959), 357–58, 361, 363, 365–69.

26. Knoxville dispatches, Chicago *Tribune*, November 8, 1873; Chicago *Times*, November 6, 7, 1873; Cincinnati *Commercial*, November 6, 7, 1873.

27. *The New York Times*, January 24, February 20, 1874; *Railroad Gazette*, January 31, February 21, 1874, pp. 40, 66. The strike finally ended when the workers signed an agreement under which the road's receivers would lease the road so that the net earnings of the line could be applied to the payment of back wages as a first lien.

28. Scranton *Times*, March 11, 1874.

When four hundred freight depot hands in New York City demanded predepression wages and special overtime rates from the Erie Railroad, a Catholic priest encouraged them.[29] Similarly, striking brakemen on the Chicago and Alton Railroad were aided by Bloomington, Illinois, citizens in June 1874.[30]

During the Pennsylvania Central dispute, the disaffected engineers and firemen also found a good deal of sympathy from nonstrikers. An Indianapolis militia officer complained that the Logansport authorities were helpless because the "public" actively sided with the railroad workers. He also found that the Indianapolis troops sent to Logansport had no heart in their work and wanted to go home. A Dennison, Ohio, resident repudiated charges that local strikers behaved like "drunken rioters" and insisted that the Steubenville militia, sent to put down "violence" in Dennison, was embittered over its task. Cincinnati socialists demonstrated in support of the strikers, and in Columbus, nonstriking engineers promised the strikers half of their wages. Enthusiastic numbers of Indianapolis workers defended and even aided the strikers. Local trade unions, such as the Iron Molders' Union, the Carpenters' and Joiners' Union, and the Indianapolis Trades' Assembly, commended their "pluck against acts of tyranny," and the Indianapolis Typographical Union, after urging the strikers "to resist the unjust demands of this [railroad] monopoly to the bitter end," voted them $300. Members of the Machinists' and Blacksmiths' International Union in the Indianapolis repair shops refused to fix damaged Pennsylvania engines, and John Fehrenbatch, the union's national president, visited the city and defended the engineers and firemen.[31]

29. *The New York Times*, March 21, 22, 23, 25, 26, 27, 29, 1874; Chicago *Tribune*, March 24, 1874.

30. *Ibid.*, June 3–6, 1874; Chicago *Times*, June 3–6, 1874.

31. Daniel Macauley, Logansport, to Governor Thomas A. Hendricks, Indianapolis, December 29, 1873; D.M., Logansport, to the mayor and sheriff, Logansport, n.d.; Mayor S. L. McFadden, "A Proclamation," n.d.; and other details printed in the Indianapolis *Daily Sentinel*, December 29, 30, 31, 1873; Resolutions of the Printers' Union, the Carpenters' and Joiners' Union, the Iron

The Indianapolis strikers also attracted substantial backing from the nonlaboring population. The mayor, a prominent local judge, and several members of the city council attacked the Pennsylvania Railroad. General Daniel Macauley, who had just returned from Logansport where he headed the Indianapolis militia and restored order, joined other local dignitaries who "extended their sympathies to the engineers" and encouraged "them in their efforts to break up the monopoly which has been oppressing them." Letters in the local press generally favored the strikers: one asked if the railroad officials were "gods that mortal men dare not speak to?" The Indianapolis *Daily Sentinel*, a Democratic newspaper, called the railroads an "oligarchy . . . more powerful . . . than the absolutism of the Napoleons." Harking back to Jacksonian concepts, the *Sentinel* blamed the strike on "the great interests" and "the grasping and imbecile management of the great corporations." [32]

Many of Susquehanna Depot's 8,000 inhabitants, although dependent on the Erie Railroad whose shops dominated the local economy, also supported and aided the strikers. When railroad officials announced the dismissal of the strike leaders and demanded that M. B. Helme, the Lackawanna County sheriff, organize a posse and drive the shopmen from the railroad's properties, Helme refused to act until the strikers received all the wages due them. Soon after, when Helme and a thirty-five-man posse arrived near the shops, the strikers refused to talk with them unless they came disarmed. Helme surrendered their arms to the strikers, who then allowed the police to stay in the shops and "preserve order." Local law enforcement

Molders' Union, the Machinists' and Blacksmiths' International Union, and the Indianapolis Trades' Assembly, printed in *ibid.*, January 2, 4, 7, 1874; John Fehrenbatch's visit is described in *ibid.*, January 3, 1874; and the Chicago *Tribune*, December 31, 1874; the Dennison details are revealed in H. B. Keffer, Dennison, to the editor, December 30, 1873, Cincinnati *Commercial*, January 3, 1874. See also Indianapolis *Daily Sentinel*, December 29, 1873 and January 11, 1874; Chicago *Times*, December 30, 1873; Chicago *Tribune*, December 29, 30, 1873.

32. Indianapolis *Daily Sentinel*, January 3, 4, 5, 8, 1874.

authorities also thwarted the company's importation of two hundred "special police" from New York and New Jersey. Scranton reporters called these two hundred men "a gang of ruffians of the no-profession-in-particular class." Together with a number of strikers, Sheriff Helme intercepted the strangers outside of the town, disarmed them of their "billies and revolvers," and, after threatening their arrest, shipped them back home.[33]

At the same time, other local citizens supported the strikers. A prominent officer in the state militia told Governor John Hartranft that the shopmen had "the sympathy of nearly if not all the citizens of the town." As a result, a friend of the Erie company exploded, "The Commune could do no more." "Public sympathy is with the men," wrote the Scranton *Times*, "and *'vox populi vox dei'* is a fairer law than many of our statutes embody." When Governor Hartranft agreed to send troops, leading local citizens, including a justice of the peace, a town burgess, an assistant postmaster, and a physician, assailed his decision. Why, asked one critic, were troops needed if the strikers were "quiet [and] orderly and the mails . . . allowed to run?" A petition signed by a majority of the city's prominent residents charged Hartranft with "supporting the interests of a corporation against our own citizens, who ask nothing but their hard-earned wages." "In the name of humanity," the petitioners asked him to withdraw the soldiers.[34]

33. Scranton *Times*, March 29, 1874; Scranton *Republican*, March 30, 1874; "Statement of J. C. Clarke," New York *Tribune*, April 9, 1874.

34. Scranton *Republican*, March 30, 1874; S. H. Daddow, Scranton, to the editor, March 30, 1874, *ibid.*, March 31, 1874; Scranton *Times*, March 31, 1874. General E. S. Osbourne, Susquehanna Depot, to Governor J. F. Hartranft, Harrisburg, March 29, 1874, printed in Adjutant General of Pennsylvania, *op. cit.*, 20; ESO, Wilkes-Barre, to Major-General James Latta, Harrisburg, October 1, 1874, *ibid.*, 23–24; W. H. Telford, Susquehanna Depot, to Governor JFH, Harrisburg, March 28, 1874; WHT, S. Mitchell, A. M. Falkenberg, C. Ovidor, and Dr. Leslie, Susquehanna Depot, to JFH, Harrisburg, March 29, 1874; petition enclosed in Burgess William J. Falkenburg, Susquehanna Depot, to JFH, Harrisburg, March 29, 1874; *ibid.*, 18–20. A copy of the petition also appeared in the Scranton *Republican*, March 30, 1874. The petitioners told the

In neighboring Scranton, the *Times* and the *Republican* backed the shopmen, too. Admitting that their seizure of property was illegal, the *Times* still defended the workers:

The law is an uncertain, tedious, and expensive means of reaching a powerful corporation. It was an insult to these men to retain their wages upon which most of them were dependent for their bread—bread for their families. "The laborer is worthy of his hire" and he should have it.

To withhold his wages was "an insult . . . to his dignity as a citizen and to his worth as a workman." "An insulted man," the *Times* concluded, "don't [*sic*] think about law and legal redress . . . Erie has wronged its labor grossly and got its blow." [35]

The popular support afforded the strikers expressed itself in many ways. Citizens housed marooned Erie passengers. A local minister preached a severe Sunday sermon against the Erie company. After the state troops arrived, many merchants refused to sell them provisions, and some soldiers suffered "for want of food." The Susquehanna Depot *Gazette* accused the

governor: "The peace of this community is not disturbed, and the sheriff has been assured by the strikers that if any arrests are to be made, they will assist him if called upon." The petitioners also protested "against the employment of troops under the command of the paid counsel of the company," William Jessup, "in whose interests they are to be used." Hartranft, however, insisted that troops were necessary. He accused the shopmen of trying to "obtain their rights by violence" and not respecting "the laws of the country." "As an individual," Hartranft explained, "I may sympathize with your people in their misfortune in not receiving prompt payment of their dues, but as the chief Executive of this State, I can not allow creditors . . . to forcibly seize [the] property of their debtors and hold it without due process of law. . . . Whenever the laws of this Commonwealth shall provide that the employees of a railroad company may suspend all traffic upon it, until their wages are paid, I will acquiesce, but I cannot do so while the law refuses to contemplate any such remedy. . . ." (Governor JFH, Harrisburg, to WHT, Susquehanna Depot, March 28, 1874; JFH, Harrisburg, to WHT, Susquehanna Depot, March 29, 1874; and JFH, Harrisburg, to WJF, Susquehanna Depot, March 29, 1874; printed in Adjutant General of Pennsylvania, *op. cit.*, 20–21.)

35. Scranton *Times*, March 31, 1874. See also editorials in Scranton *Republican*, March 30, 31, 1874.

troops of stealing cigarettes and liquor and called them "Molly Maguires," who insulted citizens and created "forty times more disturbance than the strikers." Among the militia itself, a large majority were reported in sympathy with the shopmen. In light of all this hostility toward the Erie Railroad, it was not surprising that company officials bitterly complained of the "bad advice . . . certain citizens of this place" gave the workers.[36]

The railroad strikes in 1873-74 created a number of difficulties for management. In many of the strikes, the employers learned that they had a rather tenuous hold on the loyalties of their men. Something was radically wrong if workers could successfully stop trains for from two or three days to as much as a week, destroy property, and even "manage" it as if it were their own. The law itself seemed insufficient. *Iron Age* called for new legislation modeled after the English Master's and Servant's Act and prohibiting "surprise" strikes. *Railroad Gazette* suggested an even harsher remedy: the strikers were "ignorant and violent," had no respect for "law," and deserved only "bayonets." [37]

Except in the Hornellsville strike, the railroad companies declined to compromise with the strikers.[38] Unemployment was especially severe in the industry during the early months of the depression. In many instances, therefore, the companies brought in new workers. When five hundred Buffalo freight handlers, brakemen, carpenters, painters, and track hands struck for back wages as well as a regular payday, Erie Railroad officials simply fired more than half of them.[39] Disaffected Chicago and Alton

36. Scranton *Times*, March 30, 31, 1874; Scranton *Republican*, March 30, 31, 1874; Susquehanna Depot *Gazette*, n.d., reprinted in *ibid.*, April 8, 1874; J. C. Clarke, Susquehanna Depot, to President Lucius D. Robinson, New York, March 30, 1874, printed in Scranton *Times*, April 1, 1874.

37. *Iron Age*, January 8, 1874, pp. 16–17; "Railroad's Seized by Strikers," *Railroad Gazette*, April 4, 1874, p. 122.

38. *Ibid.*, March 7, 1874, p. 87; Chicago *Tribune*, March 7, 1874; *Woodhull and Claflin's Weekly*, March 14, 1874, pp. 8–9.

39. *Railroad Gazette*, March 14, 21, 1874, pp. 94, 100; Chicago *Tribune*, March 4, 5, 6, 1874; *The New York Times*, March 6, 1874; Scranton *Times*, March 6, 1874; *Locomotive Engineer's Advocate*, March 14, 1874, reprinted in *Workingman's Advocate*, March 21, 1874.

Railroad brakemen also lost their jobs.[40] In New York City, after four hundred freight depot hands struck against the Erie Railroad, the company hired Italian and German workers. Hungry unemployed Italians also replaced discontented tunnel builders on a Delaware, Lackawanna, and Western Railroad project near Hoboken, New Jersey. Most of them had been "unemployed for a long time because of hard times" and "manifested great eagerness to begin work." [41] New engineers and firemen also took the jobs of many strikers on the Pennsylvania Railroad system. In Crestline, Ohio, a small railroad town where many workers lived, company officials ordered them "to surrender unconditionally to the company's order or . . . leave the services of the road for all time." The Indianapolis *Daily Sentinel* found that widespread unemployment dealt a "death blow" to the engineers and firemen.[42]

If it proved difficult to bring in new workers, the railroad managers used other techniques to defeat the strikers. In one instance, according to the engineers, the Pennsylvania Central tried to halt mail trains so as to force federal intervention against the strikers.[43] More common employer instruments were the blacklist and the iron-clad contract. Before striking New York City freight depot workers could return, they had to pledge never to join a union or strike.[44] During the East Tennessee, Virginia, and Georgia Railroad strike, the company fired all workers belonging to ". . . any league, body, organization, or combination which instigates . . . acts of disorder, violence, and wrong." At the same time, representatives of twenty Southern

40. Chicago *Times*, June 3–7, 1874; Chicago *Tribune*, June 3–7, 1874.

41. William Jessup, New York, to the editor, April 1, 1874, *Workingman's Advocate,* April 11, 1874; *The New York Times*, March 21, 22, 23, 24, 25, 26, 27, 29, 1874; Chicago *Tribune*, March 24, 1874.

42. Indianapolis *Daily Sentinel*, January 5, 14, 1874; Chicago *Tribune*, December 31, 1873; Chicago *Times*, December 30, 1873; Cincinnati *Commercial*, December 31, 1873.

43. Indianapolis *Daily Sentinel*, December 31, 1873 and January 1, 1874; Chicago *Times*, December 29, 1873.

44. *The New York Times*, March 21, 22, 23, 25, 26, 27, and 29, 1874; Chicago *Tribune*, March 24, 1874.

roads met in Chattanooga and unanimously decided not to hire workers discharged for "insubordination or combination to stop the operations on any road by intimidation or interference with others willing to work." These companies also drew up a list of proscribed workers and circulated it throughout the region.[45] When the strikers, led by the engineers, sought a compromise, they were ordered to surrender their union charter. Twenty-two of them, who signed an iron-clad contract, publicly declared:

> We now acknowledge that we have been beaten, and that we were in error. . . . We have withdrawn from the organization known as the "Brotherhood of Locomotive Engineers," and if you think it proper to employ us again, we will work for you as faithfully as we ever did before, notwithstanding the reduction in wages. . . .[46]

Leaders of the strike against the Pennsylvania system also were blacklisted. The Chicago *Times* found men returning to work after they learned that the company had "marked some of the bell-wethers . . . of this strike for the shambles." Some strikers, such as the Columbus men, held out in the hope of "forcing the employment of even the leaders," but the company's threats proved effective. The company sent the names of the strike leaders "through the length and breadth of the country." Although the Brotherhood of Locomotive Engineers warned of a bitter "conflict," the workers on the Pennsylvania Railroad remained quiet until the violent uprisings of 1877.[47]

State militia put down some of the more truculent strikers. Troops went to Dennison, Ohio, and Logansport, Indiana,

45. Knoxville dispatches, Chicago *Times*, November 7, 8, 1873.

46. The entire correspondence between the engineers and the railroad officials is found in the *Brotherhood of Locomotive Engineers' Monthly Journal*, 7 (December 1873), 579–80 and *ibid.*, 9 (January 1875), 33–34.

47. Chicago *Times*, December 29, 30, 31, 1873; Cincinnati *Commercial*, January 3, 1874; Indianapolis *Daily Sentinel*, January 3, 1874; *Brotherhood of Locomotive Engineers' Monthly Journal*, n.d., reprinted in *Coopers' New Monthly*, 1 (July 1874), 14.

during the Pennsylvania Railroad dispute. On the second day of the strike, Indiana Governor Thomas A. Hendricks answered an appeal for aid from the Logansport sheriff and sent two companies of militia. Led by General Daniel Macauley and armed with breech-loading repeater rifles, the soldiers guarded the depot, tracks, and trains. They accompanied trains leaving the city and quieted "large crowds of excited men." Though some railroad workers "proffered their sympathy" to Macauley, he arrested a number of strikers, swore in special deputies, had Hendricks send a detachment of Indianapolis city police, and convinced the Logansport mayor to issue a riot proclamation that ordered citizens "to their several homes or places of business in order that peace . . . be preserved." Within a few days, the militia and police restored normal traffic and left Logansport.[48]

In Susquehanna Depot, state troops also were used. After Sheriff M. B. Helme refused to ask Governor John Hartranft for militia, William H. Jessup, the Erie's lawyer in Susquehanna Depot and a ranking officer in the Pennsylvania National Guard, telegraphed the governor that "a mob of 1000 have seized the railroad trains, stopped the mails, and are causing terror." Jessup asked for seven hundred soldiers. Hartranft reminded Jessup that only the sheriff could ask for militia and rejected his plea. A day later, amid unsubstantiated "rumors" that Sheriff Helme had been "bribed" by the railroad firm to "betray" the shopmen, Helme publicly ordered the strikers to let the passenger trains through. He advised them that the road would pay them back wages and then discharge them. The shopmen agreed to allow the trains to move. Yet, when it *appeared* that they were stalling, Helme wired Hartranft to send 1,500 soldiers armed with "plenty of ammunition." Dispatching the Wilkes-Barre militia, Hartranft told its commanding officer,

48. The correspondence between the Logansport sheriff and mayor, General Macauley, and Governor Hendricks is found in the Indianapolis *Daily Sentinel*, December 28, 29, 30, 31, 1873, and January 4, 1874. For other details see *ibid.*, December 27, 1873, to January 5, 1874; Chicago *Times*, December 30, 1873; Chicago *Tribune*, December 30, 1873.

"Use every effort to restore order without bloodshed. Suppress the riot, disperse the rioters, and afford security and protection to the owners of property in its lawful use." [49]

Even though prominent citizens protested, Susquehanna Depot soon became an armed camp. Major-General E. S. Osbourne, the head of the Wilkes-Barre militia, admitted that the shopmen were "not disposed to commit violence," but he asked Hartranft for more troops, and the governor sent the Philadelphia First Regiment. Special trains supplied by the region's coal railroads brought the Philadelphia soldiers, and Susquehanna Depot, a town of 8,000, was patrolled by 1,800 soldiers and an artillery group with thirty pieces of cannon. The militia took over the railroad properties and worked closely with company officials. Martial law was proclaimed, and no one could walk on company property without a special pass. Erie Vice President James C. Clarke fired all the workers and promised them their wages after the trains left town. The shopmen let several loaded passenger trains through, but hesitated about the freight trains. At the same time, they overwhelmingly rejected the company's terms of settlement and asked it to rehire them all. "I shall run the road," Clarke telegraphed President Lucius Robinson in New York. "I am through [with] compromise. I have offered everything but the right of the company to operate its own property subject to the laws which created it." [50]

---

49. The correspondence between Jessup, Helme, and Hartranft, as well as the communications to the militia leaders, is printed in Adjutant General of Pennsylvania, *op. cit.*, 17–18, 22. See also Scranton *Republican*, March 30, 1874. The Erie Railroad took a false public position regarding its request for state troops. According to James Clarke, who issued a statement that appeared in the New York *Tribune* of April 9, the company did not ask for troops until Saturday, March 28, after the strikers had reneged on their promise to let all trains through the city. Jessup's telegrams, however, are dated March 27, 1874.

50. The vote by which shopmen rejected the company offer was either 476–11 or 478–48. Details on the events after the troops arrived are found in Adjutant General of Pennsylvania, *op. cit.*, 20, 23–24; Scranton *Republican*, March 30, 31, 1874; Scranton *Times*, March 30, 1874; J. C. Clarke, Susquehanna Depot, to L. Robinson, New York, March 30, 1874, printed in *ibid.*, April 1, 1874.

The strikers remained firm for a few more days, but it was to no avail. Twelve hundred shopmen paraded the streets and demanded to be rehired. But the company paid and discharged all of them. The militia formed "a cordon of bayonets on both sides of the depot and track for half a mile" while the men were paid off. Clarke announced that four hundred new workers were needed. No strike leader was to be taken back, and only family men with suitable references were advised to apply for jobs. At first, the strikers held off, "determined to stick to their resolution of 'work for all or none.'" The company thereupon announced that unless some of the old hands accepted its terms the shops would move to Elmira. A number of business people and other residents, undoubtedly fearing that the local economy would collapse without the repair shops, turned against the shopmen and formed a committee of sixty to protect the railroad's interests. "They see," wrote the Scranton *Republican*, "that unless they keep the shops running their businesses will be ruined." The leader of these businessmen was a local politician, who a few days before had protested to Governor Hartranft when he sent the militia. Now, he furnished the Erie Railroad's counsel with the names of leading strikers for possible criminal prosecution. When the shops reopened on April 1, four hundred and six old hands showed up. In the end, the company took back all but one hundred and fifty of the strikers. It denied work to the leaders of the strike, who left the town in search of jobs. Clarke insisted that only those men "interested in the success and welfare of the community in which they lived" were rehired. By effectively combining military power (which cost the Pennsylvania taxpayers $25,000 because the soldiers received salary for half a month although they served only five or six days) with economic coercion, the Erie restored its position in Susquehanna Depot.[51]

Several brief but pertinent observations may be made about

51. *Ibid.,* April 1, 2, 1874; Scranton *Republican*, April 2, 1874; "Statement of J. C. Clarke," New York *Tribune*, April 9, 1874; Chicago *Times*, April 1, 1874; Adjutant General of Pennsylvania, *op. cit.,* 24–27; Pennsylvania Bureau of Labor Statistics, *op. cit.,* 309–10; *Army and Navy Journal*, May 2, 1874, p. 653.

the 1873-74 railroad strikes. First, local discontent sparked the strikes; they were neither centrally directed nor national in scope. Two of the strikes involving engineers, in fact, were condemned by the head of the Brotherhood of Locomotive Engineers, who publicly assailed the strikers and advised other workers to replace them.[52] Secondly, the ability of workers in so

52. Wilson ran into difficulty after he attacked the striking engineers on the East Tennessee, Virginia, and Georgia Railroad and on the Pennsylvania Railroad. The leaders of other national unions called him a friend of "scabs" and "unjust employers," and they blamed him for the defeat of the workers. The *Iron Molders' Journal* labeled him "a grand corporosity." During the Pennsylvania Railroad strike, Wilson publicly announced: "No dishonor will be attached to any man who accepts a situation from Pennsylvania Railroad during the present strike." Engineers in Columbus, Louisville, and other cities denounced him, but the urban press and business weeklies said he was a model labor leader and not "molded . . . on the European plan." After the Pennsylvania strike ended, Wilson continued his attack on the strikers and argued that "strife between labor and capital" could but be ended by "civil war." Enraged Pittsburgh engineers published an eight-page monthly, the *Locomotive Engineers' Advocate*, which sharply attacked his policies, and, finally, in February 1874, he was removed from office by the nearly unanimous vote of delegates to a special convention of the BLE. Peter M. Arthur, who was to dominate the union for the next quarter of a century and give it a distinctly conservative flavor, replaced him as the "reform" candidate. Wilson's behavior in the two strikes is found in Chicago *Times*, November 9, 1873; CW, "Remarks," *Brotherhood of Locomotive Engineers' Monthly Journal*, 7 (December 1873), 379-80; "Law and Order," *Iron Molders' Journal* (December 1873), 165-66; CW to the Public, Cleveland *Herald*, n.d., reprinted in the Chicago *Tribune*, December 29, 1873; CW to the Associated Press, Cincinnati *Commercial*, December 29, 1873; Chicago *Times*, December 31, 1873; Indianapolis *Daily Sentinel*, January 6, 1874; "The Strike and the Brotherhood," *Railroad Gazette*, January 3, 1874, 4-5; Cleveland *Leader*, January 12, 1874. Criticism of Wilson is found in *Workingman's Advocate*, December 27, 1873, January 3, 1874; *Machinists' and Blacksmiths' Journal*, n.d., reprinted in *ibid.*, February 7, 1874; *Coopers' New Monthly*, 1 (January 1874), 13-14; *Iron Molders' Journal* (January 1874), 200. Wilson's defense is presented in CW, "General Statement," *Brotherhood of Locomotive Engineers' Monthly Journal*, 7 (January 1874), 29-30; CW to the editor, Cleveland *Leader*, January 5, 1874; CW and E. S. Ingram to the Members and Officers of the BLE, *Railroad Gazette*, February 21, 1874, pp. 59-60. The later attack on Wilson is found in L. B. Greene, "To the Brotherhood," *Brotherhood of Locomotive Engineers' Monthly Journal*, 8 (February 1874), 86; "The Locomotive Engineers," *Iron Molders' Journal* (February 1874), 243-44 and *ibid.* (March 1874), 273. Wilson's removal is described in Cleveland *Leader*, February 21-28, 1874, and Chicago *Tribune*, February 21-28, 1874.

many different towns and regions to stop trains and "take over" railroad properties as well as the degree of public support tendered these men indicates that certain institutional and ideological factors added to the strength of the workers and temporarily, at least, weakened the power of the employers and created additional obstacles for them to surmount. The sympathy the workers found in Waverley, Manchester, Indianapolis, Logansport, and Susquehanna Depot often came from property owners who supported the strikers even though their spontaneous protests (the response to deeply felt grievances and the absence of experienced trade-union leadership) were extreme and often violent. Not unusual, for example, was the attitude reflected in an editorial in the Scranton *Times* during the strike on the Pennsylvania system:

> Labor is the great moving power of the world and has the same right to unite for its own advancement that capital has to mass itself for the aggrandizement of the few who control it. . . . [If the railroads] have the right to reduce the wages of workmen, the workmen themselves have the right to dissolve the partnership and take their labor out of the firm. Capital and labor together earn a certain profit which should be equitably divided.[53]

In many small towns in the 1870s, and in sharp contrast to the larger cities of that time, the discontented worker still was viewed by his fellow citizens as an individual and was not yet the stereotyped "labor agitator," who so often stirred an automatically negative reflex from his more fortunate observer. The support tendered these railroad workers in 1873-74, furthermore, was not unique to the structure and reputation of that industry. Similar attitudes shaped the behavior of nonindustrial property owners during conflicts that involved coal miners and iron, textile, and glass workers in the 1870s.[54]

53. Scranton *Times*, December 31, 1873.
54. Supporting data is found in the articles by the author cited in footnote 25. See also Herbert G. Gutman, "Social and Economic Structure and Depression:

Finally, even though the troubles that railroad operators faced in 1873-74 were small and insignificant compared with those that developed in July 1877, the same essential patterns of behavior that were widespread in 1877 were found in the 1873-74 strikes. Three and a half years of severe depression ignited a series of local brush fires into a national conflagration that seared the conscience as well as the confidence of the entire nation. The 1877 railroad strikes are put into their proper historical context only when measured against the events that took place in 1873-74.

American Labor in 1873 and 1874," unpublished Ph.D., University of Wisconsin, 1959, v–xvii, 1–203.

7

Two Lockouts in Pennsylvania, 1873–1874

THE INDUSTRIAL HISTORY of Pennsylvania after the Civil War is characterized by a series of problems and crises that shaped the development of the new economy. There is no single pattern in this process, for each area faced its own difficulties and resolved them in a different way. Moreover, the social structure within which industry emerged differed between regions and affected the various patterns and subpatterns of economic development.

Soon after the 1873 depression started, two lockouts occurred in coal-mining areas. One involved the giant Cambria Iron Works in Johnstown, the other the mine operators in Tioga County. The issues were the same: the coal diggers had turned to trade unionism for self-protection. Both areas were semirural and isolated from the major centers of Pennsylvania industry. The employers in both Johnstown and Tioga County, furthermore, had constructed a seemingly all-powerful system of social control. Still, the outcome was different. The reasons for these dissimilar results offer certain insights into the many-sided character of industrial development after the Civil War.

Readers of *The New York Times* in 1874 learned that the Cambria Iron Works in Johnstown was "the finest iron works in

This article, in part, developed from research made possible by a fellowship granted by the Social Science Research Council.

the country and one of the glories of Pennsylvania industry." There was much truth in this observation, for by 1873, just twenty years after the firm was founded, it was already a huge enterprise. Built on the main line of the Pennsylvania Railroad, seventy-eight miles east of Pittsburgh, the Cambria Iron Works owned about forty thousand acres of valuable mineral lands in the region surrounding Johnstown and nourished itself with needed supplies of iron ore, semibituminous coal, and limestone. The company displayed a degree of vertical integration rare at the time, and used these raw materials in a complex that included four modern blast furnaces and forty-two double-turn puddling furnaces. The Johnstown company, not surprisingly, produced more iron rails than any other of the nation's eighty-odd rail factories. In 1871, for example, 160,373 tons of wrought iron, mostly rails, came from its furnaces. In that same year, it opened one of the country's first Bessemer steelworks. A firm as large and well-integrated as the Cambria Iron Works needed a huge labor force, including coal and ore miners, blast furnace operators, and rolling mill hands. In good times, when the demand for iron rails was brisk, six thousand men and boys worked in the Johnstown mills and mines. By any standards of the day, the Cambria Iron Works was a large and efficient industrial organization.[1]

Contemporaries marveled at the scope of the Johnstown company and praised it and its general manager, Daniel J. Morrell. Albert Bolles, a close student of American industry, for example, called the firm "a magnificent enterprise," while popular biographer and lecturer James Parton told an audience at the New York Cooper Institute that Morrell irrefutably proved that "a king of business is a king of men." Parton said

1. *Saward's Coal Circular*, n.d., reprinted in *Frank Cowan's Paper*, December 24, 1873; Special Correspondent, Johnstown, April 14, 1874, *The New York Times*, April 21, 1874; Cambria, Johnstown, April 16, 1874, Chicago *Times*, April 20, 1874; Pennsylvania Bureau of Labor Statistics, *Second Annual Report, 1873–1874* (Harrisburg, 1875), 254–87; James MacFarlane, *The Coal-Regions of America* (New York, 1873), 176–78; and Victor S. Clark, *History of Manufactures in the United States* (New York, 1929), 2: 16, 71, 77, 82, 99, 150, and 232.

that Morrell was "a judge of men who knows how to pick the men he wants and keeps them by treating them as he would like to be treated in their place." [2] Others reiterated this theme. In his exhaustive study *The Coal-Regions of America*, James MacFarlane insisted that men like Morrell were "greater benefactors of our race" than "those who bestow millions on the starving and destitute." Morrell illustrated "all that capital, enterprise, and science" could do "for the prosperity of a country." "What greater blessing," MacFarlane asked, "can be conferred on a locality, in a material aspect, than the building of a vast industrial centre" such as Johnstown's Cambria Iron Works? [3]

In and near Johnstown, the Cambria Iron Works and little else counted, for the iron mill, almost of necessity, dominated the life of that city and its environs. For one thing, it so towered over nearby mining and manufacturing companies that local and regional competition was almost nonexistent. Like many other semirural manufacturing and mining enterprises, furthermore, the Cambria Iron Works could attract its labor force only if it supplied it with certain necessities. The company built and owned most of the houses, stores, schools, and even libraries that dotted the Johnstown landscape.[4] As a consequence, it held almost unexampled economic and social power in the region. Morrell, finally, was not an absentee owner, for he lived in Johnstown and tried to model the community in his own image. He said he wanted to create "a civilized, intelligent, Christian community" and not live "in the midst of ignorant and turbulent savages." Moreover, since the American worker was free and "subject to no fetters of class or caste," he deserved to "live in a house not a hut" and to "wear good clothes and eat wholesome and nourishing food." At least in Johnstown, Morrell concluded, industry and labor alike would be "organized into a distinct American system." [5]

2. Albert S. Bolles, *Industrial History of the United States* (Norwich, Conn., 1881), 209, and James Parton, "Kings of Business," New York *Tribune*, October 15, 1874.

3. MacFarlane, *op. cit.*, 176–78.

4. Parton, *op. cit.*

5. "Speech of Daniel Morrell," n.d., *Iron Molders' Journal* (April 1875), 295–96. See also Parton, *op. cit.*

The conception that Morrell had of a model industrial community allowed for company-sponsored schools and libraries, but there was little room for trade unions in Johnstown. For one thing, the labor force grew so rapidly that the stability needed for permanent labor organizations hardly existed. During the prosperous years before 1873, only the skilled puddlers and coal miners had unions. The puddlers belonged to a branch of the Sons of Vulcan, but no record exists of successful bargaining by that union.[6] The coal miners, however, were more fortunate, and after starting a local union in 1871 successfully negotiated a sliding wage agreement with the company under which the wage of the coal digger rose or fell according to the price of iron rails in New York. Although the union fell apart in June 1873, the wage agreement remained intact through the fall months of that year.[7]

The center of the semibituminous coal industry after the Civil War was in Tioga County, Pennsylvania. Since most of these valuable coal deposits were near the town of Blossburg, contemporaries referred to the Tioga product as "Blossburg coal." As early as 1792, coal had been mined in Tioga for local use, and, starting in the 1840s, began to be shipped out of the region. From then on, Tioga County and Blossburg coal grew in economic importance. The output of coal increased steadily, and in 1871 no less than 815,079 tons came from the Tioga mines. In 1873, according to James MacFarlane, "few other places in the United States" had turned out so much bituminous coal "from within the same limited area." [8]

The importance of Tioga County as a coal-producing area turned on two fundamental economic considerations. First of all, Blossburg coal was a much-desired fuel because it had "a wider range in its uses than any other kind of coal." Entirely free of sulphur, semibituminous coal had an enormous heating

---

6. *Vulcan Record*, 1 (Summer, 1874), 24–25.

7. Trampled Down Miners, Johnstown, to the editor, March 30, 1874, *Workingman's Advocate*, April 11, 1874.

8. MacFarlane, *op. cit.*, 6, 134, 151.

power and made "a good hollow fire." Puddling furnaces found
it useful, as did blacksmiths and ironsmiths. Blossburg coal,
however, was most valuable for generating steam in stationary
engines and locomotives, and both the railroad and iron
industries eagerly bought up supplies of Tioga coal. Apart from
having an extremely useful product, the Tioga region had
another economic advantage, for it lay on the New York-Penn-
sylvania border and so was near the expanding industries and
railroads of Western New York. A valley adjacent to the Tioga
River reached northward and made this New York market
easily accessible. After 1840, a railroad ran through the valley
and connected Blossburg with Corning, New York, and, later
and more importantly, with the western division of the Erie
Railroad. Blossburg coal, therefore, had a nearby market, and
the demand for semibituminous coal went up as industrial
enterprise increased in Western New York. Most of the puddling furnaces in Troy and Albany used Blossburg coal, as did
the large Syracuse salt companies. More than half of Tioga's
coal, however, went to such Western New York railroads as the
Erie, the New York Central and Hudson River, and the
Rensselaer and Saratoga.[9]

Three firms—the Blossburg, the Morris Run, and the Fallbrook Coal companies—owned and operated all the Tioga coal
mines in 1873. Unlike the Cambria Iron Works, these companies
each had absentee owners, for, just as the market for Blossburg
coal lay in Western New York, so did the initiative and capital
that built up the Tioga mining industry. The three companies
had their offices in Watkins, a shipping town on Lake Seneca,
Corning, and Syracuse, and the owners had almost nothing to
do with the everyday running of their firms. That job was turned
over to managers and supervisors who lived in the small mining
villages.[10]

By 1873, the Tioga coal industry had located itself in four tiny

9. *Ibid.,* 134–38, 151–59, and table on p. 158. See also Edward A. Wieck, *The American Miners' Association* (New York, 1940), 44.

10. MacFarlane, *op. cit.,* 141, 143–44, 146.

towns near the city of Blossburg and was functioning smoothly and efficiently. Since the entire region except for Blossburg was covered with a heavy forest of hemlock and hardwood timber, it was expensive to start mining operations there. Beginning in 1860, however, when the market for Blossburg coal increased rapidly, each of the companies cleared some land, brought in mining equipment and coal diggers, and built small villages near the deposits. A number of company-built and company-owned highways and railroads connected these towns with nearby Blossburg and with the major railroad in the region, the Blossburg and Corning Railroad. In 1860, the Fallbrook Coal Company, which owned this railroad, built the town of Fallbrook and twelve years later, in 1872, started a second village called Antrim. In the meantime, Morris Run was built by the Morris Run Coal Company, and the Blossburg Coal Company established the village of Arnot. Starting such towns was costly, for the companies had to construct houses, stores, roads, schools, churches, saw mills, and other nonmining units, as well as mine shafts and coal chutes. According to James MacFarlane, the Morris Run Coal Company, for example, spent half a million dollars exclusive of the cost for mining equipment. The expense was nevertheless essential, for it was the only way to start up the mines and bring in the necessary labor force.[11] In spite of the costs involved, the companies proceeded apace. In 1873, Antrim, only a year old, already had twelve hundred residents. The other towns, Morris Run, Fallbrook, and Arnot, each housed around two thousand persons.[12] Most of the coal miners were European immigrants. Some were English and others were Irish, German, French, and even Swedish, but the great majority came from Wales and Scotland.[13]

11. *Ibid.*, 138–50, and Pennsylvania Bureau of Labor Statistics, *Third Annual Report, 1874–1875* (Harrisburg, 1876), 162–69.

12. *Ibid.;* MacFarlane, *op. cit.,* 141, 143–44, 148–50; and D. W. Knight, manager, Fallbrook Coal Company, to the Deputy Commissioner of Labor Statistics, December 2, 1873, printed in "Labor Troubles in Tioga County," Pennsylvania Bureau of Labor Statistics, *First Annual Report, 1872–1873* (Harrisburg, 1874), 480–81.

13. Unidentified letter from an official of the Miners' and Laborers' Benevo-

A kind of industrial feudalism and paternalism permeated the entire atmosphere of the Tioga mining towns. The three coal companies dominated and controlled the social and economic institutions of the region, and the degree and character of their power astonished even contemporaries. Property ownership lay entirely in the hands of the coal companies, which claimed full and final authority in the use of their land. W. S. Nearing, the superintendent of the Morris Run Coal Company, told an official of the Pennsylvania Bureau of Labor Statistics that every man (meaning, of course, the company owners) had "a right to do what he would with his own" property and that dissatisfied workers were "at liberty" to move out of the "jurisdiction" of the coal companies.[14]

In their policies, the Tioga companies treated these towns as private property and considered them only as adjuncts to the successful mining of a commercially useful product. Land was rented, not sold, to the miners and, at the same time, the companies refused to rent land to other businesses. This policy gave the operators a special kind of power. During an extended lockout in the Tioga region in 1865, the local coal operators had pushed through the state legislature a bill that made it possible to dispossess a worker from a company-owned house on only ten days' notice if he failed to fulfill the terms of his labor contract.[15] All the Tioga miners lived in company houses, and no house or tenement in the region was rented on "any terms that . . . leave the occupant anything but a tenant at will to be dispossessed at ten days' notice." [16]

lent Union of Tioga County to the Pennsylvania Bureau of Labor Statistics, n.d., printed in *ibid.,* 479–80. See also D. W. Knight, Fallbrook, to the Deputy Commissioner of Labor Statistics, December 2, 1873, printed in *ibid.,* 480–81.

14. "Interview with W. S. Nearing," *ibid.,* 488–90; D. W. Knight, Fallbrook, to the Deputy Commissioner of Labor Statistics, December 2, 1873, printed in *ibid.,* 480–81; James MacFarlane, Elmira, to T. J. Bigham, Harrisburg, January 10, 1874, printed in *ibid.,* 500–503; and John Siney, St. Clair, Pa., to the editor, February 8, 1874, *Workingman's Advocate,* February 21, 1874.

15. The entire set of events that led to the passage of the "ten-day eviction law" is clearly and carefully described in Wieck, *op. cit.,* 162–72 and 287–93.

16. "Testimony of Fallbrook coal miners," December 24 (?), 1873, Pennsylvania Bureau of Labor Statistics, *First Annual Report, 1872–1873,* 482–83.

The power to dispossess was only one part of the so-called "Tioga system." The coal firms also exercised their authority in other ways. John Siney, the president of the Miners' National Association, insisted that the operators "only allow the house of God to be used for such purposes as they see proper." [17] The roads and highways entering the four towns were often closed to unwelcome visitors. Superintendent Nearing insisted that none of the roads was "a highway for the public." The companies had built the roads, he went on, and company officials therefore had the right to chase anyone from them who was "distasteful to the manager." If the person refused to leave, he could be arrested "as a trespasser." [18] Nor was this all. The coal firms also owned all the stores that sold provisions and equipment to the miners, and though the workers were free to purchase goods elsewhere, company officials discouraged such efforts. Not one of the companies allowed merchants and shopkeepers to build competing stores in its towns, and miners who bought foodstuffs and wares from neighboring farmers and traveling peddlers were often fined, discharged, "or else forced to carry back the foods to where they got them." [19] Local Blossburg merchants, as well as businessmen from outside of the Tioga region, were not welcome in the mining towns. A sample agent from the Corning Glass and Bottle Factory tried to sell some glassware in Morris Run, but the mine superintendent warned him: "I strictly forbid you from coming here again to sell anything. This is private property and you are a trespasser." To cite another of many similar examples, a Blossburg shoemaker who went to Fallbrook was advised by an official that miners buying shoes from him would lose their jobs.[20]

17. John Siney, St. Clair, to the editor, February 8, 1874, *Workingman's Advocate*, February 21, 1874.

18. *Ibid.*, and "Interview with W. S. Nearing," n.d., Pennsylvania Bureau of Labor Statistics, *First Annual Report, 1872–1873*, 488–90.

19. "Testimony of Fallbrook and Morris Run coal miners," n.d., *ibid.*, 482–85, and John Siney, St. Clair, to the editor, February 8, 1874, *Workingman's Advocate*, February 21, 1874.

20. Numerous affidavits, including those used in the text, appear in Pennsylvania Bureau of Labor Statistics, *First Annual Report, 1872–1873*, 494–97.

The companies also forced their workers to buy in company-owned stores by extending store credit to them between monthly payments of cash wages. If the purchases of a miner fell below the amount of credit granted him, he received the difference in the form of "a 'bogus' money . . . stamped out of 'gutta percha.' " Coal diggers who preferred legal tender to company currency found that the company money was discounted at 90 percent of its face value. Ten dollars in store currency was worth only nine dollars in actual cash. At the store, however, miners could buy goods for the full value of the company money.[21] Nearing admitted that the companies "promoted" patronage of their stores and thereby "kept" the miners "from going out where they could get access to liquor and indulge in drunkenness." [22] "The operation," wrote a state official who disagreed, "amounts practically to a tax . . . on the workmen for the privilege of buying from whom they please." [23]

Apart from discounting store credit at less than its face value, the coal firms drew income from the miners in two other ways. First, although tax assessors, collectors, and supervisors were publicly elected officials, the companies deducted road, school, county, and state taxes from monthly wages and then sent the money on to the authorities.[24] Money was also taken from the miners through a system of fines. "It is and always has been the custom in all this coal region," said D. W. Knight, the manager of the Fallbrook Coal Company, in 1873, "for the manager to

21. Unidentified letter from an official of the Miners' and Laborers' Benevolent Union of Tioga County to the Pennsylvania Bureau of Labor Statistics, n.d., printed in *ibid.,* 479–80; D. W. Knight, Fallbrook, to the Deputy Commissioner of Labor Statistics, December 2, 1873, printed in *ibid.,* 480–81; *Mahoning Valley Record,* December 20, 1873, reprinted in *ibid.,* 481–82; "Testimony of Fallbrook, Morris Run, and Arnot coal miners," *ibid.,* 482–85 and 492–93; and James MacFarlane, Elmira, to T. J. Bigham, Harrisburg, January 15, 1874, printed in *ibid.,* 500–503.

22. "Testimony of W. S. Nearing," *ibid.,* 488–90.

23. John Tomlinson made this observation after a careful study of the way the companies discounted their currency. It is discussed in *ibid.,* 489–90.

24. "Testimony of Fallbrook and Morris Run coal miners," *ibid.,* 482–85, and John Siney, St. Clair, to the editor, February 8, 1874, *Workingman's Advocate,* February 21, 1874.

make rules for carrying on the work." The miners, therefore, paid fines for "misdemeanors which, in the manager's opinion, merit punishment." The worker who misbehaved or was otherwise troublesome and "unruly" in the eyes of one of his supervisors received the following note: "We shall charge your account $—— for damages to property (or drunkenness and fighting) upon the ——th inst. Should you remain in the company's employ, this will be a legal collection." If a miner refused to pay the fine, he lost his job, was evicted from his home, and then was "sent down the road." [25] While company spokesmen insisted that this system was essential for the efficient operation of their enterprises, many miners complained that supervisors frequently abused their authority and imposed arbitrary, unnecessary, and harsh fines. One miner told of being fined for beating a mule. Another complained that his firm made him pay fifteen dollars for holding a dance in his home.[26] "If two children differ," John Siney wrote, "their father is fined and the money appropriated to the company's use." Siney and the miners were convinced that in the Tioga region there was "no law or justice but the law and justice made by the Superintendent[s]." [27]

Whatever critical judgment may be made of the behavior of the Tioga coal operators, in the prosperous post-Civil War years their system of social and economic control worked. In spite of the complaints of the miners, the entire region was free of any labor difficulty between 1865 and the fall months of 1873. No strikes occurred, and trade unions did not flourish.[28] After an

25. This material is enclosed in D. W. Knight, Fallbrook, to the Deputy Commissioner of Labor Statistics, December 2, 1873, Pennsylvania Bureau of Labor Statistics, *First Annual Report, 1872–1873*, 480–81.

26. Unidentified letter from an official of the Miners' and Laborers' Benevolent Union of Tioga County to the Pennsylvania Bureau of Labor Statistics, n.d., printed in *ibid.*, 479–80, and "Affidavit of unidentified miner," *ibid.*, 494–97.

27. John Siney, St. Clair, to the editor, February 8, 1874, *Workingman's Advocate*, February 21, 1874.

28. James MacFarlane, Elmira, to T. J. Bigham, Harrisburg, January 15, 1874, printed in Pennsylvania Bureau of Labor Statistics, *First Annual Report, 1872–1873*, 500–503.

extended visit to the Tioga towns in 1873, John Tomlinson, the deputy commissioner of the Pennsylvania Bureau of Labor Statistics, concluded that "the state of things" was "a very great anomaly in the midst of a free country." He declared that the operators had created "absolute personal government in the midst of a republic." [29]

The social and economic structures of Johnstown and the Tioga coal region were similar in most respects. There were three firms in the Tioga area and each was absentee-owned, but little else was different. In both areas, the entrepreneurs exercised great economic power, which created and dominated a well-integrated social structure. Almost no institution in either Johnstown or the Tioga towns was free of entrepreneurial influence of one kind or another. Trade unions were either weak or nonexistent, and company-owned services thrived. The traditional sense of independence and self-reliance so closely associated with the American Dream was absent. The employers seemed powerful enough to meet any challenge from discontented and disgruntled workers. When the 1873 depression led to labor difficulties in both Johnstown and Tioga the managers in both localities reacted in the same way, using all their resources to suppress a demand for trade unions. There was no reason to suspect that the results would be different.

Soon after the "panic" began, the market for iron rails fell away, and the Cambria Iron Works faced serious economic difficulties. The Johnstown firm adjusted to the situation by lowering costs, cutting production, and laying off workers. Wages dropped. At first, they were cut 10 percent, and then in mid-November a further cut of 21 percent was announced. The sliding scale of the coal miners was revised downward. Finally, the company paid the entire new wage in store goods and credit rather than cash. Company officials advised dissatisfied men to find other jobs,

29. Tomlinson's observations were made during a conversation with W. S. Nearing. *Ibid.,* 488–90.

and told the rest to accept the new wage or face unemployment.[30] The Cambria Iron Works thus sought to weather the early months of the depression. Its actions, however, irritated the coal and iron ore miners, who reorganized their defunct union as a local of the newly established Miners' National Association. Within a short time, four hundred miners had joined.[31]

The owners of the Cambria Iron Works refused to accord any recognition to the Johnstown local. Several times during the winter of 1873 and 1874, union representatives pleaded with company officials for a wage increase, but in each instance they were put off. Finally, in February 1874, the company resumed paying cash wages and a month later restored part of the wage cut. The ironworkers, who had not complained about company policy, received a wage increase of at least 17 percent, but the wages of the dissident and union-conscious coal and ore miners rose less than 8 percent. There were rumors that the company wanted to destroy the union. In mid-March, after the miners held a large protest meeting and demanded an equitable wage increase and threatened to strike, Morrell and his associates closed down the entire Cambria Iron Works.[32] *Frank Cowan's Paper*, a Pittsburgh weekly, insisted that Morrell had punished his men "for creating trouble to the company," while the Pittsburgh *American Manufacturer* said that men like Morrell had taken "advantage of the present condition of things." Since the demand for iron rails was low, it mattered little whether or not the firm remained in operation. Market conditions favored the "course adopted at Johnstown . . . no employment or no unionism." [33]

30. Trampled Down Miners, Johnstown, to the editor, March 30, 1874, *Workingman's Advocate*, April 11, 1874; *Pittsburgh Post*, November 1, 1873; *Frank Cowan's Paper*, November 26, 1873; and *Johnstown Tribune*, n.d., reprinted in the *Workingman's Advocate*, February 7, 1874.

31. Trampled Down Miners, Johnstown, to the editor, March 30, 1874, *Workingman's Advocate*, April 11, 1874.

32. *Ibid.*; Johnstown *Tribune*, March 18, 1874, reprinted in *Frank Cowan's Paper*, March 21, 1874; Johnstown *Tribune*, n.d., reprinted in *Iron Age* (March 26, 1874), 11; *Workingman's Advocate*, April 11, 1874; and Pittsburgh *Gazette*, March 31, 1874.

33. *Frank Cowan's Paper*, March 21, 1874, and *American Manufacturer*, April 30, 1874.

It was much the same story in the Tioga mining towns. The demand for semibituminous coal sagged badly, and income fell off. The three companies withheld cash wages, and for three months the coal miners subsisted on store credit. In late November 1873, the firms offered the men one month of back wages in cash if they signed an agreement not to ask for any more cash until the following May.[34] The miners rebuffed the offer. They appointed a committee of eleven to meet with the operators, formed a local union called the Miners' and Laborers' Benevolent Union of Tioga County, and planned to affiliate with the Miners' National Association.[35] The three companies, working together, reacted quickly to such a threat to their so-called "Tioga system." Nine union leaders were fired, and when the rest of the miners remained firm, the operators ordered them to leave either the union or their jobs.[36] On December 11, the companies posted the following notice near each of their mine shafts and ordered the workers to answer it within two days:

First, Are you a member of the Union of miners proposed in Tioga County, Pennsylvania, or any society of similar character?

Second, Are you willing and do you pledge yourself not to join any such society?

Third, If the party is a member, he will be asked: Are you willing and do you pledge yourself to dissolve your connection with such society without delay and not to join the same again?

The miners were told that unless they answered the questions properly they would have to "settle their accounts and vacate

34. "Testimony of Arnot Miners," Pennsylvania Bureau of Labor Statistics, *First Annual Report, 1872–1873,* 492–93. See also "Testimony of Morris Run Miners," *ibid.,* 484–85.

35. "Testimony of Fallbrook and Morris Run Miners," *ibid.,* 482–85.

36. "Testimony of Arnot Miners," *ibid.,* 492–93. See also "Testimony of W. S. Nearing," *ibid.,* 488–90, and the *Mahoning Valley Record,* n.d., reprinted in *ibid.,* 481–82.

our houses." [37] When the workers demurred, the operators closed the mines. More important, they ordered the miners and their families to leave the company-owned houses within ten days.[38] It was mid-December, and the miners had been without cash wages for a few months. The operators undoubtedly believed that the men would surrender quickly and unconditionally.

The Cambria Iron Works had little trouble in defeating the new miners' union. Soon after the lockout began, the company offered its men their jobs back if they signed a new contract in which they forswore trade-union membership and accepted the final authority of the firm's managers with regard to wages and working conditions. Under the new contract the company could fine workers for violations of all sorts. Men guilty of "dishonesty, drunkenness, [and] insubordination," of "quarrelling," of "stealing" company-owned timber or coal, of damaging company-owned houses beyond ordinary wear and tear, and of "destroying or injuring any property of the company . . . [by] careless or reckless conduct" would be fined the first time and discharged after the second offense. Dismissal, furthermore, meant immediate eviction from the company-owned house, and the discharged worker was listed publicly as "not employable" by the Cambria Iron Works. A repudiation of labor organizations of all kinds was also written into the contract:

. . . Any person . . . known to belong to any secret association or open combination whose aim is to control

37. "Company Questionnaire," Fallbrook, Arnot, Antrim, and Morris Run, December 11, 1873, enclosed in A Victim, Arnot, Pa., to the editor, January 27, 1874, *Workingman's Advocate*, February 14, 1874. The questionnaire was reprinted in the Pennsylvania Bureau of Labor Statistics, *First Annual Report, 1872–1873*, 483.

38. *Mahoning Valley Record*, n.d., reprinted in *ibid.*, 481–82, and "Testimony of Fallbrook, Morris Run, and Arnot Miners," *ibid.*, 482–85 and 492–93.

wages or stop the works, or any part thereof, shall be
promptly and finally discharged. . . . Persons quitting work,
or inducing or attempting to induce others to quit work, . . .
shall forfeit whatever wages may be due . . . to such . . .
persons absolutely.[39]

The managers of the Cambria Iron Works rejected compromise of any kind, waited the workers out, and whipped up
hysteria against the new union. When John Siney arrived in
Johnstown to plead for the miners, Daniel Morrell refused his
request for arbitration.[40] Efforts by the locked-out iron and steel
roll hands to discuss the issue with Morrell also were fruitless.
Sending them a copy of the new contract, he simply told them,
"An 'explanation' on your part is not deemed necessary." [41] In
the meantime, Morrell talked and acted vigorously against the
union. After charging that the miners planned violence and were
going to blow up the mines, he deputized and armed one
hundred "special policemen" and told them to protect company
property. Even though Siney complained that Morrell had hired
"bloated rascals" and "supplied them with rotgut whisky and
weapons," the company remained adamant.[42] Morrell charged
that the miners sent him "Ku-Klux" letters that warned him "to
prepare for death." He complained that the new union—"this
secret Union, this mysterious power, this veiled Gorgon"—
"threatened, insulted, assaulted, and almost murdered" the men
who supported the company.[43] When the miners held a ball to

39. "Rules and Regulations of the Cambria Iron Company," April 6, 1874,
printed in *Iron Age* (December 31, 1874), 14–15.

40. Trampled Down Miners, Johnstown, to the editor, March 30, 1874,
Workingman's Advocate, April 11, 1874.

41. "Statement of D. J. Morrell, general manager, to the Iron Heaters and
Rollers," Johnstown, May 4, 1874, printed in the *Cooper's New Monthly*, 1 (July
1874), 11.

42. *Raftsman's Journal*, April 22, 1874; *Cooper's New Monthly*, 1 (July 1874),
10–11; and "Speech of John Siney in Union Hall, Johnstown, Pa., on the Ninth
of May 1874," *Workingman's Advocate*, May 30 and June 6, 1874.

43. Special correspondent, Johnstown, April 14, 1874, *The New York Times*,
April 21, 1874, and "Mr. Morrell on Trade Unions," *Iron Age* (July 16, 1874), 14.

raise needed funds, company officials telegraphed state authorities that a riot was imminent.[44] Morrell continually harped on the danger of the union and claimed that hundreds of men "dreaded to go to work for fear of suffering violence." The Johnstown *Tribune*, a local daily newspaper, supported him, and argued that "labor writers and orators are, one and all of them, apologists for crime." [45]

The Cambria Iron Works attracted nationwide attention in its struggle against trade unionism. *The New York Times* called Daniel Morrell "a hero," and a number of important national business weeklies encouraged the Cambria Iron Works in its battle against the "pernicious and debasing" labor unions that were "instruments of oppression . . . possessed of a giant's power." *Iron Age* advised its readers that Morrell's new contract, a model agreement, was "the easiest and best means" for solving labor troubles, for it told the worker that he could not "serve two masters." To deny him a job for belonging to a trade union hardly violated "the rights of man." "Desperate diseases," *Iron Age* explained, "require desperate remedies." "The trade union evil," it concluded, "must be rooted out or its noxious growth will poison our political, industrial, and social systems, give us anarchy for order, and drive capital out of manufacturing and into other and safer investments." [46]

The locked-out workers, too, found some outside encouragement and support. In nearby Pittsburgh, the *National Labor Tribune* printed advertisements advising men not to work for the Cambria Iron Works.[47] John Siney and John James, the national leaders of the Miners' National Association, scathingly attacked the Johnstown managers. James said they were asking the

44. "Capital and Labor," *Miner's National Record*, 1 (November 1874), 12. A company of militia was alerted in Pittsburgh but not sent to Johnstown.

45. "Mr. Morrell on Trade Unions," *Iron Age* (July 16, 1874), 14, and Johnstown *Tribune*, n.d., reprinted in *Cooper's New Monthly*, 1 (July 1874), 10.

46. *The New York Times*, April 21, 1874; "Capital vs. Unionism," *American Manufacturer* (April 30, 1874), 3; and *Iron Age* (May 7, 1874), 14, (July 16, 1874), 14.

47. Cited in "Mr. Morrell on Trade Unions," *ibid.* (July 16, 1874), 14.

workers "to give up all their citizen rights and make the Cambria Coal and Iron Company lords and rulers over them." Siney visited Johnstown twice during the lockout, and each time publicly challenged the company to submit the issues to an impartial referee.[48] At the same time, the *Iron Molders' Journal* and *Cooper's New Monthly* called Morrell "a worse slave driver than any that cracked the whip in the palmy days of negro slavery," and condemned his company as "one of the most . . . soulless corporations in the United States." [49]

In spite of this outside interest and support for both the miners and the company, the success or failure of the lockout depended to a large extent on local conditions in Johnstown. There the company had the overwhelming advantage. The nonstrikers in Johnstown offered the miners little support. A local minister attacked Morrell and his policies, but that was all. There is no record of similar criticism by other nonstrikers.[50] Morrell and his associates, furthermore, took advantage of the craft distinctions of the men they employed. Soon after the lockout started, they reopened the iron mill and offered jobs to those old employees who would sign the new contract. They also brought in men from the outside. The mill and furnace men resumed work, and production soon started up again. Finally, the firm effectively weakened the strikers by bringing coal into Johnstown from distant areas, thus demonstrating that it could dispense with the services of its discontented coal miners. The miners were isolated and powerless; it was only a matter of time before they would admit defeat.[51]

48. John James, Indiana, to the editor, April 24, 1874, *Workingman's Advocate*, May 9, 1874, and John Siney, "Speech . . . in Union Hall . . . ," *ibid.*, May 30 and June 6, 1874.

49. "The Cambria Iron Works," *Iron Molders' Journal* (June 1874), 357–58, and *Cooper's New Monthly*, 1 (July 1874), 10.

50. *Iron Molders' Journal* (August 1874), 11.

51. Johnstown Miners, Johnstown, "To the Coal Miners Whom It May Concern," May 14, 1874, enclosed in John James, Cleveland, to the editor, May 26, 1874, *Workingman's Advocate*, June 6, 1874; John James, Cleveland, to the editor, May 4 and June 2, 1874, *ibid.*, May 16 and June 13, 1874; and "Mr. Morrell on Trade Unions," *Iron Age* (July 16, 1874), 14.

Protests by the miners were of little consequence. They persuaded a number of new workers not to take employment at the mill, but they could not prevent the company from bringing in supplies of coal from other areas. Pathetically, they pleaded with the men who mined this coal. "Do not let a few dollars earned at our expense . . . cause you to act against principle and against the fraternal ties which should exist between workingmen everywhere. . . . Brothers, whether you are Union men or not, remember that our defeat, which you are directly contributing to, means your defeat, our success, your success. . . . Refrain from sending any more coal, and do not let any one call you demoralized niggers." The Miners' National Association was too weak to enforce the demands of the Johnstown miners, and the local union gave up the fight.[52] In late July 1874 the Johnstown *Tribune*, which had sided with the company throughout, announced the end of the lockout, reporting that the Johnstown workers had "completely rejected" the "principle of trade unionism." The workers had learned that they had no right to interfere with the management of the Cambria Iron Works. "Their money," wrote the *Tribune* of the workers, "did not build it."[53]

The locked-out Tioga County miners faced problems similar to those in Johnstown, but local conditions in the Tioga region worked to their advantage and success. The Tioga lockout lasted nearly three months. Although the miners were evicted at the start of winter, except for a few of the Swedish coal diggers they all held out.[54] "If the company waits for fifty years," one angered

52. Johnstown Miners, "To the Coal Miners Whom It May Concern," May 14, 1874, enclosed in John James, Cleveland, to the editor, May 26, 1874, *Workingman's Advocate*, June 6, 1874.

53. Johnstown *Tribune*, July 31, 1874, reprinted in *Iron Age* (August 6, 1874), 5.

54. "Testimony of Fallbrook Miners," Pennsylvania Bureau of Labor Statistics, *First Annual Report, 1872–1873*, 482–84, and James MacFarlane, Elmira, to T. J. Bigham, January 15, 1874, printed in *ibid.*, 500–503.

miner wrote, "I am certain that the miners now out of work will never sign such an infamous document." [55] Some of the men and their families left the Tioga region for other mining areas. A few actually returned to Scotland.[56] The great majority of them, however, stayed on in the Tioga region to challenge the power of the coal companies. They contended that their employers were forcing them "to put on a badge of absolute serfdom by signing an agreement not to do what we have as clear and complete a right to do as they have to organize their companies." [57]

In the beginning, the operators were as stubborn as the coal miners. "We are justified in our proceedings . . . to our consciences and before God and man," insisted a Fallbrook Coal Company official.[58] W. S. Nearing declared that the companies would never "permit any workmen's organization to exist on their property." [59] When John Siney visited the region and intervened in behalf of the locked-out workers, company officials refused him permission to speak in local schools or churches. Siney finally addressed the miners from a platform erected near a railroad station. Only after much difficulty could he arrange a conference with some company officials, but at this meeting they simply reiterated their opposition to the union.[60] Similarly, efforts by John Tomlinson, of the Pennsylvania Bureau of Labor Statistics, to bring about a compromise also failed. Tomlinson advised both sides to give in a bit. He told the operators to rehire the discharged miners and withdraw their hostility toward the union. At the same time, he urged the miners to accept the right of the companies to hire nonunion

55. A Victim, Arnot, to the editor, January 27, 1874, *Workingman's Advocate*, February 14, 1874.

56. James MacFarlane, Elmira, to T. J. Bigham, Harrisburg, January 15, 1874, printed in the Pennsylvania Bureau of Labor Statistics, *First Annual Report, 1872–1873*, 500–503.

57. "Testimony of Fallbrook Miners," *ibid.*, 482–84.

58. James MacFarlane, Elmira, to T. J. Bigham, Harrisburg, January 15, 1874, *ibid.*, 500–503.

59. "Testimony of W. S. Nearing," *ibid.*, 488–90.

60. John Siney, St. Clair, to the editor, February 8, 1874, *Workingman's Advocate*, February 21, 1874.

men and to have "free and exclusive [and] lawful and just management of the collieries." Tomlinson also offered a scheme of arbitration for the peaceful settlement of grievances. The miners accepted all his recommendations, but the coal operators turned him down, rejecting "any interference on the part of any public officer of the State." [61]

Officials of the Bureau of Labor Statistics criticized the Tioga operators, but had little influence on them. T. J. Bigham, the head of the bureau, minced no words. To one of the operators he wrote that their companies were run by "madmen" and that their actions "cut them off from all public sympathy." "If the miners are willing to work," Bigham told the officers of the Fallbrook Coal Company, "let them work. When they actually strike will be time enough to turn them out." His advice fell on deaf ears.[62] The operators undoubtedly believed that the eviction of the union miners and their families in the middle of winter and at the start of a serious business depression would create such hardship that the union would collapse and the men would return on company terms.

The operators, however, had entirely misjudged "public" sentiment in the Tioga Valley. Herein lay one significant difference between the Tioga trouble and the crisis in Johnstown. The central, determining factor in the Tioga lockout was neither the stand of the miners nor that of the operators. It was the behavior of the nonmining population in Tioga County. In a perhaps unexpected manner, the power of the coal operators was decisively checked by the residents of Blossburg and the farmers of the area. Local businessmen in Blossburg, possibly antagonized by the refusal of the coal operators to allow them to

61. The recommendations by Tomlinson appear in detail in Pennsylvania Bureau of Labor Statistics, *First Annual Report, 1872–1873*, 490–92. The acceptance of the recommendations by the miners is noted in *ibid.*, 487. The operators' reaction is described in *ibid.*, 492. The statement rejecting state intervention is from James MacFarlane, Elmira, to T. J. Bigham, Harrisburg, January 15, 1874, *ibid.*, 503.

62. T. J. Bigham, Harrisburg, to James MacFarlane, Elmira, January 10, 1874, printed in *ibid.*, 499.

trade freely with the miners, together with other townspeople aided the evicted miners and their families. The Blossburg Odd Fellows Society raised funds for them. An eminent Harrisburg lawyer was hired to test the eviction proceedings in court. Nor was this all. Blossburg residents and some farmers housed the homeless miners and their families. When there was no more available room, a row of tenements was built out of common rough slabs. Finally, 2,577 Blossburg citizens, "among them large numbers of the most prominent men (business and otherwise) of the county," petitioned Governor John Hartranft and his attorney-general to "interfere to secure the enforcement of the laws and the protection of these people from these oppressions." After visiting Blossburg, John Siney wrote of the close relationship between the miners and the townsfolk: "So deep is the sympathy that the business community of the 'city of refuge' entertains for them, that all aid within their power . . . is extended to the refugees." [63]

Another development further weakened the Tioga operators. In Johnstown, the Cambria Iron Works was able to start up its mill without its miners by bringing in supplies of coal from other regions. The Tioga companies could not begin operations again without bringing in new miners. In spite of the severity of the depression and the large number of unemployed miners, the operators found it hard to attract workers. John Siney and the Chicago *Workingman's Advocate*, a labor newspaper that circulated in the Western states, both pleaded with coal miners to stay away from Tioga County. The operators, wrote the Chicago weekly, opposed labor unions "for the same reason that the Southern planter was opposed to the education of his chattel." [64] Siney made the same point. "Nowhere," he wrote, "has the same oppression been imposed since the day that the whip was wrenched from the hand of the slave driver of the South." In

---

63. James MacFarlane, Elmira, to T. J. Bigham, Harrisburg, January 15, 1874, printed in *ibid.*, 500–503; "Petition of Blossburg Citizens," n.d., *ibid.*, 503–504; and John Siney, St. Clair, to the editor, February 8, 1874, *Workingman's Advocate*, February 21, 1874.

64. "The Tioga Outrage," *Workingman's Advocate*, February 21, 1874.

Tioga, he went on, "it is an issue whether the white workingmen of America shall be placed in a worse condition and treated with less respect than ever the Negroes of the South were treated by their masters." [65] The success of his plea cannot be measured, but by the end of January 1874, almost two months after the lockout had started, only five new miners worked in the Tioga mines.[66]

In spite of the structural rigidity of the "Tioga system" and the power that was thought to inhere in that system, the operators lost out to the miners. Blossburg's citizens checked part of their power. The system itself discouraged outside miners from working there. Siney insisted that the operators were "indignant that the good citizens of Blossburg . . . befriended the sufferers" and claimed that they "grieved" because they could not make the nonminers "their victims as well." [67] When business picked up somewhat in March 1874, three months after the lockout had started, the operators admitted defeat and recognized the union. Meeting with a committee of strikers, they withdrew the disputed questionnaire. Soon after, the coal miners resumed work, and celebrated the success of their new union.[68] Tioga and Johnstown each went its own way following the lockouts of 1873 and 1874. Trade unionism entirely disappeared in Johnstown, and the power of the Cambria Iron Works went unchallenged during the entire depression period. When a large number of rail orders came in in 1875, the company put its men on a seven-day week. A year later, the wages of unskilled laborers fell to seventy-five cents a day, and skilled miners earned only half as much as before the depression.[69] Daniel

---

65. John Siney, St. Clair, to the editor, February 8, 1874, *ibid.*

66. A Victim, Arnot, to the editor, February 8, 1874, *ibid.*, February 14, 1874.

67. John Siney, St. Clair, to the editor, February 8, 1874, *ibid.*, February, 21, 1874.

68. Pennsylvania Bureau of Labor Statistics, *Ninth Annual Report, 1880–1881*, 308.

69. *Frank Cowan's Paper*, January 16, 1875; *Workingman's Advocate*, March 20 and July 17, 1875; *Iron Molders' Journal* (September 1876), 79; and

Morrell nevertheless still talked of his "American system," though he admitted that American industry had to "exact some temporary sacrifices" to guarantee "general prosperity and true national independence." [70] In the eyes of many trade unionists, however, Morrell personified the tyranny of the all-powerful entrepreneur. Calling him "a canting hypocrite," the *National Labor Tribune* noted, "He can sing of our country, but he can also lash his workmen like a slave driver." The *Iron Molders' Journal* wrote of Johnstown, "If there is a town in Europe to compare with it in the actual serfdom of its inhabitants, we have failed to hear of it." [71]

Conditions were somewhat different in the Tioga mining towns. When John Siney visited them in December 1874, almost nine months after the triumph of the trade union, company officials were at first reluctant to allow him to speak. Permission was finally granted, however, and the subsequent meeting, Siney wrote, "was literally packed with our own men." "The change in Tioga County," he concluded, "appears . . . almost miraculous, comparing times now with one year ago." [72] Within a few years, the miner's union in Tioga County disappeared, but its disintegration had little to do with the so-called "Tioga system." Hard times and the prolonged severity of the depression were responsible, for it was difficult to maintain a union when its members worked as few as four or five days a month, and when union funds had to be spent to feed hungry families. [73]

Whitefoot, Gallitzen, Pa., to the editor, September 2, 1876, *National Labor Tribune*, September 9, 1876.

70. "Speech of Daniel Morrell," *Iron Molders' Journal* (April 1875), 295–96.

71. *Ibid.*, and *National Labor Tribune*, March 10, 1877.

72. John Siney, St. Clair, to Friend James, December 25, 1874, printed in the *Miner's National Record*, 1 (January 1875), 42.

73. See, for examples, *National Labor Tribune*, February 6, 1875; A Miner, Fallbrook, to the editor, December 17, 1874, *Miner's National Record*, 1 (January 1875), 45; *ibid.* (March 1875), 75; Pennsylvania Bureau of Labor Statistics, *Second Annual Report, 1873–1874*, 435–36; *Third Annual Report, 1874–1875*, 162–69.

Index

HERBERT G. GUTMAN is a professor of history at the City College of New York and the Graduate Center–City University of New York. A member of the Executive Board of the Organization of American Historians, he also represents the American Historical Association on the National Historical Publications and Records Commission. He is spending the 1976–1977 academic year as the Harrison Visiting Professor of History at the College of William and Mary.

Professor Gutman is the author of *Slavery and the Numbers Game: A Critique of Time on the Cross* (1975) and *The Black Family in Slavery and Freedom, 1750–1925* (1976). He has also completed a study of the emancipated slaves during and after the Civil War and is presently at work on a social history of working people in America.

VINTAGE POLITICAL SCIENCE AND SOCIAL CRITICISM